KU-323-898

112788

The Iraqi Aggression Against Kuwait

The Iraqi Aggression Against Kuwait

Strategic Lessons and Implications for Europe

EDITED BY

Wolfgang F. Danspeckgruber

WITH

Charles R.H. Tripp

WestviewPress

A Division of HarperCollins*Publishers*

Published under the auspices of
The Liechtenstein Colloquium on European and International Affairs,
The Center of International Studies, Princeton University, and
The LCM Foundation on European Affairs, Inc.

This book is the second in the LCM Liechtenstein Series.

All rights reserved. Printed in the United States of America. No part of this publication may be reproduced or transmitted in any form or by any means, electronic or mechanical, including photocopy, recording, or any information storage and retrieval system, without permission in writing from the publisher.

Copyright © 1996 by Westview Press, A Division of HarperCollins Publishers, Inc.

Published in 1996 in the United States of America by Westview Press, 5500 Central Avenue, Boulder, Colorado 80301-2877, and in the United Kingdom by Westview Press, 12 Hid's Copse Road, Cumnor Hill, Oxford OX2 9JJ

A CIP catalog record for this book is available from the Library of Congress
ISBN 0-8133-8623-3 (hc)

The paper used in this publication meets the requirements of the American National Standard for Permanence of Paper for Printed Library Materials Z39.48-1984.

10   9   8   7   6   5   4   3   2   1

In Memory of
Edouard and Elise Dettwiler-Dettwiler

Contents

Foreword

Abdlatif Y. Al-Hamad

As the decade of 1990s dawned, the promise of a healthier and more peaceful new world filled the air. The transformation of relations between East and West provided a unique opportunity for a new kind of cooperation in the face of global challenges. Détente between the superpowers promised a peace dividend by freeing up substantial resources from military expenditures. In Europe, countries that had been longtime rivals moved toward greater cooperation and established an economic union in 1992. Eastern Europeans discarded the shackles of communism and of central governments bogged down by bureaucracy and inefficiencies. In Asia, Japan became the world's new financial superpower and the leader of an important industrial bloc consisting of the emerging new industrialized countries in East Asia.

On the Arab scene, the 1990s looked equally promising. Several Arab countries had entered into economic partnership, culminating in the formation of two regional economic blocs in addition to the then eight-year-old Gulf Cooperation Council. These were the Arab Cooperation Council, which brought together Jordan, Iraq, Egypt, and Yemen, and the Maghreb Cooperation Council, formed between Algeria, Morocco, Tunisia, Libya, and Mauritania. These institutional frameworks were viewed as the catalyst that would bring about more realistic and sustainable economic integration among Arab states. By then, Egypt, which after the Camp David accord had been isolated from Arab forums, was once again fully reinstated in Arab mainstream activities. The Arab countries were looking forward to a buoyant decade especially as the 1988 cease-fire between Iraq and Iran had removed the greatest source of instability in the region. Oil prices, which had crashed in 1986, were stabilized, and there was the likelihood of increase throughout the 1990s.

This great promise and hope was shattered with the march of the Iraqi army into Kuwait on August 2, 1990. That act of aggression and the ensuing crisis not only brought dismal and total catastrophe to both countries and to their neighbors, but it also proved to be the catalyst that brought the economy of many countries to the brink of collapse, especially in East Asia and the Middle East. The losses and suffering inflicted on the Kuwaiti and Iraqi economies have, indeed, been enormous, and the recovery will be extremely difficult. The adverse impact of the Kuwait crisis on the economies of Egypt, Jordan, Turkey, Syria, and Yemen will be severe and long lasting.

The losses incurred by the Kuwaiti oil sector alone could amount to $100 billion, of which between $15 to $20 billion will be the cost of reconstruction of the oil industry. With no fewer than 750 damaged oil wells, Kuwait's daily losses during the Iraqi occupation and the ensuing combat were between $90 and $100 million from fire and spillage. It is estimated that between four and six million barrels of oil a day were lost. The damage to the oil refineries was estimated to be around 20 percent of their capacity, which had been seven hundred thousand barrels of oil per day. The damage to Kuwait's infrastructure, industry, agriculture, transportation, and other facilities was estimated by a UN special mission at no less than $15 billion. But Kuwait's losses far surpass these physical and financial damages, as the cost of the immense environmental destruction and human suffering could not be accurately assessed.

Iraqi losses are no less daunting. These include the thousands of casualties resulting from the Iran-Iraq War and the invasion of Kuwait. Of the $100 billion Iraq spent on arms since 1980, more than $80 billion was provided by foreign borrowings, of which $50 billion came from Saudi Arabia, Kuwait, and other Gulf countries. Iraq has nothing to show for this major economic burden: It has to rebuild its infrastructure, oil installations, power plants, and electric networks, which were destroyed by military action in the Gulf War. In addition, the physical destruction and production losses in Iraq due to the Iraq-Iran War, estimated to be in the range of $37 billion, require major reforms and investments in the economy if a reasonably productive capacity is to be restored.

The invasion of Kuwait not only affected Kuwait and Iraq but also inflicted serious damage on the economies of neighboring countries. The stability of the economies of Arab countries in the region that either supplied labor to the Gulf countries or relied heavily on external economic and financial support from the Gulf countries was seriously damaged. The full effect of the Gulf crisis on these countries could lead to economic disruptions and social upheaval. It is estimated that the losses incurred by Egypt, Jordan, and Syria total about $13 billion—$8.5 billion for Egypt and $2.2 billion each for Jordan and Syria.

Workers' remittances from abroad constitute on average about one third of Jordan's foreign exchange earnings ($872 million per annum during the period between 1986 and 1989). The average is about $2 billion annually for Egypt, thus accounting for 40 percent of its total foreign exchange receipts, and about $1 billion for Syria. These countries rely on the Gulf states as well for substantial financial assistance to support budget deficits and improve balance of payments positions. Financial assistance of the Gulf states to other Arab countries was on average about $6.4 billion per annum from 1985 to 1989, of which 86 percent was from Saudi Arabia and Kuwait alone. Jordan received about $1.7 billion; $1.8 billion went to Syria; and the Sudan and Yemen received $741 million and $500 million, respectively.

Whereas financial assistance and the export of goods and services dominated the economic activities of the public sector, the impact of workers' remittances was more pronounced in the private sector. According to national sources, about two-thirds of recorded workers' remittances constituted the sole source of income for over three million Egyptians, two million Jordanians, three million Yemenis, and one million Syrians. These remittances contributed indirectly to about 40 percent of the income of another two and a half million Egyptians, Jordanians, Yemenis, and Syrians. Over two thirds of the financial institutions and around 70 percent of today's incorporated businesses in these four countries would not have been fully financed without these remittances. Workers' remittances have been a major source of foreign exchange for the commercial banks in these countries and constituted over 45 percent of their foreign exchange earnings in 1989 and 54 percent at the end of July 1990.

Furthermore, the insecurity currently associated with the region has brought to a halt direct foreign investments and tourism receipts, which has seriously affected such countries as Egypt, Morocco, and Tunisia. But more importantly, the labor market in these countries suffered severe setbacks. The deterioration in the economic and social conditions of Arab expatriates in Kuwait and Iraq was disastrous. The misery of these expatriates was not limited to the loss of jobs; it also extended to the loss of savings, service remunerations, and personal assets.

These returnees not only affected the employment situation in their own countries but also aggravated the pressures on social services, the economic infrastructure, and resources in major population centers in Egypt, Syria, and Jordan. In Egypt, Cairo, with its population of fourteen million, accounts for almost 25 percent of the total Egyptian population. The greater Amman area has a population of about 1.3 million, or around two thirds of the total urban population, and greater Damascus accounts for over 12 percent of the Syrian population. The Kuwait crisis added further burdens to these cities because most of the returnees have settled there. The effect of these developments on the precarious environment in the cities may be enormous, particularly in Cairo, where urban services had already been extended to their utmost limits.

The damage caused by the Gulf crisis has not been limited to the front-line states; other countries such as India, Sri Lanka, the Philippines, and Pakistan have also suffered seriously. The economies of these countries have been strained by the increase in oil prices, the decrease of workers' remittances from the Gulf region, the costs of repatriation of their nationals, and the decline in export earnings due to the embargo on trade with Iraq and Kuwait. Three countries in the Gulf area—Saudi Arabia, Kuwait, and Iraq—employed more than 650,000 Indians, 700,000 Pakistanis, 600,000 Philippinos, and 300,000 Bangladeshi. Estimates of remittances flowing from these countries to the immigrants' home countries are estimated to have been between $4 and $5 billion annually.

The aftermath of the 1991 war in the Gulf will negatively affect the people of the region for years to come. Such has been the devastation in human, economic, and environmental terms that children yet unborn will pay the price. Much developmental progress, painstakingly achieved over several decades, lies in ruins, and no one can yet say how much time reconstruction will take, nor calculate its price in dollar terms.

What has happened in the Gulf is more than a political, economic, and social disaster; it is also the biggest environmental catastrophe witnessed to date. There were two major contributors to this catastrophe. First was Iraq's deliberate discharge of oil from Kuwait's storage tanks, loading platforms, and tankers. The release of oil from the offshore loading terminal at Mina al Ahmadi was a deliberate act by Iraq on January 24, 1991; 200,000 to 500,000 barrels of oil were dumped per day until January 27, 1991, when the Allied forces successfully stopped the discharge. It is estimated that no less than 4.5 million barrels were dumped into the Gulf during that period. This discharge created a giant oil slick estimated to be about 150 kilometers long and 30 kilometers wide.

This was probably the largest deliberately created oil slick in history. The 1979 blowout at the Ixtoc wellhead spilled about 4 million barrels over a period of ten months, the damage at the Norwuz and Ardeshir oil fields resulted in a spill of between 1.5 and 2.0 million barrels over a period of seven months in 1983, and the tanker accidents involving Amoco Cadiz (1987) and Exxon Valdez (1990) spilled approximately 1.3 and 0.24 million barrels, respectively.

The second, yet more drastic, catastrophe was the burning of more than 750 oil wells. The fires, with flames climbing as high as 500 feet above ground, destroyed between three and six million barrels a day of Kuwait's oil. This amount was almost four times the daily production of Kuwait before the invasion. The environmental destruction associated with the burning of this amount of oil is hard to assess fully, as burning on such a massive scale is historically unprecedented. How localized or how global the effect will be, no one can venture to predict. Clearly, however, the environmental damage to the region will be unequaled in its scale and duration. The Gulf War is testimony to the fact that peace and security are the most important prerequisites for an environmentally stable world.

The Kuwait War has also demonstrated to the world that a serious policy of demilitarization is critical for the Middle East. Currently, $700 billion is spent annually on weapons in the Middle East, that is, thirty times the amount of money spent on development assistance. Most of that money goes into making the weapons ever more efficient and ever more deadly.

A new global security order must be devised. But it must be one that holds to a wider concept of security, one that deals with threats that stem from failures in development, environmental degradation, and lack of progress toward democracy. Only with such a broader approach toward security can we find ways to a lasting world peace.

The Arab countries share with the developing world at large a number of pressing problems. Heading the list is poverty, which directly causes a pervasive reduction in the quality of life and provokes destructive practices while leaving countries and people without the means to cope with the ensuing results. Environmental disarray in developing countries cannot be eliminated without attacking poverty and related problems, especially uncontrolled population growth, at their roots. Few issues accentuate the interdependence of nations as much as the environmental issues.

Oil is at the center of most crises in the Middle East; however, water will become the cause of future conflicts if water disputes escalate into major problems. Water is a scarce commodity in the Middle East and particularly in the Arab countries. Fresh water represents only about one-thousandth of all the water on the planet. Although renewable water resources in the Arab world are estimated to be less than 1 percent (0.715) of total world resources, the total surface of the Arab countries is 9.4 percent of total world area. Water resources in these parts are about 1,475 cubic meters per capita, compared with a world average of 12,900 cubic meters. Add to this the uneven distribution of water in the Arab states, where scarcity is more critical for some countries than for others. The problem is further accentuated by the fact that other than the three major rivers, the Nile, the Tigris, and the Euphrates, which have a total water flow of approximately one billion cubic meters, there are no major renewable water systems in the region. Furthermore, these three rivers have their principal sources outside the region. These facts provide a clear indication of how closely linked the issues of water and security are in the Middle East.

Another area of special concern to the Arab countries is the conservation of marine resources. Coastal waters have been exposed to increasing levels of industrial contamination and poor development practices. More importantly, they are threatened by total degradation as a result of the Gulf crisis. The pollution of the region's coastal zones is therefore a source of great concern.

Finally, the Arab world must more seriously address the issues of human resources. With population imbalances and inadequate human resources development, the pressures on the already strained political, economic, social, and environmental systems are greatly exacerbated.

Population issues cannot be addressed in isolation. They are intimately linked to economic and social progress. In the aftermath of the Gulf crisis there is a growing recognition of the seriousness of the population and human resources development issues, both in the oil-rich but scarcely populated countries and in the non-oil, densely populated countries. These issues have proved to be at the core of development sustainability in each of these two groups. Governments will have to integrate population variables within their development strategies explicitly and courageously.

Democracy and human rights have also proved to be major determinants of sustainable development. These will become still more important issues in the coming years. Only in social and economic regimes that recognize the aspirations and the potential of the people, at both the collective and individual levels, can development efforts stand a chance of succeeding. It is clear that democratic practices are crucial to sustainable development. Constitutional governments, transparency in decision making, and accountability are essential components of a successful process. In 1990, the South Commission, concerned with Third World development problems, published the South Commission Report which, in its last paragraph, expresses this clearly:

In the final analysis, the South's plea for justice, equity, and democracy in the global society cannot be dissociated from its pursuit of these goals within its own societies.

Commitment to democratic values, respect for fundamental rights, particularly the right to dissent, fair treatment for minorities, concern for the poor and underprivileged, probity in public life, willingness to settle disputes without recourse to war, all these cannot but influence world opinion and increase the South's chances of securing a new World Order.

Foreword

General Walter E. Boomer, USMC

The successful war fought by the United States and its Coalition partners to liberate Kuwait after the invasion by Iraq was unique in many ways. It therefore offers a new model for crisis resolution that deserves careful analysis and study. This book provides great insight into the volatile Middle East on the critically important political dimension and an outstanding analysis of the events that culminated in the formation of a Coalition under United Nations auspices. Fundamental questions are raised regarding the political future of the region, its economic viability, as well as the role and impact of outside powers. This compendium also offers an outstanding study of strategic lessons of modern campaign planning, the various intricacies of opposing strategies, the application of military power, and the employment of sophisticated defense technology and war-fighting techniques. The book provides an excellent summary and serves as a remarkable starting point for further analysis.

From a U.S. military perspective, the successful Kuwait operation banished the ghost of Vietnam and validated U.S. joint warfare doctrine. The superior training, weapons systems, and tactics of the U.S. forces were there for the world to see. This was possible because the military asked for and received clearly defined objectives from its political leadership. On the international level this successful operation against Iraq was accomplished with the U.S. allies and the United Nations in the form of resolutions that delineated response options based upon political and grand strategic consensus.

The authors in this volume also debate the important implications and lessons of the Kuwait crisis on the role of such emerging powers as Germany and Japan and the future of Mediterranean and European relations.

I do not believe that it is too soon to draw major theoretical and practical conclusions from the Kuwait crisis and the ensuing war, as the chain of events from diplomatic failure to military action was relatively short and the war itself was a showcase for the decisive application of superior military power.

Acknowledgments

This book is the result of a protracted and rather complex process. The idea for the subject and the Second Liechtenstein Colloquium developed naturally by sheer force of events out of the dramatic impact of Iraq's aggression against Kuwait to which I came painfully close through Ahmad Al-Hamad, who became my student and friend seven days after the event in August 1990. The Second Liechtenstein Colloquium on European and International Affairs a few weeks after the liberation of Kuwait united (for the first time) all involved parties around one table in Vaduz, Liechtenstein.

It is customary to thank various individuals and institutions at this point, and it is a very happy obligation for me to express my gratitude to several persons without whose patience, understanding, and enduring personal and financial support neither this book nor the Liechtenstein Colloquia would have been possible. I would like to express my particular gratitude to H.S.H. Prince Hans Adam II of Liechtenstein with whom I began the entire endeavor, and whose interest and support is deeply appreciated; furthermore, to my friend Henry Bienen; to the Al-Hamad family, especially Abdlatif Al-Hamad; and to Philippe Cothier, Richard Falk, Robert Gilpin, Edgar Rachlin, Bernard J. Reverdin, Richard Ullman, John Waterbury, and William Wohlforth.

My particular thanks go to my co-editor, Charles R.H. Tripp; our long-standing friendship has resulted in this unique volume.

I also express my gratitude for financial and administrative support to the American Re-Insurance Company, the Austrian Cultural Institute/ Austrian Federal Ministry of Foreign Affairs, Werner Keicher, the Center of International Studies, Princeton University, the government of Liechtenstein, Matra S.A., Herbert Batliner, the National Bank of Kuwait, the Union Bank of Kuwait, Prince Torki Bin Saud al Kabeer, and the Swiss Federal Military Department, especially Theodor Winkler. I am most grateful to the Fürstliche Sekretariat, Schloss Vaduz; to Liselotte Berner-Dettwiler and Susanne Nüchtern; to Martina Michel-Hoch of the Liechtenstein National Tourist Office; to the management of Hotel Schlössle; and to the Colloquia's sponsoring airline, *Swissair*, particularly its office in Philadelphia, as well as to the management of the Bank in Liechtenstein, Vaduz.

For various kinds of administrative and secretarial support, I would like to express my thanks to my friends at Princeton University, its Center of International Studies, and the Woodrow Wilson School of Public and International Affairs.

For invaluable editorial assistance I thank Elsbeth Lewin, Ilene Cohen, Christopher Klaus, Anna Sims, and Erik Yesson, and also Claire del Medico. My particular appreciation goes to Marianne Donath, who has supported me, this and other projects beyond expectation through calm and hectic, funny and less pleasant moments and who certainly contributed more than her share. For the actual production, I acknowledge Barbara Ellington and Patricia Heinicke of Westview Press.

The main burden of more or less continuous and animated considerations, discussions, and reflections—aside from all the other aspects of marriage to a husband who is simultaneously teaching and involved in private diplomacy in various European capitals—had to be carried by my beloved wife, Annegret. She has supported and encouraged me, my ideas, and my projects over time while advancing her own demanding career in neuroscience. To my lovely daughters I offer my gratitude for the many Saturdays we spent together over pages of "Papa's other book."

To my mother, Maria Danspeckgruber, I express my warm gratitude for everything, but to Edouard and Elise Dettwiler-Dettwiler, my late in-laws, I dedicate this second volume of the LCM Series. They both offered stability, tradition, continuity, and a highly appreciated set of noble Central European values, and continuously demonstrated confidence in my projects—a wonderful and most appreciated kind of encouragement from generation to generation.

Wolfgang F. Danspeckgruber

1

Introduction

Wolfgang F. Danspeckgruber and Charles R.H. Tripp

A crisis in international relations is a useful reminder of some of the problems that beset the international system at any given moment in history. It is also frequently a reminder that problems exist in understanding or explaining the workings of that system. In both respects, the crisis caused by the Iraqi invasion of Kuwait in the summer of 1990 was no exception. As a relatively recent occurrence, it has the capacity, in retrospect, to shed light on the condition of the principal actors at that particular moment, raising questions about the significance of that specific juncture of events in world history. At the same time, the crisis could be said to throw light forward into the near future, providing clues about the dominant patterns of international behavior. Clearly, an interpretative challenge of two different kinds exists. For those who remain key actors in the political realm touched by the forces that shaped and defined the Kuwait crisis of 1990–1991, the lessons learned remain central to their own political strategies. Equally, for those interested less in questions of immediate advantage and security in the conduct of international relations than in the analytical framework within which such questions might usefully be examined, the lessons provide a challenge of interpretation. As in most questions of international relations, or indeed of politics generally, one of the abiding interests of the Kuwait crisis is the light it sheds on the nature of power. Whether viewed on the level of the states, of the regional subsystem, or globally, an understanding how power was perceived, handled, and projected underlies the various possible interpretations of the crisis. Of particular interest is the complex relationship between power and authority in the international system. Understanding this relationship requires, first, examining the ways in which the nature of the authority of the ruling groups or institutions of the major protagonists gave rise to beliefs in the utility of particular projections of power. Second, one must look at the authority of the principal institutions and rules of the international system itself and the capacity of such norms, if consistently internalized, to regulate the behavior of international actors. Third, one must look at the utility of sanctions—direct, possibly coercive uses of power—for upholding a particular international order. Furthermore, surrounding all of these dimensions are clusters of more specific issues that also illuminate the often problematic nature of the relationship between power and authority at various levels.

In the two states most intimately involved in the crisis—Iraq and Kuwait—there were clearly different perceptions about the authority of the rules governing bilateral relations between states. These differences can be explained in large part by the differences in the relative power of the two states. Kuwait, a weak state in the international system despite its considerable financial resources, had always been somewhat circumspect with regard to its northern neighbor. During the 1980s, however, the effects of Iraq's war with Iran began to change the nature of the relationship between the two countries. First, the financing of the Iraqi war effort fell in part on Kuwait, so that by the end of the war in 1988, Kuwait was one of Iraq's main creditors. Second, Iraq's determination to enlist international and regional support for its war against Iran had led it to a markedly conciliatory stance with regard to both the international and the regional rules of the game. Baghdad's new position appears to have reassured the Kuwaiti government—and others. In assessing how far to pursue its economic interests, the Kuwaiti government seems to have believed that its weakness relative to Iraq in other fields was somehow neutralized by Iraq's acceptance of the authority of international norms.

As the events of August 2, 1990, demonstrated, Kuwait remained weak vis-à-vis Iraq. The government of Iraq viewed the question of authority relative to power in different terms than Kuwait did. The massive increase in Iraq's military power during the war with Iran had been accompanied by its financial enfeeblement. At the same time, the rules of the international game Iraq had so assiduously cultivated, as well as the Arab state order it had so enthusiastically endorsed, were now threatening to foreclose on it. In Iraq's relations with external powers and in its relations with its Arab creditors, the authority of the rules of the international and regional systems seemed to be working against the immediate interests of the Iraqi government. Consequently, to have accepted their authority would have undermined the authority of the Iraqi regime itself. In such a situation, Iraq's use of military power seemed to make sense, since its relative advantage in the bilateral relationship with Kuwait appeared to be overwhelming. Indeed, in the context of the region, whether defined as the Persian Gulf or the Arab world more generally, nothing was likely to match Iraqi military power.

In invading Kuwait, Iraq attempted in a number of ways to keep the conflict within a setting that would maintain its massive relative advantage. First, it challenged the authority of an international state system founded on the interests of departed European imperial powers. Thus, Iraq's the old claim resurfaced that Kuwait was really part of Iraq, unjustly severed from the Iraqi state by British imperial map making. Iraq therefore depicted the invasion as merely the reassertion of its "national rights," too long denied by an unjust world order. Viewed in this light, Iraq could represent the Kuwaiti occupation as nothing more than the reconquest of part of Iraq itself, and could render the whole affair an internal matter, wholly within the jurisdiction of the Iraqi state. In this sphere, of course, the power of the Baghdad regime was absolute and the authority by which it claimed to be acting was merely that of national sovereignty.

Whether any members of the Baghdad regime seriously expected other states to accept this reasoning is unclear, although the supine reaction of the world community in 1980 when Iraq invaded Iran on similarly spurious grounds may have provided encouragement. Moreover, accompanying Iraq's claim that the invasion of Kuwait was merely an internal affair was its equally vehement assertion that it was an affair internal to the Arab world alone. This claim found greate sympathy within the region and gave rise to the call for an "Arab solution" to this allegedly distinctively Arab problem. In making this claim, Iraq sought to confine the crisis to an arena in which it believed it had the relative advantage, since, if the claim were accepted, it would have negated the authority of any non-Arab power to act in the matter.

Essentially, therefore, Iraq asserted that the authority of the international system did not apply in this case. Instead it advanced an alternative principle of national self-determination, which could be understood as applying either to an Iraqi framework or to a pan-Arab framework. Although this notion achieved a certain currency in some of the Arab states, others perceived it as a way for Iraq to attempt to hold what it had already seized. Any illusions that Egypt, Saudi Arabia, or Syria had entertained about the capacity of a distinct set of norms to restrain the behavior of one Arab state toward another had been shattered in August 1990. Paradoxically, therefore, the Iraqi government had demonstrated by its actions against Kuwait that no distinct normative order governed the relationships between the Arab states. Its use of military power to invade—indeed, to annihilate—a fellow Arab state had demonstrated clearly that the situation was not distinctly an Arab problem that could be resolved by an "Arab solution." It had become, instead, a crisis of international proportions in which the authority of the international system was to be used to justify the means of power by the dominant states in a bid to reverse the effects of Iraq's use of coercive power against Kuwait.

Having created a crisis of global significance, Iraq was forced to suffer the consequences of a global response. In this enlarged sphere, Iraqi power counted for little. A diverse array of regional states had a strong interest in seeing Iraqi power checked, if not wholly broken. Most directly for Saudi Arabia and the other Gulf Cooperation Council (GCC) states, but also for Egypt, Syria, Iran, and Israel, the prospect of blocking Iraqi ambitions and curbing Iraqi power was eminently desirable. Iraq's military actions had demonstrated that the Iraqi government rejected the rules that might be said to underlie even a minimal regional order (although Iran scarcely needed any reminders). Iraqi actions had threatened simultaneously the authority of the international order and the economic and strategic interests of the dominant industrialized states that had constructed and maintained that order. However, Iraq's actions also appeared to threaten the rules of that international order, the maintenance of which is in the national interest of the states that enjoy a dominant position within that order. In other words, by flouting this authority, Iraq challenged the very rules of the international game.

For the United States and its allies Iraq's actions provided a potent incentive for response. The speed, thoroughness, and coordination of that response testified to their view of the gravity of the Iraqi government's action. The imposition of sanctions, the mobilization of global support, and the rapid transfer of military forces to the Gulf made it clear that the United States and its allies felt that Iraq had not simply challenged the power of particular states: It had challenged the principles upon which that power claimed to be founded. In their view, Iraq had flouted the authority of the global order and, indirectly, the authority of those governments that constituted the ruling hierarchy.

Iraq had few resources to deploy in response to this reaction. It no longer had recourse to the assistance of an international patron that was on a par with the Coalition rapidly forming against it. Iraq's invasion of Kuwait coincided with the twilight of the USSR and a time of disintegration of the logic of the Cold War. Iraq was alone against the dominant global powers and the world order associated with them. During the crisis the Iraqi government questioned the authority of that order in a number of ways. It argued that its invasion of Kuwait was aimed at redressing the imbalance in power between rich and poor, not simply in the region, but also in the world. Further, Iraq persistently attempted to link its occupation of Kuwait with the Israeli occupation of the West Bank, Gaza, and Golan in 1967. The Iraqi government promised to consider withdrawing from Kuwait only after significant steps had been taken by the international community to ensure the Israeli withdrawal from the territories occupied in 1967. Its challenge was intended to serve a twofold purpose. First, a positive response by the dominant world powers to the Iraqi suggestion would have prepared the way for an honorable withdrawal from Kuwait—a withdrawal that the Iraqi authorities came to realize was increasingly inevitable. In other words, Iraq's initial use of power would have been shown to have laid the foundation for the authority of the Iraqi government that had devised this strategy, both in Iraq and in the Middle East.

Second, if the international community did not agree to Iraq's suggestion, as was the case, then the Iraqi government would have grounds for leveling a charge of hypocrisy and double standard. Indeed, this theme was in evidence throughout the crisis. Iraq's intention was presumably to challenge once again the authority of the world order by demonstrating that, for all the talk of principles by the dominant powers, in the event of military occupation, when their own interests as world powers were concerned, they could ignore the authority of those principles. The Iraqi government was attempting to demonstrate that the crisis over Kuwait was not about the authority of the rules of international behavior, but about power politics. Iraq argued that the dominant states would not act against Israel because that country was useful to the projection of their own power. However, because Iraq had dared to challenge that power, it was to be subjected to the full force of Western military might, thinly veiled by the claims of protecting the authority of an international order. Again, one cannot ascertain whether the Iraqi government seriously thought that its accusations would divide the international Coalition and confuse some of its members, but Baghdad did reiterate the theme again and again. The charge of a "double standard" became the rallying cry of various groups in various places against the military action being planned by the American-led Coalition. It also induced some members of that Coalition to press for acknowledgment of the possibility of "linkage" between the Kuwait crisis and the Arab-Israeli conflict. Even those who most vehemently denied the possibility of "linkage," such as the United States itself, felt they had no choice but to signal a willingness to attend to the Arab-Israeli conflict once the Kuwait crisis was resolved. Although this response did not signify acknowledgment of the Iraqi idea of consequential linkage, it did link the two issues sequentially and thereby indicated some sensitivity to the charge.

Nevertheless, this sensitivity was largely pragmatic. The impression given by the Bush administration and others was less that a true contradiction existed in their attitudes toward the two issues than that the belief that such a contradiction might exist was in some way damaging to the effectiveness of the Coalition against Iraq. Thus, American gestures or references made toward the Arab-Israeli conflict in the course of the Kuwait crisis had more to do with reassuring less certain allies than with an attempt to cover up an alleged case of a double standard. Indeed, the whole issue of double standards seems to have been the result of a misunderstanding about the nature of power and authority in the international system.

For the governments of the dominant world powers, as for those of all states, the national interest is the single standard by which to judge the worth of any given arrangement. In the final analysis, the national interest is the authority by which all states act. They may cede a degree of authority to other, nonnational bodies but only because they believe that such a concession is in their long-term interest, however defined. Thus, the world order is inevitably based on the values and proclivities of the dominant states. That many other states subscribe to those principles clearly enhances their authority. However, this authority is not some form of an ethical absolute. On the contrary, it has been constructed in the image of the great powers within a system designed to serve their purposes. That there may be a large degree of agreement about those purposes and, therefore, the value of the system of rules in which they may legitimately be pursued is testimony as much to the real power of the dominant states as to the abstract authority of the system as a whole.

In some respects, this highlights one of the problems facing the Iraqi government in 1990–1991. Having flouted the rules of one system and the authority by which those rules were invoked, the Iraqi government could not escape the logical consequences of its actions. For one thing, its charge that the dominant powers adhered to a double standard could have little effective purchase. These powers were acting according to the single standard of national interest. To this end, they invoked the rules of the world order that they themselves dominated, since Iraq had so obviously and unequivocally broken the rules of that order. At the same time, because Iraq's action had materially affected the specific regional interests of particular states and had demonstrated an intention to project power that was unrestrained by anything other than prudential considerations, the immediate foundations of the power of these regional states appeared to be put at risk. The nature of the Iraqi action—the context of its occurrence and the dual character of the threat it represented—suggested both the nature of the response and the authority invoked to justify that response. Furthermore, Iraq simply did not have the moral resources or the material capacity to back up its government's claims to be acting in the name of a new, more just world order. It was therefore confronted by the unmediated military power of the alliance ranged against it.

As the military campaigns of the Kuwait War demonstrated, Iraq's power, although formidable in certain contexts, was less than that of the Coalition. Military operations are, of course, an exercise in power, but they also have an authoritative component. On both levels, the armed forces of the Iraqi state were found wanting. Precisely because the Iraqi government's power failed so spectacularly, its long-standing deterrent effect within Iraq evaporated. In much of the country no authority structure existed to maintain domestic order when military power collapsed. The consequences were the widespread uprisings in the north and south of the country in March 1991.

It was during these uprisings that the question arose whether the international Coalition that had liberated Kuwait should use its probably unstoppable power to capture Baghdad, thereby ending the rule of Saddam Hussein. Once again, the problematic relationship between power and authority in international relations surfaced. It was generally believed that only the Iraqis themselves have the authority to change their government. But, in 1991, those Iraqis who wished to change their government *and* had the authority to do so clearly lacked the power to carry this project through. They appeared to require the assistance of the foreign Coalition forces.

For the United States and its allies, however, the situation raised two problems. First, they could not be certain that the Coalition that had been assembled to uphold the sovereignty of Kuwait and to use force to reestablish that sovereignty would accede to undertaking a massive intervention in Iraq in an attempt to establish a particular form of political order in the country. The Coalition's intervention in Iraq might not have made much difference in terms of the power needed to effect a decisive change in the power of the Iraqi government's forces. It would, however, have posed a challenge to the authority America and its allies would have had to invoke to justify such an exercise of power. Second, the situation touched on another aspect of the relationship between power and authority—the realization that the use of power to dismantle one political order, such as the regime of Saddam Hussein, would not automatically result in the suggestion of an authoritative successor. Indeed, many people feared that powerful and profound intervention by external forces might complicate and indeed delay the emergence of any new authoritative structures in Iraq, leaving the foreign forces with the task of maintaining order without the backing of any accepted Iraqi authority.

The potential consequences of this course of action, redolent as they were of other inconclusive and ultimately damaging military interventions, were enough to discourage the Bush administration from undertaking military involvement on this scale. Instead, the order restored to the

Gulf in the aftermath of the crisis over Kuwait reflected the predilections and interests of the principal players. This outcome should not be surprising, since Iraq's challenge to that order is what provoked the crisis in the first place. The UN and hence Washington and the international community had used power to restore the disrupted order, invoking the authority of the United Nations as justification for the continued use of that power.

As a consequence of the Kuwait crisis, Iraq's military power has been reduced or restrained in certain areas. Its ballistic missile program and its programs for developing weapons of mass destruction have been severely curtailed, possibly terminated, by the intrusive activities of UN teams. Under the terms of the Security Council resolutions, the Iraqi armed forces have been constrained from reestablishing central government control in the northern Kurdish areas of the country. Similarly, the Iraqi air force has been prohibited from operating in areas of the south, although central government control has been reestablished there. All of these measures, as well as the continuing economic sanctions, have been implemented in the name of the United Nations; all of them, however, are backed up and made a reality by the power of the United States. The latter is the power that Iraq has felt whenever its government has been tempted to defy the impositions placed upon it; consequently, Iraq perceives the invocation of UN authority as merely a cover for the power of the United States.

In other words, Iraqi attitudes toward the authority of the international order do not seem to have changed much. On the contrary, the experiences of the Kuwait crisis and its aftermath appear to have reinforced the Iraqis' belief that power—expressed as states' interests and backed by coercive might—is the decisive element in international relations. The principles of international order are unrecognized and the authority of those who act to enforce those principles is unacknowledged. Some might attribute this to the fact that more than three years after the crisis, the regime that initiated it is still in power in Baghdad. Others might see these principles of international order as a more enduring legacy of the Kuwait crisis, unconnected to the nature of the particular government that rules in Baghdad. Insofar as other legacies may combine to arouse the suspicions and the sense of grievance of subsequent Iraqi governments, there is concern that order in the Gulf cannot be maintained by any authoritative structure of mutual restraint but must instead be guaranteed by the power of military deterrence.

In particular, this concern focuses on the future relationship between Iraq and Kuwait. It is clearly going to be the key to understanding the degree to which power, as opposed to the authoritative norms of international behavior, will govern interstate relations. In the aftermath of the crisis, the balance of advantage between the two states would seem to lie with Kuwait. Iraq has been weakened militarily and economically. Iraq's earlier debts remain, and to them has been added the bill for war reparations. Iraq's territorial integrity is in question, whereas that of Kuwait has been consolidated. The border between Kuwait and Iraq has been demarcated, having been redrawn in certain important areas in Kuwait's favor. Kuwait has entered into military cooperation agreements with the major Western powers, most extensively with the United States, and has embarked upon an ambitious program of weapons acquisition. Although its military capability will obviously never match that of Iraq, it seems that the Kuwaiti government intends to compensate for its shortfall in relative power by relying on the power of its Western allies, i.e the United States. The question that remains, however, is whether for Iraq all of these manifestations of power will override the absence of an authoritative structure of international restraint. The disturbing possibility exists that these manifestations of power—the reparations, the military alliance with the West, and the border settlement—may, in the eyes of such a government, further undermine the authority of the international order, the very principles of which are invoked as the justification for their imposition on Iraq. The question any future Kuwaiti government must ask is whether Kuwait can base its future relations with Iraq on the assumption that the power that rescued it in 1990–1991 will be as readily available in changed circumstances in the future. This question is particularly relevant if one considers a future Iraqi government, resentful at what it regards as disabilities forced on it by the Kuwait crisis, that pursues its objectives and deploys its power in a more prudent way than did the regime of Saddam Hussein.

These are questions for the future, but they are questions raised by the behavior of all the actors involved in the crisis of 1990–1991. As discussed in this introduction, it could be argued that the Kuwait crisis was caused by a misperception on the part of a number of key states of the relationship between power and authority at different levels of the international system. In particular, the uncertainty displayed by many of the actors regarding the underpinnings of authority in international relations, as well as regarding the limits to power, were striking themes of the crisis and its aftermath. These aspects of international behavior are addressed in differing ways in the following chapters. The authors examine the crisis from the perspectives of Iraq and the Arab states; the various military dimensions of the conflict; the effects of the conflict on economic power, expressed in terms of oil resources; and the reactions of outside powers and the world order associated with their interests. All of the authors share a common concern to explain and to understand the ways in which the relationships between particular forms of power and particular conceptions of authority shape the dominant international order. It is hoped that through an understanding of the potential, but also the limitations, of both power and authority internationally and regionally, Iraq and Kuwait will not find themselves again locked into the logic of the events of 1990–1991 at some time in the future.

The Kuwait Crisis and Its Implications—a Summary

This book presents an overview of selective, significant issues in the causes, developments, and implications of the Kuwait crisis from 1990 to 1994. Part I elaborates on specific national and regional aspects of the crisis.

In the initial chapter of Part I, Charles Tripp analyzes the interaction between perception and strategy within Iraq. He contends that the way decisions were made by Baghdad during the conflict, and the reasoning behind those decisions, may have been significantly different than generally assumed. Saddam Hussein's strategy had priorities other than the territorial occupation of Kuwait, and the fact that the Coalition powers chose to fight plunged Iraq into a war that Saddam may have believed would never materialize. Tripp concludes that this crisis is a useful reminder that "political power is as much about the capacity to retain control of the symbolic universe that lends credibility and authority to leadership as it is about control of the material resources of economic and coercive power."

Then Laurie Mylroie elaborates on the events leading to the Iraqi aggression. She argues that although the timing of Iraq's invasion of Kuwait may have been dictated by its internal and financial problems, Saddam's hope really was to establish control over the oil on the Arab side of the Gulf.

In the final chapter of Part I, Gudrun Krämer discusses the implications of the Gulf War on the Arab state system. She argues that Saddam Hussein managed relatively early in the crisis to create some form of support from the Arab imaginaire—Arab Islamic solidarity—and that rather than creating a new order, the crisis demonstrated the primacy of national interest and of breaking the last taboos of Arab consensus. However, it also brought the relative end to superpower confrontation and altered the balance of power in the Gulf region. Although the USSR and then Russia normalized relations with some former opponents, they reduced their support for former allies as well. All of these factors would allow for fresh approaches to conflict management, especially in the Arab-Israeli case. Various approaches were tried in the postwar order, as, for instance, a six-plus-two proposition (excluding Jordan, Iraq, and Iran), which failed, though the Palestinian-Israeli solution appears by now to work, and bilateral agreements throughout the region are proliferating.

Any new Middle East order, however, has to rest on several premises, including the nonuse of force, privacy of negotiation, and the formal recognition of Israel. Even more important, compliance with peaceful negotiations should be rewarded and noncompliance punished—but who would sanction these agreements?

Power, Strategy, and Technology

Part II examines implications of the concept of power, strategy, and technology, and looks at their relationship with particular focus on the lessons learned from the Kuwait War. It compares strategies used during the war with the effects of military technology, grand strategic concepts, defense trade, and energy supply (that is, oil).

In Chapter 5, "How Kuwait Was Won: Strategy in the Gulf War," Lawrence Freedman and Ephraim Karsh demonstrate that the Gulf War's "most important feature in military terms was its decisive, overwhelming character." The Coalition strategy was a relatively protracted systematic air campaign followed by a land campaign based on envelopment and maneuver. Iraq's strategy was to threaten the United States with a "second Vietnam" and to absorb the air offensive.

On many occasions, Saddam Hussein was in a state of military defensiveness, but politically he was nearly always on the offensive, using the hostages as human shields and threatening to use gas and missile attacks on Israel.

A major surprise of the war for the liberation of Kuwait was the flight of the best planes in the Iraqi air force to Iran, which illustrates Saddam's restraint in the employment of air power (he may have ordered the flight speculatively in preparation for the time after the war). Another surprise was the absence of a valid Iraqi counter-strategy in the land war, which was ended successfully for the Coalition after the 100th hour and the "turkey shoot" of Iraqi units trapped on the road to Basra.

According to Freedman and Karsh, the Iraqi leader thus made major miscalculations, although once the war was over, he unleashed a vicious campaign to put down the postwar insurrections in Iraq.

The authors also argue that the Bush administration accepted General Colin Powell's plea to employ a sufficiently large force in the Gulf and "to refrain from engaging in political micro-management." Further, despite President Bush's perception that the successful campaign would also eradicate Vietnam malaise in the United States, the authors contend that a real difference existed between Vietnam and the Gulf in the political and military context.

In the next chapter, Erik Yesson discusses the relationship between politics, technology, and military force. He argues that "technology made a difference in the Gulf War, not because the quality of Coalition personnel or doctrine was irrelevant but because technology allowed ... the Coalition's strategy to control important political dimensions of the war." Yesson states that the new systems employed drew upon the latest technologies, which offered vastly improved capabilities, and contends that "it was the technological sophistication of the weapons that allowed Coalition leaders to retain political control over the war."

Yesson debates various strategic developments in the course of the war, accepts the Coalition's amphibious landing in Kuwait proper as a rather effective strategy, and believes the destruction of the Iraqi air force and its formidable ground-based air defense was the Coalition's major achievement. He is critical of the effectiveness of the Coalition's defense against the Scud Iraq missiles, as only 70 percent of Scuds Iraq launched against Saudi Arabia and only 40 percent of those it fired against Israel were intercepted. In referring to Theodore Postol's study, he claims that Patriot SAMs (Surface to Air Missiles) may have even "intensified the damage to Israeli cities."

Yesson provides and explains numerous fascinating, technological details of the air, ground, and sea combat, and argues that technology was critical in mastering Iraq's countermeasures and any friction in the conduct of war that was decisive and also influenced the politics after the cease-fire.

Gustav Däniker offers remarkable strategic comments and asks pertinent questions in his chapter, "Classical Campaign in a Difficult Environment." He states that General Norman Schwarzkopf repeatedly referred to Hannibal's legendary victory at Cannae and argues that Schwarzkopf's combat concept was therefore to "cut off and kill." The Coalition forces employed the "air and battle doctrine" including a twofold strategic operation—a "small pincer movement" in Kuwait and a "big encirclement" across Iraqi territory. Both operations were executed with the highest military professionalism. Däniker also explains that the outflanking of Iraq's defense positions was modelled after Field Marshall Bernard Montgomery's operation at El Alamein during World War II. The Iraqi soldiers were demoralized by the enormous bombardment and terrible logistical conditions. The Coalition leadership, however, overrated their combat power to the very end. Däniker argues that the Coalition's "obvious fixation on annihilation and rigid operational planning led to strategic negligence."

He contends that there was at least some neglect by the Coalition's (U.S.) military leadership of enemy psyche and environment, saying, for example, "In the battle damage assessment (BDA), the important qualitative psychological component seems to have been missing." Was there a lack of operational flexibility? Däniker concludes that in the future, punitive operations by the UN will have to be of a highly differentiated nature: Indeed, he states that there ought to be a warfare "costing as few human lives as possible" and aimed at minimizing enemy losses, which may make a durable peace easier to obtain and maintain.

Christian Catrina elaborates on the effects of the Gulf War on the transfer of conventional arms. He concludes that the war "occurred at an intersection of two major currents," namely, "the frequent use of military force in the Third World and the winding down of the East-West conflicts, which allowed a more forceful intervention." The major weapons suppliers to Iraq were the Soviet Union, France, and China; hence, Catrina assumes some Iraqi hope may have rested on possible support from Beijing.

Regarding regional arms trade, he claims that the image of Russian weapons systems has been hit hard due to their poor performance during the war. Certainly, Moscow quickly pointed out that bad Iraqi tactics and poorly trained operators may have been the real cause for defeat. Nevertheless, Catrina predicts a significant arms race in the Middle East, despite the fact that an imminent military threat has diminished. The lessons learned from the war, especially that the Western sophisticated defense systems perform very well, have greatly stimulated the purchase of advanced systems by Gulf states. Catrina urges stronger control of arms transfers and advocates strict international monitoring.

In the last chapter of Part II, Robert Lieber discusses potential implications of the Kuwait War for the world oil market and global energy security. He concludes the war will have few effects in these areas for three reasons: Future military threats can be minimized, the supply and price of petroleum are manageable, and the elasticity of both supply and demand appear to ensure that world energy markets can cope with potential disruptions.

But the war could have posed one real danger: Had Iraqi forces promptly driven into Saudi Arabia, a longer and much more costly war would have been triggered. However, having remained untouched, Saudi Arabia has alone made up for the loss of Kuwaiti and Iraqi oil through an increase in production by 3 million barrels a day. Nevertheless, oil prices tripled from $13/barrel in May 1990 to over $40/barrel in early autumn and fell back to $20/barrel by spring 1991.

Lieber discusses the concept of oil as a problem in international political economy and contends that a solely economic perspective remains seriously deficient. He quotes Robert Gilpin's assumption that political scientists tend to overlook markets and that economists tend to neglect the importance of power. He also shows that members of the Organization of Oil Producing Countries (OPEC) were able to absorb the higher oil costs only because of the absence of Iraqi and Kuwaiti oil and the equally reduced output from Soviet sources. Lieber recognizes the remaining potential dangers and instability, including regional terrorism and Islamic fundamentalism, and, in light of the issues of Iraq's clandestine weapons programs, notes that the West has to brace itself for any such new developments.

Outside Powers and the Emerging Order

Part III elaborates on the impact of the Kuwait crisis on outside powers and the emerging order. The authors discuss a unipolar security system; the role of the Soviet Union and subsequently Russia in the Kuwait-Iraq relationship; the behavior of, and effects of the crisis on, Germany and the European countries; the EC; the effects of the crisis on Japan's international position; the role of the UN; and the interrelationship of the Kuwait crisis, the fall of the Soviet Union, and the disintegration of Yugoslavia.

The U.S. role in Gulf security is discussed by Amin Saikal, who claims that of all U.S. presidents since Truman, George Bush did the most to establish U.S. dominance in the Gulf. Saikal explains the unipolar security system the United States has established in the Gulf and questions its contribution to peace and stability. He suggests that another, more effective system could be established by creating a comprehensive collective security arrangement in which all constituent states could participate without the military involvement of outside powers, that is, the United States.

Saikal contends that "the real purpose underlying Washington's containment of Iraq is to let Saddam's regime go on indefinitely ... as a weak, demonized and chastised force to which Washington could point to substantiate its perception of regional enemy." With regard to Iran, he feels the Clinton administration essentially follows a policy "with a high degree of venom" that has been in place ever since the success of the Islamic Revolution in 1979. In Saikal's opinion, Iran is searching for a better relationship with the West as it faces a disastrous economic situation with potential for widespread social unrest, the result of being situated almost like an "island... surrounded by regions of active instability."

Saikal sees several dangers facing the region in the late 1990s, including problems arising from political suppression, administrative corruption, lack of political accountability, human rights violations, problems in healthcare, social divisions, the plight of ethnic minorities (Kurds, Palestinians, Shi'i) and their migration, political dissidents, and environmental hazards.

William C. Wohlforth asserts that the situation in the Gulf represented the last major foreign policy crisis for the Soviet Union and that it rang in its demise. With regard to President Gorbachev's personal leadership, Wohlforth perceives that he espoused, on the one hand, a "dual policy" and, on the other, a high degree of ambiguity. In Wolforth's analysis, ambiguity formed an important part of Gorbachev's "new thinking" on foreign policy and helped prevent the domestic opposition that is typical in declining powers. Nevertheless, ambiguity has its time limits, and costs accrue over time. The unification of Germany, the Kuwait War, and its disastrous outcome for Iraq (as a Soviet ally) all contributed to a loss of credibility, and in December 1991 the "façade collapsed" and the USSR dissolved.

In her view from Moscow, Irina Zviagelskaia maintains that unprecedented Soviet-U.S. cooperation existed during the Kuwait crisis, although it became an additional cause for political struggle in Soviet society. The Soviet Union's cooperation with Washington reflected the outcome of Gorbachev's (pro-Western) new thinking and the USSR's complex client relationship in the Middle East. But the developing Kuwait crisis aggravated the acute political struggle occurring in the USSR, causing, among other things, the sudden resignation of Foreign Minister Eduard Shevardnadze in December 1990 in protest against "advancing dictatorship." According to Zviagelskaia, criticism of Shevardnadze's cooperative Gulf policy also contributed to his decision to resign. She contends that the Iraqi aggression came at a time when a new, much clearer Soviet Middle East policy was in the making (as part of a new foreign policy) that included a clear demonstration of the USSR's geostrategic interests and its national and religious structure. Today, however, many of the independent former Soviet republics are devising their own foreign policy, directed by economic and strategic considerations. Zviagelskaia also contends that the Gulf needs a working security system, the main burden of which will have to be shouldered by the United States. It seems, therefore, that Moscow has accepted a global division of spheres of influence between U.S. and Russian interests.

In Chapter 13, Helmut Hubel evaluates the impact of the Kuwait crisis on the Europeans and especially on the newly unified Germany. He argues that despite the far-reaching changes in Central and Eastern Europe since 1989–1990 and the unification of Germany, the 1991 Gulf War shocked Europeans and their leaders—and the experience was intensified by the violent breakup of Yugoslavia immediately following. He notes that all of the European countries—Germany included—supported the operation of the Coalition with money, transport facilities, and even military equipment and troops. Even neutral Austria and former Warsaw Pact countries such as Hungary facilitated allied operations. In addition, the Western European Union (WEU) and the European Political Cooperation (EPC) played an important part in focusing EC policy on aiding the allied effort, and the British advocated a strong response in support of the United States. For France, however, the crisis posed a problem, since Paris and Baghdad were major trading partners and France had become Iraq's strongest supporter while Iraq had become France's largest debtor. President François Mitterrand eventually preferred close cooperation with the United States in the operations against Iraq to keep the U.S. engagement in Europe.

Germany—according to Hubel—felt it important to keep the unification process in motion and not to upset Moscow. Although the German people were overwhelmingly opposed to involving German soldiers in the conflict, Germany did send an air force detachment and air defense equipment to Turkey and supported the Coalition financially and with military hardware. Hubel claims that Germany actually contributed much more than is generally known by the public. The Kuwait crisis became an important catalyst for Germany to participate in international operations in a way that matched the expectations of its allies and in opposition to the domestic limitations imposed by the constitution and party politics. It also provided a catalyst for participation in international peacekeeping and in NATO's out-of-area operations.

In Chapter 14, Masaru Tamamoto, with the support of Amy Cullum, contends that the Kuwait crisis was the first real trial of Japan's pacifist ideal as set forth in its constitution. The question for Japan was, how should it become involved in the Coalition's efforts? The U.S. pressure on Japan to "join the team" and send minesweepers and oil supply ships grew stronger as the crisis continued; the Bush administration thought a show of Japanese flag in the Gulf would be beneficial and indicated that merely sending money was not enough. By September 1990, Prime Minister Toshiki Kaifu had arranged to contribute U.S.$4 billion, but the U.S. pressure to display the Japanese flag in the Gulf remained.

The Japanese problem was its foreign policy orientation to Gandhian peace, which was reflected in the constitution, parliament, and public opinion. According to the authors, the United States "had demanded Japanese participation ... , mistakenly assuming that the Japanese would readily agree to this demand because they wanted and needed U.S. protection. But there was a growing Japanese understanding that their country did not need American protection ... this was new to the U.S.-Japanese relationship."

Tamamoto and Cullum contend furthermore that the Japanese public was not ready to "fully support the military response chosen by the U.S." Postwar Japan has shown a willingness to negotiate when its citizens are taken hostage by terrorists, whereas the United States has been willing to sacrifice its citizens.

Generational differences also emerged during the debate over Japanese participation in the Coalition's efforts: The older generation rejected a military option, and the younger was more concerned about good relations with the United States. Although the debate continued throughout and after the conflict because of, among other things, renewed participation requests including requests for financial help after the war, four Japanese minesweepers were dispatched to the Gulf in April 1991. In the end, Japan had contributed $9 million and some military representation, but, of most importance, it agreed to send a battalion to Cambodia for the UN operation of 1992.

During the Kuwait crisis the United Nations was not really in the "driver's seat," Helmut Freudenschuss argues in the next chapter, but the United States steered the Security Council with vision and skill. The American leadership contributed to the speedy and decisive action by the Security Council. China abstained from most Council decisions, though cooperation among the P-5 reached an unprecedented peak during the crisis and contributed to a new limitation of the role of the nonpermanent members in the UN Security Council.

Freudenschuss does not believe that Desert Shield and Desert Storm are good examples of a working system of collective security, nor of such a UN system. In his view, collective security means applying more regulations of the UN Charter than just Articles 40 and 41; it means applying also Articles 42 to 45, including the formation of a UN high command, a UN military, and staff committee. According to Freudenschuss, none of these latter articles have been applied and he finds it difficult to believe that they will be applied when there are representatives of fifteen countries (or more) in the Security Council. He therefore concludes that a new system of collective security forces in the international system has emerged and that the United Nations and its legal administrative dimension require major revamping.

In the last chapter, Wolfgang Danspeckgruber argues that the Kuwait crisis not only rang out the Cold War in the areas of perception, operation, and international cooperation but also introduced a new unstable and unpredictable phase in the international system. Problems in peace making and peacekeeping, humanitarian assistance, intervention, ruthless leadership, geopolitical expansion, national interest, and so forth, have emerged. Most importantly, however, traditional geopolitical interests including hegemony and spheres of influence and alliance formation have intruded into the international system. For Danspeckgruber, the Kuwait crisis was in many ways part of an international triple crisis that included the rapid intensification of the inner-Yugoslav crisis and the disintegration of the Soviet Union. Also, he contends that a last-minute rescue attempt by Mikhail Gorbachev to stabilize the Soviet Baltic republics faltered due to the real-time capabilities of modern international media, much in contrast to the successful Soviet operation of 1956 in Hungary under Khrushchev. Today's forceful presence of CNN in Europe is another result of the Kuwait war.

Media, leadership interests, geographic proximity, and strategic calculations played major roles in the Kuwait conflict and contributed to its expansion. All these considerations also supported the forging of cooperation between Yugoslavia and Iraq, which, according to Danspeckgruber, explains why Iraq could rebuild its armed forces so quickly and efficiently, with a result being the new "show of force" in October 1994.

PART ONE

National and Regional Dimensions

2

Symbol and Strategy: Iraq and the War for Kuwait

Charles R.H. Tripp

To understand the strategies pursued by Saddam Hussein and the Iraqi leadership during 1990–1991, analysts have made much of utilitarian and material considerations. Financial crisis, oil-related ambitions, territorial expansionism, and calculations revolving around the real or imagined military capabilities of Iraq have all been examined for their part in influencing the strategies of the Iraqi leadership. There can be little doubt that elements of all of these factors played a part in shaping the policy choices that constituted Iraqi strategy. The emphasis placed on one of these factors rather than another has largely depended upon one's interpretation of the priorities of the ruling regime. These priorities may vary depending upon the circumstances, but, by and large, it has been suggested that Iraq's invasion of Kuwait was an overwhelmingly pragmatic endeavor geared to maximizing perceived and generally agreed advantages.

While not denying the importance of these approaches and their contribution to understanding the material parameters within which the Iraqi leadership made the decision to invade Kuwait and then chose to stick with it until driven out by force, there is also another aspect to these decisions to be considered, —that is, the meaning of Saddam Hussein's and the ruling elite's decisions within their moral universe. Although there may be general agreement about Iraq's objective and the observable features of Iraq's situation as a state both before and after the invasion of Kuwait, the reasoning behind the Iraqi government's responses or reactions to these circumstances cannot be easily explained.

In a system of power such as that established by Saddam Hussein in Iraq, a good deal of obscurity exists concerning the processes by which policy is determined. In part, this obscurity is the natural outgrowth of the secrecy and conspiratorial nature of the system itself. In Iraq, it is in part (at least since Saddam Hussein became president) the result of his determination not to appear to be acting on behalf of, or to be answerable to, any ideological agenda or sociopolitical grouping not entirely of his own making and under his own control. In part, also, it has been a feature of Saddam Hussein's style, in which his declared objectives bear a contingent, rather than a necessary, connection to his actual objectives. Using this style, Saddam Hussein has consistently endeavored to create the room for maneuver that he appears to believe is necessary for his political survival and at the same time has sought to enthuse those around him and the population of Iraq for the order he claims to represent.[1]

Analysts have little doubt that during the war the formulation of Iraqi strategy remained firmly in the hands of both Saddam Hussein and a small, trusted inner circle whose perspectives were almost identical to his. However, in a larger sense those perspectives and strategies were products of the political world of Iraq—a world composed not simply of the leader but also of the structures of Iraqi political society and the ideational environment, or political culture, in which those structures make sense and that they, in turn, help to reproduce.

Because all developments both within Iraq and outside its borders are in some fashion filtered through the state's ideational environment, it constitutes the setting in which Saddam Hussein and those close to him assign significance to those developments. In this respect, the strategies of war become indicators of meaning in Iraqi politics, privileging certain glosses over others and making some courses of action more desirable than others. Frequently, as clearly happened in 1990–1991, apparent disconnections between courses of action and their presumed intended effects can be disconcerting for outside observers. As much of the comment on Iraqi strategies has indicated, such discrepancies can lead to bewilderment and a feeling that the decisions in question are being taken by someone wholly out of touch with "reality."

One must, therefore, think about the nature of the "reality"—the rules, conventions, and values—according to which Saddam Hussein operated. Once the events that occurred are considered from this perspective, the rationale behind them may become clearer. Consequently, this chapter examines the symbolic importance of the war in the context of Iraqi politics and the kind of regime that Saddam Hussein constructed to dominate the Iraqi state.

During the invasion of Kuwait, as at other times, Saddam Hussein was indisputably the autocrat who dominated the system in a way unequaled by any other figure within the regime. However, like any other autocrat, he needed a circle of more or less trusted lieutenants to do his bidding and provide him with the degree of social control that he required. Because of the power that he perforce delegated to them, these men were best placed to advise Saddam Hussein and, by the same token, to remove him should the occasion have warranted it and the opportunity presented itself. Avoiding such occasions and denying others such opportunities have been the preoccupation of all rulers of Iraq, including Saddam Hussein. To remain in power they need both skill at playing upon the imaginations of those whose obedience makes their power possible and skill at controlling the mechanisms of coercion that allow disobedience to become a threat.

Saddam Hussein has exhibited these skills in abundance and has deployed them with a resourcefulness and ruthlessness that have ensured his political survival under improbable circumstances. His knowledge of the Iraqi political world and his ability to manipulate it to his own advantage—regardless of the cost to the Iraqi state or its population—have been notorious. Despite defections, executions, and conspiracies, he has succeeded in maintaining within his regime a more or less cohesive inner core that has seemed to give him great latitude in his dealings with others. At various times, he has sacrificed territory, ideology, or the economic future of his state in the belief that all that does not immediately serve his purposes can be jettisoned. If the center can hold, according to this thinking, then all is possible. The war with Iran was likely based on these premises. So, too, was the war over Kuwait and the events that followed it.

Collective Myths and the Impulse to Invade Kuwait

A number of themes came to the fore in Iraq both before and after the invasion that shed light on what the invasion meant for Saddam Hussein and his circle. First, there was the resonance of Arab nationalism, which was used by Saddam Hussein in a number of ways to indict the Kuwaiti government and to justify Iraq's occupation of the country. Second, and often simultaneously, there was an apparent distinctive Iraqi nationalism concerning the territorial claims of Iraq and the relative importance of the interests of Iraq and Kuwait. Although these themes were publicly proclaimed and often aimed at relatively wide audiences, Saddam Hussein was also addressing—and was certainly more concerned about—constituencies closer to the inner core of his regime.

The common cultural inheritance shared by these constituencies seems to have given rise to a third theme, one that ran through much of Saddam Hussein's rhetoric—namely, resentment of the arrogance and pretensions of the al-Sabah and other Gulf dynasties. In another culture and another setting, such resentment might have been labeled "class hostility," but in this case it seemed to have more to do with the sharply felt differences in status between different clans and families. In this respect, Iraq's action against Kuwait was aimed as much at the Al Sa'ud and the wealth and power of Saudi Arabia as at Kuwait's al-Sabah.

A fourth theme, which clearly was connected to the latter, concerned Saddam Hussein's standing among his supporters in Iraq: He had to maintain their support and respect to remain powerful. To that end, he had to act boldly and to humiliate common enemies. In many ways this motivation has been a constant theme of Saddam Hussein's behavior in recent years and has often led to actions that have puzzled outsiders precisely because some of the adverse consequences have appeared, on the surface, to defeat the objectives.

If one examines the invasion of Kuwait and Iraq's subsequent strategies for dealing with the consequences of that invasion in the light of these themes, one can better understand Iraq's choices of targets and strategies throughout the crisis. Arab nationalism, for example, has been a central feature of the publicly expressed ideological commitment of successive Iraqi regimes. For all Ba'thist regimes, including that of Saddam Hussein, it is the principal public raison d'être, although, as in all such cases, interpretation of the consequent obligations and actions lies with the ruler—in this case, Saddam Hussein.[2] In domestic Iraqi politics, all ruling elites since the country's creation, have asserted an Arab nationalist identity. Coming as they unfailingly have from the Sunni Arab 24 percent of the population, they have done so as a means of integrating themselves into the larger Sunni Arab majority in the Arab world as a whole. Their assertion of an Arab national identity has effectively transformed them, in their estimation at least, from an unrepresentative minority into representatives of the overwhelming majority.

Arab nationalism has also been useful in emphasizing the overwhelmingly Arab nature of Iraqi society and therefore encouraging a feeling of solidarity, which in theory can overcome sectarian and other differences among the 78 percent or so of the population who are Arab. For the same reason, it has been embraced enthusiastically by large numbers of secular Shi'i and Christians who want to become integrated into the dominant power structure of Iraq and are mistrustful of the confessional political creeds espoused by some of their coreligionists.[3] The assertion of a common Arab identity was critical in Iraq during the war with Iran in the 1980s, serving as a social cement within the country, and providing a link with the rest of the Arab world, which supplied resources for the Iraqi defense effort. Arab nationalism and its associated themes consequently resonate on multiple levels in Iraqi society.

The Kuwait crisis demonstrated the degree to which the expression of Arab nationalism helps to frame the rationales for Iraqi policy, not simply in an instrumental sense, but also in an expressive sense as one of the rhetorical languages in which the Iraqi government formulates policy justifications. The instrumentality of Arab nationalism could be seen both in the way in which Iraq initially sought to settle its differences with Kuwait through the Saudi-mediated meetings that preceded the invasion and in the way in which it attempted to handle the post-invasion crisis within distinctively Arab forums, repeatedly asserting that this was an "Arab" problem in need of an "Arab" solution. It could also be seen in the Iraqi government's assertion of "linkage," whereby it tried to link any withdrawal from Kuwait with some kind of progress toward Israeli withdrawal from the Occupied Territories. In this light the invasion of Kuwait was seen as a means to a greater end, conforming with Arab nationalist aspirations: The liberation of occupied Palestine. An (old) Arab nationalist theme also recurred in Iraq's rationalizations for the invasion: It was necessary to redraw frontiers to rectify the fragmentation of the Arab world that had been contrived by the imperialists. The argument ran that the "union" of Kuwait and Iraq was the first step on the path to a more widespread political union among the states of the Arab world.[4]

The strength of the reaction to the invasion by people in many parts of the Middle East at different levels of society indicates that all of these Arab nationalist themes found echoes throughout the Arab world. In certain crucial ways, they made sense to large numbers of Arabs, since they played upon themes that had been at the heart of the dominant Arab nationalist discourse for more than a generation (and which had, *grosso modo*, been adapted by the new Islamist discourses with which Saddam Hussein also sought to engage). Linkage with the Palestine issue, the feeling that non-Arabs should not use the Kuwait crisis as a pretext for further intervention in the Arab world, and even the "unification" argument seemed to combine with a resentment of the Kuwaitis and a readiness to believe that they had been less than enthusiastic in playing their part as Arabs, because they had not disposed of their wealth as other, poorer Arabs might have wished. However, despite the heady populist mixture that exploded in various places during the months of the Kuwait crisis[5] and despite the replaying of these themes by the Iraqi government and media, the governments of many of the other Arab states remained unmoved. Iraq's proclamations of Arab nationalism failed to weaken the participation of other Arab states in the multinational Coalition ranged against Iraq. Evidently, the themes of Arab nationalism were not particularly effective for the Iraqi government's instrumentalist purposes.

As mentioned previously, Arab nationalist themes have an expressive function as well that relates to the self-image of the Iraqi regime as a

whole. Within the Ba'th Party, within the Iraqi armed forces, and, one sus-
pects, among the most senior figures of the regime, it is important to represent oneself, even to one's most intimate confidants, as infused by the
spirit of Arab nationalism. To know the obligations of this creed is one of
the chief declared roles of the "Leader-Necessity," (one of the epithets
applied to Saddam Hussein) and to conform with his commands in the
name of the cause is prudent and usually desirable. Since the Ba'th came
into power in Iraq, but also under previous regimes to some extent, the
language of Arab nationalism has been the language of politics. No other
discourse has been allowed to displace it from its dominant place, even
though both Iraqi nationalist and Islamic themes have been used with
increasing frequency since the early 1980s.[6]

Arab nationalism was therefore not simply a theme picked up by
Saddam Hussein and the Iraqi leadership to confuse the rest of the Arab
world about the real issues at stake in the invasion of Kuwait. To the contrary, it *was* one of those real issues; it was because of Arab nationalism
that the invasion of Kuwait made sense in a certain moral universe. Thus,
it is quite possible that the Iraqi leader and those closest to him were genuinely surprised by the vehemence of the reaction against the invasion
among many of the Arab states as well as by the hostile response of the
majority of Kuwaitis. As Saddam Hussein had remarked on an earlier
occasion: "As long as we place Iraq at the core of the Arab nation, we are
not afraid that strengthening Iraqi identification would occur at the
expense of the Arab nation, much as we talk, with great pride, of Iraq's
present, past and future."[7] Indeed, the commonly held view in the Iraqi
government seems to be that whatever is good for Iraq must be good for
the Arab world as a whole.

The use of Iraqi nationalist themes in the planning of the invasion and
during the invasion itself seems to have had two major purposes within
Iraq. The first was to prepare Iraqis for the invasion and occupation of a
fellow Arab country. To that end, the discourse played upon the distinc-
tiveness of Iraq's sacrifices during the years of war with Iran, the way in
which Kuwait had benefited from those sacrifices, and the way in which
Kuwait was now seeking to advance its own national interest at the
expense of Iraq. A vivid illustration was the claim that Kuwait's insistence on loan repayments and its maintenance of a low oil price on the
world market were effectively sabotaging the Iraqi economy. According
to this discourse, Kuwait's relentless pursuit of its interests at Iraq's
expense justified the assertion of Iraq's national rights, particularly since
these were claimed to have a greater legitimacy in the larger "community" of the Arab nation than those of Kuwait.[8] The second purpose was
to convince the population that all Iraqis had an interest in "reclaiming"
Kuwait since that country was really a part of Iraq—the nineteenth prov-

ince—and that the invasion was intended simply to rectify a historical mistake. As Saddam Hussein put it in September 1990: "Kuwait is Iraqi ... they are a people who have returned to the fold; a land that has been restored to its people."[9] In cultural-political terms, this contention merely revived a sentiment present in Iraqi politics since the foundation of the state after World War I. The ruling elite of the time quickly came to see the separate existence of Kuwait as part of a plot by the British authorities to restrict Iraq's free access to the waters of the Gulf and to deny Iraq the oil resources of Kuwait. The composition of this elite has changed substantially during the past seventy years, but the sense of historical injustice has been faithfully transmitted from one regime to the next, finding its latest expression in the pronouncements of Saddam Hussein.

As the crisis unfolded following the occupation of Kuwait, Iraqi nationalist slogans and exhortations were used with increasing frequency, with two themes in particular coming to the fore. The first was the identity of Iraq's national will and that of the Iraqi leader, Saddam Hussein. As in the propaganda of the preceding years, the discourse suggested that Saddam's understanding of the Iraqi national interest was qualitatively different from—and superior to—that of other Iraqis and that all Iraqis therefore had a special duty to obey his commands. The second was the reiteration that this battle was one of all Iraqis against an impressive array of international enemies, all of whom were intent on destroying Iraq because of its open defiance of imperialism, Zionism, and other forms of oppression. As conflict became increasingly likely, the inevitability of war breaking out was reiterated with some desperation by the regime as a way of avoiding responsibility for disastrous decisions and of convincing all Iraqis to make common cause.[10] In this connection Saddam Hussein made frequent use of ridicule and contempt in references to the al-Sabah, the Al Sa'ud, and other Gulf dynasties. Metaphorically, if in no other way, the Iraqi leader was seeking to include all Iraqis—and perhaps many other Arabs—in the collective identity closest to his heart: that of membership in a once disadvantaged rural clan despised by people with more impressive pedigrees and greater wealth. In the language Saddam Hussein used to cast down the al-Sabah and others, one hears the resentments of a man of lower status: satisfaction that the tables have been turned and a determination to assert implicitly that the Al Bu Nasir (Saddam Hussein's clan) is as worthy of respect as the al-Sabah.

In speaking this language, Saddam Hussein struck a chord of sympathy among many, not just from his clan or from within Iraq but also from outside Iraq. He was, after all, speaking the language of the rural clans and communities that had seized power throughout the Middle East. They had succeeded in moving into the machinery of the armed forces and had displaced the old elites in the wave of radical coups and revolutions of the 1950s and 1960s. For Saddam and others, the al-Sabah and the Al Sa'ud—with their wealth, pedigrees, overweening power, and close connections with the Western powers—resembled the classes that the rural clans had displaced within Iraq and other states in the Middle East. Attacking them could be portrayed as continuing the revolution, a marked feature of the talk of rich and poor alike in the Arab world.[11] Again, although there may have been an instrumentalist aspect to the use of this rhetoric and these images of inequality, the language also appears to have expressed something close to the heart of Saddam Hussein and his clannish entourage.

The Iraqis' resentment of the old elites seems to have been a factor in their treatment of Kuwait and the Kuwaitis under occupation. It is quite possible that the main target of the Iraqi forces in the first hours of the invasion was the Kuwaiti ruling family. Saddam Hussein likely felt that removing the ruling family from Kuwait would leave the followers of the al-Sabah (that is, the citizens of Kuwait) with no choice but to redirect their loyalty to him. He had practiced this form of ruthless patrimonialism with some success inside Iraq, and he probably felt it would work with the Kuwaitis too. Be that as it may, the Kuwaiti ruling family received enough warning to escape to Saudi Arabia, with the exception of one of the ruler's brothers, who did indeed die at the hands of the Iraqi forces.

If partrimonialism was a strategy in Kuwait, it was unsuccessful. Shortly after the invasion, it became apparent to the Iraqi occupiers that they faced opposition abroad and that few Kuwaitis were willing to welcome them and attach themselves to the following of Saddam Hussein. The Iraqi strategy shifted to ritual humiliation of the Kuwaitis and spoliation of the domain of the al-Sabahs. The Iraqi forces applied the brutal methods typically used by the Iraqi security services in Iraq, systematically harassed the Kuwaiti population, looted public and private assets, and ransacked houses and other properties that caught the eye of Iraqi officers. One senses an officially sanctioned license that allowed the Iraqi forces to do as they wished with a people who had put themselves beyond the pale by refusing to identify with Saddam. The Iraqi forces were allowed—even encouraged—to give vent to a collective expression of envy and resentment reminiscent of crowd behavior during the Iraqi revolution of 1958.[12]

This strategy continued throughout the period of occupation. Kuwait became a zone in which behaviors severely repressed and punished in Iraq became permissible. As the activities of the Kuwaiti organized resistance came more to the notice of the Iraqi authorities, Iraqi repression grew worse and attempts to cultivate the Kuwaitis to delegitimize the claims of the al-Sabahs were abandoned. With the onset of the war, it rapidly became clear to Iraq that its forces would have to leave Kuwait. It was then that Iraqi forces carried out their destruction: A number of public buildings in Kuwait City were blown up and a large proportion of Kuwait's oil wells were set on fire. The explosive charges had apparently been laid very early in the occupation, which suggests that these were not last-minute acts of spite but rather were part of a planned strategy, the goal of which appears to have been the public humiliation of the al-Sabah.[13] As far as Saddam was concerned, if Iraq was to gain nothing of value from the invasion and occupation of Kuwait, it would at least destroy Kuwait's assets. The destructive acts had no military significance; on the contrary, their importance was wholly symbolic, intended to signify the resolve, ruthlessness, and contempt of Saddam Hussein and the Iraqis for "the hypocrites and Croesuses ... the companions of evil and the eaters of the bitter tree of hell."[14]

Myths of Leadership and War Strategies

Undoubtedly, the myths of collective identity were important to Saddam during the Kuwait crisis, both instrumentally and as appropriate forms of expression for himself and his entourage. Equally important to him, however, were the myths of his own leadership, that is, the versions of reality, actual and potential, that justified his hold on power. In some respects, they were derived from the myths of collective identity. Saddam claimed, after all, to be uniquely suited to interpret and act upon the imperatives of Arab nationalism, Iraqi nationalism, and socioeconomic justice. This belief influenced a number of his actions and strategies, for example, the measures he ambitiously took to create a constituency in the wider Arab world and to retain and mobilize his existing populist constituency in Iraq. More important to him, however, than the general and unspecific populace, whether in the Arab world or in Iraq, were the groups of Iraqis whose support had been crucial to his political success: Saddam Hussein needed to sustain their continued belief in his indispensability.

These people constitute the circles of power in Iraq. Any leader of the country must cultivate them to remain in power—though without necessarily being accountable to them. He must manipulate their fears, ambitions, and rivalries in a way that will create for him a vital space of decision and control—and thus of access to the resources that make patronage possible.[15] Further, he must expend much energy ensuring that this terrain remains his exclusively. Those who are permitted into this turf understand that they are there on sufferance and that, in the final analysis, it is the leader who decides their fate.

Like many leaders of Iraq before him, Saddam Hussein has drawn chiefly, although not exclusively, upon his family and clan for the members of this innermost circle. Because of their identification with him, they are unlikely to oppose him on any vital question of policy—nor can they afford to do so, since all other Iraqis regard them as his creations. The relationship could be called one of complicity as much as one of trust. Although Saddam Hussein is not systematically answerable to them, his policies and strategies must "make sense" to them, and he must demonstrate to them his resolve to maintain their privileged positions within the state. Individually, they can become greedy, ambitious, or foolhardy without necessarily compromising his power, since he can demote, disgrace, or eliminate them. Should his behavior begin to compromise the security of their collective position, they would likely attempt to replace him with someone better fitted to guarantee their continued domination of Iraq.

Spreading out from those in this inner circle are networks of patronage cultivated by them and sustained by their access through their association with the president to the treasury and offices of the state. This patrimonialism, which underpins a large structure of privilege in Iraq, makes many willing and rewarded accomplices of Saddam Hussein and his style of rule. They are aware of the darker side of the regime, but they are also confident that they know how to negotiate the networks of patrons and clients and can, no doubt, justify their participation in such a system by referring to its "stability" and "order." Iraq's experience of alternative systems is, after all, extremely limited. Patrimonialism appears to deliver the goods and enjoys the respectability of tradition; it fits neatly into the patterns of communal power and privilege of Iraqi society and history. Saddam has helped to make the system work through his ability to speak to collective concerns that underpin the multiple identities of these wider circles of Iraqis and his demonstrated capacity to maintain the resources and the credibility that sustain the client networks they represent.

To manage these important underpinnings of his power, the Iraqi leader is obliged to play a number of roles, all of which left their mark on Iraqi government strategy during the crisis over Kuwait and in the aftermath of the war. It appears that Saddam Hussein had to convince those around him that he was uniquely qualified to fulfill two principal functions. The first was that of the decisive and, if necessary, ruthless leader, who could seize the initiative and take command of events. These qualities reassured those around him that they had placed their faith in someone who could protect and advance their interests. Without them, he would become a patron of diminishing utility, and they would likely come to believe that there might be others in the ruling circle who could do a better job of delivering the expected goods. The second major function was that of protector of his followers against the forces of disruption, discord, and enmity that threatened their identities and their interests. In the demonology of the regional, parochial identities in the country, Iraqi nationalism, and Arab nationalism, these forces range from tribal, ethnic, and sectarian communities and their associated political organizations within Iraq to the regional enemies of the Iraqi state to the ever-watchful forces of world imperialism. Many Iraqis perceive that these forces are in league with one another; thus, in their eyes, the function of the leader is to ensure that such forces do not bring about the internal upheavals or the breakup of the Iraqi state that they are allegedly conspiring to achieve.[16]

If Iraqi strategies during the Kuwait crisis and its aftermath are looked at from these perspectives, some of Saddam Hussein's actions make more sense—even if the consequences for Iraq's objective position vis-à-vis the Coalition were almost wholly negative. One such strategy was the detention of Western hostages in Kuwait and Iraq. It is possible that the Iraqi leadership believed that their detention would contribute to the paralysis of Western decisionmaking, but it seems more probable that Saddam Hussein saw their detention as a way of regaining the initiative and forcing Western countries to react. His action made him appear ruthlessly and fearlessly in command. Within Iraq, it was presented as a key move that prevented the Western alliance from attacking Iraq immediately. More important for Saddam's prestige and credibility, a procession of Western politicians made its way to Baghdad to supplicate him for the release of the hostages. His release of the hostages in batches, in apparent magnanimous response to the supplications of these humbled Westerners, was surely calculated to enhance his stature within Iraq. His much publicized reception of one Western politician after another, as well as the curious films made of his encounters with some of the hostages, created for some months an ongoing *tableau vivant*, that illustrated his power and status as guardian of Iraq and challenger of the West.

As far as Iraq's interests were concerned, the response of the outside world to the detention of the hostages was wholly disastrous. Iraq's action hardened opinion against the Iraqi government and made it easier to maintain the unity of the coalition against Iraq in the UN. It is unlikely that Western opinion was ever reported to Saddam, however, or that he saw any connection between Iraq's adverse predicament and the detention of the hostages. When, in December 1990, he released the remaining hostages, Iraq's situation was objectively worsening; but as far as Saddam was concerned, the hostages had served their purpose and a "new game" was afoot. The new game, in his opinion, was created by the U.S. decision the previous month to double the strength of its forces in Saudi Arabia and by the passage of UN Security Council Resolution 678, which sanctioned "all necessary means" to expel Iraq from Kuwait if Iraq did not order an unconditional withdrawal before January 15, 1991.

The deadline set by the United Nations for the unconditional withdrawal of Iraqi forces from Kuwait created a problem for the Iraqi leader. He could not comply with the deadline precisely because it was imposed by outside forces. Not only would compliance have annulled all that he had sought to achieve through the invasion of Kuwait, but it also would have given a fatal impression of vacillation and weakness on his part. It would have seriously weakened his hold on members of the inner core of his regime and, in turn, would have undermined their networks of obligation and deference within Iraq. Their claims would have appeared hollow, and, more damagingly, their competence in controlling events politically would have been thrown into doubt.

In addition, it is quite possible that Saddam Hussein believed the deadline was simply a device for drawing attention to a diplomatic solution, to the ultimate advantage of Iraq. In any case, it appeared that the regime was unprepared for the aerial bombardment launched by the allies on January 16, 1991. Given the nature and scale of the attack, there did not appear to be much that Iraq could do in response: Its air defense capacities were rapidly overwhelmed. The regime had not, however, lost all initiative. On the contrary, it became more important than ever for Saddam and his government to demonstrate their resolve.

Apparently, this determination underlay Iraq's decision to launch the first of the Scud missiles against Israel. Analysts have variously interpreted the Scud attacks. One interpretation holds that they were a ploy designed to provoke Israeli retaliation and thereby complicate the position of the Arab allies in the anti-Iraqi coalition. Although this motivation may have played into the attacks, more effective ways of ensuring Israeli military involvement in the war—steps never taken by the Iraqi leadership—existed at the time. For example, Iraqi troops could have been sent into Jordan, an act that the Israeli government had clearly indicated would provoke an Israeli military response.[17] Further, even if the Iraqi leadership could not see that it was very much to Israel's advantage to exercise self-restraint, the Syrian government soon made it clear that Israel would be acting within its rights if it retaliated.[18] A more plausible explanation is that the Scud attacks were primarily a political demonstration aimed at the many constituencies that Saddam was cultivating. Within Iraq, he had to show command, resolve, and fearlessness to the inner circles of the regime and to the Iraqi public. Externally, a show of strength may also have been a consideration, but equally potent was the idea of sending a message throughout the Arab world that this struggle was really against Zionism. Saddam may have hoped thereby to discredit the leaders of the Arab states ranged against him and to provide a powerful demonstration of the linkage he had been trying to make between Iraq's occupation of Kuwait and Israel's occupation of Arab territories.

In this light, the launching of the missiles could be viewed as a political demonstration aimed at bringing pressure to bear on the allies to negotiate conditions for an advantageous Iraqi withdrawal—rather than a military strategy to reduce the threat against Iraq. Alternatively, it might have been intended to prepare the way for an "honorable" military defeat, if defeat were already seen to be inevitable. In both cases, the firing of a few missiles at Israel might then have been a tactic to raise the whole struggle to the level of the fight against Zionism. To be driven from Kuwait in such circumstances could be interpreted as a withdrawal of Iraq's forces so that they could face the traditional enemy to the west. It is, of course, impossible to judge how effective the missile launches were in achieving these goals, but the launches were evidently thought to serve a useful political purpose at the time.

The military strategies available to the Iraqi ground forces following the Scud attacks were clearly limited. They had little choice but to await an allied offensive. The small-scale Iraqi operation on January 29, 1991, in which Iraqi forces seized the border town of Khafji and held it for a few days, bears the stamp of Saddam Hussein's "strategic genius" (the most obvious precedent is the brief capture of Mehran by Iraqi forces in 1986).[19] It is almost certain that the Iraqi high command knew that such an operation would expose Iraqi forces to allied air power and would, in the end, be futile, even if in the short-term some square kilometers of Saudi territory could be captured. However, it seems that it was necessary and important for Iraq to proceed seriously with the operation (and, as far as one can gather, to plan follow-up operations). The Iraqi high command may have been acting under the direct orders of Saddam Hussein, or it may have been pressured to come up with a plan that would demonstrate that the Iraqi forces were not cowed by the allied air attacks. The Khafji operation seemed to provide such an opportunity, although its military effect was nil. Once again, therefore, the symbolic or demonstrative effect of the use of military power dominated Iraq's military strategy.

For Iraq, the indefensibility of its position in Kuwait was becoming more apparent each day. In February 1991 the Iraqi government attempted to arrange a diplomatic solution by offering to withdraw Iraqi troops on February 15. However, it hedged the offer with conditions that had been long rejected by the alliance and stood no chance of acceptance. Following the predictable rejection of the offer, Saddam Hussein must have decided that his best political option was to allow the war for Kuwait to begin—even though it is unlikely that even the most optimistic Iraqi army commanders believed that the Iraqi army would be able to retain control of Kuwait once the allied ground offensive began. On the basis of the logic that had previously shaped Iraqi strategy, the idea of sacrificing the Iraqi troops defending Kuwait to give the impression of heroic resistance and a fighting withdrawal would certainly have made sense; as in earlier instances, Saddam would have been using armed force to make a political point. However, the campaign developed in ways that the Iraqi high command did not appear to have anticipated: The withdrawal from Kuwait turned into a rout, and the allied forces overran large areas of the south of Iraq itself. In doing so, of course, they changed the game. The war was no longer for the defense of Kuwait; Iraqi forces now had to fight for the defense of their own state.[20]

The Iraqi government had long prepared for the defense of the regime. The units involved and the strategy behind their deployment had little to do with the forces defending Kuwait. Saddam had kept certain key divisions of the Republican Guard in reserve in Baghdad and in the Sunni Arab heartland, areas from which the regime drew its most uncritical support. These divisions were psychologically and militarily prepared for any enmity or opportunism of forces in Iraqi society that would seek to take advantage of any setback suffered by the government. Thus, when rebellions erupted in the Kurdish north and the predominantly Shi'i south soon after the withdrawal from Kuwait, the Republican Guard divisions were far from demoralized. Indeed, they were exactly the kinds of rebellions for which these units had been created and prepared.

The nightmare of ethnic and sectarian revolt combined with predatory foreign intervention had become a reality and Saddam Hussein was not the only one fighting for survival. Many people clustered around the only government they knew and the only leader with whom they were familiar, including all those who had been accomplices of the regime in some measure in the preceding twenty or so years as well as those who had benefited even modestly from its patronage networks and those who feared the anarchy and sectarian violence threatened by insurrection and invasion. The scale of the disaster and its nature had transformed Saddam's plight into the plight of large numbers of people in central Iraq.

Under these conditions, the regime could present the decision by the allied forces to halt their advance into Iraq as evidence of its resolve and that of the armed forces. The regime claimed that the allied forces did not dare proceed farther into Iraq, and with that discourse the loss of Kuwait faded into relative insignificance despite its prominence for the preceding seven months. Further, the failure of the allies to materially assist the Kurdish or Shi'i resistance forces as they rose up against the regime allowed the latter to suppress the rebellions. The regime presented this suppression, too, as evidence of the ruthless competence of the leadership—it had prevented the suspect communities of Kurdish nationalists and Iranian-connected Shi'i from making common cause with the allies to bring about the destruction of the Iraqi state. The future of Iraq had been saved by steadfast and decisive leadership.[21]

Conclusion

The strategy of the Iraqi leadership was based on a set of priorities that had little to do with the obvious object of the war, that is, the territorial occupation of Kuwait. Delighted as Saddam Hussein most likely would have been had the world acquiesced in his permanent annexation of Kuwait and its resources, he declared this objective, paradoxically, only after the almost universal condemnation of the invasion. It could be argued, therefore, that territorial occupation was his objective all along. Alternatively, it could be argued that the invasion was simply a move to underline the seriousness of his purpose and oblige the rest of the world to make substantive concessions to Iraq to persuade him to withdraw. Because the Iraqi leader was pursuing a course that had as its ultimate aim the enhancement of his own power and authority in Iraq, he could change the material objectives appropriate to that pursuit to suit the demands of the moment. In some respects, the way in which he dealt with the world was as important as the material benefits that his strategies were intended to derive.

Saddam Hussein's rule of Iraq has been based on his ruthless command of all economic and coercive resources within the country. In the patrimonial system he heads, his style of command has lent him authority among sufficient numbers of Iraqis to sustain his rule. When dealing with the outside world, where his control is obviously less, he must ensure that its intrusion into Iraq is mediated by the same symbolic vocabulary that he uses in his domination of the state. In line with a potent theme of Iraqi politics, through rhetoric and gesture he must give the impression that he is the one in command of events, even when the initiative clearly lies with others. If that becomes too difficult to sustain, he can begin to stress the other potent symbolic theme of Iraqi politics: The precarious nature of the state and the international conspiracies aimed at its destruction. Both of these themes were plainly visible in the strategies pursued by Iraq in the invasion and occupation of Kuwait and in the war that followed.

When the Coalition powers chose to fight, Iraq was plunged into a war that Saddam Hussein may have believed would never materialize. In the conduct of that war, two Iraqi strategies became apparent. The first concerned Iraq's defense of Kuwait, or at least the creation of circumstances for an advantageous withdrawal. The second was more intimately related to the survival of the political order in Iraq and was dominated by the concerns, prejudices, and wary trust of its chief beneficiaries. This second, more fundamental set of priorities and stratagems became increasingly prominent. It had, in any case, underlain much of the strategy devised for the defense of Kuwait, which seemed, therefore, to have a dual purpose: It should be effective, if possible, in its apparent aim, but above all it must contribute to the reinforcement of Saddam Hussein's power within Iraq and do nothing to shake the order on which it relied. This double purpose marked all of the Iraqi initiatives between January 16 and February 28, 1991: The Scud launches, the Khafji episode, the flight of Iraqi planes to Iran, the destruction wrought in Kuwait. Even the Iraqi troops stationed in Kuwait bore the stamp of a leadership that regarded the war as manageable, whatever the military outcome, as long as it was not permitted to threaten the underpinnings of the regime itself. The success, in the short term at least, of this strategy among Iraqis, despite its apparently suicidal consequences outside of Iraq, is testimony to the single-minded ruthlessness of those who devised it as well as their capacity to judge the priorities of Iraqi politics. Similarly, the behavior of the Iraqi regime in the years following the defeat in Kuwait—in its periodic confrontations with the outside world and its repression of internal dissent—have borne the stamp of the same strategy. Iraq's behavior during and after the invasion is a useful reminder that political power is as much about the capacity to retain control of the symbolic universe that lends credibility and authority to leadership as it is about control of the material resources of economic and coercive power.

Notes

1. This ruling style was made evident in the Ninth Ba'th Party Regional Congress (the first since Saddam Hussein became president of Iraq) in 1982. See particularly the Arab Ba'th Socialist Party, Iraq, *The Central Report of the Ninth Regional Congress June 1982*, trans. SARTEC, Lausanne (Baghdad, January 1983), 23–40. It was also a message that Saddam Hussein took pains to drive home, especially to all party members. See his address to the mayors of Najaf, Misan, and Karbala provinces, quoted in *BBC Summary of World Broadcasts (SWB) Middle East (ME)* July 16, 1987, A/11–12.

2. See, for example, Saddam Hussein's interpretation of Arab nationalism in the speech he made in July 1989 to commemorate Michel Aflaq, the late founder of the Ba'th Party; Saddam Hussein, *Al-Mu'allafat al-Kamila*, Pt. 18, 1988–1989 (Baghdad: Dar al-Shu'un al-Thaqafiyya al-'Amma, 1989), 365–371.

3. H. Batatu, *The Old Social Classes and the Revolutionary Movements of Iraq* (Princeton: Princeton University Press, 1978), 966–973, 1003–1017.

4. For a good example of this mixing of Iraqi national interests and pan-Arab or Arab nationalist outrage, see Tariq Aziz's letter to the secretary-general of the Arab League concerning Kuwait, *BBC SWB/ME*, July 19, 1990, A/4–7.

5. See the charges leveled at the emir of Kuwait by Republic of Iraq Radio, which accused him of failing to be a true Arab nationalist and of being a lukewarm supporter of the Palestinians. Republic of Iraq Radio also charged that instead of investing in the Arab world, the Kuwaiti government had invested

chiefly in the United States and the United Kingdom, thereby indirectly investing in Israel. *BBC SWB/ME*, August 15, 1990, A/8–9.

6. See, for example, *Central Report of the Ninth Regional Congress* and the speech by Saddam Hussein in November 1988, "Al-Haqq yasru' al-Batil" (Truth brings down falsehood), Saddam Hussein (*Al-Mu'allafat al-Kamila*, Pr. 18, 1988–1989), 61–70.

7. Quoted in A. Baram, "Culture in the Service of Wataniyya," *Asian and African Studies* 17 (1983), 266.

8. See Tariq Aziz letter of July 1990, *BBC SWB/ME*. July 19, 1990 A/4–7.

9. Republic of Iraq Radio, September 24, 1990, quoted in *BBC SWB/ME*, September 27, 1990, A/1.

10. See Republic of Iraq Radio, September 7, 1990, quoted in *BBC SWB/ME*, September 10, 1990, A/3; and Saddam Hussein's Army Day speech on January 6, 1991, in which he spoke as if Iraq were already at war and had been dragged into a war not of its own making, Republic of Iraq Radio, January 6, 1991, quoted in *BBC SWB/ME*, January 8, 1991, A/1–3.

11. Clearly, this talk of rich vs. poor was something that touched a raw nerve with the Saudis, as can be seen by King Fahd's retort that when his own forebears were grindingly poor, no other Arab felt impelled to come to their aid. See King Fahd's speech of December 21, 1990, quoted in *BBC SWB/ME*, December 24, 1990, A/7–8.

12. See Kanan Makiya, *Cruelty and Silence* (London: Jonathan Cape, 1993), 31–56.

13. See the report from Agence France Presse in August 1990, quoted in *BBC SWB/ME*, August 21, 1990, A/9.

14. Saddam Hussein's Army Day speech on January 6, 1992, Republic of Iraq Radio, quoted in *Foreign Broadcast Information Service (FBIS)* NES-92-M5, January 8, 1992, 18.

15. See Saddam Hussein's portrayal of and justification for his own leadership, *Al-Thawra*, August 23, 1986, 4–5.

16. Such a perception is both reflected in and encouraged by the official rhetoric of the regime. See, for instance, the broadcast of the Iraqi News Agency accusing "traitorous reactionaries" of being in league with the United States and with Zionism, with the aim of destroying Iraq, quoted in *BBC SWB/ME*, December 15, 1990, A/2.

17. L. Freedman and E. Karsh, *The Gulf Conflict, 1990–1991* (London: Faber and Faber, 1993), 331–370.

18. Ibid., 340–341.

19. See S. Chubin and C. Tripp, *Iran and Iraq at War* (London: IB Tauris, 1988), 118–119.

20. The parallel here is with the changed nature of the Iran-Iraq War in 1982, when Iran went on the offensive and, after recapturing Khorramshahr, began to threaten the territory of Iraq itself. Signaling this change, and making explicit reference to the events of 1982, an Iraqi military spokesman sought to rally the Iraqis at the end of February 1991 by stating

"They thought [it] ... would open the door for them to humiliate Iraq and its people," quoted in *BBC SWB/ME*, February 28, 1991, A/1.

21. See Saddam Hussein's speech on the anniversary of the 1968 revolution in July 1991, broadcast on Iraqi National Radio, quoted in *BBC SWB/ME*, July 18, 1991, A/8–12.

3

Saddam Hussein's Invasion of Kuwait: A Premeditated Act

Laurie Mylroie

For mine own good, All causes shall give way.
— Macbeth, 3.4.135

Why did Saddam Hussein invade Kuwait? Some analysts have argued that his move was largely defensive, taken on the spur of the moment and driven by mounting economic and political pressures. An extreme version of that argument runs that Saddam's aggression against this neighboring state, as when he invaded Iran in 1980, had less to do with a premeditated grand design than with his often seen sense of insecurity. In both cases, war was not his first choice and he made the decision to use military force only shortly before the outbreak of hostilities.[1] Other analysts have suggested that "a series of provocative acts by Israel" contributed to Saddam's motives.[2]

However, there is no consensus that the invasion of Kuwait was a largely defensive act. In fact, it appears more likely to have been an unprovoked act of aggression driven above all by the ambitions of one man, Saddam Hussein, and his relatively small coterie of sycophants and advisers.

When the Iraqi leader attacked Kuwait in August 1990, he had concrete goals: to increase Iraq's access to the sea, to resolve his country's economic problems by taking control of Kuwait's assets and its oil resources, and to establish control over the oil on the Arab littoral of the Persian Gulf.

The Gulf contains two thirds of the world's oil supplies, four fifths of which lie on the Arab side. Control of that region's oil brings with it power, not just money, because it means controlling access to the most important commodity in the modern industrial world. If Saddam Hussein had succeeded in establishing a position from which he could dictate access to the 40 percent of the world's oil lying on the Arab side of the Gulf, he would have become one of the most powerful people on earth.

This chapter describes Saddam Hussein's motives for attacking Kuwait and the steps leading up to the invasion.

Saddam Hussein and the Greek View of Tyrants

The ancient Greeks gave tyranny its name: They understood that a tyrant's ambition and insecurity were closely linked, as Aristotle's discussion of tyrannical rule in *The Politics* makes clear. Indeed, Aristotle's analysis of tyranny provides as good a description of Saddam Hussein's regime as any: First, he said, tyrants lop off the heads of outstanding men, not for what they do, but for their talents, which could make them a challenge. Second, tyrants "make every subject as much of a stranger as possible to every other," so that they cannot combine together. Third, they inure the people "to humility by a habit of daily slavery." Fourth, they maintain a secret police "to get regular information about every man's sayings and doings." Fifth, they impoverish their subjects "to keep them so busy in earning a daily pittance that they have no time for plotting." Sixth, they pursue war "with the object of keeping [their] subjects constantly occupied and continually in need of a leader."[3]

But in the Greek view, tyrants are moved by far more than insecurity and a desire for survival. Like those analysts who stress the defensive nature of Saddam's invasion of Kuwait, Book 8 of Plato's *Republic* discusses the insecurity of tyrannical rule. But Book 9 begins with an assertion of the insufficiency of that view: "We haven't adequately distinguished the kinds and numbers of the desires and with this lacking, the investigation we are making will be less clear," said Socrates before he began a discussion of tyrants' insatiable appetites.[4] Likewise, Aristotle explained, "Men do not become tyrants in order to avoid exposure to the cold."[5] It would seem that Saddam, like the Greek tyrants, was motivated by more than insecurity.

Saddam's Aim: Controlling Gulf Oil

In all that has been said and written about why Saddam invaded Kuwait, insufficient attention has been paid to the role of oil. Yet, as Egyptian president Hosni Mubarak explained in July 1991, Gulf oil had been on Saddam Hussein's mind for over a decade. According to Mubarak, "Saddam believed that the [September 1980] operation against Iran would last only one month, and then he would either control the Gulf states politically or control the oil fields. The war against Iran lasted eight years instead of several weeks, thus postponing the occupation of Kuwait."[6] Furthermore, Mubarak said, "Saddam believed that the invasion of Kuwait [in 1990] would only cause verbal protests and then he could calmly attack the oil wells in the Kingdom of Saudi Arabia and, after swallowing them, attack the oil wells of the United Arab Emirates."[7] In short, by invading Kuwait, Saddam Hussein sought to establish control of the oil on the Arab side of the Gulf.

The War with Iran: Saddam's First Attempt

Until the Iranian Revolution of 1978–1979, the shah of Iran, backed by the United States, kept Iraq in check and limited Saddam Hussein's ambitions. Historically, Iran has been much stronger than Iraq. It has three times Iraq's territory and population and greater access to the sea. Whereas Iraq has only narrow access to the sea, Iran fronts the entire Persian Gulf and the Gulf of Oman as well. Throughout the shah's reign, Iraq would have been unable to successfully defend its borders against a determined Iranian attack.

But in 1978, as domestic unrest increasingly preoccupied the shah, opportunities arose for Saddam Hussein that were enhanced by the September 1978 Camp David Accords. Two months after the Camp David meetings, Saddam Hussein convened an Arab summit in Baghdad, where, with the support of Syrian president Hafiz al-Assad, he engineered the Arab ostracism of Egypt. Although the Arab Gulf states hesitated to join Iraq in ostracizing Egypt (in fact, a high-ranking Saudi intelligence official, Kamal Adham, reportedly told Egyptian president Anwar el-Sadat that the Gulf states secretly supported the agreements),[8] they eventually complied. Backed by Assad, Saddam Hussein pressured them into agreeing to break ties with Egypt if Sadat finalized the Egyptian-Israeli peace treaty that constituted the core of the accords.

The shah left Iran in January 1979. Sadat signed the peace treaty six weeks later, and the Arabs promptly broke ties with Egypt. Shortly thereafter, Sadat denounced them, making public what had transpired in Baghdad. The Saudis, Sadat explained, had "been threatened by Husayn al-Tikriti of Iraq [Saddam] and the Alawites of the Ba'th party in Syria and the Palestinians." The Syrian president, Sadat said, told the Arabs that he would "transfer the battle to [their] bedrooms if they did not break ties with Egypt, and Saddam threatened to occupy [Kuwait]."

"Suppose Iraq were to attack Kuwait tomorrow," Sadat asked, "what position would Saudi Arabia adopt? ... Can Saudi Arabia defend Kuwait?"[9]

So what were Saddam Hussein's motives in Iraq's September 1980 invasion of Iran? Some were defensive. Radical Persian mullahs were calling for Saddam Hussein's overthrow and promoting terrorist attacks on Iraqi officials. But some of his motives were offensive. Indeed, a former Iraqi ambassador, now in opposition to the regime, recalled a discussion with Saddam Hussein before the war, in which he advised Saddam Hussein to improve ties with Ayatollah Khomeini. Saddam Hussein's reply was, "We don't have any intention to fight Iran, but if we are forced to, we will win." Arguing that Khomeini had destroyed the Iranian army, Saddam concluded, "We are not afraid of Iran." The ambassador left the conversation believing that Saddam Hussein wanted war.[10]

King Fahd of Saudi Arabia told a similar story. Fahd visited Iraq in August 1980, shortly before the Iran-Iraq War. According to the Saudi Press Agency (in 1991), "he sensed that Saddam [intended] to enter a war against Iran" and "advised Saddam to speak to Iran as a Muslim country," but Saddam told him that the Iranians were fighting among themselves and that it would be his only chance (to attack).[11]

Indeed, once the war with Iran had commenced in September 1980, Saddam Hussein expected Khomeini's regime to collapse swiftly and the oil of Arab-populated Khuzistan to fall to Iraq. Had that happened, the Gulf monarchies would have been in dire straits. With the shah gone, no force existed in the area that was powerful enough to protect them. And the United States, still recovering from the trauma of the Vietnam War and uncertain whether to conciliate or confront the revolutionary Iranian regime, also lacked the capability to protect the Gulf states. Washington did not even begin to develop the capability to project force quickly into the Persian Gulf until the December 1979 Soviet invasion of Afghanistan. If Iraq had defeated Iran in 1980, Saddam Hussein would have been in a position to dictate to all the Gulf Arabs, and he could have attacked with impunity for disobedience. In effect, Saddam would have gained control over much of the Gulf's oil.

Yet by November 1980 it was clear that quick victory over Iran had eluded Saddam Hussein. Six weeks into the war with Iran he admitted, "If you asked me now if we should have gone to war, I would say it would have been better if we had not gone to war."[12] The war with Iran lasted eight years, and at times it seemed that Iraq might lose. Iraq's losses were horrific—nearly 400,000 casualties, or over 2 percent of the Iraqi population—the per capita equivalent of five million Americans.

When the war ended with Khomeini's surprise acceptance of a United Nations-sponsored cease-fire in July 1988, the Iraqi population was ecstatic. Iraq's tangible gains from the war were meager, however. Saddam Hussein laid claim to the entire Shatt al-Arab, but Iraq did not actually possess it, and the disputed river border remained closed to maritime traffic. Yet the Iraqi population was immensely relieved that the fighting had ended. Iraqis looked forward to peace, a modicum of prosperity, and a relaxation of the wartime repression.

Saddam Hussein made gestures in the direction of those aspirations, but they were only gestures. In mid-November 1988, as the talks between Baghdad and Tehran that followed the cease-fire faltered, Saddam Hussein announced to a conference of Arab lawyers in Baghdad that he would initiate a new program of democracy for Iraq, including constitutional reform, freedom of speech, and pluralism, permitting the formation of other political parties besides the Ba'th. High-level committees were established to study the three issues and four months later, in April 1989, the National Assembly elections were more open than any previously held. Although all candidates were carefully screened bu the security services, Ba'th Party members won only 40 percent of the seats. In addition, a new constitution was promulgated on July 30, 1990, but it was suspended three days later after Iraq invaded Kuwait. Even as the constitution was being promulgated, Saddam Hussein knew that it would soon be a dead letter.

Kuwait: The Second Attempt

It is unclear when Saddam Hussein decided to invade Kuwait. Perhaps he already thought of it during the war with Iran,[13] even though he went out of his way when the Iran-Iraq War ended to assure the Gulf states that Iraq would not pose any threat to them. In an address to a conference of Arab information ministers in Baghdad on September 6, 1988, he essentially told those assembled that the long war with Iran had caused Iraq to renounce its former ambitions as well as its earlier Ba'thist commitment to Arab unity by any means: "We Arabs," he said, "have many systems and inclinations. However, what is required of all of us is not to cancel the present structure and tear up the present fabric but to place a large tent over all other tents. Thus, this large tent will encompass all the other tents without harming our national tents whether in Iraq, Kuwait, Qatar, or the UAE."[14]

Ironically, Kuwait, Qatar, and the UAE were the very states that were threatened by the prospect of an Iraqi invasion two years later. Had Saddam Hussein been sincere, or was he seeking to allay the fears of those states while all the while planning his next project?

After the Iraqi invasion, Saudi Arabia's King Fahd cited a March 1989 Iraqi-Saudi treaty of nonaggression as evidence of Saddam Hussein's preparations for attacking Kuwait. Fahd reported being surprised at Saddam's proposal of the pact, as the Arab states tended not to have such treaties.[15] It would be the equivalent of Canada and the United States signing a treaty of nonaggression. To what end would they sign such a treaty, since the presumption is one of peaceful relations?

As the Saudi information minister, Ali al-Shaer, explained, Saddam Hussein asked King Fahd what he would think about signing a nonaggression treaty. King Fahd responded that such a treaty had existed for years and did not need to be put down in writing. The Iraqi leader, according to his information minister, replied: Let us sign it and keep it for the coming generations. The king agreed. In retrospect, the treaty turned out to be something of a smoke screen.[16]

The Saudis later came to see the treaty as an attempt to ensure Saudi neutrality after Iraq occupied Kuwait. In fact, Baghdad invoked the pact twice during the Kuwait crisis: First, to deny any hostile intent toward Saudi Arabia and therefore to deny the need for foreign intervention to protect the kingdom's territory and, second, as grounds for objecting to the launching of the war against Iraq from Saudi territory.

In any event, in early 1990 Saddam Hussein began to act. He demanded that Kuwait pay Iraq U.S. $10 billion and forgive its wartime debts. The demands were so unreasonable that one could speculate Saddam intended them to serve as an excuse for the invasion. After all, if Kuwait had conceded, more demands for equally fantastic sums would likely have followed.

One can see a clear path from Saddam Hussein's exorbitant demands for money to the invasion five months later. At the February 23, 1990, Arab Cooperation Council (ACC) summit in Amman, Jordan, Saddam warned the presidents of Egypt and Yemen, as well as Jordan's King Hussein, that it was not enough for the Gulf states to forgive their wartime loans to Iraq. "Go tell them in Saudia and the Gulf," he reportedly said, "that I need $30 billion in fresh money, and if they don't give it to me, I will know how to take it."[17]

Returning from the summit, the Yemeni president, Ali Abdullah Salih, stopped in Saudi Arabia and Jordan's King Hussein toured the sheikhdoms, including Kuwait, before continuing to Iraq. Although it is not known what these leaders told the Gulf rulers, it seemed likely that they relayed Saddam Hussein's threats, which would explain the widely held conviction in the Gulf that the Jordanian and Yemeni rulers were privy to Saddam's plans.

At the same meetings, Saddam Hussein also began raising tensions with the West and Israel, generating an atmosphere in which the Gulf states were more susceptible to Iraq's pressure. Saddam made two public appeals at the ACC summit. First, he called for the United States to leave the Gulf even though the expanded U.S. naval presence, which protected Kuwaiti tankers against Iranian attack, had helped end the Iran-Iraq War and despite the fact that those ships had largely been withdrawn and the U.S. naval presence reduced to peacetime levels by the time of his remarks. Second, he called for the Arabs to liberate Jerusalem, a topic about which he had been silent during most of the Iran-Iraq War.

The next month, the CIA reported that Baghdad had, early in the month, constructed fixed Scud launchers at a base in western Iraq, H-2, putting such weapons within range of Tel Aviv for the first time.[18] According to another report, on March 3, 1990, Saddam ordered his military command to draw up plans for massing forces on the Kuwaiti border.[19]

Then, on March 9, Iraq brought a British-based, Iranian-born journalist to trial for espionage, and six days later he was hung. Farzad Bazoft had been imprisoned for investigating a suspicious explosion at a major Iraqi munitions plant in August 1989, even covertly gaining access to an area around the plant from which he took soil samples.[20] There was no need to try, let alone hang, Bazoft. Imprisoned, he posed no threat to Baghdad, and his imprisonment was not a source of tension in Iraq's relations with other states. However, the hanging triggered a predictable flurry of denunciations from the West and equally predictable proclamations of Arab support for Iraq, including support from Kuwait.[21]

Developments beyond Baghdad's control also contributed to tensions. On March 22, 1990, Gerald Bull, the Canadian artillery genius behind the supergun, was assassinated outside his home in Brussels, perhaps by Israeli agents. Further, in a sting operation at London's Heathrow airport six days later, U.S. and British customs officials intercepted a shipment of nuclear triggers en route to Iraq. Baghdad used these incidents to portray the rising tensions as the result of the West's hostility and not Baghdad's initiative.

Then, on April 2, Saddam asserted in a long, rambling, nearly incoherent speech that Iraq had the capacity to manufacture "dual" chemical weapons and threatened to "make the fire eat up half of Israel if it fired anything against Iraq."[22] Although Saddam's words were defensive, Baghdad's Information Ministry omitted the defensive language when it published the speech, saying only that Saddam threatened to make the fire eat up half of Israel. In doing so, the ministry created an international uproar.

Saddam Hussein appealed to King Fahd of Saudi Arabia to send an emissary, and the Saudi ambassador to Washington, Prince Bandar bin Sultan, was dispatched to Baghdad. Saddam Hussein told Prince Bandar that he had spoken in self-defense and sought assurances that Israel would not attack Iraq. In passing, the Iraqi leader cautioned against the "conspiracy" being peddled by "imperialistic-Zionist forces" that he had "designs" over his neighbors. He requested mediation in the dispute, which led to an exchange of assurances between Iraq and Israel that neither would launch a first strike against the other. Within a year, however, Baghdad broke that pledge.

After Iraq invaded Kuwait, Prince Bandar reflected that Saddam Hussein had been setting the stage to attack. He had sought and received U.S. and Israeli assurances that Iraq would not be attacked. He had protected his western flank with Israel, freeing him to do what he wanted on the east with Kuwait. Bandar concluded that the Saudis and the Bush administration had been set up, a belief that was reinforced when he learned that Saddam did not have a single soldier on his western flank at the time that Iraq invaded Kuwait.[23]

The Iraqi leader's threat to use chemical weapons against Israel also served another purpose. It allowed him to tout Iraqi possession of such weapons of mass destruction in the one way that was somehow acceptable among the Arab states. But Saddam Hussein's boasting could have meant to intimidate the Arbs as well. In any event, the prospect of Iraq using chemical weapons was a factor that all members of the anti-Saddam coalition had to consider following the invasion.

The May 28, 1990, Arab summit in Baghdad proved to be yet another step leading toward Iraq's invasion of Kuwait. In a closed session of the summit that Iraq later made public, Saddam Hussein chastised Kuwait for producing more oil than its Organization of Petroleum Exporting Countries (OPEC) quota and thereby causing a precipitous decline in oil prices. He warned that war is "also done by economic means," and he threatened, "We have reached the point were we can no longer withstand the pressure." Indeed, the emir of Kuwait, Sheikh Jabir, later recalled a curious incident related to the summit. While in Baghdad, he reminded Saddam that he had yet to reply to an outstanding invitation to visit Kuwait. Saddam Hussein replied that he would indeed visit Kuwait in the coming months and that the visit would be a surprise.[24]

In the spring of 1990, Israeli intelligence learned that Iraq had accelerated its centrifuge program—the only one of its four covert nuclear programs that was known at the time—and had offered European firms making centrifuge parts twice the original price to complete their work by September of that year. By June, according to the Israelis, Iraq was bankrupt. It was no wonder that Saddam needed money and was demanding it from the Gulf states.[25]

Further evidence of Saddam Hussein's preparations for moving against Kuwait can be found in his dealings with Iran. In January 1990, after eighteen months of stalemated negotiations following the cease-fire to the Iran-Iraq War, Saddam publicly offered a peace plan to Iran. The gesture seemed to be largely propaganda, but on April 21, Saddam Hussein revived his initiative in a letter to Iranian president Ali Akbar Hashemi Rafsanjani. An exchange of notes followed, leading to a meeting on July 3 between the Iraqi and Iranian foreign ministers. The Iraqi diplomacy culminated on August 15, two weeks after the invasion of Kuwait, with Saddam Hussein's acceptance of the 1975 Algiers accord (Iran's central demand) and the neutralization of the Iran-Iraq frontier for the duration of the Kuwait crisis (Iraq's demand).

Still other events also suggest the premeditated nature of the Iraqi assault on Kuwait. One such event was the raid launched on a Tel Aviv beach on May 30, 1990, by the Abu Abbas faction of the Palestine Liberation Organization (PLO). The terrorists had trained in Libya, but Abu Abbas also had close links with Baghdad. Edward Said, then a member of the Palestine National Council, charged in a letter to the *New York Times* that Iraq was also behind the raid. When the PLO proved unwilling to condemn the raid—as required by the terms of the United States-PLO dialogue—despite U.S. attempts for nearly a month to coax such a statement from PLO chairman Yasir Arafat, the Bush administration reluctantly suspended U.S.-PLO dialogue on June 20. A little more than a month later, when Iraq invaded Kuwait, the Iraqi leader could more readily refer to the invasion as the only answer to the Palestinian problem.

Additional evidence for Saddam Hussein's premeditation is Iraq's purchase of high-definition satellite photographs of Kuwait and Saudi Arabia from Spotimage, a French company. The contract was signed in 1988, and photos were delivered through May 2, 1990. The nature of Iraq's last request for photos, however, suggested that they could be used for military planning, and Spotimage ceased deliveries. As the *Financial Times* later concluded, "This tends to confound Iraq's claim that the invasion was unpremeditated and was instead provoked by Kuwaiti intransigence."[26]

In late June, the Iraqi minister of state for foreign affairs, Sadun Hammadi, toured the sheikhdoms, ostensibly pressing for adherence to OPEC quotas but in reality pursuing a different agenda. Kuwait had told Iraq it did not have the liquid assets to pay the huge sums of money it was demanding. Hammadi came to Kuwait with a detailed list of Kuwait's assets to prove that it did.[27]

The denouement came the next month. An "emergency" meeting of the Arab League foreign ministers was held July 15 at the request of the PLO, which had already adopted a strong pro-Iraqi position. Iraq's foreign minister, Tariq Aziz, circulated a memorandum describing offenses committed by the United Arab Emirates and, especially, Kuwait against Iraq.[28] In addition to accusing the two principalities of producing oil beyond their OPEC quota, the Iraqi document accused Kuwait of encroaching on Iraqi territory and Iraq's oil fields. The Iraqi complaints about territorial issues, it turns out, were far removed from reality.

It was scarcely a secret that over the years the Ba'thist regime had been taking over Kuwaiti territory. The UN postwar border commission confirmed, after prolonged study using the most advanced technology, that the border had drifted nearly a kilometer southward. The revised border demarcated by the UN border commission proved more disadvantageous to Iraq than the line that had prevailed before the war.

Saddam Hussein made the charges in Tariq Aziz's memo public in a July 17, 1990 speech, marking the twenty-second anniversary of the Ba'thist takeover in Iraq. Intense Arab mediation followed as Iraq began massing troops on the Kuwaiti border. But the Iraqi leader focused the dispute on oil prices and deluded the world into believing that oil was the issue at stake.[29] That problem, of course, could be addressed at the upcoming OPEC meeting (to be held July 26 in Geneva).

At the meeting Kuwait and the UAE agreed to Iraqi demands, yet two days later Iraq charged that Kuwait was cheating again. As a former U.S. ambassador familiar with the oil markets wrote, "This was assuredly not true; it was impossible that Iraq could have had evidence two days after the agreement that Kuwait was overproducing ... Indeed, what evidence was available showed exactly the contrary. Kuwait had told its Asian customers that, for reasons of force majeure, it was cutting deliveries by some 25 percent."[30]

Mediation continued over Baghdad's other complaints—over territory and money. During the mediations, the Iraqi leader assured the principal Arab mediator, president Hosni Mubarak, that he would not attack Kuwait. The UAE, meanwhile, asked for an American show of support. In a move that was described as a "training program agreed upon previously," a joint U.S.-UAE refueling maneuver was hastily organized and was held July 24.[31]

The next day Saddam Hussein called the U.S. ambassador to Baghdad, April Glaspie, for her first private audience with the Iraqi president. Perhaps the refueling maneuver prompted Saddam Hussein to want to take a better measure of the U.S. position. Nothing in Glaspie's discussion with Saddam Hussein would have discouraged him from carrying out the attack on Kuwait. Glaspie was, in fact, following the conciliatory line laid down by the White House and the U.S. State Department. However, she misread Saddam Hussein's invitation as an indication of peaceful intentions, as he probably hoped, thereby reinforcing the misperception that prevailed in Washington.[32]

On July 25, 1990, President Mubarak announced that his mediation efforts had proved fruitful. There would be a meeting between representatives of Kuwait and Iraq in Jidda, Saudi Arabia, at the end of the month. He cautioned the United States to avoid doing anything that would increase tensions in the meantime.

However, when the Iraqi-Kuwaiti meeting was held on July 31, it proved stillborn. The Iraqi envoy, Izzet Ibrahim al-Duri, laid out a set of demands and claimed that he did not have authority to negotiate. Two days later Iraq invaded Kuwait. As one analyst concluded, "Iraq's behavior at Jidda indicates that the die had already been cast."[33]

Conclusion

Although the timing of Iraq's invasion of Kuwait may have been dictated by internal problems, Saddam Hussein's goals went far beyond merely addressing those problems. His hope was to establish control over the oil on the Arab side of the Persian Gulf. Controlling the Gulf's oil had been a factor behind Iraq's 1980 invasion of Iran. It is doubtful that Saddam Hussein had abandoned that ambition.

Notes

An earlier version of this article appeared in *Orbis*, Winter 1993.

1. "Why Saddam Hussein Invaded Kuwait," *Survival* (January–February 1991), 18, 29. For less extreme versions of this argument, see International Institute of Strategic Studies, "War in the Middle East," in *Strategy Survey 1990–1991*, Sidney Bearman, ed. (London: Brassey's 1991); Pierre Salinger and Eric Laurent, *Secret Dossier: The Hidden Agenda Behind the Gulf War* (New York: Penguin, 1991).

2. Stephen Pelletiere and Douglas V. Johnson II, "The True History of the Gulf War: An Exchange," *New York Review of Books*, March 26, 1992.

3. Aristotle, *The Politics*, 5.9.

4. *The Republic of Plato*, trans. Allan Bloom (New York: Basic Books, 1968), 251.

5. Aristotle, *The Politics*, 2.7.13.

6. Middle East News Agency, July 14, 1991, in Foreign Broadcast Information Service, Near East and South Asia (hereafter *FBIS-NESA*), July 15, 1991.

7. Middle East News Agency, October 1, 1990, in *FBIS-NESA*, October 2, 1990.

8. "Frontline," April 21, 1992. PBS documentary.

9. Cairo Domestic Service 1 May 1979 *FBIS-NESA* 2 May 1979.

10. Iraqi opposition figure, to author, December 1992.

11. Saudi Press Agency, November 6, 1991, in *FBIS-NESA*, November 8, 1991.

12. Radio Baghdad, November 4, 1980, cited in Uriel Dann and Ofra Bengio, "Iraq," *Middle East Contemporary Survey, 1980–1981*, 579.

13. According to a well-informed Middle Eastern journalist, Saddam had thought about war with Saudi Arabia during that time. Complaining of the lack of support from the Gulf states, after Iraq's February 1986 loss of Fao, Saddam

swore before a group of Iraqi diplomats, "The first one I will attack after this war is over is Saudi Arabia."

14. Baghdad Domestic Service, September 6, 1988, in *FBIS-NESA*, September 7, 1988.

15. *Middle East Mirror*, February 20, 1991.

16. In *FBIS-NESA*, November 8, 1990. Al-Musawwar, October 26, 1990.

17. Interview with Arab opposition figure, April 1990. This information was confirmed the next month by Muhammad Wahby, then head of the Egyptian press office in Washington. Saddam Hussein's demand for $30 billion is noted in Laurie Mylroie, "Tough Words Mean Tough Times in Baghdad," *Boston Jewish Times*, May 3, 1990. The timing is significant, as these reports were not invented after the fact.

18. *New York Times*, March 30, 1990.

19. Salinger and Laurent, *Secret Dossier*, 11.

20. One author even reported that Bazoft was working as a spy; see Simon Henderson, *Instant Empire: Saddam Hussein's Ambition for Iraq* (San Francisco: Mercury House, 1991), 208.

21. "Minister Defends Iraq in Bazoft Execution," Iraqi News Agency report on remarks by Kuwait's information minister, March 19, 1990, in *FBIS-NESA*, March 22, 1990.

22. Voice of the Masses, Baghdad 2 April 1990, *BBC/SWB ME/0730 A/1–4*, 4 April 1990.

23. Bob Woodward, *The Commanders* (New York: Simon and Schuster, 1991), 202, 239. Prince Bandar subsequently confirmed the Woodward account in an interview with me.

24. This story was related by King Fahd, Riyadh television, March 5, 1991, in *FBIS-NESA* March 6, 1991.

25. Interview with Israeli officer in June 1992.

26. *Financial Times*, January 11, 1991.

27. Interview with Kuwaiti ambassador, Nasir al-Sabah, Fall 1990.

28. The memorandum was reprinted by the Baghdad Domestic Service, July 18, 1990, in *FBIS-NESA*, July 18, 1990.

29. Ofra Bengio, "Republic of Iraq," *Middle East Contemporary Survey, 1990*, 401.

30. James Akins, "Heading Toward War," *Journal of Palestine Studies* (Spring 1991), 20.

31. Uzi Rabi, "The United Arab Emirates," in *Middle East Contemporary Survey, 1990*, 694.

32. See A. Ayalon (ed.) *Middle East Contemporary Survey 1990* 27–28. The Pentagon was much more skeptical and favored a harder line.

33. Bruce Maddy-Weitzman, "Inter-Arab Relations," in *Middle East Contemporary Survey, 1990*, 148.

4

Order and Interest: The Kuwait War and the Arab State System

Gudrun Krämer

From the onset, Iraq's invasion of Kuwait and the international reactions to it were charged with fears, hopes, and high expectations of fundamental structural and psychological change in the area. International and, to a lesser extent, regional reactions to the Iraqi aggression were seen as a test of superpower entente in the post-Cold War era. The allied victory was viewed as an opportunity, and indeed an obligation, to install a new regional order—if not simply order writ large— reflecting the rules of the new world order to be established by the international community. According to the well-known view of war as the "father of all things" and a catalyst for change, the Kuwait War was bound to constitute a watershed in Middle Eastern politics.

The crisis and war triggered by Iraq's aggression against Kuwait certainly provided for a disruption of the existing order. Indeed, such a disruption had been desperately sought by all who had long felt that the existing state of affairs, both within the individual states of the Middle East and in the region at large, was intolerable by all standards—social, economical, political, and moral.[1] Nonetheless, the Iraqi invasion came as a shock to the regimes in power and to large sections of the general public and was widely condemned by governments and opposition groups alike, including segments of the Islamic opposition groups as an act of aggression by one Arab state against another. And yet, within a relatively short time, Saddam Hussein managed to give a new meaning to the aggression by linking it to core issues on the Arab political agenda: the search for justice and equity, for Arab and Islamic solidarity, strength, and unity, and for a just solution to the Palestine conflict. In response to Saddam Hussein's skillful propaganda, and as a reflection of deep-seated frustration and despair, people of diverse origins and persuasions—from unemployed youth to prominent and even highly sophisticated intellectuals—supported Saddam Hussein, the commander of the strongest Arab military machine, as the prospective agent of change. They did so virtually without thought to his personal characteristics, qualifications, and credibility, expressing in their support criticism of their own governments rather than approval of Saddam's person and policies. Their dismay at seeing an Arab leader invade and annex another Arab country and then at seeing him defeated by an American-led Coalition that included several Arab states and Israel as a de facto (if silent) partner, was profound. The dismay was felt, although in certain circles the defeat was later denied or reinterpreted as a victory, or at least a partial or moral victory.

One had to wonder then, and to a large extent still must wonder, whether the shock and dismay would prove to be cathartic, as expected by many, and would prepare the ground not only for a new regional balance of power but also for new political thinking that would be reflected in the creation of structures and mechanisms of conflict management and resolution. In view of the intensity of popular involvement in the crisis and the magnitude of the defeat, expectations for change were possibly even higher than after the war of June 1967. At that time, after a period of self-scrutiny and reluctant readjustment among the states of the region, the regional balance of power shifted in favor of the conservative oil states, and political approaches to the Arab-Israeli conflict gradually began to be contemplated. The latter trend was counterbalanced, however, by the surge of autonomous Palestinian activism and Islamic reassertion.[2]

I argue here that Iraq's invasion of Kuwait and the war that followed, rather than creating a new regional or other order, brought to full light the primacy of "national" (i.e., by and large, regime) interests in the region, breaking the last taboos, constraints, and fetters of Arab consensus without, as yet, replacing that system with a coherent one of regional security, cooperation, or even interaction. With regard to the first point, a postwar system based on passing alliances and inherently unstable balances of power cannot be considered a new order. With regard to the second point, the open pursuit of national interest may be lamented or welcomed. It can be lamented as a definite break with the ideals of Arab unity and solidarity, as treason based on selfishness.[3] Indeed, the Iraqi invasion was premised on accommodation with U.S. hegemony in the area and the adoption of diplomatic rather than confrontational approaches to the Arab-Israeli conflict. Alternatively, it can be welcomed as a token of realism and pragmatism and as an escape from compulsive hypocrisy. There is a condition, though: Reduced commitment to the Arab cause should be compensated for by greater devotion to internal (within-state) problems of economic performance and political organization.

The crisis and war put into stark relief the primacy of domestic sources of strength and weakness within the individual states and regimes and the stability of the regional order. The domestic sources of stability and legitimacy, of course, could not be entirely divorced from the Arab-Israeli question, as was evident enough in the cases of Israel's immediate neighbors— Syria, Jordan, and Lebanon—and was again demonstrated during the 1991 Gulf War.[4] Still, the war made clear, or should have made clear, to domestic and international audiences that socioeconomic and political conditions within the individual states, and not the issue of borders (complicated and unresolved as that issue may be in various places), are at the root of violence and instability in the area. Although that statement would appear to be a truism, international reactions to and interpretations of the events suggest that the relevance of domestic politics to Arab policies has still not been universally recognized.[5] Indeed, one of the most common assumptions has been that the Kuwait crisis and war would destroy the regional order and sweep away its artificial states and borders. Its effect has so far been the opposite. Rather than tearing down the borders between the existing states, both natural and artificial, the war apparently confirmed their presence.[6] Once again, the remarkable resilience of Middle Eastern states and regimes in the face of grave challenges at home and abroad was demonstrated. Their pursuit of "selfish" interests was seen particularly in the Arab Gulf states' implementation of vindictive policies against their neighbors after the war and their resuscitation of long-standing border disputes. The case of Syria is a glaring example.

The Postwar Arab Order: Old Rules, New Alliances

The end of superpower confrontation and the Iraqi defeat have visibly altered the regional balance of power in the Middle East. While the former Soviet Union normalized its relations with prior opponents such as Israel and Saudi Arabia, it reduced its support for prior allies, among them most notably Syria, Iraq, and the Palestine Liberation movement— Israel's most determined critics and enemies. Theoretically at least, the end of superpower confrontation held the promise not only that it would lead to the formation of new alliances reflecting the changed balance of power but also that it would allow for fresh approaches to conflict management and resolution on a regional as well as an international level.

Against this background, the impact of the 1991 Gulf War may be described as having been primarily preventive: Iraq's defeat prevented it from exploding the regional balance of power and the rules of interstate behavior in the area.[7] Had Iraq been able to develop the full range of its military potential, from conventional and chemical to nuclear armament, it would have been the first Arab state to reach parity with Israel on a military level. By the same token, it would have become the hegemonic power in inter-Arab relations and in the Gulf area, with undisputable ascendancy over its longstanding rivals, Iran and Saudi Arabia.

Instead, the defeat of Iraq set back the dynamics of inter-Arab relations to the point where each of the major powers once again seeks security, influence, and (if possible) regional hegemony until checked by its rivals, either individually or collectively, with or without the support of non-Arab actors. The resultant shifting lines of cooperation, tension, and confrontation have been so bewildering to many observers that they have assumed them to be based on irrationality. However, the maneuvers have not been irrational in the majority of cases. Amid all the flux, one motive has stood out: the determination of the ruling elites to stay in power, no matter what the cost in terms of loss of life, property, credibility, or honor.[8] So far, the search for survival, self-assertion, and domination in the region has been synonymous with intensive armament; indeed, rearmament has been one of the most prominent features of early post-Kuwait War developments.[9]

The Iraqi aggression against Kuwait and interstate relations after the war have once again exposed the limits of inter-Arab conflict regulation both within the framework of the Arab League and based on individual efforts of mediation and conciliation (of which there had, incidentally, been no lack). Although the implementation of the cease-fire agreement and continued international supervision may for a certain time prevent Iraq from adopting revisionist policies vis-à-vis its neighbors, the unstable situation within Iraq keeps alive its sense of vulnerability and insecurity. The most prominent member states of the Gulf Cooperation Council (GCC)—Saudi Arabia, the United Arab Emirates, and Kuwait—attempted to reduce their risk through a number of measures. At the home front, for example, they announced drastic reductions in the number of foreigners allowed in their countries, a measure that affected most notably Arab workers and professionals. The citizens of states that had refused to side with Kuwait and Saudi Arabia in the conflict—i.e., Palestinians, Yemenis, and Jordanians—were particularly hard hit. In addition, Saudi Arabia, the smaller GCC countries, Egypt, and Syria engaged in large-scale rearmament and most intensified cooperation with their wartime Western allies in military and security matters. The risks involved in this policy package (it would be bold to call it a strategy) are obvious: The massive expulsion of Arab expatriates was bound to strain relations with the expatriates' countries of origin, two of which (Jordan and Yemen) were direct neighbors of Saudi Arabia, and to aggravate domestic tension in those countries and inject yet another element of regional instability. Furthermore, the extensive rearmament by Iraq's Kuwait War opponents was sure to affect the regional military balance, inevitably drawing Iran and Israel into the renewed arms race.

Despite massive military spending, the security guarantees sought by the Arab Gulf states have ultimately rested on external actors. In the spring and summer of 1991, an Arab solution to what was essentially an Arab problem seemed to be emerging in the form of the so-called Six-Plus-Two pact, an alliance of the six member states of the GCC plus Egypt and Syria.[10] The immediate aim of all partners was to secure their wartime gains and to perpetuate the postwar status quo. Egypt was attempting to make itself indispensable to both U.S. and conservative Arab interests in the area.[11] Syria tried to draw closer to the conservative oil states and the United States by continuing its intense rivalry with neighboring Iraq.[12] For all involved, the alliance promised to be beneficial: The vulnerable Gulf states would gain a certain degree of military protection and security from Egypt and Syria; those states, in turn, would receive substantial financial assistance, investment, cooperation, and job opportunities from the Gulf states. Like the short-lived Arab Cooperation Council (founded in February 1989 to include Iraq, Egypt, Jordan, and former North Yemen—and hence to exclude Syria), the alliance would not have been based on common ideological grounds, but would have brought together regimes both radical or moderate, progressive or reactionary. Also, the alliance would have been based on shared but volatile interests—on realpolitik as practiced with remarkable skill and success by the Syrian leadership.

The projected alliance would therefore have represented one more variation on the established pattern of Arab alignments that, with the exception of the Union du Maghreb Arabe (founded in 1989), have been formed against one or several other Arab states. Not only would it have been openly directed against Iraq; it would also have left out Jordan, thus punishing it for its noncommittal stand during the Gulf crisis and war. (Jordan had acted in the only way it could have to maintain its role as a buffer between Israel and Iraq, a role well understood by policy makers and analysts elsewhere.) The alliance would also have excluded Iran, even though, in the aftermath of the war, it increasingly claimed to be consulted in Gulf security policies.[13] The Six-Plus-Two formula thus reflected not so much Egyptian and Syrian policy objectives as the long-standing Saudi policy of excluding Iraq and Iran from formal security arrangements in the Gulf. In view of the alliance's transparent political objectives, one could expect that it would have been as unstable as virtually all of its predecessors. It is difficult to envision it as becoming the nucleus of a comprehensive Arab (or regional) security system providing a stable framework for negotiated conflict resolution.

In the end, the Six-Plus-Two pact failed because of the depth of distrust and resentment among the participants: The weaker Gulf states feared they would be subjected to continued interference and extortion on the part of Egypt and Syria, which were vastly stronger militarily but were notoriously in need of financial aid and investment. In addition, the former were not convinced of the latter's military competence. In a characteristic move, the Gulf states turned to out-of-area powers rather than regional ones to secure the protection they thought they needed.[14] Despite their deep-seated aversion to military alliances with non-Arab and non-Muslim powers, the smallest and weakest of the GCC members, Kuwait and Bahrain, decided to shed their traditional discretion and opt for close military cooperation with the United States, Great Britain, and France. Only Saudi Arabia did not invite a permanent U.S. military presence in its territory. In the long run, events may prove that it is not necessary for the Gulf states to create a comprehensive formal security pact or structure, but without such a structure in place, little progress has been made in the Gulf on the path toward peace and stability.

Hidden Merits of Selfishness?
Fresh Approaches to the Arab-Israeli Conflict

Although policies based on narrowly defined national (regime) interest seem to have precluded the establishment of a stable order in the Gulf, the "selfishness" of Iraq and other states may in the end produce more positive results in the realm of Arab-Israeli relations. (This view, of course, would not be shared by Arab nationalists and Islamic activists seeking full recognition of Arab Palestinian rights.) The Arab states' selfishness, the unavowed U.S. policy of "atomizing Arab politics,"[15]— openly supported by Israel—and the decline of the former Soviet Union all seem to have played a part in enhancing Arab-Israeli relations.

After Egypt's withdrawal from the Arab front in 1978–1979, Syria assumed the role of central player against the "Zionist entity." With the Soviet decline, however, Syria found itself squeezed between two neighbors of superior strength and uncertain designs—Israel to its south and Iraq to the east. Presumably, the Syrian regime would have been obliged to adjust to U.S. hegemony after the end of superpower competition; however, Iraq's defeat in the Gulf War made that accommodation much easier. Freed from a menacing rival that had given support to Syria's critics and opponents in Lebanon and among the Palestine Liberation movement, the Syrian regime was able to move toward the United States and its conservative Arab allies without having to face charges of treason from influential foes and rivals. It was handsomely rewarded by international acquiescence in its newly asserted hegemony over Lebanon.[16] In turn, Syria's volte-face made it possible for Jordan and the Palestinians to engage openly in peace negotiations with Israel.

Substantive changes caused by the Kuwait War, therefore, can be found in Arab-Israeli relations.[17] It is in that domain that the psychological and political effects of the Iraqi defeat have been felt most strongly. Although there are no indications that the use of force has been discredited, there seems to be a growing realization that certain vital issues cannot be solved militarily. The repercussions of progress in the Arab-Israeli conflict are potentially enormous, for only in conjunction with a settlement of the Arab-Israeli dispute(s) can the wider regional issues of economic cooperation, the use of dwindling water resources, the protection of the environment, and the problems of refugees, arms control, and arms reduction be addressed with any chance of success.

Justice, Equity, and Democratization?

It is obvious that peace and stability in the Gulf will require the reduction of poverty, inequality, and injustice within and among the various Arab states. In fact, the call for justice constituted one of the main issues raised during the Kuwait crisis, although it was skillfully exploited by Saddam Hussein, who interpreted it as a call for more equal distribution of oil wealth in the Arab Muslim world rather than as a call for structural change at home. The demands for political liberalization and for safeguards of human rights, which, in the 1980s and 1990s emerged as some of the core concerns of political opposition groups, professional unions, and human rights leagues all over the Arab world figured less prominently on Saddam Hussein's agenda.[18] Nonetheless, together with the Arab-Palestinian cause, the call for political participation, government control, and accountability—no matter whether it was called democracy, "Islamic democracy," or *shura* (referring to the Islamic ideal of participation via consultation)—constituted the common theme of all opposition forces. Safeguards of human rights cannot solve the problems of ethnic or religious minorities, but they may help to defuse them. Greater political participation, by placing stricter limits on corruption, clientelism, and nepotism, may also help increase economic efficiency and enhance system legitimacy. Therewith the attraction of foreign policy activism (if not adventurism) as the primary instrument of resource mobilization, regime maintenance, and legitimization may thus be reduced.

Unfortunately the prospects for redistribution of wealth and for liberalization and democracy in the Arab world continue to be questionable. In the wake of the war, a new dividing line was drawn across the so-called Arab camp pitting those who had supported the alliance and the conservative Arab Gulf states (all of whom have since been generously rewarded for their engagement) against those who had refused to do so (without, however, giving military support to Iraq)—notably, Jordan, Yemen, Sudan, and Tunisia. The latter group of states were punished by the former through isolation and the withdrawal of financial support and work permits for their citizens. In addition, not only have the financial reserves of the Arab oil monarchies been depleted, at least temporarily limiting their largesse, but aid and investment has been more openly politically conditioned so as to reward the "good" and punish the "evil."[19] Not incidentally, social cleavages, poverty, and frustration have been particularly severe in some of the countries that did not support the anti-Iraq alliance. Region-wide economic stabilization, which would provide the basis for greater political stability, can be reached only if and when those countries, too, are included in economic cooperation and reconstruction.

In the immediate aftermath of the war, other domestic problems were also compounded in most states in the area. The changed balance of forces, together with exacerbated economic pressures and crises, obliged the regimes to seek a rapprochement with the new hegemonic forces. In states that had previously embarked on a course of controlled political liberalization (Jordan, Yemen, and Tunisia in particular), domestic conflict and instability seemed most imminent. Rather than having created conditions for stability and legitimacy, the Gulf War thus sharpened internal tensions. The conflict between Iraq and the international alliance, which in much of the Arab world was largely perceived and presented as a conflict between all Arabs or Muslims and the West, mobilized what is alternatively called "public opinion," "the street," or "the masses" on a wider scale than had any other recent event.[20] Wherever their respective governments allowed, "the masses" (with the significant exception of those of Egypt) gave vent to their frustrations—whether social or political in nature—in primarily Arab nationalist or Islamic terms.

The violent outbursts of protest may have been a passing phenomenon, but they may also have strengthened the existing opposition movements and organizations. Antagonism to Western military intervention seems to have bridged, for the time being at least, the differences between the major opposition movements (Islamic activists, Arab nationalists, leftists, and liberals) that share such concerns as the Palestinian cause, social justice, and the protection of human rights as well as such enemies as

Israel, imperialism, and the states and groups considered to be their local allies. As a result of this general mass involvement, the commitment to Arabism has been reaffirmed as has the powerful though vaguely defined undercurrent of anti-Western feeling. The reaffirmation of Arabism has not, however, aimed at the dissolution of colonial borders and the merger of the existing Arab states into one; rather, it has focused on what are perceived to be common concerns of all Arabs and Muslims. It is possible that the medium- and long-term effects of accumulated tension and frustration will be felt in the Maghreb even more than in the Arab east and that therefore France rather than the United States will see its position and influence harmed the most.[21]

Paradoxically, the reaffirmation of ideology at the popular level, emphasizing Arabism, Islam, authenticity, and the rejection of foreign intervention, has coincided with a marked trend toward de-ideologization at the regime level that has translated into closer cooperation with the West in economic, political, and military matters and movement toward a negotiated settlement of the Arab-Israeli conflict on the basis of land-for-peace. How the two trends can be reconciled is difficult to see. Nowhere has the clash between popular demands and external restraints on government policies, both foreign and domestic, been more marked than in Jordan.[22] There, the conflicting exigencies of exacerbated socioeconomic crisis, domestic pressure for political participation, and dependence on external forces have critically restricted the regime's room for maneuver. They have made Jordan's cautious drive toward (controlled) liberalization for the maintenance of the regime even more difficult.

Public attention has understandably been fixed on the possible impact of the Gulf War on the Islamic movement in the area. Like many Arab nationalists, a majority of Islamic activists have condemned both the Iraqi invasion of Kuwait and the allied campaign against Iraq that culminated in war. The Islamic activists have been in a much more difficult position than the nationalists, however, because the anti-Iraq alliance included Saudi Arabia, which had for many years funded their activities, particularly in the Maghreb and Jordan. The reduction or wholesale withdrawal of Saudi support was bound to impair their capacity to offer services to present and prospective adherents. It must be emphasized, however, that the attraction of Islamic ideology and activism is not based solely on external support; it is also based on domestic sources of disaffection, such as social inequality, political repression, and cultural alienation, which continue to exist and to be felt as strongly as ever.

The confluence of these various forces can be seen, for instance, in Algeria. The greatly enhanced military and political presence of the United States and the setbacks in the process of political liberalization in that country in the late 1980s have created fertile grounds for radical Islamic groups' operation and their political ascendancy at the expense of what has been termed the moderate wing of the movement, rendering economic reform and political liberalization even more problematic. Still, the "moderates" advocating nonviolent strategies of cooperation and integration have by no means been eclipsed.

Conflict Resolution

Beyond aspects of structural reform within the regional states, peace and stability in the Gulf will require the introduction, implementation, and eventual institutionalization of rules of conflict resolution that transcend the established pattern of power politics based on shifting regional balances and alliances. Conflict will have to be settled through negotiation without resorting to the use of force, or the threat of its use; conflict resolution would have to be based on a reciprocity of interest rather than on unstable balances of power. It will have to be linked to regional arms control and reduction, and it will eventually have to be integrated into a collective security system (or at least arrangement) to provide a stable framework that can guarantee the underlying principles.

To be stable, the new order will have to rest on a number of premises. First, the actors involved will have to reach the conclusion that conflict (over territory, water, minority rights, and so forth) cannot be solved, and their proper interest cannot be secured through the use of force; furthermore, they will have to realize that both material and other costs of the use of force are always higher than the cost of negotiation. This stage seems to have been reached with regard to the Arab-Israeli conflict but not with respect to other issues, such as the Kurdish question. Second, all states in the region, including Israel, will have to be formally recognized as legitimate actors, and Israel will have to accept the principles of land-for-peace and self-determination for the Palestinians—irrespective of how these conveniently vague and controversial principles are defined. Here, progress has been clearly visible, as seen in the bilateral peace negotiations and multilateral talks on the Palestinian end of wider regional issues. Third, compliance with the principle of negotiated conflict resolution will have to be rewarded and noncompliance punished. The same is true with regard to the region-wide redistribution of wealth and political liberalization. At this point it is difficult to see who among the regional actors will be able and qualified to furnish the rewards and sanctions required, particularly in the fields of human rights and economic restructuring. It is equally difficult to see how external actors (such as the UN Security Council, the United States, and the European Union) can be formally involved without overtaxing their resources and capabilities and without creating too much regional opposition to their involvement.

Conclusion

The war against Iraq has been won, and its declared aims have been achieved: Kuwait has been liberated and its former regime reinstalled. Iraq is, at least for the time being, unable to pose a military threat to its neighbors, both Arab and non-Arab (i.e. Iran and Turkey); neither is it able to dictate oil prices and production quotas to the Arab Gulf producers and Iran. To that extent, the war was a success. However, in view of the high costs involved in the military action against Iraq and its original moral purpose—civil war in Iraq, the mass flight of the Kurds, economic devastation, and ecological damage in the Gulf—results have not been considered satisfactory by Arab, European, and U.S. publics.[23]

Indeed, in the aftermath of the war, it has been quite common to hear that although the war had been won, the peace had been lost. More had been hoped for, including creative, constructive action that would supplement and build on preemption and destruction to create the conditions for "international peace and stability in the area" that were envisaged in UN Security Council Resolution 678. For those conditions to be created peace and stability would have to embrace more than a solution to the most urgent interstate issues. It would also require more than the creation of a viable postwar order in the Gulf that secured stability in the vital oil-producing area and more than a settlement of the Palestine conflict. Peace and stability would ultimately have to rest on a reduction of poverty and inequality within and among the regional states, on political liberalization, and on the acceptance of new rules of negotiated conflict resolution and of arms control and limitation.

In light of these high expectations, the postwar developments were sobering. The immediate aftermath of the Kuwait crisis and war was dominated by attempts to stabilize the postwar status quo by containing Iraq and its wartime sympathizers rather than by concerted efforts to redefine regional challenges and establish new rules of conflict management and resolution. Contrary to widespread hopes and expectations, the 1991 Gulf War did not discredit the established (negative) rules of the political game; nor did it destroy the existing pattern of interstate relations. So far, it has merely redistributed the cards without rewriting the rules of the game. It has brought forth new alignments rather than new structures. The issues of social inequality, political repression, and the widespread use of force in domestic and interstate conflict still remain to be addressed. Against this somber background, it is, ironically, the Arab-Israeli issue that offers a ray of hope.

Notes

1. See, e.g., Ann Mosely Lesch, "Contrasting Reactions to the Persian Gulf Crisis: Egypt, Syria, Jordan, and the Palestinians," in *The Middle East Journal*, Vol. 45, No. 1, Winter 1991, 30–50; Alain Roussillon, "L'opposition égyptienne et la crise du Golfe," *Maghreb-Machrek*, No. 130, October–December 1990, 79–98; M. alAhnaf, "L'opposition maghrébine face à la crise du Golfe," ibid., 99–114; Maha Azzam, "The Gulf Crisis: Perceptions in the Muslim World," *International Affairs*, Vol. 67, No. 3, July 1991, 473–485. For further references, see Gudrun Krämer, "Der irakische Überfall auf Kuwait und seine Vorgeschichte," in Wolfgang Wagner et al. (eds.), *Die Internationale Politik 1989–1990* (Munich: R. Oldenbourg, 1992), 193–209; Udo Steinbach, "Der Verlauf des Krieges," 210–223, and *Current History*, No. 561 (The Middle East, 1992), January 1992. For political and strategic analyses of the Kuwait crisis and 1991 Gulf War, see The International Institute of Strategic Studies, *Strategic Survey 1990–1991* (London, 1991), 49–102, and *Strategic Survey 1991–1992* (London, 1992), 84–116; also Roland Dannreuther, *The Gulf Conflict: A Political and Strategic Analysis* (London: Adelphi Papers, No. 264, Winter 1991/92).

2. For a controversial presentation of the post-1967 crisis and developments, see Fouad Ajami, *The Arab Predicament: Arab Political Thought and Practice Since 1967* (Cambridge: Cambridge University Press, 1981); for the effects on inter-Arab relations, see Alan Taylor, *The Arab Balance of Power* (Syracuse, N.Y.: Syracuse University Press, 1981).

3. See, e.g., Yezid Sayigh, "The Gulf Crisis: Why the Arab Regional Order Failed," *International Affairs*, Vol. 67, No. 3, July 1991, 487–507.

4. For an earlier analysis, see Valerie Yorke, *Domestic Politics and Regional Security: Jordan, Syria and Israel* (London: Gower, 1988).

5. See also Yezid Sayigh, "Arab Regional Security: Between Mechanics and Politics," *RUSI Journal*, Vol. 136, No. 2, Summer 1991, 38–46.

6. See the excellent article by Iliya Harik, "The Origins of the Arab State System," in Giacomo Luciani (ed.), *The Arab State* (London: Routledge, 1990), 1–28.

7. For a fuller examination of this point, see G. Krämer, "Konfliktmuster und Konfliktmöglichkeiten im Nahen Osten und am Golf," Wolfgang Heydrich et al. (eds.), *Sicherheitspolitik Deutschlands: Neue Konstellationen, Risiken, Instrumente* (Baden-Baden: Nomos Verlagsgesellschaft, 1992), 439–457.

8. This point is well illustrated with regard to Iraq under Saddam Hussein in Efraim Karsh and Inari Rautsi, *Saddam Hussein: A Political Biography* (London: I.B. Tauris, 1991).

9. See, e.g., *The Middle East*, No. 216, October 1992, 19–22; also Burkhardt J. Huck, "Rüstung und Rüstungskontrolle im Nahen Osten. Die Region ein Jahr nach dem Golfkrieg," *Informationsdienst Wissenschaft und Frieden*, Vol. 10, No. 2, June 1992, 30–34.

10. On the prospects of the projected alliance, see the earlier comments by Sayigh, "Arab Regional Security," 39–41.

11. On Egyptian foreign policy, see G. Krämer, *Ägypten unter Mubarak. Identität und nationales Interesse* (Baden-Baden: Nomos Verlagsgesellschaft, 1986), 129–211.

12. On Syrian foreign policy under Assad, see Raymond Hinnebusch, "Revisionist Dreams, Realist Strategies: The Foreign Policy of Syria," Bahgat Korany and Ali E. Hillal Dessouki (eds.), *The Foreign Policies of Arab States* (Boulder, Colo.: Westview Press, 1984), 283–322; also G. Krämer, "Syriens Weg zu regionaler Hegemonie," *Europa-Archiv,* Vol. 42, No. 22, November 1987, 665–674, and more specifically Moshe Ma'oz, "Syrian-Israeli Relations and the Middle East Peace Process," *Jerusalem Journal of International Relations,* Vol. 14, No. 3, September 1992, 1–21.

13. For brief overviews, see Shahram Chubin, "Iran and Regional Security in the Persian Gulf," *Survival,* Vol. 34, No. 3, Autumn 1992, 62–80, and R. K. Ramazani, "Iran's Foreign Policy: Both North and South," *The Middle East Journal,* Vol. 46, No. 3, Summer 1992, 393–412; also Anoushiravan Ehteshami and Gerd Nonneman, *War and Peace in the Gulf: Domestic Politics and Regional Relations into the 1990s* (Reading: NY Ithaca Press, 1991).

14. The assessment is shared by Sayigh, "The Gulf Crisis," 504. Basing his argument on an earlier analysis of Saudi foreign policy by Ghassan Salamé, he spoke of strategic and economic disengagement of the Arab Gulf states from their "northern tier." See also Chubin, "Iran and Regional Security," and Steven Simon, "U.S. Strategy in the Persian Gulf," *Survival,* Vol. 34, No. 3, Autumn 1992, 81–97.

15. Jim Hoagland, "The Decline of Radical Arab Nationalism," *International Herald Tribune,* September 10, 1992, 4.

16. See Augustus R. Norton, "Lebanon After Ta'if: Is the Civil War Over?" *The Middle East Journal,* Vol. 45, No. 3, Summer 1991, 457–473.

17. See L. J. Duclos and J. F. Legrain, "Dossier: Vers la paix au Moyen-Orient?" *Maghreb-Machrek,* No. 134, October–December 1991, 97–127; also the special document files on "The Madrid Conference," *Journal of Palestine Studies,* Vol. 21, No. 2, Winter 1992, 117–149, and on "The Peace Process," *Journal of Palestine Studies,* Vol. 21, No. 3, Spring 1992, 126–146.

18. See, e.g., Muhammad Salim al-'Awwa, "al-'arab wa-l-shura ba'da azmat al-Khalij's," *al-Mustaqbal al-'Arabi,* Vol. 14, No. 148, June 1991, 48–55; Michael C. Hudson, "After the Gulf War: Prospects for Democratization in the Arab World," *The Middle East Journal,* Vol. 45, No. 3, Summer 1991, 407–426; and G. Krämer, "Liberalization and Democracy in the Arab World," *Middle East Report,* No. 174, January–February 1992, 22–25, 35.

19. For the economic effects of the war, see Siegfried Schönherr and Axel J. Halbach (eds.), *Der Golf nach dem Krieg: Wirtschaft, Politik, Rüstung* (Munich, Cologne, London: Weltforum Verlag, 1991).

20. See note 2. On Arabism and the Gulf War, see As'ad AbuKhalil, "A New Arab Ideology?: The Rejuvenation of Arab Nationalism," *The Middle East Journal,* Vol. 46, No. 1, Winter 1992, 22–36. For broader perspectives, see Giacomo Luciani and Ghassan Salamé, "The Politics of Arab Integration," in Luciani (ed.), *The Arab State,* (London: Routledge, 1990) 394–419; and Center of Arab Unity Studies (ed.), *The Future of the Arab Nation: Challenges and Options* (London, New York: Routledge, 1991).

21. Here, however, France's military engagement in the Gulf War has to be seen in conjunction with its stand on the aborted Algerian elections of January 1992.

22. For Jordan's role in the Gulf crisis and war, see, e.g., Amatzia Baram, "Baathi Iraq and Hashimite Jordan: From Hostility to Alignment," *The Middle East Journal*, Vol. 45, No. 1, Winter 1991, 51–70; Laurie A. Brand, "Liberalization and Changing Political Coalitions: The Bases of Jordan's 1990–1991 Gulf Crisis Policy," *Jerusalem Journal of International Relations*, Vol. 13, No. 4, 1991, 1–46. For background information, see also Rodney Wilson (ed.), *Politics and the Economy in Jordan* (London, New York: Routledge, 1991).

23. Ecological damage appears to have been more limited than initially expected. The fear of such damage may reflect a specifically German, or Western, rather than a primary regional concern.

PART TWO

Power, Strategy, and Technology

5

How Kuwait Was Won: Strategy in the Gulf War

Lawrence Freedman and Efraim Karsh

The dust has yet to settle after the 1991 Gulf War, and it may not settle for some time. After the grand finale of the 100-hour land campaign came the confusion of the Shi'ite and Kurdish insurrection and the torrent of refugees into Turkey and Iran. The accumulation of human suffering, material decline, and environmental damage did not stop with the fighting. The political futures of either Iraq or Kuwait were not settled, nor the responsibilities of the victorious powers for the peace and security of the area concluded.

Whatever the political outcome, the most important feature of the Gulf War in military terms was its decisive, overwhelming character. At no point did Iraq offer any serious resistance. Its air force retreated in the face of combat; its small navy, which had nowhere to hide, was decimated in a side-show; the army crumbled in the face of the Coalition's advance.

The strategy that led to the victory—a relatively protracted and systematic air campaign followed by a land campaign based on envelopment and maneuver—was fully advertised beforehand. So was the Iraqi strategy, which was based on threatening the United States with a "second Vietnam" and absorbing the air offensive.[1]

In this chapter we demonstrate how the strategies of both sides in the Gulf War were governed by a sensitivity to its political context, both domestically and internationally. It was widely expected that Iraqi forces would only be expelled from Kuwait following a ferocious land battle. This created the severe risk of extremely high American casualties because the United States was providing the bulk of the Coalition forces ranged against Iraq. The Bush administration was therefore under intense pressure to adopt a strategy that would minimize the Coalition's casualties. It was also widely expected that the disparate Coalition of Western and Arab states would split under the stresses and strains of war: American military strategy therefore had to be reinforced by a careful leadership of the alliance.

These demands on the Bush administration suggested opportunities for Iraq. President Saddam Hussein's strategy had to be based on increasing American casualties and sowing division within the Coalition. The consequence was a war in which Iraq was on the military defensive but on the political offensive. For either side, the political and military strands of strategy could not work independently. Success would depend on mutual reinforcement. In the end, the United States was successful because the strength of its military offensive eased the pressure on its political defenses.

The Buildup to War

U.S. forces were initially committed to the Gulf in order to deter a perceived threat to Saudi Arabia following Iraq's invasion of Kuwait on August 2, 1990. They were later joined by forces from a number of countries. By the start of the war, some 35 countries were providing assistance in one form or another. The main contributors to the Coalition (other than Saudi Arabia and Kuwait) were Britain and France from Europe, and Egypt and Syria from the Arab world. No country gave Iraq significant material support, although the Palestine Liberation Organization (PLO) declared solidarity. Of Iraq's other neighbors, Jordan showed sympathy to Iraq but was in no position economically and militarily to give much material support; Iran was generally unsympathetic (despite obtaining a favorable settlement of issues remaining from the Iran-Iraq War, including its border dispute with Iraq and the exchange of prisoners of war); Turkey cut off Iraq's oil pipeline and then offered the use of its air bases to the Coalition.

One striking consequence of the universal condemnation of the Iraqi aggression was the ability of the Western members of the Coalition—France, the United Kingdom, and the United States—to use their positions as permanent members of the United Nations Security Council to gain legitimacy for their effort to drive Iraq out of Kuwait. The Soviet Union was generally supportive, and China was at least acquiescent. After Resolution 660 of August 2, which condemned the invasion of Kuwait, demanded unconditional withdrawal of Iraqi forces, and called for immediate negotiations between the two states, the resolutions passed by the Security Council gradually hardened. The Council condemned the measure taken by Iraq to consolidate its hold on Kuwait, by declaring the annexation null and void (Resolution 662), and by insisting that foreign nationals be allowed to leave and that diplomatic missions in Kuwait were to remain open (Resolution 665). It demanded compensation for financial losses and human rights violations incurred by the invasion (Resolution 674), and prevented attempts to change the demographic structure of Kuwait by moving in Iraqi nationals (Resolution 677). There was a comparable escalation in the measures taken against Iraq; the stringent trade sanctions imposed on August 6 (Resolution 661) were reinforced on August 25 by permission to the Coalition to use limited naval forces to enforce the sanctions (Resolution 665), and a month later by a prohibition on air traffic (Resolution 670).

The blockade hurt Iraq and obliged it to adopt exceptional measures, such as rationing of food, gasoline, and motor oil supplies, and draconian legislation making the hoarding of foodstuffs for commercial purposes a crime punishable by death.[2] The weight of evidence, however, suggests that Saddam believed that he could survive the blockade, at least until his opponents were ready for compromise. The U.S. Central Intelligence Agency (CIA) judged that sanctions alone would take at least a year and possibly longer to bring Iraq to the point where it might comply with the UN resolutions.[3] There was no suggestion that success could come earlier. It was unclear how much more time Iraq might gain by plunder from Kuwait, rationing, smuggling, and a boost to the harvest. One study suggested that a realistic assessment of the impact of sanctions could not be made until March 1991, the point at which conditions for military action would be deteriorating.[4]

Iraq's defensive preparations in Kuwait convinced Coalition leaders that Saddam was preparing for the long haul. A serious offensive military option would require more forces than the United States had initially planned for. On November 8, 1990, immediately after the congressional elections, President Bush announced an effective doubling of U.S. ground forces to some 430,000.[5] Other Coalition partners soon followed suit. This was a turning point in the strategic calculations of both sides. Washington apparently was seeking to bring matters to a head.[6]

Despite official denials,[7] it was widely assumed that if the offensive option was not exercised by the end of March, the onset of the hot weather would create problems for mobile military operations until the next autumn; at the same time, it would be expensive and politically awkward to keep such large forces in the Gulf. In practice, the deadline was set by UN Security Council Resolution 678 of November 29, which authorized member states to use "all necessary means" to enforce full Iraqi compliance with all relevant UN resolutions by midnight of January 15, 1991, if this had not yet been accomplished peacefully. President Bush followed this the next day by going "the extra mile for peace" with a proposal that Secretary of State James Baker visit Baghdad and his Iraqi counterpart, Tariq Aziz, come to Washington.[8] After considerable diplomatic gamesmanship, the two men eventually met in Geneva on January 9, 1991. The meeting ended in deadlock.[9] There were desultory efforts by others afterwards—most notably a visit by UN Secretary General Jávier Perez de Cuellar to Baghdad on January 11, and a last-ditch attempt by French President François Mitterrand to engineer a UN resolution linking the Kuwait issue with the Palestinian problem. Nothing was achieved, and the allied air offensive began soon afterwards during the night of January 16–17. The failure of diplomacy indicated that both sides believed that their positions could be improved only by military action.

For the Coalition, the war strategy had been shaped by the peace strategy. It was believed that Saddam's compliance with UN resolutions depended on convincing him that if he did not comply, he would suffer an overwhelming defeat.[10] This coercive strategy did not work. Part of the explanation may lie in the shifting moods of the Iraqi leader, convinced one moment that the United States was determined to overthrow him, come what may,[11] and the next that the Americans lacked the stomach for a fight. However, these moods must also be placed in the context of Saddam's strategic perspective, shaped by his country's eight-year war with Iran.

Iraqi Strategy

Saddam Hussein should have had serious misgivings regarding Iraq's capacity to sustain a prolonged and ferocious conflict. The persistence of the Iran-Iraq War had not been of his own choice: It had been imposed on him by a fanatical foe who openly demanded his downfall. He survived the war largely by shielding the Iraqi public from its effects.[12] Iraq's much-celebrated defensive prowess was overstated. Iraqi military operations during the Iran-Iraq War had been conducted under ideal circumstances, with superior firepower and complete mastery of the air. Still, Iraq's formidable defenses had repeatedly been breached by ill-equipped Iranian teenagers, whose advance had been contained with great difficulty and at times through the use of chemical weapons.[13]

Perhaps in light of all this, Saddam's strategy from the beginning of the Gulf crisis had been geared toward preventing an armed confrontation and, had hostilities broken out, toward quick termination. But if it made such sense for Saddam to avoid war, why did he fail to seize the various face-saving formulas to withdraw from Kuwait, offered to him during the crisis, let alone fail to launch a serious diplomatic initiative of his own? An unconditional withdrawal from Kuwait, or one with a cosmetic face-saving formula added, was totally unacceptable to Saddam from the outset, since it did not address the fundamental predicament underlying the invasion of Kuwait. He had not occupied Kuwait for reasons of power-seeking or political aggrandizement, although certainly his prestige across the Arab world and among his own subjects would have grown enormously with a successful takeover of Kuwait. Rather, the invasion had been a desperate attempt to shore up his regime in the face of the abysmal economic conditions created by the Iran-Iraq War. This economic plight not only remained after the invasion of Kuwait, but was significantly aggravated by the sanctions; Saddam therefore felt that any turn-about on his part would damage his position beyond repair.[14]

By the beginning of 1991, Saddam should have been aware that the Coalition was more cohesive than he had expected: His calls for popular insurrections against the Arab members of the Coalition had produced a minimal response; his attempt to wean France away through preferential release of hostages had failed; the Soviet Union had supported a series of tough anti-Iraq resolutions in the UN, including Resolution 678. Nonetheless, Saddam apparently still hoped that the vociferous peace camp in the West, and the variety of would-be intermediaries visiting him in Baghdad, would help him avert war. He interpreted President Bush's November 30 offer of direct talks as readiness to reach a compromise. "Bush's initiative is a submission to Iraq's demand, [on] which it has insisted and is still insisting," gloated the Iraqi media, "namely, the need to open a serious dialogue on the region's issues."[15]

During this period Saddam made two decisions that undermined his military position and that must have reflected some optimism that a settlement could be reached or, at least, that war could be delayed. The first was to release all Western hostages on December 6. Saddam appears to have been persuaded by Arab supporters, such as PLO leader Yassir Arafat and visiting elder statesmen from the West (such as former British Prime Minister Edward Heath, former Secretary General of the United Nations Kurt Waldheim, and former German Chancellor Willy Brandt) that the holding of hostages was detrimental to his image, and that their release would be taken as a serious gesture of reconciliation and would generate a momentum toward a negotiated settlement which President Bush would find difficult to contain. He might also have judged that, rather than encouraging the United States to stay its hand, the holding of foreign nationals might stimulate outrage and a more ferocious reaction. On balance, the release of the hostages turned out to be a strategic mistake, as Saddam himself was to admit later with uncharacteristic frankness.[16] Their release did not weaken the Coalition's resolve to dislodge Iraq from Kuwait, and it facilitated its military planning. Despite Western statements that the location of the hostages at "strategic sites" did not affect operational plans, clearly this was not wholly true. Once the hostages were out, the U.S. Air Force added many facilities to its target list that had earlier been excluded.[17]

The second indication of Saddam's belief that war could be avoided was his decision not to attack Coalition forces in Saudi Arabia, a move which could have disrupted and confused the Coalition's own military preparations. From the beginning of the crisis he vehemently denied the American allegations of Iraqi intentions to attack Saudi Arabia, and took great pains not to threaten the Coalition with preemption.[18] Preemption would have been unlikely to change the eventual outcome of the crisis and would have made inevitable a conflict that might still have been avoided. If this latter factor was influential, then it could also indicate Saddam's hope that the start of war might be delayed.

In essence Saddam's strategy was to rely on his defenses around Kuwait and the cost that could be imposed on Coalition forces if they could be drawn into killing zones, as Iranian forces had been during the Iran-Iraq War. His initial worry was an amphibious assault, which led him to order extensive coastal defenses and mining of adjacent waters. The size of the U.S. ground forces moving into Saudi Arabia then encouraged the construction of extensive fortifications along the Saudi-Kuwait border. These followed the pattern of those developed during the Iran-Iraq War, but could not be quite the same. There, the swampy conditions allowed for areas to be flooded, thus forcing attacking forces into a killing ground. Here, berms or ridges of bulldozed sand were constructed and combined with ditches, some filled with oil, barbed wire, and a variety of other anti-tank obstacles. These were backed up by tanks and artillery (believed in the West to be an Iraqi specialty) and numerous troops. But the stark desert provided less opportunity for natural obstacles than the waters around Basra. Furthermore, these fortifications did not extend much beyond the Kuwaiti-Saudi border. Belatedly the Iraqis realized that their fortifications could be outflanked by a desert attack through Iraq, thus suffering the same fate as the Maginot Line in World War II. Although they made an attempt to extend the line to cover the whole of the border with Saudi Arabia, they achieved only limited results, and the resultant gap was later exploited mercilessly.

Saddam was able to call upon large numbers of reserves. At 19 million, Iraq's overall population was not large, but he could put together an army of about a million men because the country had been on a war footing for nearly a decade. The expedient if disadvantageous settlement with Iran made it possible to shift a number of divisions from that border. As the crisis developed, and in particular after President Bush's November 8 announcement of the U.S. buildup, the number of divisions was boosted; all young men, and then the middle-aged, were called up. There seems to have been some belief that large numbers of defenders would have a deterrent effect. This may have reflected a belief in the famous 3-to-1 ratio, held to be necessary for an attacking force against an entrenched defense.[19]

However, this buildup was geared to the protection of Iraq as a whole and not just the new Kuwaiti acquisition, and the perceived threats did not come simply from the United States. Significant forces had to remain deployed along Iraq's borders with its Iranian, Turkish, and Syrian neighbors. The elite Republican Guards, Iraq's best-equipped units of some eight divisions, were not pushed far over the border into Kuwait, for Saddam was anxious not to endanger the praetorian protectors of his personal rule.[20] Consequently, there were not enough forces for a wide front; the border defenses were manned by less capable troops while the Republican Guards were kept back as, at best, a strategic armored reserve.

The large numbers cited by Iraq never arrived in the Kuwait theater. After the end of the war, estimates suggested that there may have been as few as 350,000 Iraqi troops available prior to hostilities, despite Western estimates at the time (reinforced by Iraqi statements) of at least 540,000 Iraqi troops.[21] The numbers that the Iraqis deployed created major logistical difficulties for them; the stretched supply lines were easily disrupted by the Coalition's air strikes. Such vulnerabilities would have been magnified if Iraq had sent more troops to Kuwait.

The most obvious weakness in the Iraqi military structure was the lack of air support. On the face of it, Iraq's air force was substantial, with some high-quality aircraft. The key role it had played during the war with Iran, breaking enemy morale through sustained campaigns against strategic targets and population centers, underscored the significance of air power in modern war. The hardened bunkers prepared for the most valuable aircraft, the enormous airfields, and the redundant command-and-control system all indicated Iraq's sensitivity to the dangers of preemptive air attack, and presumably the central importance of air power in Israeli strategy.[22] And yet, even during the Iran-Iraq War, Saddam displayed considerable restraint in the employment of air power, refraining for a long time from carrying Iraq's overwhelming aerial superiority to its logical conclusion. Saddam's reluctance thus put at risk his most effective reserve of military force.[23] This insecure operational conception was extended into the Kuwaiti crisis.

Another key Iraqi underestimation was in the area of precision-guided weapons, with which Iraq's defenses proved unable to cope. This was not wholly unreasonable because many of the most modern weapons were untried and their effectiveness was widely questioned even in the West.[24] In addition, the full significance of electronic warfare was imperfectly understood.

Saddam considered missiles as his most reliable means of inflicting a painful blow on the enemy. The Iraqi stocks of ballistic missiles were extensive and, with the benefit of European technology, their ranges had been extended.[25] According to Iraqi disclosures to the United Nations after the war, Iraq had thirty chemical warheads for its Scuds.[26] Saddam had long spoken of his missile force as an "anti-Israel" capability and re-emphasized this on the eve of the war.[27] Designed to divide the Coalition by giving the crisis an Arab-Israeli dimension, these threats followed a diplomatic campaign that sought to link the occupation of Kuwait with the Palestinian problem.[28] The missiles could also be used against Saudi population centers, and to a lesser extent as a threat to the Saudi oil instal-lations.[29] They represented Saddam's best prospects of taking the war to the enemy camp.

Iraq's strategy was therefore based on deterring and if necessary rebuffing the central thrust of the enemy's campaign, by exacerbating the prospective war's stresses and strains on the political cohesion of the Coalition while absorbing the air assault.[30] There was no obvious strategy for war termination other than inflicting such discomfort that the Coali-tion would develop an interest in a cease-fire on terms other than the full implementation of all UN resolutions. Saddam strongly believed that the Achilles heel of the United States was its extreme sensitivity to casualties, and he was determined to exploit this weakness to the full. He told the American ambassador to Baghdad, April Glaspie, shortly before the inva-sion of Kuwait: "Yours is a society which cannot accept 10,000 dead in one battle."[31]

In a speech a few days before the war began, Saddam told an Islamic gathering in Baghdad that "thousands of men" at the front were "under-ground in strong reinforced positions," ready to "rise against" the enemy as soon as it attacked. He acknowledged that the coming war would be a testing ground for advanced technology, but stressed Iraq's numerical superiority and its experience of war. The Americans would "carry out acrobatics just like a Rambo movie. ... They tell you that the Americans have advanced missiles and warplanes, but they ought to rely on their soldiers armed with rifles and grenades."[32]

Coalition Strategy

The Vietnam War had as profound an influence on American calcula-tions as the war with Iran had on Iraq. Key actors in the American politi-cal process were determined not to repeat the mistakes of the 1960s: The administration was resolved not to get trapped in an unwinnable war; the military would not allow civilians to impose artificial restrictions that would deny them the possibility of a decisive victory; Congress refused to be railroaded into giving *carte blanche* for waging war to the executive; and the diplomats did not wish to find themselves supporting a military campaign in isolation from natural allies.

The administration never doubted the folly of getting drawn into a messy ground war with a Third World country. One view—the quagmire thesis—was that this was an inevitable feature of any such conflict. This view had been reinforced by the more recent relevant experience in Lebanon in 1983. Another—the escalation thesis—held that a quagmire was the unnecessary result of attempting to employ force in a graduated, incremental manner.[33]

President Bush demanded of the military that they avoid another Vietnam at all costs. On November 30 he promised the American public that any military action would not "be another Vietnam";[34] one of his first comments after the end of the war was the claim that the United States had "kicked the Vietnam syndrome."[35] This focus had an impact on Coalition strategy in both the setting of objectives and the choice of strategy designed to achieve these objectives.

Officially, the United States insisted that its primary aim was to liberate Kuwait rather than to change the Iraqi regime, despite continuing public allegations to the contrary, reinforced by the "demonizing" of Saddam Hussein. This objective would obviously require attacking targets in Iraq; the Bush administration evidently saw this as an opportunity to destroy the most threatening aspects of Iraq's military power.[36] However, Washington recognized that it would be extremely unwise to be seen as trying to change the regime in Baghdad. This would alarm the Arab members of the Coalition and also Iran, which had expressed its fear of a permanent, intrusive American presence. It would involve assuming responsibility for Iraq, which could be a long-term liability especially if there was popular opposition. Even advancing to Baghdad and taking it would involve more difficult and painful fighting than the liberation of Kuwait.

Restricting the objectives to the liberation of Kuwait did not involve the risk of a Vietnam-type quagmire, which was the consequence of fighting a largely guerrilla war in difficult terrain and under unfavorable political conditions. It is of note that when the United States began to get sucked into the postwar civil war in Iraq, it was this fear of a quagmire that was most often mentioned.[37]

However, even if the United States could fight the war on terms for which it was best prepared, a presumed lesson of Vietnam was that the public would be intolerant of high casualties. As with many other such lessons, the evidence was ambiguous.[38] Both Vietnam and the British experience in the Falklands suggested the countervailing importance of the "rally around the flag" factor once war begins,[39] and this factor became evident during the Gulf War as well.[40]

Nonetheless, prior to the war all the indications were that U.S. public opinion was most brittle on the question of casualties. An opinion poll in early January 1991 showed a strengthening of support for war—63 percent, compared to 55 percent in early December—but also continuing optimism over the possibility of a diplomatic solution. Support was less if the assumption was 1,000 American troops killed—to 44 percent in favor of war and 53 percent opposed—and it further declined to only 35 percent in favor, with 61 percent opposed, if the cost were to be 10,000 troops killed.[41]

This, as we have seen, was Saddam Hussein's main hope. Just as his strategy depended on convincing—if necessary with proof—American public opinion that the level of casualties would be unacceptably high, President Bush had to demonstrate the opposite. Few in the United States doubted that the Coalition could inflict a crippling military defeat on Iraq and eject it from Kuwait. The severity of the sacrifice depended to some extent on the quality of the Coalition strategy. An all-out assault on entrenched Iraqi positions could put casualties up to several tens of thousands; skillful use of air power, mobility, and night-fighting capability could reduce this to a fraction.[42] However, it was feared that there was still an irreducible minimum. For example, Edward Luttwak, one of the most visible and vocal opponents of a land campaign, argued that high casualties were "almost mathematically certain" even given what he deemed to be extremely optimistic assumptions (which in fact approximated the actual state of affairs when the land campaign came). High casualties, he argued, would result from "the incidentals of war: troops stepping on unmarked mines, short fire-fights with stragglers and hold-outs, mechanical accidents, and the ragged fire of some surviving fraction of the huge number of Iraqi artillery tubes."[43]

Luttwak argued that the way to avoid such casualties was to avoid a ground war and rely instead on an intensive air campaign. In this view he was not alone. However, it is important to note that there were a number of distinct air power strategies, each one reflecting a different assessment of the political character of the conflict and the role of military force in its resolution, as well as the particular attributes of this sort of warfare. In terms of air power theory, it was of interest that there were no serious proposals to attack the regime through direct assaults on the civilian population and its morale, even though, as argued below, the eventual attacks on civilian infrastructure do appear to have undermined Iraqi resolution.

All of the air power proposals assumed relatively accurate strikes against military targets, but beyond that there were significant variations.

Luttwak's objective was to denude Iraq of its military capacity, thus limiting the potential damage it could do in the future. He claimed that an air offensive directed not against ground forces but against the basis of Saddam's long-term strategic power "could literally demolish Saddam Hussein's military ambitions within a week or so, and with the loss of not more than a few dozen aircrew at most."[44] Richard Perle, by contrast, was more concerned with getting Iraq out of Kuwait, and so he proposed the use of air power to support a war of attrition, exploiting Iraq's problem of resupplying its forces of occupation.[45] Henry Kissinger also wanted to force Iraq out of Kuwait, but he conceived of the use of airpower more along the lines of traditional coercive diplomacy. It would serve as an adjunct to sanctions, raising "the cost of occupying Kuwait to unacceptable levels while reducing Iraq's capacity to threaten its neighbors." Kissinger, declaring himself "extremely skeptical about a full-scale ground assault," believed that the reduction of Iraq's military power would mean the erosion of the dictatorship's base, thereby encouraging a "negotiation more compatible with stated U.S. objectives."[46]

The most forceful case for primary reliance on airpower from within the administration came in a September interview with Air Force Chief of Staff General Michael Dugan, which led to his firing.[47] He reported what he claimed to be the conclusion of the Joint Chiefs of Staff that U.S. air power could force Iraq out of Kuwait without a bloody land war. There would be a role for ground forces, intimidating Iraqi forces and channelling them into killing zones for aircraft. However, the "cutting edge would be downtown Baghdad." The enemy had to be targeted where it hurts, "at home, not out in the woods someplace." He had been advised, by the Israelis amongst others, that "the best way to hurt Saddam" was to target his family, his personal guard, and his mistress. Because Saddam was a "one-man show" in Iraq, Dugan said, "if and when we choose violence he ought to be at the focus of our efforts." Without him, Iraqi troops "would all of a sudden lose their legitimacy and they would be back in Iraq in a matter of hours, in disarray."[48]

General Colin Powell, chairman of the Joint Chiefs of Staff, challenged proposals for "surgical air strikes or perhaps a sustained air strike" and other "nice, tidy, alleged low-cost incremental, may-work options." Their "fundamental flaw" was to leave the initiative with the Iraqi president: "He makes the decision as to whether or not he will or will not withdraw. He decides whether he has been punished enough so that it is now necessary for him to reverse his direction and take a new political tack." A second problem was that such strategies were indecisive and "not success oriented." They took no account of Saddam's demonstrable willingness and ability "to absorb punishment, to callously expend Iraqi lives and to care not a whit about what happens to the citizens of his country." Third, such strategies would allow Iraq to concentrate on one threat. Powell did not doubt "the competence and ability of our United States Air force to inflict terrible punishment." However, he said, "One can hunker down. One can dig in. One can disperse to try to ride out such a single-dimensioned attack. Recognizing that such attack will do grievous damage to the defenders after such strategy has been executed, the decision is still in the hands of the defender to decide whether or not he has had enough punishment."[49]

He also dismissed any interest in a strategy of "cannon fodder," in which "we are just going to run into fortifications without thinking our way through this."[50] In practice, the real question was not whether a ground campaign would be required, but the speed with which it should be entered into.[51] Powell indicated in advance that the conflict would begin with a decisive air campaign and that the ground war would not be simultaneous but would follow the air campaign.[52] His basic view was that there was no need for the Coalition to restrict its military options.[53]

The Bush administration had a number of advantages that made possible a decisive application of Western military power. It was possible to bring in all types of military capabilities to high levels. This was an enormous logistical effort that would not have been easy to reproduce in other locations that did not have existing garrisons of Western forces. It was possible in the Gulf, initially, because of the existence of pre-positioned stocks, but more importantly because of first-class ports and military airfields. Saudi Arabia was, in effect, one large petrol station, which dramatically eased one of the most critical logistical problems. The United States was further helped by the complete lack of interference and harassment from Iraq. The difficulties imposed on Iraq as a result of the arms embargo were considerable. Even though the Iraqi military was given priority, it was still required to husband resources and limit training and exercises. Resupply from the Soviet Union was not a possibility.

There was time to gather full intelligence and prepare plans. By the time Desert Storm began, the basic elements of the Iraqi order of battle as well as the essential elements of its communications and supply networks were well known to its opponents. By comparison, Iraqi intelligence was minimal. The Coalition had no need to consider a "second front." Neither Jordan nor Iran had any interest in taking military action in support of Iraq. Terrorism was a serious risk, but some fears were alleviated by Syria's membership in the Coalition and by the attention of the security services to Iraq's diplomatic missions.[54]

The primary political objective—expelling Iraqi forces from Kuwait—was clear and had been clarified during the buildup to direct military action.[55] It provided obvious guidelines. All of this meant that Coalition planning could follow staff college principles in an almost classic manner.

The strategy was dictated by the logic of Western air superiority, a determination to minimize Western casualties, and the objective of expelling Iraq from Kuwait.

The Coalition also had good reasons not to be overawed by Iraq's military capability.[56] The major uncertainties surrounded its readiness and ability to use chemical weapons, and the potential effects of its ballistic missile force.[57] Although fear of an eventual Iraqi nuclear capability was one of the reasons for defeating Saddam, no one thought that such a capability was then already available. Only a limited number of Iraqi divisions were considered competent,[58] and only the elite Republican Guard had modern Soviet T-72 tanks. Nearly half of the troops were mobilized reservists who had shown a readiness to surrender during the war with Iran when the opportunity arose. There was also evidence that Iraq's less capable and youngest troops were being put in the lightly defended forward positions. The air force had been ineffective in close air support and the pilots were judged to be poor. The chain of command was heavily centralized and unresponsive. Generals who had made their names in the war with Iran were retired, dead, or under arrest.[59] The defensive methods developed during the war with Iran had been based on massive earthworks combined with flooding to channel any offensive into a killing ground. The Kuwaiti border did not offer the same potential for water barriers, nor were there any natural barriers such as the Shatt al-Arab waterway.[60] It was also apparent that the Iraqi force on the border to the west was more thinly spread.[61]

From early on[62] it was recognized that the American priorities would be to achieve air superiority, eliminate missiles and Iraq's small fleet of fast patrol boats, interdict supply lines, and then engage in a fast and mobile desert campaign based on maneuver rather than attrition. In a variety of unofficial publications, the most likely targets for the air campaign were outlined and the most likely instruments of attack were indicated. The preference for flanking maneuvers rather than direct assaults on Iraqi fortifications was made clear.[63] The military options were so fully explored in the weeks before the start of hostilities in hearings held by the Armed Services Committees of the U.S. Senate and the House of Representatives that it was possible for the chairman of the House Committee, Representative Les Aspin, to produce a detailed and largely accurate forecast of the course of the war.[64]

The Conduct of Desert Storm

The war began at 03:00 Kuwait time on January 17. A million men with some 32,000 women on the Coalition side faced each other across the border, but as predicted, the initial stage of the war was turned over to the air campaign.[65] The Coalition command had earlier intended to begin with a phased campaign; the sustained attacks on ground forces were to be held back for a later stage. In the event, the considerable air armada gathered by the start of the war made it possible to begin attacks on ground forces from day one. Despite the intense speculation accompanying the lapse of the United Nations deadline, effective tactical surprise was achieved. Iraqi air defenses, confused by electronic warfare, accomplished little.[66] A high sortie rate, averaging about 2,000 per day, was achieved almost immediately and sustained thereafter.[67] A strategic phase of considerable efficiency was directed against Iraq's ability to command and supply its ground forces, and to develop and produce weapons of mass destruction.[68]

The dividing line between civilian and military targets was a thin one. There were definite rules on avoiding religious and cultural sites. Although the U.S. forces indicated that they were keeping clear of civilian structures, in a centralized state such as Iraq, civilian and military facilities can be interchangeable, and it is hard to demarcate civilian areas in garrison towns such as Basra. Oil refineries and electrical power installations were attacked, but an attempt was made to leave some power for civilian life.[69] While care was taken not to rationalize the air strategy in terms of its effects on civilian morale, such effects were seen as a bonus. Army Lieutenant General Thomas Kelly, a frequent Pentagon spokesman to the press during the war, stated that "if there is an additional effect on the civilian population, it's one that Saddam Hussein has chosen, not one that we did."[70]

Two unanticipated factors prolonged the air campaign. The first was that the worst weather in the region for twenty-five years held up many missions and made it extremely difficult to work out just how successful the initial strikes had been. Key targets had to be attacked again just in case they had been missed the first time. The second source of delay was the success of Iraq in launching Scud missile attacks against Israel and Saudi Arabia. Thirty-nine missiles were fired at Israeli civilian targets, first and foremost Tel Aviv.[71] The most serious consequence of these attacks was to create a political crisis, as fear grew that the Israeli determination to retaliate would transform the character of the war and put excessive strain on the Arab members of the Coalition. In the event, the limited yield of the Scuds, which were not used with chemical warheads,[72] the problems of actually fashioning an Israeli response in the ongoing context of a massive allied air campaign, and the evident political advantage of a conspicuous show of restraint led Israel to stay its hand.[73] Some 15 percent of the Coalition campaign became devoted to finding and destroying mobile Scud launchers. The air campaign had initially been planned to last for thirty days but in the end took thirty-nine.

Iraq had no answer to the air campaign. It is questionable whether the Iraqi air force ever really expected to engage. In the period before the onset of hostilities, barely 200 sorties a day were being flown by all types of Iraqi aircraft, and on the eve of hostilities hardly any were being flown at all. This may have represented a husbanding of resources, as a result of the embargo, but it ensured that the pilots were poorly trained for such tasks as air-to-air refueling and night flying. Few took to the air to greet the allied offensive; most that did turned and fled as soon as they became vulnerable.[74] There were also few attempts to penetrate Coalition air space to strike at Iraq's enemy, for example against relatively exposed military targets such as battleships,[75] or counter-value objectives in Saudi Arabia such as the oilfields.

Soon the Iraqi air force found that it could not survive the war within its hardened bunkers. After a week of attacks on the communication centers and the airfields, the allies began the systematic destruction of Iraq's 594 aircraft shelters. Eventually 375 were destroyed, along with 141 aircraft caught inside. Within three days the most convincing evidence of the success of the air campaign became apparent, when the cream of the Iraqi air force began its flight to Iran. Initially 27 combat aircraft departed, followed in the next three days by another 48. Thereafter the Coalition set up combat air patrols to intercept them, with partial success. The numbers fleeing to Iran eventually grew to over 100. It remains unclear who gave the order to the Iraqi pilots, for this move does seem to have been coordinated. Initially the Coalition was concerned that Iran and Iraq were colluding,[76] perhaps to help preserve air assets for the land battle. However, Western intelligence soon indicated that the aircraft were not going to be available for combat in the future, as the Iranians showed no intention of releasing the planes. The flight was therefore believed to have been an act of panic on the part of Saddam Hussein.[77]

In these circumstances, and given Saddam's fear that the war would not be confined to the front lines, the longer it dragged on, the dimmer became his chances of surviving the postwar situation. The economic plight that had pushed him to invade Kuwait was significantly aggravated after the invasion, and a protracted war was bound to deal a devastating blow to his hopes for the economic reconstruction of Iraq, on which his political survival would continue to hinge. A sustained conflict was also likely to erode national, and in consequence military, morale and to force him into a humiliating withdrawal from Kuwait.

To salvage his strategy, Saddam would have had to draw the Coalition into a premature ground offensive in Kuwait to bring the war to a quick end, even at the cost of many Iraqi lives. Such an encounter had been the centerpiece of his strategy, in the hope that heavy casualties would drive a disillusioned Western public opinion to demand an early cease-fire. He stated this objective at the start of hostilities: "Not a few drops of blood, but rivers of blood will be shed. And then Bush will have been deceiving America, American public opinion, the American people, the American constitutional institutions."[78] But even if this scenario failed to materialize, a quick but honorable withdrawal from Kuwait in the course of a bloody encounter could allow him to emerge from the conflict as a "new Nasser" who had single-handedly fought "world imperialism" and survived.

Missile strikes against Israel were Saddam's foremost attempt to lure the allies into a premature ground assault. Striking at Israel's main population centers would be cheered by the Arab masses, put the Arab members of the Coalition in a difficult position, and also lay the ground for an Israeli retaliation. To preempt the latter, the Coalition might move earlier than planned to a ground offensive in Kuwait. But this ploy failed, in part because the Israeli government realized that retaliation could only play into Saddam's hands.

Almost simultaneously with the attack on Israel, Saddam sought to press the allies through another means: oil.[79] As early as October 1990, Iraq sent tankers filled with oil down to the Kuwaiti port of Mina al-Ahmadi. In December Iraqi experts had experimented with explosions on wellheads in the area of the Ahmadi loading complex to perfect the means of their destruction. There then followed intensive engineering and explosives work, wiring together all the wellheads in the Kuwaiti fields. The first use of the oil weapon came on January 16 when Iraqi artillery hit an oil storage tank at al-Khafji in Saudi Arabia. This action was limited. More serious consequences resulted from a sustained campaign of environmental warfare, which began on January 19 when the valves were opened on the Sea Island Terminal and then the tankers' load was dumped into the Gulf. Flowing at the pace of 200,000 barrels a day, the oil slick soon became one of the worst ever oil-related ecological disasters, covering an area of at least 240 square miles.[80] Two days later the al Wafrah oil fields and storage facilities were set on fire, producing large amounts of smoke.

While this action made some military sense by creating a smoke screen that could complicate allied operations and might also have been in retaliation for Coalition attacks on Iraqi oil installations, its main aim was to underline to the Coalition the devastating consequences of a protracted war for the world oil market and the region's ecology. It took until January 22 for the Coalition to appreciate what was going on. But, in another display of precision bombing, which also served to demonstrate allied command of the air, the Sea Island pump was shut down.[81]

Frustrated with the failure of his latest ploy, Saddam began to castigate the Coalition for the harm caused by the air campaign and to taunt it for cowardice in refusing to go ahead with the land campaign.[82] Having initially pushed out the bulk of the Western media, supposing (correctly) that it was helping the Coalition to assess damage,[83] he soon invited them back and sent them on guided tours of civilian damage.

This, too, giving him no great success, Saddam decided to take a rare military initiative by ordering a limited ground encounter in Saudi Arabia. Such a move entailed grave risks, but the potential advantages were compelling. Saddam would be seen to have seized the initiative from the allies, at least temporarily, so giving the morale of his battered troops in Kuwait a much-needed boost, but it might also create a momentum that would suck the reluctant Coalition into a ground offensive. The Iraqi attack on the Saudi border town of Khafji in late January provided one of the few authentic battles of the war.[84] The attack initially was a boost to the Iraqi position, demonstrating that Saddam was fully in charge (the Iraqi communiqué credited him personally with the plan), and was capable of seizing the initiative and catching the Coalition by surprise. However, the most important aspect of Khafji was that it failed, with severe casualties and a demonstration of the vulnerability of Iraqi land forces to allied air power.[85] It confirmed Saddam's growing desperation to force the Coalition into the decisive ground encounter. This, in turn, reinforced the Coalition's conviction not to play into Saddam's hands.[86]

The only factor that began to create pressure to get the land campaign underway was unease in the West over the judgment, implicit in the massive air campaign, that any number of Iraqi deaths was worth the reduction of risk to Coalition forces. The early claims made by Coalition commanders with regard to the precision of Coalition bombing, and the contrast with Saddam's indiscriminate missile attacks, meant that any evidence of substantial civilian damage was highlighted. The concern over damage to Iraqi civilians grew as the attacks moved on to the supply lines, which meant striking roads and bridges. Aggravating this effect were reports that Iraqi military systems were being collocated with schools or archaeological monuments. The most controversial attack, on the Amiriya command bunker/air raid shelter, led to around 400 civilian deaths.[87]

While contrary to the Coalition's strategic philosophy, the bunker attack might have had a beneficial strategic impact. Those occupying it may have been the families of senior officials in the Ba'ath Party; if so, the attack may have begun to bring home the costs of war. It is also of note that the general dislocation to civilian life caused by the bombing may also have made Saddam concerned about his political base.[88]

More seriously for Saddam, the attacks on Iraqi ground forces were starting to tell. "Preparation of the battlefield" by the air campaign involved cutting off supplies, which was relatively straightforward; destroying existing stores of forward supplies and equipment; and "softening up" the troops. An objective was set of the destruction of 50 percent of the Iraqi fighting capability, but at first the dispersion of the Iraqi units and their readiness to remain under cover made this difficult. Gradually allied tactics improved and the success rate increased markedly. However, bomb damage assessment is an uncertain art and there were a number of controversies over the progress of the allied campaign.[89] In the end, it was more an informed judgment that the battering received by Iraqi forces must have seriously degraded their ability to cope with a land offensive, rather than confirmed evidence, that gave the Coalition commanders their confidence. By mid-February, intelligence estimates suggested that more than 100 tanks a day were being caught on the ground and destroyed. The furor over the civilian casualties in Baghdad almost obscured a series of remarkably upbeat briefings from the U.S. military in which the Iraqi position was described as "precarious."[90]

Saddam reached the same conclusion. Rather than his opportunity, the imminent land battle seemed set to confirm his overwhelming defeat. The Coalition had not fallen for his various ploys and appeared content to carry on with an air campaign, gradually unravelling Iraq's military infrastructure, destroying its supply system and its front-line capability. The prolongation of the first stage of the war had left Iraq in no fit state to prosecute the second, where Saddam had assumed his forces could be employed to their greatest advantage. Hence, on February 15, Baghdad radio announced that the Revolutionary Command Council was now prepared "to deal with Security Council Resolution 660, with the aim of reaching an honorable and acceptable solution, including withdrawal [from Kuwait]."[91] Since Saddam wrapped up his cease-fire proposal with a series of conditions (such as a demand for international recognition of Iraq's historical rights in Kuwait) that nullified the letter and spirit of Resolution 660, Bush quickly spurned his initiative as "a cruel hoax," and the allies continued to demand implementation of all UN resolutions.[92]

The next week saw a flurry of diplomatic activity as the Soviet Union worked to get Baghdad's agreement to a face-saving formula, which still fell short of the Coalition requirements.[93] In the end President Bush brought the issue to a head by setting a twenty-four hour deadline for Iraq to accept all UN resolutions. His task was made easier by reports of murder in Kuwait and the firing of oil wells: The U.S. military announced on February 22 that over 100 oil wells had been set on fire over the previous twenty-four hours. Saddam ignored the deadline and on February 23 the ground war began on schedule (a schedule determined, in part, by expected conditions of weather and moonlight).

The Ground War

Again the Coalition plan reflected the military logic recognized in many of the prewar debates. Although a campaign based on maneuver and envelopment had been anticipated,[94] U.S. Commander General Norman Schwarzkopf's "Hail Mary" play was nonetheless remarkably bold.[95] A rapid move westward enabled a flanking action far deeper into Iraq than expected, to separate the in-theater Iraqi forces from their home base; direct thrusts were intended to liberate Kuwait City and to take on the more capable Iraqi divisions. The Iraqi command was disoriented by two diversionary moves—a pretended amphibious landing,[96] and a feint up the Wadi al-Batin corridor, along the Iraqi-Kuwaiti border, which had been assumed to be the obvious invasion route.

Some Iraqi units, especially those placed along the anticipated Coalition invasion route, put up a serious fight but they had no answer to the vastly superior firepower and mobility of the Coalition. It was apparent after the first day that the land war would be in effect a walkover. Movement was rapid; the Iraqi response was minimal; Coalition casualties were slight. There was slight evidence of Iraq's much-vaunted artillery, let alone its chemical weapons capability. In fact, chemical weapon stocks do not appear to have been issued to field commanders.

Saddam had no strategy for this stage of the war other than to get through it as quickly as possible with whatever he could salvage of his military power. As the land war developed, Iraqi political concessions came steadily and rapidly. Within less than 48 hours after its start, around midnight of February 25, Saddam publicly ordered his troops to withdraw "in an organized way" from Kuwait. Two days later, he had agreed to honor all UN resolutions.

The land war was a race between the Coalition's determination to destroy as much as possible of the Iraqi military capability and Saddam's awareness of the requirement to accept all UN resolutions unequivocally. This came to a head with the Iraqi withdrawal from Kuwait City. The withdrawing forces were a disorderly rabble. They were trapped on the road to Basra and attacked by waves of aircraft, destroying hundreds of vehicles and causing thousands of casualties, in what was described as a "turkey shoot." General Schwarzkopf later indicated that he would have preferred to continue the fight,[97] but President Bush, sensing that any more carnage would lead to public revulsion and, having been told that the coming hour would represent the land campaign's hundredth, called a halt.

Greatly relieved by the American decision, Saddam lost no time in telling his subjects that the cessation of hostilities was the result of their glorious stand against "world imperialism":

O Iraqis, you triumphed when you stood with all this vigor against the armies of 30 countries. ... You have succeeded in demolishing the aura of the United States, the empire of evil, terror, and aggression. ... The Guards have broken the backbone of their aggressors and thrown them beyond their borders. We are confident that President Bush would have never accepted a cease-fire had he not been informed by his military leaders of the need to preserve the forces fleeing the fist of the heroic men of the Republican Guards.[98]

Saddam's Objectives and Miscalculations

From the outset of the Kuwaiti crisis in the summer of 1990, there was an absolute certainty in Saddam's mind of what could not be sacrificed—his political survival. Kuwait, the Palestinian cause, Iraqi lives: All were important only so long as they served the perpetuation of Saddam. So was his military strategy and deployment: Key units had been held back from the start for this purpose, and he was clearly anxious that as many units as possible who had been caught in the Kuwait/southern Iraq theater would get back to save the regime rather than make a gallant last stand.

A less obvious objective was Saddam's desire to ensure that the ruling al-Sabah family would not get Kuwait back intact, but that their country would be left permanently damaged; thus, the mining of the oil wells and the campaign of vandalism and murder which began even before the Moscow peace initiative had run its course.[99] Another objective, in which he was far less successful, was to attack Israel's nuclear capability, possibly in retaliation for the Israeli destruction of Iraq's nuclear capability.[100] These objectives represented an attempt to recoup something from the war in terms of hurt to opponents, even though, at least in the case of the action against Kuwait, this gave the United States a helpful argument to reject negotiations and accelerate the ground war.

The Gulf War is viewed as the first real "electronics war." The sight of cruise missiles and smart bombs roaming to their destination with pinpoint accuracy has created a widespread impression of an uneven match between a high-tech power and a hapless, ill-equipped, and backward Third World army. However intriguing, this notion is largely misconceived. While the war clearly represents a military victory of a technological society over a non-industrialized one, such an astounding outcome was by no means a foregone conclusion. The Iraqi army, it is true, proved to be a far cry from the formidable power portrayed in the West prior to the war, and it was inferior to the Coalition forces in crucial technological respects, but the fact that it fought so badly was mainly the outcome of more "traditional" factors, such as a poor combat performance along with incompetent politico-military leadership and war strategy.

The main cause of Iraq's military debacle lies in Saddam's personality and the nature of his regime. As aptly noted by General Schwarzkopf, Saddam is no strategist, nor a soldier. His poor understanding of military affairs, and his complete subordination of military strategy to the ultimate goal of political survival, drove him to fight a political war with one eye set on his postwar survival. He was cautious when it came to initiatives, reluctant to hazard his air force,[101] and did not want to commit the Republican Guards to an offensive move that could decimate them, because he needed them for the postwar situation, as illustrated by their brutal repression of the later Shi'ite uprising in southern Iraq.

The flawed strategy reflected a fundamental misunderstanding of the lessons of the Iran-Iraq War. Saddam's failure to distinguish between the Coalition forces confronting him and the poorly equipped and ill-trained Iranian army led him to the mistaken belief that Iraq's defensive posture would suffice to inflict unacceptable pain on the enemy. Secondly, he failed to appreciate the decisive role of air power on the modern battlefield.[102] Thirdly, the substantial desertions in the first months of the Iran-Iraq War, after Saddam had voluntarily surrendered the initiative, should have warned him of the consequences of a collapse of morale.

Saddam's vicious success in putting down the postwar insurrection in Iraq took the shine off Bush's victory, but the American military strategy was largely vindicated. Casualties on the Coalition side were extraordinarily light. Early analysis suggested that 8 to 10 percent casualty rates could be anticipated.[103] On the eve of the ground war President Bush was warned to expect some 5,000 casualties.[104] In the event, U.S. battle deaths were under 150. As many American lives were lost in the air campaign as in the land campaign.[105]

Still Graduated Response

The Gulf War offered a unique opportunity for the exercise of military force on a decisive scale. The strategic options available to the Bush administration were quite different in kind from those confronting the Johnson administration in Vietnam. In this sense, the claim that the Gulf War represented a break with the old concepts of graduated response has to be treated with care. According to this view, the failure in Vietnam could be attributed in part to the policy of graduated response, understood as a strategy of incremental pressure, with a series of restrictions on targets that were imposed by the politicians. At each stage, the opponent was to face a choice between compliance and further pressure until eventually its breaking point was reached. The critique of this strategy argues that these small steps merely provide the opponent with time to adjust and develop forms of counterpressure.[106]

From the early decision to introduce ground forces into Saudi Arabia, Powell urged Bush not to go for a minimum force but to ensure sufficient numbers to cope with all eventualities,[107] and also to refrain from engaging in political micro-management. The administration accepted both these arguments.

To avoid charges of micro-management, civilian officials avoided amending the target list for the air campaign (a practice that had been judged to be a particular fault of the Johnson administration), although the commanders were expected to show political sensitivity.[108] It was reported that Bush was not informed of the detailed target set.[109] However, after the raid on the Amiriyah bunker, Secretary of Defense Dick Cheney ordered General Powell to review all subsequent missions over Baghdad, and a number of the "softer" targets that might have contained large numbers of civilians were removed from the list.

While Bush may have felt that his strategy represented a sharp break with that adopted in Vietnam, the real difference lay in the political and military context, which was altogether simpler in the Gulf. The debate over escalation in Vietnam had largely developed in connection with the Rolling Thunder bombing campaign, which began in February 1965. This was adopted initially as a means of boosting the morale of the South Vietnamese government, as an alternative to dealing with the government's main problems, its weakness and corruption and its inability to counter communist strength. Those who believed that the bombing campaign would help differed as to whether this would be done by persuading the North Vietnamese government to cease this support for the infiltration routes. In the attempt to coerce the North, the Johnson administration still did not want to provoke China or the Soviet Union into direct intervention. No serious negotiating track was available to take advantage of any move from Hanoi toward concessions. Not surprisingly, the bombing campaign was soon recognized to be inadequate by itself and attention turned to the introduction of substantial ground forces, although here the process was shaped by Johnson's anxiety to play down the significance of the move.

The political situation in the Gulf was in all respects easier; the Kuwaiti people were all clearly opposed to the Iraqi occupation. The military basis of the Iraqi occupation was evident, including the supply lines through which it was sustained. So long as U.S. objectives did not extend to a change of regime in Iraq, the Soviet Union and China were generally supportive, and at least in the Soviet case were willing to supply intelligence information on their former client.[110]

In the Gulf, the administration was still obliged to follow a version of graduated response in order to develop a domestic and international consensus supporting direct military action. The pressure on Iraq was built up in stages, first with economic sanctions; then with naval blockade, air blockade, and the threat of direct military action; followed by the offer of negotiations. Even once the war began, there was a clear break between the air and the land campaigns during which time there was a flurry of diplomatic activity. In strict terms the key threshold in terms of violence was passed by the imposition of a blockade, for this is an act of war. The only reason it did not become serious was because of Iraqi reluctance to try to break it.[111] Most of the controversial decisions surrounded moving from one stage to the next, especially the move to direct military action. The challenge to President Bush was in developing the political support to transcend this threshold.[112]

Conclusion

The ferocious and comprehensive nature of the eventual employment of force raised the question whether the Coalition could have achieved its objectives with a greater economy, and whether the air campaign on its own could have decided the war. It is arguable that Iraq was already on the ropes when the land war began and that it merely provided Saddam with his main opportunity to inflict pain on American forces to counter the pain the U.S. Air Force could undoubtedly inflict on Iraq. Against this argument, three points can be made. First, if the Western presence in Saudi Arabia had been smaller, then Saddam's opportunities to extend the war would have been greater. Second, an air offensive directed solely at purely military targets might not have moved Iraq, especially if it could counter with missile attacks against Israel and Saudi Arabia, however ineffectual they might be in strict military terms. To put pressure on Saddam required imposing real distress on the civilian population, and there could have been no guarantee that Saddam could not turn the consequential unease in the West to his political advantage. Third, it was the ground campaign that ensured rapid Iraqi agreement to all UN resolutions. The argument over air power will therefore rumble on, but it does so after a convincing demonstration that chronic inferiority in this area is a strategic liability for which it is almost impossible to compensate in regular conventional warfare.

Simply because he was leading a disparate Coalition rather than a unitary state, President Bush was on the political defensive. This provided Saddam with his main strategic opportunity. The pattern of employment of U.S. air power was shaped by this political context. Direct military action was required because Bush could not be sure that the cohesion of the Coalition could withstand a long wait for sanctions to bite, and then it had to be swift because the Coalition, and Bush's support at home, would have been strained by a prolonged conflict. When it came to using air power to undermine Saddam's ability to resist a ground offensive, Bush had to depend upon international tolerance of the spectacle of a largely unopposed air bombardment continuing day after day. When he called for a cease-fire, it was because he was aware of a growing unease at the carnage inflicted upon Iraqi troops, and because his basic objectives had now been achieved, even if the future of Saddam himself was left unresolved.

Saddam by this time had been deprived of a strategy other than one of political survival. The blunting of his political offensive had exposed the weaknesses of his wholly inadequate military defense.

Notes

The authors wish to express their thanks to David Boren, Yosef Meckelberg, and Michael McNerny for their assistance in gathering materials for this chapter.

Reprinted with permission from *International Security,* Vol. 16, No. 2, (Fall 1991).

1. In discussing the shaping of Coalition strategy this [chapter] must inevitably concentrate on the United States, which provided some 90 percent of the forces and also took upon itself the task of forging the various concerns of its Coalition partners into a coherent strategy. We focus on the substance of the strategic calculus of the two sides and not the processes of policy formation.

2. *Baghdad Radio*, October 19, 22, 28, 1990, published in *Foreign Broadcast Information Services: Near East and South Asia* (FBIS-NES), October 19, 1990, 26; October 22, 1990, 8–12; October 29, 1990, 23.

3. See testimony by William Webster, director of the Central Intelligence Agency, on December 5, 1990, in U.S. House of Representatives, Hearings Before the Committee on Armed Services, *Crisis in the Persian Gulf: Sanctions, Diplomacy and War* (1991) [hereinafter referred to as *House Hearings*].

4. Susan Willett, *The Gulf Crisis: Economic Implications, London Defence Studies* (London: Brassey's/Centre for Defence Studies, University of London, November 1990), 33. See also Clyde R. Mark, *Iraq: U.S. Economic Sanctions* (Washington, D.C.: Congressional Research Service, January 22, 1991).

5. The highlights of the President's decision were to add two armored divisions and elements of a third, an infantry division, a Marine Expeditionary Force, three carrier battle groups and an additional 14 fighter squadrons, two bomber squadrons, and 11 support squadrons. See Staff Dispatches, "U.S. to Send 700 More Tanks," *International Herald Tribune*, November 9, 1990, 1; "Bush Adds to Gulf Build-Up," *International Herald Tribune*, November 9, 1990, 1.

6. The logistical strain of sustaining substantial numbers of troops in the Gulf led to expressions of concern such as that of General David Jones, former chairman of the Joint Chiefs of Staff. He feared that because of the extra troops the

United States might be forced "to fight prematurely and unnecessarily—their very presence could narrow our options and our ability to act with patient resolve." U.S. Senate, Hearings Before the Committee on Armed Services, *Crisis in the Persian Gulf Region: U.S. Policy Options and Implications* (1990) [hereinafter referred to as *Senate Hearings*], 190.

7. In an interview that appeared on November 29, General Schwarzkopf said: "If the alternative to dying is sitting out in the sun for another summer, that's not a bad alternative." Cited by Senator Nunn in *Senate Hearings*, 681 (from *Los Angeles Times*). Bob Woodward's account of the U.S. policy process during the crisis indicates that the military leadership, including the chairman of the Joint Chiefs of Staff, General Colin Powell, would have preferred a sustained containment strategy, allowing sanctions to take their course, with troop morale problems eased by rotation of units. Bob Woodward, *The Commanders* (New York: Simon and Schuster, 1991), 299–300.

8. For text, see Staff Dispatches, "Iraqi Envoy Welcomes Offer of a Baker Visit," *International Herald Tribune*, December 1–2, 1990, 1.

9. William Drozdiak, "Baker, Aziz Describe Six Hours of Talking Past Each Other," *Washington Post*, January 10, 1991, A23.

10. The United States asserted that Saddam's main reward for complying with UN resolutions was that Iraq would not be attacked. See, for example, James Baker's remarks on NBC's *Meet the Press*, reported in E.J. Dionne, "Baker Says Baghdad Can Avoid U.S. Attack," *International Herald Tribune*, December 3, 1990, 1.

11. Iraqi Foreign Minister Tariq Aziz told an interviewer after the war that the ruling elite in Iraq "developed a fatalistic feeling about war; we found ourselves in a position where we could not do anything about it." William Drozdiak, "Iraqi Says Regime Made 'Mistakes,'" *Washington Post*, May 8, 1991, A1.

12. Because of Iran's inability to extend the war to the Iraqi rear, and to generous financial help to Iraq from the Gulf states, Saddam Hussein managed to keep the war confined to the battlefield and to preserve, by and large, an atmosphere of "business as usual" for the Iraqi population.

13. On the military lessons of the Iran-Iraq War, see Efraim Karsh, *The Iran-Iraq War: A Military Analysis*, Adelphi Paper No. 220 (London: The International Institute for Strategic Studies, 1987).

14. For a detailed discussion of the reasons for the Iraqi invasion, see Efraim Karsh and Inari Rautsi, *Saddam Hussein: A Political Biography* (New York: Free Press, 1991), chap. 9.

15. See, for example, *Baghdad Radio*, December 4, 1990, in *FBIS-NES*, December 5, 1990, 24. Prince Bandar bin Sultan, the Saudi ambassador to the United States, warned the administration that this message would be received in Baghdad as a sign of weakness. Woodward, *The Commanders*, 336.

16. Saddam interview with the Baghdad correspondent for the Cable News Network (CNN), Peter Arnett, January 28, 1991. Elements of the hostage situation had become farcical, with every visiting dignitary expecting to take home a brace of nationals to justify his trip.

17. Despite public assertions to the contrary, Saddam's placement of hostages at missile sites, ammunition plants, chemical complexes, and oil refineries in Iraq

and Kuwait led U.S. military planners to remove these sites from the target list in order to minimize casualties. The sites were reintroduced after the hostages had been withdrawn. John M. Broder, "With the Hostages Out, U.S. Revises Its List of Targets," *International Herald Tribune*, December 14, 1991, 1. Iraq's revised awareness of the potential of "human shields" was indicated when some of the first allied military prisoners of war were sent to strategic facilities to deter air raids.

18. While threatening the Coalition with harsh retaliation should it attack Iraq, the Iraqi media never implied any predilection for offensive measures beyond the Kuwaiti frontier. See, for example, *Iraqi News Agency (INA)*, August 3, 7, 1990, *FBIS-NES*, August 6, 1990, 38–39; *Baghdad Radio*, August 6, 1990, Ibid., August 7, 1990, 28–29.

19. INA on November 19 reported the view of the Iraqi Armed Forces General Command that "even without considering the state of morale, the difference in supply sources, and other considerations, all of which are in Iraq's favor—if the battle starts, the wicked U.S. administration would need a ratio of three to one to become technically able to launch an attack against the valiant and faithful God's forces." This, it noted, would raise the U.S. force requirement to three million. *FBIS-NES*, November 19, 1990, 9.

20. The Guard had been expanded from a brigade in 1982 to eight divisions in 1990. With higher pay, better training, and access to better equipment, the Guard was considered to be the most professional of the Iraqi forces and the most loyal to the Ba'ath regime.

21. The calculation of Iraqi strength appears to have been based on the simple formula of counting the number of divisional flags (around 38) and multiplying by the standard divisional "paper strength" of 15,000. It would seem that many divisions were in fact 80% and in some cases 50% of full strength. Christopher Bellamy, "Arithmetic of Death in the Wake of the Gulf Conflict," *Independent* (London), March 20, 1991. Many conscripts appear not to have joined their units or not to have rejoined them after leave. There may have been considerable desertion.

22. Israel had, after all, attacked and destroyed the Osiraq nuclear reactor in 1981.

23. Karsh, *The Iran-Iraq War*, 38.

24. Following the initial Desert Shield deployments, there were many reports in the West that high-technology systems were suffering in the heat and dust of the desert environment. See, for example, Molly Moore, "Too Hot, and Sandy, to Fight," *International Herald Tribune*, September 4, 1990, 1.

25. The U.S. intelligence community was not sure how many upgraded Scud-Bs (with a range of 615 kilometers) Iraq possessed, but the estimates were between 800 to 1,000. Woodward, *The Commanders*, 285. Even after the war there was still great confusion as to Iraqi stocks.

26. Leonard Doyle and Edward Lucas, "Saddam's Nerve Gas Arsenal," *Independent*, April 20, 1991. There may have been some problems with fusing that would have prevented the effective dispersal of the toxic agents. See "No Chem Scuds," *Armed Forces Journal International*, March 1991, 23. At the end of July, a UN commission reported that Iraq had about 46,000 pieces of field chemical munitions and 3,000 tons of precursors and intermediate materials, including missile warheads outfitted with nerve gas. U.S. Information Agency, August 1, 1991.

27. In April 1990 Saddam threatened to "burn half of Israel" should it attack Iraq's nuclear installations. *Baghdad Radio*, April 2, 1990, in *FBIS-NES*, April 3, 1990, 35. On the Iraqi threats against both Israel and Saudi Arabia during the crisis, see *INA*, August 9, *FBIS-NES*, August 9, 1990, 30–32; *Baghdad Radio*, August 8, 11, 1990, *FBIS-NES*, August 8, 1990, 28–30; *INA*, September 18, 1990, *FBIS-NES*, September 24, 1990, 19–20.

28. The "linkage" of the Kuwait crisis to the Palestinian problem was first made by Saddam on August 12, 1990. For a succinct Iraqi explanation of the essence of this linkage, see *Baghdad Radio*, December 17, 1990, *FBIS-NES*, December 18, 1990, 25–26.

29. Saddam's first response to Bush's November 8 announcement had been to threaten to turn Saudi Arabia into a battle zone. The fear of missile attacks on Saudi installations, which was given considerable credibility by some analysts, was in part responsible for the expectation that oil prices would rise when the war began. The euphoria in the international oil and financial markets which followed the first day of the war reflected confidence, which turned out to be justified, that the "oil war" would not be extended into Saudi Arabia.

30. See, for example, *INA*, August 20, 1990, *FBIS-NES*, August 21, 1990, 6–7; *Radio Baghdad*, January 7, 1991, *FBIS-NES*, January 8, 25–27. Unofficial Translation of Key Excerpts of Statement by Revolutionary Command Council, "Saddam: 'The Blood of Our Martyrs Will Burn Evil Doers,'" *Financial Times*, August 9, 1990.

31. John Bullock and Harvey Morris, *Saddam's War: The Origins of the Kuwaiti Crisis and the International Response* (London: Faber and Faber, 1991), 11.

32. Patrick Cockburn, "Warlike Saddam Defies 'Infidels,'" *Independent*, January 12, 1991; Tony Walker and Lamis Andoni, "Saddam Jeers at U.S. 'Rambos,'" *Financial Times*, January 12–13, 1991. With regard to the air threat, Saddam claimed that enemy aircraft needed to get within three miles of their target to inflict damage but that Iraq could shoot them down from 18 miles away.

33. These theses are discussed in Lawrence Freedman, "Escalators and Quagmires: Expectations and the Use of Force," *International Affairs* (London), Vol. 67, No. 1 (January 1991), 15–32.

34. "This will not be a protracted drawn-out war. The forces arrayed are different; the opposition is different; the resupply of Saddam's military would be very different; the countries united against him in the United Nations are different; the topography of Kuwait is different, and the motivation of our all-volunteer force is superb." Text of President Bush's statement, "Bush: 'Go the Extra Mile for Peace,'" *International Herald Tribune*, December 1–2, 1990, 6.

35. Edward Lucas, "In Victory U.S. Buries 'Vietnam Syndrome,'" *Independent*, March 2, 1991.

36. Indeed, it was suggested that a preemptive Iraqi withdrawal that denied the Coalition this opportunity would be a "nightmare" because Saddam's power would be left intact. Judith Miller of the *New York Times* used the term in October 1990, attributing it to a "European diplomat" describing attitudes in the Bush administration. See Judith Miller, "And What If Saddam Really Pulled Out?" *International Herald Tribune*, October 9, 1991. The term was soon in frequent use. See, for example, "The Dangers of Peace" (editorial), *International Herald Tribune*, October 26, 1990. It was still in use on the eve of the UN deadline. John J. Fialka

and Gerald F. Seib, "In This Scenario, Retreat by Saddam Would Be Nightmare: Allies Fear Partial Withdrawal Could Turn Public Opinion and Preserve Iraqi Army," *Wall Street Journal*, January 11, 1991.

37. At a joint news conference with Japan's Prime Minister Toshiki Kaifu on April 5, 1991, Bush said: "I condemn Saddam Hussein's brutality against his own people. But I do not want to see United States forces, who have performed with such skill and dedication, sucked into a civil war in Iraq." Staff Dispatches, "Bush: No Obligation to Kurds," *International Herald Tribune*, April 6–7, 1991, 3.

38. It took a number of years for disillusionment with the Vietnam War to set in, and then this was largely because casualties were being taken in pursuit of a flawed strategy and not because of casualties *per se*. See John Mueller, *War, Presidents and Public Opinion* (New York: Wiley, 1973).

39. On the British experience in the Falklands, see Lawrence Freedman, *Britain and the Falklands War* (London: Basil Blackwell, 1988). The British government was less troubled by the prospect of casualties than the American. Brigadier Patrick Cordingley, commander of the British 7th Armoured Brigade, considered it important that public opinion was prepared for high casualties. He told journalists: "There are going to be a lot of casualties and inevitably one has to be prepared for unpleasant things to unfold." Worst-case British estimates were of some 1500 Army casualties out of a force of 25,000, assuming a "head on" attack against entrenched Iraqi positions. Michael Evans, "Britain Must Face Horror of War," *Times* (London), November 30, 1990.

40. A survey by CBS and the *New York Times* of 412 American adults on January 17, 1991, found that 78 percent considered that the United States had done the "right thing in starting military actions against Iraq," compared with only 47 percent approval of the military option from the same group of people on January 5–7. The later poll showed that while 33 percent thought that casualties would be under 1000, 29 percent thought that they would be between 1000 and 5000, and 16 percent thought more than that. By February 25, the start of the ground war brought only marginal slackening of support. A CBS telephone poll of 517 adults showed 73 percent support for the ground war. Even if "several thousand American troops" were to lose their lives in the ground war, 50 percent of those sampled would consider it "worth it," although by this time 45 percent actually judged that casualties would be below 1000. *CBS News*, New York.

41. Nationwide poll of 1057 randomly selected adults conducted for the *Washington Post* and ABC on January 4–6, reported in Richard Morris, "Gulf Poll: Most Americans Want Hill to Back Bush," *Washington Post*, January 8, 1991, A12.

42. See, for example, testimony by former Secretary of Defense James Schlesinger, *Senate Hearings*, 116, and by Admiral William Crowe, Ibid., 229. Some estimates were extraordinarily precise even if not accurate. For example, Joshua Epstein calculated an optimistic case of 15 days' intense combat with 3,344 casualties and 1,049 dead; and a pessimistic case of 21 days with 16,059 casualties, of which 4,136 would be dead; Joshua Epstein, *War With Iraq: What Price Victory?* (Washington, D.C.: Brookings, January 1991). Colonel Trevor Dupuy gave a low of 300 American dead and 1,700 injured and a high of 3,000 dead and 15,000 injured. Trevor Dupuy, *How to Defeat Saddam Hussein: Scenarios and Strategies for the Gulf War* (New York: Warner, 1991). The Center for Defense Information, assuming an

overland drive to Baghdad, expected 10,000 dead. Center for Defense Information, "U.S. Invasion of Iraq: Appraising the Option," *Defense Monitor*, Vol. 19, No. 8, 7. It is interesting to note that an article published on the eve of the land campaign and generally prescient with regard to its character and duration postulated "probably less than 1,000 fatalities" among Coalition forces; John Mearsheimer, "Liberation in Less Than a Week," *New York Times*, February 8, 1991, A31.

43. Luttwak's optimistic scenario involved an elegant envelopment operation that cut off the Iraqi forces in Kuwait, with no frontal dislodgement attacks, highly effective softening-up operations by air power and even naval gunfire, any major Iraqi counter-stroke broken by air attacks before it could reach U.S. forces, no Iranian volunteers joining the fighting "when the U.S. offensive reaches its necessary end-point at the borders of Iran," hundreds of thousands of Iraqi troops on each side of the U.S. offensive thrust not attempting "to converge against it, [even] if only by dribs and drabs, [even] if only to make good a retreat," all equipment working perfectly, operational plans cunning, tactics sound. See *Senate Hearings*, 325. Luttwak later admitted that he concocted his estimates: "I was not going to give my real forecast of casualties. ... As an advocate, you only make forecasts when they are conducive to your advocacy." Joel Achenbach, "The Experts, in Retreat: After-the-Fact Explanations for the Gloomy Predictions," *Washington Post*, February 28, 1991, D1.

44. Luttwak's proposed targets were weapons production and storage facilities, including those associated with Iraq's missile, chemical, biological, and nuclear ventures, as well as ammunition depots and POL [Petroleum, Oil, Lubricants] storage sites, "insofar as they are not greatly dispersed and well camouflaged." This would not be a "surgical strike" but rather a sustained air operation, with thousands of sorties over several days. Luttwak argued that an option against ground forces had been undermined by allowing Saddam time to get his stores dispersed and his troops dug in, so that now "to destroy, say, 50 percent of the Iraqi army some tens of thousands of sorties would be needed, in protracted air operations lasting some weeks, and which would entail the loss of dozens of aircrew in operational accidents alone." *Senate Hearings*, 325–326.

45. Perle testified: "It would seem to me an entirely plausible approach, if force becomes necessary, to execute air strikes against critical Iraqi installations, to achieve control of the air over Iraq and Kuwait. And then, over many weeks or even months, if necessary, to interdict the supply of Iraqi forces in Kuwait to the point where we could hope to force surrender without engaging the Iraqi army on the ground." He advised against engaging the Iraqi army on the ground, and expressed doubts about the recent build-up of U.S. forces. Ibid., 335.

46. Kissinger testimony, *Senate Hearings*, 268–269.

47. Dugan interview by Rick Atkinson of the *Washington Post*, reprinted in "A Prime U.S. Air Force Target: Saddam Hussein," *International Herald Tribune*, September 17, 1990, 1. See also John D. Morrocco, "U.S. War Plan: Air Strikes to Topple Hussein Regime," *Aviation Week and Space Technology*, September 24, 1990, 16–18. On the repercussions of the Dugan interview, see Woodward, *The Commanders*, 290–296.

48. In sacking Dugan on September 17, Secretary of Defense Dick Cheney observed: "There are certain things we never talk about. We never discuss opera-

tional matters, such as the selection of specific targets for potential air strikes. We never talk about the targeting of specific individuals who are officials in other governments. That is a violation of the executive order. We never underestimate the strength of opposing force or reveal previously classified information about the size and disposition of U.S. forces. Nor do we demean the contributions of the other services." Iraq's comment was that Dugan's remarks would "neither shake the fronds of Iraqi palm trees nor awaken a sleeping girl." Staff Dispatches, "Cheney Fires General Over Iraq Remarks," *International Herald Tribune*, September 18, 1990, 1.

49. *Senate Hearings*, 662–663.

50. Ibid., 664.

51. Sam Nunn, also drawing a "lesson" from Vietnam, made this point: "We should hit military targets with awesome power at the beginning of any conflict, as well as knocking out power and communications, electrical, nuclear and chemical facilities. At the same time we should not 'overlearn' the Vietnam lesson. We in America like instant results. We want fast food and fast military victories. However, our nation places a higher value on human life, especially on the lives of our men and women in uniform. Depending upon developments after the first wave of air attacks, a short war may be possible and save lives. But we must avoid 'instant victory' demands and expectations that could cause a premature and high-casualty assault on heavily fortified Kuwait by American ground forces." Sam Nunn, "War Should Be a Last Resort," *Washington Post*, January 10, 1991.

52. During the House hearings Representative John Kasich asked Powell whether "you believe we have to go with all the forces at once." General Powell replied, "I didn't say that, Congressman … I never said 'at once,'" *House Hearings*, 594.

53. There was little real difference here with many of those preferring a primary stress on the air campaign. Eliot Cohen, for example, argued that it would be wise to preserve the ground option while being prepared for the "possibility that an air campaign might do the trick." *House Hearings*, 391.

54. Nonetheless, the anticipated terrorist campaign, which never materialized, had some impact on Western behavior, particularly with regard to air travel.

55. Marine Corps Major General Robert Johnson noted in a briefing on February 8, 1991: "This will not be like Vietnam. We can measure our success here because our objectives are to get the Iraqis out of Kuwait. That's measurable in terms of real estate somewhere down the road." Transcript, CENTCOM Briefing, Major General Robert B. Johnson, Riyadh, Saudi Arabia, February 8, 1991.

56. Tom Marks, "Iraq's Not-So-Tough Army," *Wall Street Journal*, August 22, 1990. "Time and again during the [Iran-Iraq] conflict, Baghdad displayed shortcomings in military leadership that crippled its forces. The over-centralized chain of command failed to make even the most mundane tactical decisions in a timely and advantageous manner. Inter-service and inter-arms coordination was rudimentary."

57. In general the Scud force was played down prior to the war. For example, Edward Luttwak, who expected that they would be fired said: "So, I do not think the 10, 12, 15 Scuds you would expect—upgraded Scuds—would escape destruc-

tion in the first air strike. I would be amazed if they inflicted significant damage." *Senate Hearings*, 348.

58. One U.S. intelligence official gave the following anonymous assessment to a British newspaper in October: "One of the significant unknowns is the general level of quality of the Iraqi forces. My assessment is that the Republican Guards forces are quite good—that's seven divisions. There are another eight to 10 divisions in the regular army which are quite competent. After that the quality falls off quite quickly. Many of the assessments tend to exaggerate their capability. There are nowhere near 50 competent divisions. I think there is a core of highly competent military forces, particularly in the defensive. I think the Iraqis would be a very tough nut to crack." Christopher Bellamy, "Tactical Use of Pessimism by the Pentagon," *Independent*, October 31, 1990.

59. Saddam had been reluctant to keep any senior commander in his post for sufficient time to build up a personal following or to get into a position where he could conspire with others.

60. See, for example, John Keegan's assessment in "Framing a Gulf Strategy," *Daily Telegraph* (London), August 22, 1990: "Building fixed defences in the desert is less profitable than in the marshes and waterways of the Shatt al-Arab. Sands will not make trenches or anti-tank ditches. Any sort of fixed defence will, however, encourage infantry, particularly poor infantry, to sit tight." He noted that infantry sitting tight could be bypassed by a mobile attacker. Israel had found with the Bar-Lev line in 1973 that a thin line, even if fortified, creates considerable problems for a defender.

61. This feature of the Iraqi defenses became the basis of Schwarzkopf's strategy for the ground war.

62. See, for example, Christopher Bellamy, "First Target: Destroying Iraq's Air Forces," *Independent*, August 22, 1990.

63. Admiral Crowe, *Senate Hearings*, 207. He suggested that the total campaign would take 35 to 40 days. See also Crowe, "On Jan. 15, We Must Stand United" (op-ed), *Washington Post*, January 7, 1991: "I assume that the fighting will commence with an intensive air campaign. This effort should be structured to accelerate the quarantine's effects and soften the resistance to subsequent ground attack, if it proves necessary. We have never fought a country as isolated as Iraq. The results of a sustained and heavy air attack should be successful."

64. "The war is likely to begin with an air campaign against strategic and military targets in Iraq and then proceed to a sustained air campaign against Iraqi military forces in or near Kuwait. The final phase of the campaign would involve the commitment of ground forces. Advocates of air power will likely get a full opportunity to see if air power can win by itself. But the U.S. military has made sure that sufficient ground force capability is available to do the job, if air power does not force Iraq's withdrawal from Kuwait." Representative Les Aspin, *The Military Option: The Conduct and Consequences of War in the Persian Gulf,* January 8, 1991; reprinted in *House Hearings*, 905.

65. Before the war, Iraq's air force was credited with 700 combat aircraft, including some 360 fighter ground-attack planes, nearly 300 air defense fighters, and some elderly bombers. The air defense system had 300 SA-2 and SA-3 sur-

face-to-air missile launchers, a further 400 mobile missile launchers and over 4,000 anti-aircraft guns. The in-theater force was believed to consist of 540,000 men in 42 divisions, 4,200 tanks, and 3,100 artillery pieces (although it is now believed that the troop numbers were inflated). Against this, U.S. personnel in the Gulf numbered some 500,000, with 1900 tanks, 930 artillery pieces, and 456 attack helicopters. IISS, 1990–91 *Strategic Survey* (London: Brassey's/IISS, 1991). The British contribution was 35,000 troops, 163 tanks, and 48 aircraft; that of France 10,000 troops, 40 tanks, and 36 aircraft. The total allied contribution, including those from the states of the Gulf Cooperation Council (GCC), was put at over 670,000 troops, 3,600 tanks, and 1,740 aircraft. *International Herald Tribune*, January 3, 1991.

66. The Iraqi air defenses were shut down in the first 24 hours of the air war by Coalition electronic warfare techniques, helped by a pre-war feint which obliged Iraq to activate its air defense system.

67. By the end of the war Coalition aircraft had flown a total of 109,876 sorties (by all types of aircraft, not just those delivering weapons). Compare this 43-day air campaign with its most intense predecessor: 1,945 air sorties were flown against 59 targets in North Vietnam during the twelve days of Linebacker II, December 18–29, 1972.

68. According to U.S. briefings, by January 20, Iraq's nuclear and chemical plants had been "gravely damaged," and by January 23, the two nuclear reactors were "inoperative." IISS, 1990–91 *Strategic Survey,* 69. After the war, it was discovered that the Iraqi nuclear project was more extensive than appreciated previously and that some elements had survived the bombing campaign. This became a major issue in the implementation of Resolution 687.

69. General Schwarzkopf observed on January 30 that the intention was not to destroy all of Iraq's electrical installations: "Because of our interest in making sure civilians did not suffer unduly, we felt we had to leave some of the electrical power in effect, and we've done that." He also indicated that the oil industry had suffered more because "we certainly wanted to make sure they didn't have a lot of gasoline for their military vehicles." CENTCOM Briefing, General Norman Schwarzkopf and Brigadier General Buster Glosson, Riyadh, Saudi Arabia, January 30, 1991.

70. U.S. Department of Defense News Briefing, Lieutenant General Thomas Kelly, Washington, D.C., February 11, 1991.

71. This is the estimate by Martin Navias, *Saddam's Scud War and Ballistic Missile Proliferation, London Defence Studies* (London: Brassey's/Centre for Defence Studies, University of London, August 1991), 21. Others put the figure at 40, see Ma'ariv (Tel Aviv), *Israel in the Gulf War*, March 29, 1991, 41; or at 38, *Jane's Defence Weekly*, April 6, 1991.

72. There has been considerable speculation as to why the Iraqis did not use chemical warheads on Scuds or indeed any chemical munitions. Technical difficulties may be one explanation. However, a fear of retaliation appears the most likely reason. Israel had given dark threats as to what it might do in the event of a serious chemical attack. More significantly, the Bush administration had given indications that any use of weapons of mass destruction would provide justification for a formal extension of the war aims to the elimination of Saddam's regime.

Given Saddam's preoccupation with his survival, this would have been a formidable deterrent threat. In the letter from Bush to Saddam that Baker attempted to hand over to Aziz on January 9, 1991 (which the latter refused to accept; however, the contents were still widely publicized), the president stated that "the United States will not tolerate the use of chemical or biological weapons, support of any kind of terrorist actions, or the destruction of Kuwait's oil fields and installations. The American people would demand the strongest possible response. You and your country will pay a terrible price if you order unconscionable actions of this sort." *New York Times* Service, "This Choice Is Yours to Make," *International Herald Tribune*, January 14, 1991. It has to be noted that this threat did not save the Kuwaiti oil fields.

73. The political danger to the Coalition was taken very seriously at the time. President Bush put considerable effort into convincing the Israeli government not to retaliate and providing reassurance—through the hunt for Scuds and the delivery of Patriot air defense missiles—that the threat was being dealt with. It is by no means clear whether Israel's retaliatory options were extensive or whether, so long as the retaliation was not disproportionate, the Arab members of the Coalition would have been obliged to reconsider their position. Immediately after the first attack on January 18, Israel was ready to retaliate against the Scud bases in western Iraq. Without American cooperation this would have been impossible. Either the Coalition campaign would have had to [have been] suspended for the duration of an Israeli attack, or the Israelis would have needed access to the American codes so as not to be mistaken for Iraqi aircraft. The Israelis were eventually persuaded that there was little that they could do that the Americans were not doing already. Small rocket attacks from Palestinians based in Lebanon gave Israel the opportunity to reassert its policy of retaliation. The freedom of maneuver of the Arab governments was restricted. Having committed themselves to the anti-Iraq cause, any move that made it likely that Saddam could survive the war with something that could be described as a victory was more dangerous for them than one that fed accusations that the Arab members of the Coalition were conniving with the Israelis. The Syrian Minister of Defense thus ridiculed Saddam: "You are free to fight the entire world alone, but you are not free to claim reason and wisdom. You are especially not free to call on other people to join you in this folly." *Al-Thawra* (Damascus), January 21, 1991. Syrian Foreign Minister Farouq al-Shara reassured foreign ambassadors in Damascus that Syria would not be dragged into war with Israel in order to satisfy Saddam, even in the event of Israeli retaliation. Juan Carlos Gumucio and Michael Knipe, "Assad Defies Saddam's Attempts to Break Up American-Led Alliance," *Times*, January 21, 1991.

74. There were only limited opportunities for the Coalition air forces to take on Iraqi aircraft. By the end of the war some 35 Iraqi aircraft had been destroyed in air-to-air engagements. No Coalition aircraft were lost in these encounters.

75. On January 24, three Iraqi aircraft attempted to mount an Exocet missile attack. Two were shot down by a Saudi F-15.

76. The move does not seem to have been checked with Iranian President Ali Akbar Hashemi-Rafsanjani in advance, and the Iranians appeared reluctant hosts.

77. At the beginning of the Iran-Iraq War, Saddam had sent some of his aircraft to Jordan for safekeeping. On the Iraqi flights to Iran, see Richard Ellis, "Two

Dozen Iraqi Planes Defect to Iran," *Sunday Times*, January 27, 1991; Michael Evans, "Saddam Sends His Best Planes to Iranian Shelter," *Times*, January 29, 1991; Hugh Carnegy, "Israel Says Iraq's Feared Bombers Have Fled to Iran," *Financial Times*, January 30, 1991.

78. INA, January 18, 1991, in British Broadcasting Corporation (BBC), *Summary of World Broadcasts* (SWB), January 18, 1991, ME/0973/A1.

79. This discussion of the environmental aspects of the war has benefited from William Arkin, Damian Durrant, and Marianne Cherni, *On Impact: Modern Warfare and the Environment (A Case Study of the Gulf War)*, Greenpeace study prepared for a conference on "A 'Fifth Geneva Convention' on the Protection of the Environment in Time of Armed Conflict," London, June 1991.

80. Martin Fletcher and Elaine Fogg, "U.S. Accuses Iraq of Creating Vast Oil Slick in the Gulf," *Times*, January 26, 1991.

81. A bombing raid by F-111 aircraft destroyed two oil terminal pressure controls on January 27, slowing the flow of oil into the Gulf.

82. See, for example, *Baghdad Radio*, January 31, 1991, in SWB, February 1, 1991, ME/0985/A1.

83. Lt. General Charles Horner, in charge of the air campaign, observed: "You know some people are mad at CNN. I used it. Did the attack go on time? Did it hit the target? Things like that." "The Secret History of the War," *Newsweek*, March 18, 1991, 21.

84. Khafji, a small town close to the border with Kuwait, had been evacuated early in the conflict because of its vulnerability to Iraqi artillery. The fact that it was abandoned and only lightly defended by Saudi and Qatari troops was advertised in the Western media. On the night of January 29–30, four minor Iraqi incursions were repulsed, but one armored brigade reached Khafji. This succeeded in occupying the town for a while and was expelled by February 1, with some degree of effort by U.S. and Saudi troops. IISS, 1990–91 *Strategic Survey*, 74. There is evidence that Iraq was prepared to follow up this attack in strength, but the fate of the initial attack served to deter it. See *Baghdad Radio*, January 31, 1991, in SWB, January 31, 1991, ME/0984/A1-4.

85. The lack of air support may have come as an alarming revelation to the local Iraqi commanders who were calling for air support during the battle.

86. See, for example, President Bush: "We are on course, we are on schedule, and things go well." Susan Elliot, "Bush's Tribute to Dead Sets the Moral Agenda," *Times*, February 2, 1991.

87. After this raid the U.S. briefer declared himself "comfortable" with the attack because he was convinced that as a communications center it was a legitimate target. However, the intelligence appears to have been out of date, and the target, which had not been of the highest importance earlier, was only attacked because more important targets had already been destroyed. James Adams, "Pentagon Admits Error on Bunker Hit," *Sunday Times*, February 17, 1991, 2. Senior officers recognized that the whole episode had been poorly managed; the result was to lead to unease in the allied camp over targeting procedures.

88. Tariq Aziz denied that the raid killed some relatives of officials close to Saddam. "Nobody in my family was injured, nor were any of those from other members of the leadership." William Drozdiak, "Iraqi Says Regime Made 'Mis-

takes,'" *Washington Post*, May 8, 1991, A1. However, this does not mean that the families of second-ranking officials were not among the victims. Aziz did acknowledge that the Iraqi leadership was surprised by the extent of the devastation: "We were watching the American buildup, and we expected the conflict to be severe. But we did not think the United States would try to destroy all of our telephone exchanges and the rest of our civilian infrastructure."

89. The controversy was discussed on BBC, *Panorama*, March 25, 1991. Another folk memory of Vietnam was of the loss of credibility resulting from persistent over-optimism.

90. See Lawrence Freedman, "Allies Advance in the Psychological Battle," *Independent*, February 16, 1991. It was claimed that 1300 tanks, 800 armored personnel carriers, and 1100 artillery had been destroyed, equivalent to about one-third of Iraq's deployed forces.

91. *Baghdad Radio*, February 15, 1991, in SWB, February 16, 1991, ME/0998/A1-3.

92. These included provisions relevant to Iraq's annexation of Kuwait (Resolution 661), compensation for the harm inflicted on Kuwait and others by the occupation (674), the attempt to change the demographic balance in Kuwait (677), and the continuation of sanctions (661).

93. The Soviet-Iraqi plan involved a full and unconditional withdrawal from Kuwait beginning on the second day after the cease-fire and taking place in a fixed time-frame. After two-thirds of Iraq's forces had been withdrawn, all economic sanctions would cease to apply and at the conclusion of the withdrawal, all Security Council resolutions would be deemed redundant and cease to be in effect. Prisoners of war would be released immediately after the cease-fire, and the withdrawal of forces would be monitored by countries not directly involved in the conflict under the aegis of the Security Council. Associated Press, "8 Points of the Soviet-Iraqi Peace Plan," *International Herald Tribune*, February 23, 1991; for analysis of the politics of the plan see Peter Riddell, "Bush Regains the Initiative," *Financial Times*, February 23–24, 1991; and Joseph Fitchett, "Sweeping Away the Tangled Web of Negotiations," *International Herald Tribune*, February 23, 1991. For a Soviet perspective see Anatoly Repin, "The Chance Has Been Missed," *Novosti Gulf Bulletin* (Moscow), February 27, 1991.

94. See, for example, testimony of James Blackwell, *House Hearings*, 464–478.

95. As Schwarzkopf explained it: "When the quarterback is desperate for a touchdown at the very end, what he does is, he steps behind the center and every single one of his receivers goes way out and they all run down as fast as they possibly can into the end zone, and he lobs the ball." Barry James, "A Flanking Attack Foiled the Iraqis," *International Herald Tribune*, February 27, 1991, 1. The initial plan had assumed the necessity of a direct attack on Iraqi positions. According to Bob Woodward, Schwarzkopf had been persuaded of the feasibility of the indirect approach when shown that the desert was hard enough to support the movement of a tank army. Woodward, *The Commanders*, 348.

96. The marines wanted to make the landing real, but although the Iraqi navy was no longer an obstacle, the mine-clearing operation would have taken many days to complete, and without it casualties could have been substantial. See Will Bennett, "Marines Poised to Storm Ashore," *Independent*, February 25, 1991.

97. See Schwarzkopf's remarks in interview with David Frost, reported in Patrick E. Tyler, "Schwarzkopf on War: He Differs With Bosses," *International Herald Tribune*, March 28, 1991, 1.

98. *Baghdad Radio*, February 28, 1991, in SWB, March 1, 1991, ME/1009/A4-5.

99. Analysis of satellite images indicated a plume of smoke emerging from al Shu'aybah, a Kuwaiti oil processing center, at 7:30 GMT on February 21, followed by the intensification of an existing fire at the al-Burqan oil field at 9:00 and a new one at the oil processing center of Mina al-Ahmadi at 10:00. That afternoon Saddam gave a defiant speech which was followed, at 16:00, by fire near the city of Mina Abdallah and then at 19:00 at the al-Sabiriyah oil field. Foreign Minister Tariq Aziz arrived in Moscow at 21:00. Vipin Gupta, "METEOSAT Lifted Fog of War to Expose Reality in Gulf," *Defense News*, March 18, 1991.

100. On February 16 and February 25, a total of three missiles landed harmlessly in the Negev. On February 17, Iraq claimed that its missile force had launched "three destructive missile strikes on the Israeli Dimona nuclear reactor dedicated to war purposes." Staff Dispatches, "Iraq Targets Israeli A-Plant," *International Herald Tribune*, February 18, 1991.

101. Given the absolute nature of Saddam's personal rule, probably no military commander dared to question his view: The unhappy fate of those generals who had forced Saddam in 1986 to let them win the Iran-Iraq War in spite of himself, and who were later purged, was apparently fresh in their mind.

102. Saddam did not have to look only to the Arab-Israeli wars, where airpower often determined the outcome, for this lesson. It was the sustained Iraqi air campaign against civilian targets which gradually led to the collapse of Iranian national morale in 1988. And if the zealous Iranians eventually broke down under the pressure of the not-very-effective Iraqi air force, how could the less resilient Iraqis expect to withstand an onslaught of the most lethal aerial force assembled in modern history? See Efraim Karsh, "Military Lessons of the Iran-Iraq War," *Orbis*, Vol. 33, No. 2 (Spring 1989), 209–223.

103. Admiral Crowe, the former chairman of the Joint Chiefs of Staff, indicated that the U.S. estimates may have been based on Israeli experience. *Senate Hearings*, 229.

104. "The Secret History of the War," *Newsweek*, March 18, 1991, 25. The "worst-case" American plans were for 20,000 casualties, including about 7,000 killed in action. Woodward, *The Commanders*, 349.

105. At the end of the campaign the following allied losses were listed informally:

	Total	U.S.	U.K.	Arab	Others
Killed in Action	139	79	16	44	
Wounded in Action	432	213	13	206	
Missing in Action	56	35	10	10 Saudi	1 Italian

"Debriefing: Day 43," *The Observer*, March 1, 1991. These figures were later refined, especially as prisoners were returned. Arkin, Durrant, and Cherni, *On Impact*, 44, suggest a final U.S. total of 266 deaths for the whole operation from early August (including 122 accidental non-combat deaths), with 357 soldiers wounded in action and six missing. Later Pentagon reports put the U.S. toll at 148 battlefield deaths and 467 wounded in action. Barton Gellman, "Gulf War's Friendly Fire Tally Triples—Pentagon: 35 Died in Accidental Attacks," *Washington Post*, August 14, 1991, A1, A28. These figures provide a picture of the scale of the casualties, especially when put against Iraqi casualties crudely estimated at over 100,000 by a senior U.S. military official with access to battle damage assessment and intelligence reports. Associated Press, "100,000 Iraqi Troops Died, U.S. Officials Say," *International Herald Tribune*, March 23–24, 1991. Other estimates have ranged from half to twice this number; see, e.g., John H. Cushman, Jr., "Military Experts See a Death Toll of 25,000 to 50,000 Iraqi Troops," *New York Times*, March 1, 1991; James Adams, "Iraqi Toll Could Be 200,000 Dead," *Times*, March 3, 1991. However, as estimates of the numbers of Iraqi soldiers in place at the start of the battle came down, so did the estimates of casualties. Patrick Cockburn, citing a U.S. Army source, suggests that the realistic figure of Iraqi dead may be 20,000–25,000. Patrick Cockburn, "Triumphant Army Marches to the Rumble of Defeat," *Independent* (London), June 8, 1991. Estimates of Iraqi civilian casualties also vary enormously from 5,000–50,000. Arkin, Durrant, and Cherni, *On Impact*, 46–47, estimate civilian deaths at 5,000–15,000. Forty-two allied fixed-wing and rotary-wing aircraft were lost in combat during the 42 days of the war. Another 33 were lost to non-combat causes. John D. Morrocco, "War Will Reshape Doctrine, But Lessons Are Limited," *Aviation Week and Space Technology*, March 11, 1991. The most serious single American loss came when one part of an elderly Scud which had broken up in flight hit a U.S. barrack in Dhahran. Nine of the 16 British casualties were the result of "friendly fire" from two U.S. A-10 aircraft.

106. This critique can be found, for example, in Alexander Haig, *Caveat* (London: Weidenfeld and Nicholson, 1984), 125.

107. Woodward, *The Commanders*, 260.

108. To reduce the temptation, Powell kept as much targeting information out of Washington as possible. Woodward, *The Commanders*, 368. One of the few examples was Dick Cheney's removal of the monument of Saddam Hussein in central Baghdad from the target list because this was considered gratuitous. The al-Rashid Hotel had been identified as a command-and-communication facility, but the fact that the Western media had made it their headquarters saved it from attack. "The Secret History of the War," *Newsweek*, March 18, 1991. In Dugan's interview, he mentioned that the Air Force had identified three "culturally very important sites" in Iraq—possibly religious centers—that the United States would avoid. "We're not mad at the Iraqi people and when this is all over we don't want the Iraqi people to be mad at us and the rest of the allies we've brought together."

109. Maureen Dowd, "Bush at War: Seeking to Be Not Too Detached, Yet Not Gripped by Detail," *New York Times*, January 23, 1991, A8. Marlin Fitzwater, the White House spokesperson, said in January: "I don't think you would ever see George Bush going over targeting charts. He's not involved in that kind of micro-management," Melissa Healy and Mark Fineman, "U.S. Forced to Defend Basic Targeting Goals," *Los Angeles Times*, February 14, 1991, 1.

110. For a comparison, see Patrick Tyler, "Vietnam and Gulf Zone: Real Military Contrasts," *New York Times*, December 1, 1990. Among numerous studies of U.S. decision-making in connection with escalation in Vietnam, see Larry Berman,

The Planning of a Tragedy: The Americanization of the War in Vietnam (New York: Norton, 1983); Wallace J. Thies, *When Governments Collide* (Berkeley: University of California Press, 1980); and William Conrad Gibbons' remarkable series, *The U.S. Government and the Vietnam War: Executive and Legislative Roles and Relationships,* 3 vols. to date (Princeton: Princeton University Press, 1986), which had reached July 1965 in its third volume.

111. The initial basis of the concept of graduated response was the successful management of the Cuban missile crisis in October 1962. The first step taken by Kennedy was to impose a quarantine around Cuba to prevent the introduction of offensive military forces.

112. Many of those who were part of the Kennedy administration when the original concepts of graduated response were developed were cautious about the step to direct military action in the Gulf crisis. George Ball, "The Gulf Crisis," *New York Review of Books,* December 6, 1990; McGeorge Bundy, "Against Iraq, Patience Is the Best Weapon," *International Herald Tribune,* October 13–14, 1990; Theodore Sorensen, "A Draft Declaration of War, But No Carte Blanche," *International Herald Tribune,* January 11, 1991.

6

Politics and Military Technology: Explaining the 1991 Gulf War

Erik Yesson

History has recorded few wars won as rapidly and with as few casualties for the winner as the 1991 Gulf War. An American-led Coalition opened this phase of the Gulf crisis on January 17, 1991, with a massive aerial attack on Iraq. The subsequent U.S. and allied ground force attack lasted five days, February 24–28, and succeeded in destroying a large portion of Saddam Hussein's army. The Coalition forces suffered fewer than 200 dead and 500 wounded during all phases of combat operations.

That the United States and its Coalition partners defeated Iraq on the battlefield is hardly controversial. *Why* they won is another matter. Almost from the day the guns fell silent, analysts have cited a long list of factors that purportedly explain the victory in the Gulf. These include the relative quality and morale of the two opposing armies, the Coalition's unchallenged dominance of the air and extensive satellite reconnaissance capabilities, a desert terrain that offered ideal conditions for armored and air operations, and the Bush administration's diplomatic skill in organizing and maintaining the cohesion of a disparate group of allied states.[1]

Perhaps the most heated debate surrounds the relative impact of technology and what is termed the "human element." Some postwar analyses and reports have cited recent developments in military technology as the key to the Coalition's success; others have argued that more traditional human factors—such as the relative quality of leadership, training, personnel, and strategy—produced the victory for the Coalition.

Warfare always has involved, and most likely always will involve, human beings wielding material implements. In this chapter I argue that technology made a difference in the Gulf War because it allowed those who designed and implemented the Coalition's strategy to control important *political* dimensions of the war.

Technology and Military Affairs

Despite wide attention in academic scholarship and the popular media to the phenomenon of "technology," what technology actually is, and the role it plays in military conflict remain shrouded in myth and misinterpretation. Most people who argue that technology plays a considerable role in military conflict equate technology with specific weapons or military capabilities, but they thereby fail to explain how technology influences the political conduct of war.

Before examining how technology can shape warfare, one must pin down exactly what "technology" means. To do so, it is necessary to draw a distinction between technology and technics. *Technology* is the accumulation of knowledge that conditions the fabrication of specific kinds of implements or artifacts. As one author put it, technology comprises "a knowledge of techniques, methods, and designs that work, and that work in certain ways and with certain consequences, even when one cannot explain exactly why."[2] This knowledge is separate from the tools, or *technics*, that are fashioned on the basis of this knowledge.[3]

In the sphere of military conflict, technological development involves the application of knowledge about new techniques and practices to the production of weaponry and related military systems. Consider a prominent example from the nineteenth century: The knowledge of metallurgy and the engineering skills that conditioned the production of high-strength steel tubes would be considered technology; the artillery pieces that resulted would be technics.

Preserving the distinction between technology and technics is essential in explaining the course of military conflict. To equate the concept of technology with particular weapons systems is to use circular reasoning: One country's forces prevailed (their weapons were more effective) because they possessed superior technology (their weapons were more effective).

The most common rejoinder to this critique is that superior technology leads to better performance: Technologically advanced systems are faster, more accurate, have greater range, and so forth. But these criteria do not explain how, if at all, technology affects the *political* conduct of warfare. When considering the role of technology as a causal mechanism in military conflict, it is important to understand an underlying relationship—the relationship between technology and war as a political phenomenon.

The centrality of politics in warfare means that the stronger side (in numerical terms) does not always prevail. Military history is full of examples of dominant military powers that failed to achieve victory over weaker opponents because the latter could manipulate the political terms of the conflict. Where technology influences the outcome of wars, it does so by forestalling one side's exploitation of the political forces it could use, in resisting its opponent.

Social scientists generally offer three contending hypotheses on the relationship between technology and politics. *Technological determinism* holds that technology shapes the political world in distinct and predictable ways. In this view, technology acts as an autonomous force, or "independent variable." A second basic thesis, *social determinism*, views technology as an outcome, or "dependent variable," that is formed by social and political interests. In this perspective, the nature of technology is shaped by the social interests of those who produce it. A third thesis, *instrumentalism*, holds that technology is simply a means to unspecified ends, a neutral instrument that either side can use, depending on its needs. In this view, technology is neither an independent nor a dependent variable; at most, it is an intervening factor between human interests and political outcomes.[4]

Proponents of the view that technology exerts an influence on the course and outcome of military conflict ultimately rest their case on some form of technological determinism. However, this position need not negate the claims of social determinists concerning their belief that technology is shaped by groups of individuals intent on promoting their interests.[5] Technological determinism rests on the idea that over time the link between human intentions and technological consequences can break, and therefore analysts can explore the effects of technology independently of the social context that produces that technology.

Technology and the 1991 Gulf War

The weapons used by the United States and the Coalition forces in the Gulf relied on technological developments in a number of areas including microelectronics, composite materials, lasers, munitions, and various types of sensors. No single technology appears to have been decisive. Rather, the military systems that were used relied upon a range of new technologies that provided them with vastly improved capabilities over their immediate predecessors.

I contend that this cluster of advanced technologies played a considerable role in giving the Coalition forces control over the battlefield and in aiding the Coalition forces to overcome both the countermeasures employed by Iraq and the natural obstacles that arose on the battlefield. The Coalition's control of key operational dimensions of the conflict closed off any opportunity for Saddam to exploit political forces that could have helped him avert a military defeat. It was not the Coalition's numerical superiority in men or matériel that led to its victory (Iraq held numerical advantages in at least two areas, tanks and artillery) [see Appendix]; rather, victory was attained because the technical sophistication of the Coalition's weapons allowed Coalition leaders to retain political control over the war.

Analyzing the Kuwait War: A Look At Alternative Outcomes

In theory, the best way to test this claim would be to compare that war with other armed conflicts that featured similar initial political and military conditions but less sophisticated technologies. However, few wars have been fought under conditions closely resembling those of the Kuwait War, hence, a secondary line of inquiry must be followed. One method of explaining the outcome of that war is to look at alternative political scenarios in which the Coalition would have fallen short of the results it achieved.

Consider the following plausible scenarios under which Iraq could have avoided defeat on the battlefield.

1. *Public Opinion* The United States becomes bogged down in a war of attrition and, although not losing battlefield confrontations outright, suffers high casualties. Over time, the conflict's unpopularity at home forces the Bush administration to accept a ceasefire without achieving its war aims.

Saddam Hussein's dominant strategy *was* clearly to swing U.S. public opinion against the war by inflicting large numbers of casualties on U.S. ground forces. Even before invading Kuwait he told U.S. Ambassador April Glaspie that "yours is a society which cannot accept 10,000 dead in one battle."[6] On another occasion, he declared that if it came to war, "not a few drops of blood, but rivers of blood would be shed. And then Bush will have been deceiving America, American public opinion, the American people, the American constitutional institutions."[7]

Polling data lend some credence to the idea that U.S. public opinion would not have tolerated high casualties. In a survey taken on January 4–6, 1991, of 1,057 randomly selected adults, 53 percent of the respondents opposed and 44 percent supported the war if casualties were assumed to total 1,000 killed. Opposition increased to 61 percent (35 percent in support) with the assumption of a loss of 10,000 American lives.[8]

2. *Third Party Intervention* In an extended war of attrition, the Soviet Union or the European Community intervenes and negotiates a cease-fire.

Prior to Operation Desert Storm, the Soviet Union and the European Community (EC) did actively seek to negotiate a settlement that would avert a shooting war. In October 1990, President Mikhail Gorbachev sent an envoy to Baghdad to negotiate a diplomatic settlement of the crisis. And as late as January 10, 1991, the EC extended an invitation to Iraq to conduct talks on a proposed regional peace conference.[9] Then, on February 14, after the start of the air campaign, Gorbachev sent an emissary to Baghdad to seek Iraq's withdrawal from Kuwait so that it could avoid a ground war, and Iraqi Foreign Minister Tariq Aziz shuttled between Baghdad and Moscow via Tehran to negotiate an agreement. This mission resulted in Iraq's offer to withdraw from Kuwait if the United States and the United Nations accepted a number of preconditions.[10]

All three initiatives failed, but the fact that the Soviet Union and the European Community attempted to intervene prior to the war indicates that they might have tried again if the conflict had dragged on or had reached a stalemate. There is little doubt, moreover, that Saddam would have used negotiations with third parties to obtain a settlement if his bargaining leverage had increased in the course of a longer, bloodier war.

> 3. *Dividing the Coalition* Saddam Hussein successfully draws Israel into the conflict through Scud missile attacks. Some or all of the Arab states withdraw from the Coalition, and President George Bush judges that the risks of continuing what has now turned into an Arab-Israeli war are too great.

Saddam Hussein did seek to link the Gulf crisis to the Arab-Israeli conflict by launching missile attacks against Israel. Three intertwining strategic rationales seem to have lain behind his strikes against Israel; two were military in nature, and the third political. The first was simply to divert the Coalition aircraft from flying sorties against Iraqi ground forces. The second was an effort to draw the Coalition into a premature ground offensive and thus increase the likelihood of inflicting massive casualties on the predominantly U.S. ground force. The third was an attempt to split the Arab members from the Coalition and create new political obstacles for the Bush administration.

The Iraqi president seems to have been fully aware of these possible paths to victory that would not necessarily have involved tactical success on the battlefield. Like Robert E. Lee during the American Civil War, Saddam did not have to win the war outright; he could have benefited from simply not losing it. And, like Abraham Lincoln in 1861, American policy makers during the Gulf crisis faced the difficult challenge of overturning an undesirable status quo. That Saddam Hussein could possibly have created any of the three scenarios outlined here made this task more daunting.

The Course and Consequences of the Kuwait War

To evaluate whether technological advances played a crucial role in the Coalition's victory over Iraq, it is helpful to look at each phase of the war: the air campaign, the ground offensive, and postwar developments. In the sections that follow, special attention is paid to the influence of technology on the political climate.

The Air Campaign

Strategic bombing. During the air campaign, Coalition forces struck a number of strategic targets in Iraq, including command-and-control sites in Baghdad and elsewhere, military-related infrastructure, air force bases, air defense nodes, and fixed and mobile Scud launchers. The Coalition flew more than 109,000 combat and support sorties during the war (the United States accounting for 95 percent of these) and lost 48 aircraft.

The Coalition air strikes against Iraqi command-and-control nodes began on the first night of the campaign and continued for the duration of the war. The aircraft used to strike targets in downtown Baghdad was the F-117A Nighthawk, a piloted aircraft designed with radar-absorbing materials. The pilots used forward-looking infrared radar (FLIR) to find their way to target areas and employed downward-looking infrared radar (DLIR) sensors to aim laser-guided bombs (LGBs), which they released from an altitude of 20,000 feet.[11] The F-117A could strike highly defended targets, and Iraqi radar apparently never tracked the aircraft.[12]

FLIR was also an integral component of two other U.S. Air Force targeting and navigation systems used during the war: Pave Tack, which is carried internally on the F-111F, and LANTIRN (Low Altitude Navigation and Targeting Infra-Red for Night), which consists of two pods slung under the fuselage of the F-15E and F-16C/D.[13] All three systems allow pilots to navigate and search out targets in darkness, haze, and low-visibility weather. After detecting a target with radar, the pilot can lock on a laser designator and release LGBs.

The laser-guided bomb system was introduced in the 1960s and met with some success during the Vietnam War. Since the 1980s, electro-optic weapons designers have improved the performance of LGBs by combining this weapon with targeting equipment for use at night and in poor visibility. The advanced microelectronics of Pave Tack and LANTIRN allowed pilots to strike a range of strategic targets throughout the Kuwait War, including railroad and auto bridges spanning the Tigris and Euphrates rivers, oil refineries, and electrical power stations.

U.S. Department of Defense and civilian analysts continue to debate the effects of the strategic bombing campaign. The Pentagon maintains that Coalition aircraft equipped with these systems severely disrupted Iraqi war-planning efforts, damaged the ability of Iraq's leadership to communicate with ground forces, and crippled roads and rail lines used to resupply combat units. However, Greenpeace analyst William Arkin, after inspecting targets in Baghdad and interviewing Iraqi government officials, concluded that the strategic bombing campaign contributed little to the Coalition's victory. According to Arkin, communications with ground commanders were not severed, equipment and computers had been removed before buildings were attacked, and key army and air force personnel survived simply by avoiding command bunkers targeted by the U.S. Air Force. From his research he also concluded that the destruction of power stations and electrical grids in Baghdad contributed to the deaths of 70,000 to 90,000 civilians in the war's aftermath because electricity is critical to maintaining the water supply and sewage treatment.[14]

I contend that although these attacks on strategic political and military targets and civilian infrastructure may have contributed little to the defeat of the Iraqi military in the Kuwaiti Theater of Operations (KTO), the threat of renewed air attacks on these targets clearly gave the United States and its allies a great deal of leverage over Iraq when the Coalition began to dismantle Saddam's facilities for the production of weapons of mass destruction.

Tomahawk cruise missiles launched from naval vessels also played a role, albeit small, in the initial stages of the air campaign. The U.S. Navy launched 288 of these low-flying subsonic missiles, which employ a radar guidance system and an optical and near-infrared system that guides the weapon as it closes on the target. Because of the relative inaccuracy and small warhead of the Tomahawk, the weapon was used primarily to strike sizable targets, such as oil refineries and large buildings. The popular conception of Tomahawks making abrupt turns at intersections and flying through windows and doors is largely unfounded.[15]

The main order of business for Coalition aircraft was the destruction of Iraq's formidable ground-based air defense system and its air force. U.S. Air Force F-4G, F-16, EF-111, and Navy and Marine Corps EA-6B and F/A-18 aircraft fired more than 1,000 High-speed Anti-Radiation Missiles (HARMs) against enemy radar units, often after drones simulating the radar signature of strike aircraft lured the Iraqis into switching on their tracking radar.[16] Royal Air Force Tornado aircraft launched limited numbers of Air-Launched Anti-Radiation Missile (ALARMs) that had been rushed into operational deployment.[17]

The threat posed by Iraq's surface-to-air missile (SAM) system should not be underestimated, and its defeat by Coalition air forces held the key to the subsequent success of the air campaign, particularly against Iraqi ground units. The Iraqi network of search-and-fire control radars and missile batteries was *not* a clone of the standard Soviet air defense system. It consisted of approximately 300 Soviet SA-2 and SA-3 fixed-based SAM sites and 400 mobile SAMs, including 300 Soviet SA-7s, SA-8s, and SA-9s, 100 French-supplied Rolands, and a number of U.S. Improved Hawks captured from Kuwait. By knocking these missiles out of action, the Coalition effectively removed the SAM threat above 10,000 feet. Although Iraq's inventory of 4,000 conventional antiaircraft guns still posed a threat at lower altitudes, the neutralization of the main SAM threat allowed Coalition aircraft to conduct strikes with near impunity.[18]

The other main target, as mentioned, was the Iraqi air force. Iraq had deployed as many as 350 helicopter aircraft, including approximately 30 MiG-29s, 25 MiG-25s, and 30 Mirage F1s, all relatively sophisticated aircraft by contemporary standards. Recognizing that they were vastly outnumbered by better aircraft flown by superior pilots and backed by airborne warning and control system (AWACS) aircraft, the Iraqis decided to use their air force as part of an elaborate shell game, which they hoped would prolong the war. The Iraqi military believed that its hardened aircraft shelters—constructed by Dutch, British, and Yugoslavian firms—would withstand even direct hits by enemy bombs. By housing its fleet of high-performance fighters in these shelters, it tried to lure the Coalition into attacking every shelter in a fruitless attempt to destroy all Iraqi fighter aircraft on the ground. Knowing that U.S. Air Force doctrine placed highest priority on the destruction of the enemy's air force, the Iraqis reasoned that the shell-game strategy would delay air attacks on their ground units in the KTO.

They were right: The U.S. Air Force systematically targeted each hardened shelter; however, the accuracy of its targeting pods, in conjunction with its LGBs, proved capable of penetrating the steel and concrete shelter walls. Numerous reconnaissance photographs show that 2,000-pound LGBs such as the steel-encased GBU-27 and the GBU-24 (equipped with a delayed action warhead) easily ripped through most of these hardened shelters. The walls of the Yugoslav-built shelters, which were 10 to 12 feet in diameter, remained impervious even to direct hits, but Coalition pilots were eventually able to destroy these revetments by sending LGBs through the blast doors.[19] When it became clear that the U.S. Air Force would eliminate all of the "shells" with its highly accurate weapons, the Iraqis evacuated most of their remaining aircraft to Iran.

Combatting the Scud Missile. In addition to command-and-control centers, SAM sites, and airfields, the other priority target for Coalition forces at the start of the air campaign was the Scud missile. During the war, the Iraqis fired 86 Scuds from fixed sites and 36 mobile launchers;

their total inventory has been estimated at 400 to 1,000 missiles.[20] Nearly all of the Scuds were fired at night. Mobile scud launchers were kept concealed during the day, hidden in ravines, beneath highway underpasses, and in culverts. Under the cover of darkness, they were deployed to sites that had been surveyed prior to the outbreak of the war.[21]

According to the Pentagon, the U.S. Air Force succeeded in destroying all of the fixed sites and some mobile launchers during the war. Lieutenant General Charles Horner, the commander of allied air forces in the Gulf, stated that F-15Es equipped with LANTIRN were instrumental in defeating the Scud missile threat and claimed that LANTIRN doubled the effectiveness of the F-15E against the Scuds.[22]

It now appears that these claims were exaggerated. According to United Nations inspectors, the Coalition did not destroy a single mobile Scud launcher during the war. Furthermore, it appears that Iraq had only 19 mobile launchers, all of which were destroyed after the war by UN inspectors or by the Iraqis themselves, and that the Coalition probably destroyed only a fraction of the fixed launchers. The latter in the Western desert, it turns out, were never even used by the Iraqis.[23]

The Coalition also used the Patriot surface-to-air missile system in its efforts to neutralize the Scud threat. The Patriot is unquestionably one of the most advanced systems in the U.S. arsenal.[24] It employs a powerful phased-array radar that tracks incoming ballistic missiles and guides the interceptor to impact. In the terminal phase of the engagement, a seeker in the nose of the interceptor homes in on the radiation reflected against the target by the system's ground-based radar. The Patriot has been widely credited with minimizing damage to Israeli and Saudi cities during the war and keeping Israel out of the war.

Initial claims about the Patriot's effectiveness must, however, be discarded. Although it was claimed that Patriot missiles intercepted 80 percent of the Scuds fired against Saudi Arabia, and 50 percent of those launched against Israel, in postwar testimony before the House of Representatives, army officials revised those numbers to 70 and 40 percent, respectively.[25] A later study by Theodore Postol made clear that the Patriot's shortcomings were of an even greater magnitude. Postol contended that the Patriot failed to defend Israel against Scud attacks and may actually have intensified the damage to Israeli cities.

Postol based his assertions on a comparison of damage data from undefended and defended Scud attacks. Of the approximately 40 Scuds launched against Israel during the war, the first 13 fell on Tel Aviv and Haifa before the Patriot system was deployed in Israel. Postol's data indicate that these attacks damaged 2,698 apartments and wounded 115 people. After the Patriot system became operational in Israel, the subsequent 14 to 17 Scud missiles that fell on the country resulted in 7,778 damaged apartments, 168 wounded, and 1 fatality.[26] The remaining 10 to 13 Scuds landed in the sea or the desert.

Postol attributed the higher level of damage and casualties of the later attacks to three factors: (1) Patriot intercepts caused Scuds that would otherwise have fallen harmlessly in unpopulated areas to rain debris on population centers, resulting in significant damage; (2) Patriot intercepts that cut incoming Scuds into pieces often failed to damage the warhead, so that the combination of scattered debris and the explosion of the warhead intensified damage; and (3) some of the Patriot interceptors fell into populated areas, causing damage independent of that from the attacking Scuds.[27]

Thus, although the Patriot is a highly advanced system from a technological standpoint, its capabilities apparently did not blunt Iraq's attacks on Israel. Ironically, part of the problem was the primitive nature of the Scuds used. So that they would reach targets in Israel, Iraq modified its Scuds to extend their range. These modifications left the missile aerodynamically unstable, causing many of the weapons to break into pieces in midflight. The Patriot's targeting system was thus saturated with what were in effect multiple decoys, which made it difficult to intercept the Scud's warhead. Although the U.S. Army upgraded the software packages for the Patriot's guidance computers, this software and other features of the Patriot system may have been flawed.[28]

Was Iraq's Scud campaign against Israel and Saudi Arabia successful? From a military standpoint it was, because the United States was forced to devote over 15 percent of its air-to-ground missions to tracking down the Scuds.[29] All told, the so-called Great Scud Hunt diverted numerous Coalition sorties from other targets in Iraq and Kuwait.

So why did Iraq's Scud missile attacks fail to draw Israel into the war? One reason was the wild inaccuracy of the Scuds. Thirty-nine drifted so wide of their targets that Patriot batteries never even engaged them.[30] Also, it has been suggested that the presence of the Patriot in Israel after its demonstrated success in defending Saudi Arabia from Scud attacks led to positive political and psychological reactions among the Israeli public, making counterattack seem unnecessary.[31] On its face, this conclusion presents a paradox to the analysis presented here, as it suggests that technology can be ineffective and still yield the desired political results. However, it was the Israeli government and not the public that decided whether to enter the war. Postol's interviews reveal that Israeli military and defense officials were well aware of the Patriot system's severe shortcomings.[32] It is therefore unlikely that the public's reaction affected whether Israel entered the war.

Probably the best explanation for Israel's restraint is that the United States successfully lobbied Israeli leaders into remaining on the sidelines. When the Israelis announced they wanted to try their hand at striking Scud launchers in western Iraq, U.S. envoys convinced them that the Coalition was already attacking any potential targets that the Israeli Air Force might wish to strike and that any complications associated with the identification of friend or foe (IFF) might interfere with the Coalition's air campaign.[33] Moreover, the United States offered Israel monetary inducements for restraint: $650 million in economic assistance and $700 million in military hardware (including a Patriot missile battery).[34]

Tactical Bombing. Coalition air forces had better success against the more numerous stationary targets offered by the Iraqi ground forces. Technological advances in weapon guidance and target acquisition played a considerable role in the defeat of these units.

Smart weapons, which came into use in the mid-1980s, played a decisive role in the outcome of the Gulf War. The most significant development was the imaging infrared (IIR) seeker for air-to-ground missiles and guided bomb units (GBUs). Unlike passive infrared, which is used to home in on a heat source (such as the seeker on the Sidewinder air-to-air missile), the IIR seeker works like a camera, generating a visual image of heat-emitting objects. When mounted on the nose of a missile, the IIR seeker relays a picture of the target to a screen in the aircraft cockpit. The pilot can then lock the missile on the target, launch the missile, and take evasive action.

Two IIR weapons were used extensively in the Gulf War. The primary type was the IIR Maverick air-to-ground missile. First delivered to the U.S. Air Force in 1982, the Maverick AGM-65D was deployed in the Gulf primarily on A-10 and F-16 aircraft. A-10s launched 4,801 Mavericks during the war, more than 90 percent of the total.[35] The Maverick AGM-65G employs the earlier version's seeker and rocket motor but has a larger warhead, which enhances its effectiveness against buildings and hardened bunkers; it is also extremely effective against tanks. According to one source, the U.S. Air Force fired 100 Mavericks a day, primarily IIR versions but also some non-IIR versions, and achieved greater than 80 percent kill rates.[36]

In contrast to the earliest, non-IIR Maverick model, which employed an optical seeker (essentially a television camera), the IIR versions proved far superior in the desert conditions. Pilots reportedly found that non-IIR Mavericks did not allow them to discriminate between high-value targets (tanks) and low-value ones (personnel carriers and previously destroyed tanks), whereas the infrared versions were optimal for target identification in the blowing desert sand.[37] With the IIR Maverick, a disposable seeker mounted in the nose of the missile detects targets and relays the scene to a monitor in the cockpit. It is this system, and not the plane's conventional 30mm cannon, that is credited with most of the A-10s tank kills;[38] however, the Maverick seeker provides such a narrow field of vision that one Pentagon official likened this targeting method to peering through a soda straw.[39]

As with LGBs, weapons designers were able to marry the Maverick to targeting systems such as LANTIRN, which provided better resolution and a wider field of view. With the revised system, pilots could launch weapons like the Maverick more quickly and at longer ranges when threatened by antiaircraft fire.[40] The revised Maverick infrared targeting systems proved extremely effective for engaging Iraqi forces at night and in bad weather and for detecting concealed targets.[41]

The other IIR weapon used in the war was the GBU-15 guided bomb. The GBU-15 consists of either an IIR or an optical seeker attached to a 2,000-pound bomb modified with steerable fins. The pilot uses the IIR or optical seeker to lock the bomb on target. With the aid of an optional data link, the pilot can steer the weapon as it nears the target to gain greater accuracy.

During the course of the air campaign, the combination of FLIR sensors and IIR missiles proved particularly devastating to Iraqi army units, especially Iraqi armor. The initial air onslaught against Iraqi armor entrenched in Kuwait and southern Iraq yielded meager results: B-52 heavy bombers conducted numerous raids against these forces, but the dug-in armor remained largely untouched.[42] However, the U.S. Air Force switched tactics and began using F-16s as scout planes to search predetermined 30-mile-square "kill boxes." Once the pilots identified targets visually, they passed the positions on to other F-16s and A-10s, which went in and bombed the targets.[43]

When this method resulted in the destruction of scores of vehicles, the Iraqis dug in their armor even deeper and began using sandbags to camouflage their locations from aerial reconnaissance. But these measures were ultimately defeated by LANTIRN, Pave Tack, and Maverick missiles. Because the dug-in armor absorbed heat during the day and at night radiated it more slowly than the surrounding desert, U.S. Air Force pilots could use FLIR to detect the hot spots and could then launch LGBs to destroy the hidden vehicles. According to one report, 60 F-15Es and F-111Fs destroyed as many as 200 tanks per night using this technique.[44] Another source indicates that the Pentagon's goal of annihilating 50 percent of Iraq's equipment before the start of the ground war was exceeded by 10 percent, with F-111Fs and A-10s each destroying approximately 1,000 armored vehicles.[45]

LANTIRN has an advantage over Pave Tack, in that it is a smaller, lighter system and thus can be fitted to smaller aircraft, which constitute a large portion of the U.S. Air Force's inventory. Pave Tack is a relatively large system that requires a large air frame, like that of the F-111. Through advances in microelectronics, the scale of the navigation and targeting systems has been reduced to the point where LANTIRN can be fitted to the F-15E and F-16C/D and other smaller aircraft.

The Ground Campaign

Prelude. With wealth generated from oil sales and the impetus provided by the war with Iran, Iraq began, in the mid-1970s, to procure a vast stock of relatively advanced conventional weaponry. In 1980, it obtained its first T-72 tanks.[46] By 1985, it had added long-range artillery such as the Austrian Noriann GH N-45 and the South African G-5. These two 155mm systems outranged the best guns in the Coalition's arsenal.[47]

Although Iraq did not always acquire the most advanced versions of weapons (its T-72 tanks, for example, reportedly lacked the most advanced armor found on Soviet models[48]), by 1990 its arsenal of modern weapons was as formidable as any outside the industrialized world, with the exception of Israel and perhaps one or two other nations. Saddam's highly mechanized army could deliver withering amounts of firepower.

In purely quantitative terms, Iraq deployed more tanks and artillery in the KTO than the Coalition did. It has been estimated that prior to the Coalition's air offensive, the Iraqis deployed 4,200 tanks and 3,100 artillery pieces in the KTO, whereas the numbers for the Coalition were 3,600 and 1,200 perspectively.[49]

Iraqi ground forces were arrayed in three layers in the KTO (see Map 6.1). Infantry and artillery were deployed along the Saudi-Kuwait border, where they were protected by barbed wire, minefields, and antitank ditches. Armored and mechanized divisions were stationed to the north and west, constituting an operational reserve force. Republican Guard divisions equipped with Iraq's best armor were positioned between Basra and Kuwait's northern border as a strategic reserve.

The extent of attrition of Iraqi ground units due to air and ground attacks prior to the ground offensive is hard to gauge. According to the official Pentagon report, "the general assessment at the time was that the tactical echelon and artillery were severely degraded, the operational echelon's sustainment capability had been eliminated, and the Republican Guard somewhat degraded." In that report, the Department of Defense estimated that over 540,000 Iraqi troops were in the KTO initially and that war planners operated under the assumption that 450,000 remained at the start of the ground offensive.[50] Other reports indicated that Iraq never had more than 350,000 troops in the KTO and that as few as 200,000 troops remained on February 24.[51]

Advanced technology played a considerable role in the Coalition's destruction of Iraq's artillery and its quantitative and numerical advantages. Two methods were used. A large portion of Iraq's artillery tubes were demolished by fixed-wing aircraft, particularly the A-10. Another lethal method was counterbattery fire from conventional cannons and the recently deployed multiple launch rocket system (MLRS). The latter consists of a mobile launcher that fires twelve 227mm rockets to a distance of 40 kilometers.

Effective counterbattery fire involves immediately locating the position of the enemy guns that have fired, targeting those guns, and returning fire. Thus, it requires not only a means for locating the enemy's guns but also the ability to compute the precise trajectory at which to return fire. The Coalition's AN/TPQ-36 and -37 Firefinder radars in combination with MLRS proved devastating to Iraqi artillery batteries that fired on Coalition forces: According to Colonel Roberrt Scales, Jr., the "radars proved their ability to locate Iraqi firing positions to within a dozen meters or less and had the data on MLRS firing screens often before the Iraqi incoming rounds landed. MLRS was overwhelming and an enemy battery that gave itself away by firing and did not move immediately was doomed."[52] MLRS was particularly deadly when the system was used to dispense hundreds of explosive submunitions, which saturated target areas.[53] Iraqi soldiers reportedly referred to these salvos as "steel rain." U.S. and British MLRS units fired a total of 17,000 such rounds during the conflict.[54]

The most recent addition to the U.S. arsenal used in the ground war, the E-8 joint surveillance target attack radar system (JSTARS) aircraft, provided Coalition forces with real-time day and night reconnaissance of enemy ground forces. The Coalition's two E-8 JSTARS proved highly effective as a force multiplier by paralyzing Iraq's mechanized ground forces.

The E-8 is a modified Boeing 707 that carries a large radar under its belly. In its synthetic aperture mode, the radar scans the ground with a resolution of 3 meters. In its moving target indication mode, it can detect moving objects with cross-sections smaller than one-fifth the size of a typical tank.[55] The radar signals are then processed by the E-8's computers to provide a picture of enemy activity on the ground.

These capabilities allow JSTARS to scan 1 million square kilometers over an 8-hour period. The system was still in operational testing when Iraq invaded Kuwait, but the Pentagon rushed the system to the field before it had reached full-scale development.[56] One of the two aircraft deployed to the Gulf logged nightly 12-hour missions in the skies over

Saudi Arabia. The planes flew a total of 49 sorties, providing targeting information for 750 air-to-surface missions.[57]

Iraqi tanks and other vehicles that had been attacked during the day could not relocate at night because JSTARS would detect their movement and call in air strikes.[58] Further, JSTARS ground stations accumulated reconnaissance histories of specific sectors. Over time, this capability allowed intelligence units to identify Iraqi decoys; a tank that appeared overnight with no history was probably a fake.[59] In addition, JSTARS imagery aided in bomb damage assessment and the surveillance of Iraqi fortifications.[60]

Operation Desert Sabre. The strategic plan of each side for the ground campaign seems apparent.[61] Iraq's strategy was to delay the Coalition forces along the belt of obstacles and

minefields on the Saudi-Kuwait border and then saturate them with artillery fire. In the meantime, its operational reserve of armor would move south and attempt to envelop the forces pinned down by the infantry and artillery. The Republican Guard would roll in from the north to repulse the Coalition's counterattacks.

The Coalition's war planners anticipated this strategy, and prepared their own envelopment plan (code-named "Operation Desert Sabre"), which relied on a sequence of attacks. The U.S. Marine and Saudi divisions would attack the Iraqi defense on the first day of the ground offensive in an attempt to draw the operational and strategic reserves southward; the XVIII Airborne Corps would simultaneously drive to the northeast to provide flank protection. Then, on the second day of the ground war, the VII Corps would begin a drive to the northeast. The delay was designed to allow time for the Iraqi armored and mechanized infantry divisions to be drawn south by the Marines and Saudis, whereupon the VII Corps and the 24th Mechanized Infantry Division would envelop them as they turned east.[62]

IIR technology enhanced the effectiveness of two U.S. Army weapon systems that played important roles in defeating Iraqi armor in all phases of the ground campaign: The M1A1 Abrams tank and the AH-64A Apache attack helicopter. The M1A1 tank was delivered to the U.S. Army in 1985. It is equipped with the same thermal sight as the M1 tank that went into service in 1980, but the M1A1 uses the German-designed 120mm smoothbore gun—a larger caliber weapon than the M1's 105mm rifled cannon. The M1A1 thus provides greater killing power at longer ranges.

The combination of the 120mm gun and the thermal imaging sight allowed the Abrams' crews to identify, target, and destroy enemy armor beyond the effective range of the T-72, Iraq's best tank.[63] The M1A1's infrared sight proved to be a vital asset during the day as well as at night,

FIGURE 6.1   Operation Desert Sabre

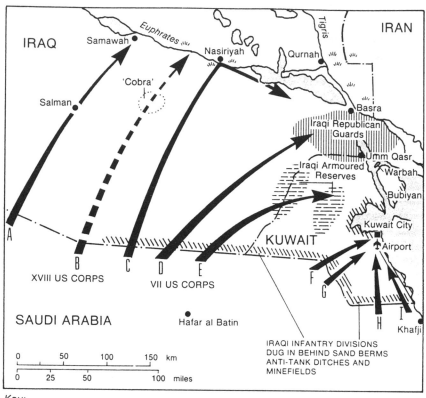

Key:

A – French Light 'Daguet' Division   E – British 1st Division
B – 101st US Air Assault Division by Helicopter   F – 1st US Marine Division
C – 24th US Infantry Division (Mechanized)   G – Combined Egyptian/Saudi Forces
D – 1st & 3rd US Armoured Division   H – 2nd US Marine Division
       1st US Infantry Division (Mech.)   I – Saudi Forces

Source: Strategic Survey 1990–1991, The International Institute for Strategic Studies, London, 1991, p 77.

for during the day, the battlefield was often obscured by smoke billowing from the hundreds of Kuwaiti oil wells set afire by the Iraqis just prior to the Coalition's ground offensive.[64] The advanced materials used in the construction of the M1A1, including composite and depleted uranium armor, also gave it a tremendous advantage. Not a single enemy round is reported to have penetrated the M1A1's armor during the war.

The AH-64A Apache attack helicopter, the other Army system that relied on thermal imaging, is equipped with a target recognition and designation sight and a pilot's night vision sensor, both of which employ FLIR technology. The Army used the Apache's FLIR navigation and targeting capabilities at the start of the air campaign to find and destroy, under the cover of darkness, Iraq's early-warning sites with laser-guided Hellfire missiles, rockets, and 30mm cannon fire. The Apache fired at least 2,900 Hellfire missiles during the war and is credited with knocking out 500 main battle tanks (MBTs) and 120 armored personnel carriers (APCs).[65]

Another important force multiplier for the Coalition during the ground campaign was the navigation capability provided by NAVSTAR GPS (navigation system with timing and ranging global positioning system). NAVSTAR consists of 16 satellites in semisynchronous orbit 20,000 kilometers above the earth (the full fleet of 21 satellites plus 3 spares entered service in 1994). These satellites carry highly accurate atomic clocks that continually broadcast time readouts and ground stations track the satellites to pinpoint their exact positions. Ground forces, aircraft, and ships are equipped with portable receivers that calculate the distance between themselves and any three of these satellites to obtain continuous updating of longitude and latitude with an accuracy to 25 meters.[66]

The navigation capabilities provided by GPS proved crucial in the Coalition's ground offensive as well as in the air campaign. Coalition aircraft equipped with GPS receivers were able to navigate toward their targets with a high degree of accuracy. Because the Gulf experienced its worst weather in fourteen years during the Kuwait War, this capability proved essential to the air campaign. The Coalition planners had estimated an average of 13 percent cloud cover during the air war, but the actual figure turned out to be 39 percent.[67] Coalition pilots used GPS to find their way through the inclement weather to the general vicinity of their targets, whereupon they switched over to infrared navigation systems.[68]

Prior to the ground offensive one of the key preparations made by the Coalition's ground forces was to accurately determine the map coordinates of their artillery tubes. The artillery units used GPS receivers to ascertain their positions precisely—the first requisite for delivering accurate fire on enemy positions. These units could then maneuver through the unsurveyed desert, come to a halt, update their positions with GPS, and continue to deliver highly accurate fire.[69]

GPS played a pivotal role in guiding Coalition ground forces around Iraq's western flank toward Basra and guiding them as they encircled Saddam's forces in Kuwait. Tanks and other vehicles were equipped with small light-weight GPS receivers (SLGRs, or "sluggers"), which enabled accurate navigation in the charge across the Iraqi desert. Microprocessors and other advanced electronics were key components in all GPS receivers: With this technology, the computational power needed for the navigational calculations fit into small, handheld receivers.[70]

Cease-Fire and Beyond

Prior to the initiation of Coalition offensive operations in the war, the commander in chief of Central Command, General Norman Schwarzkopf, stated five primary "missions" from the objectives set by the president and his advisers: to "neutralize" Iraq's national command authorities, to eject the Iraqi army from Kuwait, to destroy the Republican Guard, to destroy Iraq's ballistic missile and NBC (nuclear, biological, and chemical) capabilities, and to restore the Kuwaiti government to power.[71] These "war aims" constituted the immediate goals tied to events on the battlefield.[72] But did the United States meet its objectives?

It would appear that the United States was successful in four out of five of its stated aims. Iraqi forces are out of Kuwait, and the emir has returned to power. UN inspectors have tracked down and destroyed Iraq's NBC production facilities and weapons stockpiles.[73] It is likely that Saddam Hussein acquiesced to the inspection and dismantling of his NBC capabilities out of fear for his political survival. Although the air attacks on Iraqi military and civilian infrastructure seem to have had little impact on the conduct of the Iraqi forces during the ground war, the destruction of the infrastructure, the civilian deaths caused by the air campaign, and the threat that Coalition forces could renew those attacks severely disrupted Iraqi society. For Saddam Hussein, they must have raised the specter of being deposed by the Iraqi people or, more importantly, the Iraqi military. The economic embargo does not seem to have had the same effect; Saddam has shown an impressive ability to contend with the shortages caused by the embargo.

The main unrealized objective is the destruction of the Republican Guard. General Schwarzkopf stirred some controversy after the war by arguing that the cease-fire called by President Bush prevented U.S. forces from cutting off the retreating Republican Guard units. It is estimated that four and one-half of the eight Republican Guard divisions managed to escape across the Tigris River. These surviving forces are said to deploy 700 tanks and 1,400 APCs.[74]

Most likely the United States called for a cease-fire rather than the pursuit of these divisions across the Tigris because such advance might have looked like a full-scale invasion of Iraq—an action that neither the United Nations nor the Arab members of the Coalition would have countenanced. To eliminate or capture all eight of the Republican Guard divisions, Coalition forces would have needed to draw the units southward in Kuwait as the ground offensive began. This action would have allowed the Coalition forces on the left flank to encircle and trap these units.

One factor that appears to have prevented such a plan from being implemented was Saddam Hussein's order to his best troops to withdraw before the start of the ground offensive. Some sources indicate that he ordered Republican Guard units to withdraw as early as February 17, a full week before the Coalition launched its ground strike.[75] Another source indicates that withdrawal orders may have also been sent to other units on the eve of the ground offensive.[76] These latter troops fled northward under the threat of the oncoming Coalition forces. Their inclination to retreat so quickly can probably be ascribed to a second factor: the previous successes of the Coalition's advanced technology. Iraqi armored forces that had tried to maneuver at night had been immediately struck by Coalition aircraft[77] equipped with JSTARS and advanced targeting systems. Thus, when the ground attack began on February 24, it set off a chain reaction among Iraqi forces, whose first inclination was to flee.

Because the Marines and Saudis were making rapid progress, the Coalition's war planners decided to throw their "left hook"—the armored thrust from the west—9 hours after the attack on Iraqi positions in Kuwait instead of waiting 24 hours as initially planned.[78] But apparently General Schwarzkopf failed to appreciate that the Iraqis had been ordered to withdraw or to take into account the direction of their retreat. Had he anticipated that the Iraqis would refuse to take the bait, Schwarzkopf could have set the VII Corps in motion simultaneously with, or even prior to, the right flank's attack on Iraqi lines in Kuwait. In this instance, the Coalition's strategy was not sensitive to the superior performance of its advanced technology in destroying Iraqi army units from the air.

As mentioned previously, the Coalition could not simply march on Baghdad to eliminate the Ba'ath Party's control over the residual forces. At the end, allied forces stood a mere 150 miles from the capital. A full-scale invasion could have driven the Arab countries from the Coalition; moreover, if Saddam had been removed, the country would have been left in U.S. custody with no apparent successor regime.[79] Upon some thought, it appears that Saddam's political longevity may actually be consistent with long-term U.S. interests. Saddam's removal could upset the balance of power in the region and create a new danger, namely a resurgent Iran seeking to dominate the Gulf.[80]

The Political Impact of Technology

The advanced weapons deployed by the United States and its allies did not always perform as advertised. As the Tomahawk and Patriot systems demonstrated, advanced technology is no guarantee of tactical success in warfare. However, the destruction of the Iraqi army, its eviction from Kuwait, and the subsequent demolition of weapons facilities inside

Iraq owe much to advanced technology. With the help of such technology, the Coalition's air forces then out a sophisticated air defense system and then systematically destroyed Iraqi ground units. The Coalition's ground forces then used advanced systems to devastate what was left of the Iraqi army while minimizing their own casualties.

Technology allowed the Coalition's leaders to fight the war in a manner that preserved their *political* control over the conflict. Technology aided the Coalition in winning quickly and with relatively few casualties; it prevented the conflict from becoming a war of attrition. Even if the United States and its allies had the upper hand in a much longer and bloodier war, that kind of conflict could have unleashed political forces that might well have obstructed the Coalition's war aims.

In shaping the nature of the conflict, technology was instrumental in two areas. One was mastery over *countermeasures*, or what Carl von Clausewitz called "active" forms of resistance: the actions taken to parry the moves of an attacker. The other was the ability to surmount *friction* (or the "fog of war"), what Clausewitz described as the "countless minor incidents—the kind you can never foresee—[that] combine to lower the general level of performance, so that one always falls far short of the intended goal."[81] Whereas countermeasures are obstacles deliberately placed in the path of an opponent, friction is caused by those unintended forces—bad weather, equipment failure, and other mishaps—that intervene at inauspicious times and impede the progress of military forces in their pursuit of battlefield objectives.

Friction and countermeasures are crucial factors that influence the conduct of war. The evidence from the 1991 Gulf War indicates that the Coalition forces encountered numerous Iraqi countermeasures and a great deal of friction. With the exception of the campaign against the Scud missile, the Coalition's advanced systems met with success. Their technology allowed the United States and its allies to destroy numerous hardened aircraft shelters, air defense missiles, dug-in tanks, and minefields, as well as to overcome blowing sand, oil fires, low-visibility weather, and a trackless desert.

Conclusion

An understanding of the links between technology, friction, countermeasures, and politics should caution those looking for lessons from the Kuwait War for future policy. Technology influences but does not determine outcomes. The political context of military conflict can vary greatly. In the Gulf, the Coalition had numerous political forces arrayed in its favor at the outset and then used technology to preserve those political advantages.

The impact of advanced technology on the Gulf War has created a widespread impression that these results could be readily duplicated elsewhere. The ravages of ethnic conflict in the former Yugoslavia is perhaps the best example of this mindset. Many continue to believe the United States and its allies could have used high-tech weaponry to launch an "Operation Balkan Storm" that would have halted Serbian aggression on Bosnia. However, the Balkan war aptly illustrates the fallacy of this claim. While NATO aircraft have successfully attacked Serbian gun emplacements, ammunition depots, and communication nodes, an all-out attack on Serbia and the Bosnian Serbs would not have produced a political settlement in the region. The Bosnian Serbs took a seat at the negotiating table only once the balance of power had decisively shifted in favor of their opponents. Active cooperation between Bosnian and Croatian leaders and a rather substantial flow of arms to their respective armies have moved the Bosnian Serbs toward a negotiated settlement. The comparative perspective offered by the Bosnian experience underscores that technology never creates the political preconditions for "victory" but only reinforces and sustains initial political advantages.

Notes

I would like to thank Aaron Friedberg for helpful comments and criticism on an earlier draft of this chapter.

1. For comparable lists of factors, see Eliot A. Cohen, "In DOD We Trust," *The New Republic*, June 17, 1991, 35; James F. Dunnigan and Austin Bay, *From Shield to Storm: High-Tech Weapons, Military Strategy, and Coalition Warfare in the Persian Gulf* (New York: Morrow, 1992), 493; William J. Taylor, Jr., and James Blackwell, "The Ground War in the Gulf," *Survival*, Vol. 33, No. 3 (May/June 1991), 240–243; James O'Bryon, "Gulf Victory Provides No War Blueprint," *Defense News*, March 18, 1991, 27; Jeffrey Record, "Why the Air War Worked," *Armed Forces Journal International*, April 1991, 44–45; Gene I. Rochlin and Chris C. Demchak, "The Gulf War: Technological and Organizational Implications," *Survival*, Vol. 33, No. 3 (May/June 1991), 260–273, at 260.

2. Nathan Rosenberg, *Inside the Black Box: Technology and Economics* (Cambridge: Cambridge University Press, 1982), 143. This definition highlights the main distinction between science, which seeks to explain *why* things work, and technology. A case in point concerns superconductive materials. Scientists produced "high temperature" superconductive devices before knowing why they worked. The prevailing theory of superconductivity was then reworked to account for the new phenomenon. This process of theory readjustment illustrates the divide between technology (understanding *how* to build devices with certain physical effects) and science (understanding *why* these effects occur).

3. For further discussion on the distinction between technology and technics, see Langdon Winner, *Autonomous Technology: Technics-Out-of-Control as a Theme in Political Thought* (Cambridge, Mass.: MIT Press, 1977), 8–12.

4. These three theses are reviewed in Norman J. Vig, "Technology, Philosophy, and the State: An Overview," in Michael E. Kraft and Norman J. Vig, eds., *Technology and Politics* (Durham, N.C.: Duke University Press, 1988), 12–19.

5. See the literature summarized in Donald A. MacKenzie, *Inventing Accuracy: A Historical Sociology of Missile Guidance* (Cambridge, Mass.: MIT Press, 1990), chap. 1. Stephen Rosen's research indicates that technological innovation derives not from bureaucratic interests per se but from "environmental" constraints created by uncertainty. See Stephen Peter Rosen, *Winning the Next War: Innovation and the Modern Military* (Ithaca, N.Y.: Cornell University Press, 1990), 51–52 and chaps. 7–8.

6. Cited in John Bulloch and Harvey Morris, *Saddam's War: The Origins of the Kuwaiti Crisis and the International Response* (London: Faber and Faber, 1991), 11.

7. Statement of January 18, 1991, cited in Efraim Karsh and Inari Rautsi, *Saddam Hussein: A Political Biography* (New York: Free Press, 1991), 248.

8. Washington Post/ABC News poll, as reported in Richard Morin, "Gulf Poll: Most Americans want Hill to Back Bush," *Washington Post,* January 8, 1991, A12.

9. These negotiations are summarized in John K. Cooley, "Pre-war Gulf Diplomacy," *Survival*, Vol. 33, No. 2 (March/April 1991), 132–138.

10. For a summary of Soviet mediation efforts after the air campaign had begun, see International Institute for Strategic Studies (IISS), *Strategic Survey, 1990–1991* (London: Brassey's/IISS, 1991), 75–76.

11. See Bill Sweetman, "F-117A Excels in 'Desert Storm,'" *Jane's Defence Weekly,* January 26, 1991, 104; and Jeffrey M. Lenorovitz, "F-117s Drop Laser-Guided Bombs in Destroying Most Baghdad Targets," *Aviation Week and Space Technology,* February 4, 1991, 30. Although the Pentagon initially claimed that the F-114As accurately struck their targets 90 percent of the time, the Department of Defense later conceded that the true figure was closer to 60 percent. The improvement in accuracy over earlier systems was still substantial, however. During the Vietnam War, U.S. aircraft had to drop about 300 "dumb" bombs to gain a direct hit; the kill rate of the F-117A lowered this figure to two bombs. See Barton Gellman, "Gulf Weapons' Accuracy Downgraded," *Washington Post,* April 10, 1992, A1 and A37.

12. In Iraqi radio communications intercepted by Coalition forces, Iraqi troops referred to the F-117A as "the ghost." See Bruce D. Nordwall, "Electronic Warfare Played a Greater Role in Desert Storm Than in Any Other Conflict." *Aviation Week and Space Technology,* April 22, 1991, 68.

13. The F-16 carried only the navigation pod because there was a shortage of targeting pods. See United States Department of Defense, *Conduct of the Persian Gulf War: Final Report to Congress* (Washington, D.C.: Department of Defense, April 1992), 697.

14. The debate between Arkin and Department of Defense officials (including Major General Buster Glosson, who planned the Coalition's air campaign) is presented in "Defeat of Iraq Sparks Debate on Which Air Role Was Crucial," *Aviation Week and Space Technology,* January 27, 1992, 60–65. Mohamed Heikal in *Illusions of*

Triumph: An Arab View of the Gulf War (London: HarperCollins, 1992), 313, also asserted that communications between Baghdad and the KTO were not severed.

15. The Department of Defense initially maintained that the Tomahawk was "successful" 85 percent of the time, but its criterion for success seems to have simply been that the missile achieve flight after being dispensed from an armored box launcher aboard a surface vessel or from a submarine tube. Subsequent reports indicated that the Tomahawk struck its target little more than 50 percent of the time. See Gellman, "Gulf Weapons' Accuracy Downgraded," A37; and Eric H. Arnett, "Awestruck Press Does Tomahawk PR," *Bulletin of the Atomic Scientists* (April 1991), 7–8. The weapon's inaccuracy may in part result from the fact that the guidance system relies on late 1970s microelectronics, which cannot compensate for differences in lighting and weather. See John A. Adam, "Warfare in the Information Age," *IEEE Spectrum* (September 1991), 30–31.

16. See John D. Morocco, "U.S. Tactics Exploit Advances in Avionics, Air-to-Surface Weapons," *Aviation Week and Space Technology,* February 18, 1991, 52; Nordwall "Electronic Warfare," 68; Richard Hallion, *Storm over Iraq: Air Power and the Gulf War* (Washington, D.C.: Smithsonian, 1992), 172–173.

17. Mark Hewish, Bill Sweetman, and Anthony Robinson, "Precision-Guided Munitions Come of Age," *International Defense Review* (May 1991), 464.

18. Pierre Sprey has contended that the ineffectiveness of Iraq's SAM system was due not so much to damage inflicted by the U.S. Air Force than to the Iraqis' incompetence. He suggested that North Vietnam successfully used coordinated tactics to foil U.S. antiradiation missiles during the Vietnam War. See Pierre M. Sprey, Testimony Before the U.S. House of Representatives, Hearings Before the Committee on Armed Services, *The Impact of the Persian Gulf War and the Decline of the Soviet Union on How the United States Does Its Defense Business,* 102d Cong., 51st sess., 1991, 573. This argument overlooks the fact that the United States had developed highly sophisticated systems to counter air defenses. The U.S. Air Force and Navy greatly improved their electronic jamming capabilities and antiradiation missiles after Vietnam. For a comparison between Vietnam and the Gulf War in this respect, See Hallion, *Storm over Iraq,* 61–62, 172–173.

19. See "Allies Shift Air Attacks to Break Ground Units," *Aviation Week and Space Technology,* January 28, 1991, 21; Morrocco, "U.S. Tactics Exploit Advances in Avionics," 52.

20. "Race to Find Iraq's 'scuds,'" *Jane's Defence Weekly,* January 26, 1991, 103.

21. See Department of Defense, *Conduct of the Persian Gulf War;* R. A. Mason, "The Air War in the Gulf," *Survival,* Vol. 33, No. 3 (May/June 1991), 217.

22. Murray Hammick, "Aerial Views," *International Defense Review* (July 1991), 743.

23. This new information was presented in "Street Stories," CBS television, October 1, 1992; transcript available from network.

245. David Hughes, "Patriot Antimissile Successes Show how Software Upgrades Help Meet New Threats," *Aviation Week and Space Technology,* January 28, 1991, 26–28.

25. Eric Schmitt, "Army Cuts Back Its Estimate on Patriot Missile's Scud Toll," *New York Times,* April 8, 1992, A11.

26. See Theodore A. Postol, "Lessons of the Gulf War Experience with Patriot," *International Security,* Vol. 16, No. 3 (Winter 1991–1992), 139–145.

27. Ibid., 146–147.

28. Ibid., 153–157.

29. This percentage is based on a figure of 4,534 sorties derived from table in Department of Defense, *Conduct of the Persian Gulf War,* 165, and the figure of 27,000 total air-to-ground sorties cited in Hallion, *Storm over Iraq,* 188.

30. Postol, "Lessons of the Gulf War," 134.

31. See the comments of Joseph Shea, professor of engineering at the Massachusetts Institute of Technology and former head of research and development at the Raytheon Corporation (the Patriot's manufacturer), in Bob Davis, "Patriot Missile, High-Tech Hero in Gulf, Comes Under Attack as Less Than Scud's Worst Enemy," *Wall Street Journal,* April 15, 1991, A16; see also Hallion, *Storm over Iraq,* 184.

32. Postol, "Lessons of the Gulf War," 152–157.

33. See Patrick E. Tyler, "Israeli Jets Fly Spy Missions in Iraq, Prompting U.S. Protest," *New York Times,* October 9, 1991, A6; also *Triumph Without Victory: The Unreported History of the Persian Gulf War,* compiled by the staff of U.S. News and World Report (New York: Times Books, 1992), 246–250, 258–259. The IFF problem could have been solved if, as the Israelis requested, the United States had provided Israel with the transponder codes required to identify Israeli aircraft as friendly. U.S. officials refused to turn over these codes, however. See Hallion, *Storm over Iraq,* 180.

34. See Joel Brinkley, "Israel Asks U.S. for Extra $13 Billion," *New York Times,* January 23, 1991, A7; Dilip Hiro, *Desert Shield to Desert Storm: The Second Gulf War* (London: HarperCollins, 1992), 334.

35. Department of Defense, *Conduct of the Persian Gulf War,* 777.

36. See David Hughes, "USAF Firing 100 Mavericks per Day in Current Air-to-Ground Missions," *Aviation Week and Space Technology,* February 11, 1991, 25; Hewish, Sweetman, and Robinson, "Precision-Guided Munitions Come of Age," 459.

37. Hammick, "Aerial Views," 743.

38. See Department of Defense, *Conduct of the Persian Gulf War,* 139; Clifford Beal, Mark Hewish, Bill Sweetman, and Gérard Turbé, "Taking Aim: Airborne Targeting," *International Defense Review* (March 1992), 253.

39. Cited in John A. Morrocco, "Nighttime CAS to Pose Challenge for Air Units Once Ground War Begins," *Aviation Week and Space Technology,* February 11, 1991, 20.

40. Hughes, "USAF Firing 100 Mavericks per day," 25.

41. Though not discussed here, the U.S. Navy carrier-based aircraft and Royal Air Force Tornados also carried FLIR targeting and navigation equipment. Information on these systems is presented in Brian Wanstall, "Targeting Pods Open the Night Window," *International Defense Review* (May 1991), 483.

42. The B-52 was more successful in destroying fuel and ammunition depots and in demoralizing Iraqi troops in the field. See Hallion, *Storm over Iraq,* 154, 218.

43. Ibid., 180; David A. Fulghum, "Allies Divide Air Strike Targets into Grid of 'Killing Boxes,'" *Aviation Week and Space Technology,* February 18, 1991, 62.

44. Eric Schmitt with Michael R. Gordon, "Unforeseen Problems in Air War Forced Allies to Improvise Tactics," *New York Times*, March 10, 1991, 16.

45. "Strategic Campaign Focused on Targets and Cut Casualties, Pentagon Maintains," *Aviation Week and Space Technology,* January 27, 1992, 65.

46. IISS, *Military Balance, 1980–1981* (London: IISS, 1980), 42.

47. IISS, *Military Balance, 1985–1986* (London: IISS, 1985), 76; "Iraq's Formidable Array of Guns," *Jane's Defence Weekly,* February 2, 1991, 136.

48. Christopher F. Foss, "Piercing the Fog of War," *Jane's Defence Weekly,* June 29, 1991, 1185.

49. See Defense Intelligence Agency estimate in Department of Defense, *Conduct of the Persian Gulf War*, 254; and IISS, *Strategic Survey, 1990–1991* (London: Brassey's/IISS, 1991), 65–68.

50. See Department of Defense, *Conduct of the Persian Gulf War*, 254.

51. The figure of 350,000 appears in Lawrence Freedman and Efraim Karsh, "How Kuwait Was Won: Strategy in the Gulf War," *International Security,* Vol. 16, No. 3 (Fall 1991), p. 13, citing Christopher Bellamy, "Arithmetic of Death in the Wake of the Gulf Conflict," *Independent* (London), March 21, 1991. The derivation of the 200,000 figure from a base force of 300,000 to 370,000 troops is explicated in *Triumph Without Victory,* 404–406.

52. Colonel Robert H. Scales, Jr., "Accuracy Defeated Range in Artillery Duel," *International Defense Review* (May 1991), 473, 477.

53. One MLRS rocket contains 644 submunitions. Specially modified 203mm and 155mm projectiles fired from conventional artillery guns dispense, respectively, 180 and 88 of these bomblets. See ibid., 477.

54. See Hallion, *Storm over Iraq*, 299.

55. Beal et al., "Taking Aim," 253.

56. See Department of Defense, *Conduct of the Persian Gulf War*, 360.

57. Ibid; Edward H. Kolcum, "Joint-STARS E-8s Return to U.S.; 20-Aircraft Fleet Believed Assured," *Aviation Week and Space Technology,* March 11, 1991, 20.

58. See "Success from the Air," *Jane's Defence Weekly,* April 6, 1991, 531.

59. See John A. Adam, "Warfare in the Information Age," *IEEE Spectrum*, Vol. 28, No. 9 (September 1991), 32.

60. See David Hughes, "Electronic Systems Div. Accelerates New Systems Deployments, Upgrades," *Aviation Week and Space Technology,* February 4, 1991, 58.

61. The following discussion owes much to a conversation with General Bernard Trainor of the John F. Kennedy School of Government, Harvard University.

62. A description of this plan can be found in Department of Defense, *Conduct of the Persian Gulf War*, 243–245.

63. Michael R. Gordon, "G.I.'s Recall Destruction of Powerful Iraqi Force," *New York Times*, April 8, 1991, A6. Recounting a clash between elements of the U.S. 1st Armored Brigade and the Republican Guard's Medina Division, one study noted that "after the battle, the Americans judged the maximum range of the T-72s to be 1,800 meters. The M1A1s were getting hits at nearly twice that distance. The M1A1 thermal sights picked up Iraqi tanks at 4,000 meters, well beyond visual range in the damp and fog." *Triumph Without Victory,* 384.

64. Foss, "Piercing the Fog of War," 1183.

65. John G. Roos and Benjamin F. Schemmer, "Desert Storm Bares 'Roundout' Flaw But Validates Army Modernization Goals," *Armed Forces Journal International* (April 1991), 35; Dunnigan and Bay, *From Shield to Storm*, 207.

66. Department of Defense, *Conduct of the Persian Gulf War*, 807. GPS satellites are equipped with a feature called "selective availability." When selective availability is switched on, GPS satellites send erroneous signals that degrade the accuracy of commercially available GPS receivers. Only specially designed military receivers can decode the signals to obtain the most accurate navigational readings. Because the Department of Defense had yet to purchase military receivers in sufficient numbers at the same time of the ground campaign, however, Coalition forces had to rely almost entirely on commercially available receivers, and thus they did not activate selective availability for the duration of the war.

67. Weather data as reported in Department of Defense, *Conduct of the Persian Gulf War*, 169; Hallion, *Storm Over Iraq*, 176–177.

68. See Morrocco, "U.S. Tactics Exploit Advances in Avionics," 52.

69. Scales, "Accuracy Defeated Range in Artillery Duel," 473.

70. See M. E. Barnard, "The Global Positioning System," *IEE Review*, Vol. 38, No. 3 (March 1992), 99–102, at 101.

71. See Department of Defense, *Conduct of the Persian Gulf War*, 73.

72. These more narrow concerns contrast with the realm of "grand strategy" or "national interest," which describes the long-term goals that underlie a nation's battlefield objectives. A discussion at this broader level of analysis would focus on such issues as why the United States considers the Middle East or the Gulf to be of vital interest and why U.S. leaders believed that the invasion of Kuwait, under the international conditions prevailing at the time, merited a response in the first place. For informed speculation on these broader questions, consult Robert W. Tucker and David C. Hendrickson, *The Imperial Temptation: The New World Order and America's Purpose* (New York: Council on Foreign Relations, 1992), 80–141.

73. What the UN inspectors have found at Iraq's nuclear facilities is detailed in David Albright and Mark Hibbs, "Iraq's Bomb: Blueprints and Artifacts," Bulletin of the Atomic Scientists (January/February 1992), 30–40.

74. See *Triumph Without Victory*, 406; Hiro, *Desert Shield to Desert Storm*, 401.

75. Hiro, *Desert Shield to Desert Storm*, 371, 397.

76. See Heikal, *Illusions of Triumph*, 313.

77. One episode took place on January 22, when a convoy of 71 Iraqi vehicles moved toward Kuwait; 58 of them were destroyed by coalition air strikes called in by JSTARS. See Hallion, *Storm Over Iraq*, 220–221.

78. See Department of Defense, *Conduct of the Persian Gulf War*, 262.

79. It has been reported, however, that on the last day of the war, two Coalition F-111F bombers armed with specially designed LGBs attacked a bunker outside Baghdad where Saddam was suspected to reside. See *Triumph Without Victory*, 3–6; Department of Defense, *Conduct of the Persian Gulf War*, 165–166; and John Morrocco and David Fulghum, "USAF Developed 4,700-lb. Bomb in Crash Program to Attack Iraqi Military Leaders in Hardened Bunkers," *Aviation Week and Space Technology*, May 6, 1991, 67.

80. Iran's foreign aspirations are detailed in Youssef M. Ibrahim, "Rebounding Iranians Are Striving for Regional Leadership in Gulf," *New York Times*, November 7, 1992, 1.

81. Carl von Clausewitz, *On War*, Michael Howard and Peter Paret, eds. and trans. (Princeton: Princeton University Press, 1976), 379, 119.

7

Classical Campaign in a Difficult Environment: Remarks and Questions Regarding the 1991 Gulf War

Gustav Däniker

"Cannae" as a Model

Dick Cheney, the U.S. Secretary of Defense, General Colin Powell, Chairman of the Joint Chiefs of Staff, General Norman Schwarzkopf, Supreme Commander of Centcom and the Coalition agreed: Unlike the Vietnam combat, this war was to be conducted rapidly and was to end with a clear decision. A strategy of extensive attrition of enemy forces was out of the question, but all of the above held to the theory of war which professed that physical annihilation of the enemy is the aim of all military operations. Hence, Schwarzkopf referred repeatedly to Hannibal's legendary victory at Cannae, during which fifty thousand encircled Romans perished.

Accordingly, the combat concept characterized in short but clear terms as "cut off and kill" by General Powell was strictly implemented in operation Desert Storm. Indeed, the Coalition forces won the operational freedom of action on the first day of aerial warfare and never abandoned it, not even during the forceful tactical reconnaissance drive staged by several Iraqi brigades in the battle at Khafji on January 23, 1991. In the Coalition's operations, the rebirth of an operational philosophy observed in the actions of the U.S. armed forces during the 1980s and 1990s, the mechanics of their "Air-Land Battle 2000," and the increased flexibility of all formations proved their worth.

General Schwarzkopf in particular was unswerving in his adherence to the detailed operation plan for land warfare worked out in the fall of

1990: to contain the enemy at the front (that is, in the south) and to apply the psychologically effective measure of employing the Saudi and pan-Arabic forces side by side with units of the U.S. Marines. Furthermore, Schwarzkopf used a feigned landing operation near Kuwait City to keep important Iraqi forces at the Gulf coast of Kuwait while Coalition forces, with a powerful double flanking attack striding far to the west and supported by extensive airborne operations in the north surrounded and destroyed the occupation forces in Kuwait. In addition to a "smaller pincer movement" in Kuwait, Coalition forces took part in a "big encirclement" across Iraqi territory, which reached the Euphrates and as far northeast as Basra.

The performance of U.S., British, and French soldiers in the strategic operations demonstrated the height of military professionalism. Furthermore, the conduct and implementation of the operations displayed a totally new dimension that combined a hitherto unknown intensity of firepower with astonishing mobility and precision. The rapid large-scale movement of armored forces, the integrated cooperation of naval and air power, including airborne units and ground forces, and excellent logistics formed an offensive unity hardly ever achieved in the past.

Dunkirk as a Result

As in 1940, the "sickle cut of a left-hander"[1] led to quick success. On that occasion, the armored forces of the German Third Reich advanced through the Ardennes, where the French did not expect them, and subsequently encircled the British expeditionary corps on the Atlantic coast near Dunkirk. Similarly, the logistic accomplishment of the brilliant, more recent operation Desert Storm was realized by a huge force of armored troops supported by airborne formations pushing forward in a "leapfrog" manner.

The Desert Storm performance would have been impossible without the preceding air offensive and without the Coalition having had complete air superiority over Kuwait and Iraq. Only the latter allowed the flanking movement to proceed practically unnoticed and with almost no enemy contact. Because of its air superiority, the Coalition could move logistics and supplies by air and take the risk of also transporting by air—practically on their own and by helicopter—light mechanized forces, such as the French "Daguet" division and the air assault formations of the 101st and 82nd U.S. Divisions, to the front.

The combat zone, called "the area" in military terms, though underestimated for Desert Storm by many analysts, was assessed correctly and fully utilized by the U.S. military leaders from the beginning. Not coincidentally, one of General Schwarzkopf's models was the operation of Field

Marshal Montgomery against the Germans under Field Marshal Rommel at El Alamein. Like Montgomery's troops, Schwarzkopf's convincingly outflanked the enemy through the desert—unexpectedly and across a tremendous distance.

Favoring the allied forces was the combat-related and overall psychological weakness of the enemy. Even soldiers more hardened to stubborn endurance than the Iraqis could barely have withstood the weeks of incessant barrage by air and artillery bombardments while they remained unable to defend themselves effectively and fought under ever worsening logistical conditions.

Confronted with the unstoppable failing of their main weapons, even officers of the Republican Guards realized soon enough that an organized and coordinated resistance had become unthinkable—all the more so, because the Iraqis knew virtually nothing about the allied plans of attack but had experienced their opponents' technical superiority in practically all spheres of combat. When troops are without water and food for days, when the sand, which originally served as protection and camouflage material, increasingly turns into an enemy infringing on all functions of defense systems and matériel and even limiting tactical movements and appropriate medical services, morale collapses.

But with the benefit of hindsight, one can argue that the allied military command perhaps deliberately disregarded these developments and overrated Iraqi combat power to the very end. Likewise, it considerably overestimated the strength of enemy troops in the Kuwait Theater of Operations (KTO). Two hundred fifty thousand troops, 150,000 of which were on Kuwait territory, seems closer to the truth than the 540,000 men repeatedly mentioned by allied military sources.

Overkill?

The obvious lack of continuous evaluation of these decisive factors appears to have led the allies to a kind of "operational overkill." Despite growing indications to the contrary, the enemy concept nurtured by Saddam Hussein through the media ("fourth-strongest army in the world," tough defenses, deployment of guard elite divisions) seems to have been believed by many of the allied commanders. Indeed, this concept of the enemy apparently was never subjected to critical, objective scrutiny.

Accordingly, the allies suppressed political impatience in favor of an assumed military time requirement. The time factor was dealt with cautiously until the very end of the campaign. For example, the allied command postponed the beginning of ground operations (in order to continue strategic bombing and increase damages) even though both new incoming information on the enemy's weakness and Saddam's threat to apply the strategy of "scorched earth" during his withdrawal would have suggested quick action or at least an acceleration of operations.

Thus, the Coalition's obvious fixation on annihilation and rigid operational planning appears to have brought about strategic negligence - a flaw that was not corrected by the rather early cease-fire arranged for political and humanitarian reasons as well as in consideration of other (Arab) allies. The controversial comments by Schwarzkopf, on the one hand, and those of Bush and Cheney, on the other (on March 26 and 27, 1991), show the clash of two principles as was seen in Dunkirk when the Germans let major parts of the British Expeditionary Corps escape. Undoubtedly, a considerable number of Iraqi Guard tank units that later became crucial to the suppression of the Shi'ites and Kurds escaped from the Basra area. Despite later démentis (retractions), General Schwarzkopf clearly revealed that he was aiming at a classical battle of annihilation, a "Cannae," and was looking for complete success (total victory). Obviously, such a strategic escape would not have been a justifiable part of his plan.

But the campaign turned into a "Dunkirk" not solely because of President Bush's cease-fire order. Schwarzkopf's campaign did not fully attain its goal: It neither prevented Iraqi troops from escaping across the Euphrates nor rendered the remaining escape routes totally impassable.

Neglect of Enemy Psyche and Environment?

It would be inappropriate to utter narrow-minded criticism of a brilliant strategy and operation like Desert Storm. Many problems will come to light and lessons will be learned. But we should be allowed to measure the "ordinary military victory" (Field Marshal von Schlieffen of the imperial German army) that was won against the overall grand strategic concept. The U.S. forces and their allies, supported by the UN, set out not only to liberate an invaded country but also to punish a dictator—within the premises of a new world order—who violated international law, jeopardized regional stability, and set out to dominate Gulf oil resources. This plan should have led to the establishment of additional criteria for success as well as new solutions to problems in the military dimension of that grand strategic objective.

One problem area concerns psychological warfare. Was the maximum really achieved? Was it sufficient to use the traditional techniques of loudspeakers and leaflets, which resulted in a few thousand deserters and prisoners, and otherwise to follow the standing plan of encirclement and annihilation termed "cut off and kill," which eventually led to some thirty thousand casualties among the enemy? Was it not necessary to think beyond the immediate tactical success to the future deployment of remaining Iraqi units?

The apparent absence of such questioning seems to be a function of the methods applied. In the endlessly discussed battle damage assessment (BDA), the important qualitative-psychological component remained largely unconsidered. The prime goal was to minimize allied losses, and therefore quantitative, mathematical calculations were preferred to in-depth, all-encompassing considerations of the relevant strategic factors including the socio-psychological, socio-cultural, and socio-political.

Were Centcom and the Coalition staff not aware, despite the American advanced satellite and air reconnaissance capabilities, that a significant part of the alleged Iraqi defense potential as touted by Iraqi propaganda was pure exaggeration? Did they not know that despite Iraq's impressive field fortifications, a "Saddam wall" never existed? Indeed, this situation can be compared to Adolf Hitler's "Alpenfestung"—a German mountain fortress that also never existed but caused tremendous strategic preparations on the part of the allies in 1943–1944. And did it really escape the Coalition staff's attention that the Iraqi soldier as a determined fighter able to employ his weapons and equipment had long ago ceased to exist?

If the Coalition command was truly unaware of these facts, then what caused the failure of the intelligence services and special forces that had been smuggled into Iraq behind enemy lines for extended special reconnaissance and destruction missions? Can understated and therefore wrong information be excused if deliberate caution is the purpose? If, however, these facts were known, why were the ground operations not adapted and started earlier? Why did the Coalition wait for the end of the initial deployment, planned for mid-February, instead of proceeding much more expeditiously and thus saving time and human lives?

Lack of Operational Flexibility?

Certainly, there were reasons why the combat plan for operation Desert Storm, created in the fall of 1990, did not sufficiently consider these additional criteria and their possible development and alteration. Yet, even when the modification and actual significance of these parameters became increasingly obvious, nobody was willing to adopt or consider them. Any power that commits two airborne divisions and additional highly mobile formations to combat without retaining reserves for unexpected special needs, and that is therefore unable to react to sudden changes, must question its degree of operational flexibility.

Given the Coalition's long-term grand strategic objective of liberating Kuwait, other issues might also be raised. After a number of Iraqi formations had left the KTO rather hastily during the first phase of the air war, the Coalition, even as late as mid-February, could have adapted its conduct of operations to include considerations of psychological dimensions. Perhaps suitable bridges would have suggested themselves as routes of retreat for those Iraqi soldiers that remained and they could then have withdrawn unarmed along these "one-way streets," leaving all of their military equipment behind. It can also be assumed that with simultaneous pressure from the south, the self-disintegration of the Iraqi occupation forces in Kuwait would have begun sooner: Maybe in this or in a comparable fashion Kuwait could have been liberated much faster or at least without suffering such large-scale destruction and the taking of hostages. Also, perhaps the Iraqi army could have been separated more easily from its political and military leaders, and the large numbers of returning soldiers, bombed, beaten, and unarmed, could have brought about unpleasant domestic problems for Saddam Hussein, thereby undermining his leadership and precipitating change. Instead, today he unscrupulously uses the parts of his army unfit for battle duty against his domestic opponents.

A strategic review of the other Mideast wars since 1945 reveals that such propositions do not prove a "know-it-all attitude" by the author. Rather, the review demonstrates that a shock-type clash of excessive propaganda with the brutal and bitter reality of war—i.e., effective psychological warfare—often leads to the quick collapse of morale among highly armed military forces. Such a turning point could have been expected early in the 1991 Gulf War and was at least as predictable as the assumed number of destroyed tanks.

Was it not the duty of the supreme Coalition command to recognize a second (psychological, political) area of problems and take appropriate preventive action? After studying the Iraqi dictator's personality, the command could easily have foreseen that Saddam would put into effect his grim threats of terrorism and crimes against the environment. Indeed, on the eleventh day of Desert Storm (January 29, 1991), he began to use oil as an ecological weapon and to pollute the Gulf on a large scale; and with the beginning of Coalition ground operations, he set Kuwaiti oil installations on fire at a rate of seventy to one hundred a day. News of lootings, the taking of hostages, and torture in Kuwait abounded.

Could not the advance of the ground forces have been accelerated once the Coalition made more progress than expected and the extent of the catastrophe was finally recognized? Should not air-mobile reserves have been employed much earlier to forestall the atrocities and environmental destruction? But it seems that these crimes of a vindictive man were considered less important by the allies than the anticipated and feared counterblows by chemical or other means of mass destruction. As discussed, from the beginning it had been the Coalition command's interest to seize and keep the initiative; hence, it subsequently neglected flexible countermoves of an overall strategic nature.

Indispensability of an Overall Strategy

It seems today that even so brilliant a military victory against a totalitarian enemy as achieved by Desert Storm is simply not good enough. Not only the politician's responsibility, but also that of the soldier, goes beyond military victory. Although the performance of the U.S. military in the Gulf was outstanding, Washington overemphasized the military side at the same time that Saddam, prepared to commit the worst crimes even against his own people and the "Arab nation," was aiming at a strategy of "maximum damage"—a strategy that could not be countered by the classical art of warfare alone.

In the future, punitive operations of a world power, sanctioned by the UN, will have to be of a particularly careful nature. Even if not every future conflict takes place in such a sensitive ecological environment as was the case with the oil fields in the Gulf, many other natural and artificial sources of danger will require the "protection of life fundamentals" as a principal factor in operations planning. If such protection of life fundamentals is not taken into account, the military authorities in charge may easily punish themselves and interfere with their long-term objectives by creating an even worse evil than the one they just eliminated. And the call for warfare that costs "as few human lives as possible" and that also tries to minimize enemy losses is neither bold cynical propaganda nor humanitarian wishful thinking. Instead, it may permit a durable peace following the bloody combat by diminishing hate and thirst for revenge on the part of the defeated party.

The "Cannae principle," which has been raised to a doctrine since the times of German Field Marshal von Schlieffen and which is still taught at some military schools, must no longer be an absolute maxim for modern armed forces. Those who still think today in carefully separated phases—that is, diplomacy, destruction of a hostile army, armistice, and subsequent reconstruction—do not acknowledge the complexity of today's security problems, which are multifaceted and interconnected in unprecedented degrees.

Today's militaries must develop overall strategies aimed at a correct assessment of all security parameters and their integration into a long-term strategic view. It is hard to understand why, at the threshold of the third millennium, thousands still have to lose their lives when efforts are made to keep a paranoid criminal and his followers from abusing their power. In future instances in which a leader, population, and armed forces are equally fanatical, the planned, systematic destruction of the hostile military should be avoided. More specific and subtle strategies and means will have to be developed to discipline such regional despots and their followers.

If members of (conservative) military circles find this idea too revolutionary, they should consult works expressing the thoughts of General André Beaufre. There they will find the eternal truth that wars are nothing but the dialectical conflict between two wills, and that methods and weapons have to be adapted to the prevailing situation. And even Carl von Clausewitz,[2] at the beginning of the nineteenth century, wrote: "The armed forces [of the enemy] have to be annihilated so that they no longer can go on fighting. Let us make it clear that whenever we use the expression 'annihilation,' we mean just this and nothing but this." According to von Clausewitz, the purpose is to force the enemy to yield. He was not arguing for the renunciation of additional measures known to us from Chinese experts of war (such as Sun Tzu); indeed, only his epigones raised the battle of annihilation to a dogma.

Under a most able U.S. command, the Coalition won an outstanding victory in Desert Storm. In an almost perfect performance of military technology, the forces executed President Bush's order to liberate Kuwait quickly and to crush the Iraqi military power. That they did not take into account the implications of that task, and therefore were not successful in preventing psychological, socio-political, physical, and ecological long-term damage, seems to be the consequence of following a traditional philosophy of war. History will judge whether the Coalition's success was an adequate prerequisite for pacification or whether it was just another of those purely military victories that achieve only partial results.

Notes

This chapter was edited by Wolfgang Danspeckgruber with the assistance of Marianne Donath.

1. This is an expression common among European strategists. Holborn, Hajo, *Makers of Modern Strategy,* Princeton University Press, 1971, p. 202.

2. Carl von Clausewitz, *On War,* Princeton University Press 1976, p. 90–91, edited and translated by Michael Howard and Peter Paret.

Further Readings

Beaufre, André, *Dissuasion at Stratégie*, Paris: Armand Colin, 1964.

Clausewitz, Carl von, *Vom Kriege*, 16th edition, Bonn: Ferd. Dümmlers Verlag, 1952.

Freedman, Lawrence, and Efraim Karsh, *The Gulf Conflict 1990–1991: Diplomacy and War in the New World Order*, London-Boston: Faber and Faber, 1993.

Däniker, Gustav, *Wende Golfkrieg: Von Wesen und Gebrauch künftiger Streitkräfte*, Frauenfeld, Switzerland: Verlag Huber, 1992.

Meier-Welcker, Hans, and Graf Alfred von Schlieffen, in *Klassiker der Kriegskunst*, Werner Hahlweg, Darmstadt: Wehr und Wissen Verlagsgesellschaft, 1960.

Schwarzkopf, H. Norman, *It Doesn't Take a Hero*, New York: Bantam Books, 1992.

SSUN-DS'. "Traktat über Kriegskunst," Berlin: Ministerium für Nationale Verteidigung, 1957.

U.S.News & World Report. "Triumph Without Victory: The Unreported History of the Persian Gulf War." New York: Times Books, 1992.

Woodward, Bob, *The Commanders*, New York: Simon & Schuster, 1991.

8

The Second Gulf War
and Transfers of Conventional Arms

Christian Catrina

In the 1980s, Iraq was one of the largest arms recipients in the world. It imported large fleets of main battle tanks, armored personnel carriers, howitzers, combat aircraft, helicopters, and missiles (see Appendix). The main suppliers to Iraq were the Soviet Union (furnishing about 300 combat aircraft and more than 2,300 main battle tanks), France (furnishing more than 110 Mirage combat aircraft and close to 100 helicopters), China (furnishing 1,300 main battle tanks), Brazil (furnishing close to 2,000 armored cars) as well as Great Britain and the United States. Some of these supplies were consumed by the war with Iran, but still Iraq emerged from the 1980s with a formidable military machine, with a large inventory of fairly modern weapon systems, and with battle-experienced (though not necessarily battle-proven) military forces.

Iraq had practically no defense production capabilities for conventional arms, however.[1] The 1991 Gulf War, which caused Iraq first an embargo and then an attack from a coalition of forces including three of its five major arms suppliers (the United States, France, and Great Britain), occupies a particular place in the study of arms transfers, their impact on regional stability, and the dependencies associated with them.

For several reasons, the Gulf War was an atypical case, at least compared to wars of the past. First, the Iraqi invasion of Kuwait was a particularly blatant breach of international law: A small sovereign state, a member of the United Nations and recognized by all (including Iraq), was attacked with the openly stated objective of annexation. A more ambiguous case might have resulted in more states avoiding to take sides.

Second, Iraq's aggression confirmed an uneasiness that existed in many countries about its future plans. It had emerged from the war with Iran without political and territorial gains and saddled with a large debt, but it had retained large and relatively capable armed forces. It was therefore regarded as a revisionist power that might bring about the overthrow of other governments in the region.

Third, the Soviet Union, as the major arms supplier to Iraq, was in a weakened condition. Its politico-military position in Central and Eastern Europe had collapsed, and it was for all practical purposes suing for peace to terminate the Cold War. Thus, Iraq could no longer expect the "customary" diplomatic protection from its main arms supplier.

For these reasons, the United Nations was in a much better position than in the past to perform effectively the role laid down in its charter—that is, to take decisive action against a breach of international peace. For the first time since the Korean War, the UN provided a legitimatizing cover for military action against an aggressor.

Kuwait, with one of the largest oil deposits in the world, is economically important for Western oil-importing countries. These countries might have had the choice of buying from Iraq in the future, but Iraq's occupation of Kuwait was seen as a move to destabilize the whole oil-producing region.

In short, the Iraqi invasion of Kuwait seems to have been based on a misperception of the global political situation, and thus of the likely reaction by the West, the United Nations, and the Soviet Union. The Gulf War occurred at an intersection of two major currents in world affairs: the continuation of the frequent use of military force (and the perceived legitimacy of such use) in the Third World, and the winding down of the East-West conflict, which allowed a more forceful intervention than had hitherto been conceivable.

In this situation, the old truths were no longer valid. The Soviet Union in particular, which had in the past backed its major arms recipients politically, had revised its priorities—perhaps unnoticed by Saddam Hussein. The visit to Iraq of Yevgeny M. Primakov, as Soviet presidential envoy on a mediating mission, the visits of Soviet generals to Baghdad, and the long delay in the withdrawal of Soviet military technicians and advisers could have been read as signals of Soviet hesitation.[2] But in the end the Soviet Union decided to politically support the anti-Iraq Coalition. Its decision may have been a close one, but once made it was undisputed, and it turned out the wrong way for Iraq.

At this point, some Iraqi hopes may have rested with China. During the 1980s, that country had supplied large numbers of arms to Iraq, but it had simultaneously also supplied them to Iran, indicating that its arms exports were motivated by economics only. China might have been willing to invest limited foreign-policy capital to prevent a military response sanctioned by the United Nations, but it was not willing to be the only power in the UN Security Council to veto the relevant resolutions. If the Soviet Union had been on the same side, the outcome may have been different.

France, another major arms supplier to Iraq and a permanent member of the UN Security Council, was the third-best hope for Iraq. Its arms supplies were regarded (by Iraq, as there was a close cultural relationship) as carrying relatively little political commitment, compared to those from the Soviet Union or China (or, for that matter, the United States). For France, the choice between solidarity with its European and Western partners and an important arms customer was fairly clear-cut, although France did make efforts to prevent armed conflict through last-ditch diplomatic action up to the deadline of January 15, 1991.

The United States and the United Kingdom were the major powers pushing for the use of force, if necessary, to evict Iraqi troops from Kuwait. These countries had provided almost no weapons to Iraq but were major suppliers to Kuwait and Saudi Arabia (as was France).[3] If they had acquiesced in the overthrow of the Kuwaiti leadership, their compliance could have been perceived as paving the way for the eventual removal of moderate leaders in other Gulf countries, in particular Saudi Arabia. In view of the economic importance of this area, their acquiescence was not a possibility.

The five permanent members of the UN Security Council accounted for close to 90 percent of all arms exports.[4] Other important suppliers to Iraq—Brazil, Egypt, and Czechoslovakia—were for different reasons not able or willing to take Iraq's side, particularly not if that action would imply defying the United States and the Soviet Union. Brazilian arms exports were generally considered to be motivated by economic goals; Egypt had a vested interest in preventing the overthrow of moderate governments in Arab countries; and Czechoslovakia, after its peaceful revolution, had no desire to support a client of the former regime, especially not if such support would involve negative consequences for its relations with Western countries.

Thus, Iraq was not only not supported by its arms suppliers, but for all practical purposes it was also cut off from supplies of spare parts.[5]

Paradoxes

Arms transfers and the Gulf conflict are linked in several seemingly paradoxical ways. These are discussed in this section.

Statements by governments and statements reported in the media suggest that the Gulf War showed how arms transfers had enhanced the military capabilities of Iraq. Yet the military campaign turned out to be one-sided, indicating a significant difference between Iraq and the main Coalition countries in the possession and operation of military technology. The Iraqi air force did not put up a strong fight; moreover, Iraq lacked effective means for acquiring tactical intelligence, which had a major impact on the development of hostilities. These facts would indicate that arms transfers have less of an equalizing impact on military power than is often assumed. It has to be taken into account, however, that the Coalition forces included the main and most technologically advanced military powers. Thus, the case does not lend itself to a final conclusion that rests on a valid comparison.

Transfers of advanced weapon systems to developing countries lacking a technological and industrial infrastructure are generally considered to foster dependence. Yet the Iraqi leadership was not deterred from taking an action that—as subsequent events showed—was opposed by all significant suppliers of arms to Iraq. This paradox indicates either the limits of dependence or the fact that miscalculation can obviate the inhibiting effect of recipients' dependence on their suppliers. In the case of Iraq, neither dependence nor the political support assumed to be implicit in arms transfers stood the test. However, because of the particular circumstances of the Soviet Union at the time and the irrational character of the open aggression, it is difficult to draw generally applicable conclusions.

In another paradox, although a large coalition fought against the Iraqi invasion of Kuwait on the principle of international law, there is today greater readiness than ever to restrain or limit arms transfers in a discriminatory way—which would appear to be at variance with the spirit of international law. In addition, Iraq's defeat is different from endings of other wars; that Iraq has been found to be in violation of the Treaty on Nonproliferation of Nuclear Weapons (NPT) has added legitimacy to the international treatment of postwar Iraq.

Many commentators and politicians have said that the Kuwait War demonstrated the political and military pitfalls of arms transfers to Third World countries. Yet, an upsurge of arms transfers to the Gulf region occurred in the aftermath of the war. The assessment of the effect and utility of arms transfers is by necessity subjective and depends largely on the presumed intentions of the recipients. Nevertheless, voices have warned that the Western countries are about to commit the same mistake now for the third time—after having armed the shah of Iran as a seemingly stable pro-Western regional power in the 1960s and 1970s and Iraq as a bulwark against Islamic fundamentalism during succeeding years.

Impact on Future Conventional Arms Transfers

In the aftermath of the Kuwait War, arms transfers to the Middle East increased, even though the direct military threat to the moderate Arab states and Israel was likely to diminish with the full implementation of the UN Security Council resolutions concerning the reduction of Iraq's war-making capabilities. Having fought alongside the United States on a common front against a common adversary, countries such as Saudi Arabia and Egypt should now meet less resistance from the United States to their requests for arms than they sometimes met in the past.

In late 1990, the United States wrote off $7 billion of military debts that Egypt had accumulated. U.S. arms transfers to the Middle East, most of them still in the pipeline, submitted to Congress between the outbreak of the Gulf war on August 2, 1990, and the end of 1991, comprise conventional arms valued at close to $20 billion (see table in Appendix). On March 11, 1992, the U.S. government announced an additional transfer to Kuwait of six Hawk batteries and six Patriot batteries with 450 missiles, thus increasing its arms sales to the Middle East to about $8.5 billion since the announcement of a Middle East arms control initiative by President George Bush on May 29, 1991.[6] Even though European suppliers have so far not announced similar transfers, they can be expected to aggressively seek arms orders.[7] The currently negotiated or envisaged transfers to the Middle East are due less to military requirements than to circumstances created by the Gulf conflict. The arsenals being accumulated in the Middle East may be unnecessarily large and costly if there is no major military threat—or they may serve as mere trip-wire forces to trigger a U.S. engagement in case of war—and they may be too small for the defense of some countries against a major threat.

Several considerations may combine to reduce the attraction of Russian weapon systems to Third World countries. Russian arms, employed by the Iraqi armed forces, did not perform well against the Coalition forces. A partial explanation may be, as Russian military analysts have been quick to point out, the suboptimal tactics and deficiencies of the Iraqi weapons operators. However, the lasting impression will most likely be that Russian weapons were on the losing side and U.S. (and, to a lesser degree, West European) weapons were on the winning side. By not participating militarily in the Coalition's campaign, Russia missed an opportunity to correct this impression. In addition, the impression has long existed that the West has an edge over Russia in most areas of advanced military technology. In another arena, although Iraq was a major recipient of Soviet arms, and arms transfers are often assumed to indicate a relationship of political support, the Soviet Union sided politically (though not

militarily) with the Coalition. Iraq's unprovoked invasion of Kuwait constituted such a blatant breach of international law that the wider objectives of official Soviet foreign policy ruled out even a tacit acceptance of
this act. The Soviet Union sought to limit damage by publicly declining to
provide the United States with confidential information on Soviet-sup-
plied Iraqi weapon systems. However, Russian arms transfers may in the
future no longer be viewed to indicate Russian political support. This may
depend on the outcome of the current political evolution in Russia.

A reduction in the demand for its arms would present Russia with
economic difficulties but also with political opportunities. On the positive
side, Russia can make a virtue of necessity and present any reduction in
its arms exports as a conscious decision to exercise restraint in the interest
of peaceful settlements of regional conflicts. Such a reduction would also
tie in well with Russia's support for the UN's establishment of an international register of arms transfers. It could be presented as the logical extension of a policy of military (and, to some extent, political) disengagement
from regional conflicts in the Third World. Moreover, Russian arms
exports have been criticized within Russia on the grounds that numerous
recipients have in the past failed to pay their arms-related debts and that
subsidized arms exports are a waste of resources that Russia cannot
afford in its present situation.

On the negative side, a reduction in demand for its arms would
weaken Russia in one of the few areas of foreign trade in which it has
been competitive. In view of its desperate economic situation, such a
reduction could not come at a worse time. Having withdrawn about
77,000 major weapons systems from the European to the Asian theater to
prevent their being scrapped under the terms of the CFE Treaty, Russia
has at its disposal large quantities of arms that could, in theory, be sold to
foreign buyers. As a consequence of the CFE Treaty and of political decisions to allocate more resources to the civilian sector, the Russian military-industrial complex faces stronger economic pressures for exports
than ever. Conversion of the defense industry as a theoretical way to
reduce such pressures has so far not been effective and is still facing resistance by managers and the workforce.

One of the early military lessons of the Gulf War was that Western
high-technology weapon systems performed well. The repeatedly televised precision attacks on bridges, ammunition depots, and other military targets suggest that advanced technology not only provides clear
superiority to the side that possesses it and is able to use it but may also
help to reduce civilian casualties and collateral damage. This conclusion
contradicts the opinion that military technology has reached the point of
diminishing returns, and those countries with sufficient political clout or

economic resources might therefore place even more emphasis on the acquisition of the most advanced weapons systems. Some questions have arisen, however, concerning the apparently not so brilliant performances of the Patriot air-defense system in an Anti-tactical Ballistic Missile (ATBM) role and of the "smart bombs."[8]

Initiatives for the Monitoring and Control of Conventional Arms Transfers

After the end of the 1991 Gulf War, the governments of several major Western countries came forward with initiatives for improved monitoring or control of arms transfers. In February 1991, Canada proposed a global summit of heads of state to be held under UN auspices to discuss the reduction of arms transfers to regions of tension and conflict. Canada also proposed a conference of representatives of the main arms-supplying countries to establish an information network on arms sales. In March 1991, Italy proposed an international conference on arms sales. Prime Minister Giulio Andreotti, who made this proposal at the UN, stated that arms transfers need to be limited; otherwise they will run counter to the establishment of a new world order. In April, British Prime Minister John Major expressed support for establishing a UN register of arms sales. (The Soviet Union had already supported this idea in August 1990 in a letter by Foreign Minister Eduard Shevardnadze to the UN Secretary General.) In June, France presented a plan for arms control and disarmament that called for global supplier restraint. And on July 2, Japan announced that it would propose to the summit of the seven major economic powers (G-7) a plan requiring all nations to report their arms sales and imports.[9] The G-7 summit meeting (held in London, July 15–17, 1991) subsequently issued a Declaration on Conventional Arms Transfers and NBC Non-Proliferation, which supported the proposal for a universal register of arms transfers under the auspices of the United Nations.

The United States, in turn, launched a Middle East arms control initiative on May 29, 1991, which included a proposal to ban weapons of mass destruction in the Middle East and to regulate sales of conventional arms to the Middle East. Then President Bush urged that arms suppliers should commit themselves to observe a general code of responsible arms transfers, avoid any destabilizing arms transfers, and establish effective domestic export controls on the end use of arms to be transferred. It was suggested that the guidelines include a mechanism for consultations among suppliers, who would:

1. Notify one another in advance of certain arms sales

2. Meet regularly to consult on arms transfers
3. Consult on an ad hoc basis if a supplier believed guidelines were not being observed
4. Provide one another with an annual report on arms transfers[10]

As a consequence of these initiatives, the five permanent members of the UN Security Council (P-5) held their first meeting on arms transfers, particularly arms transfers to the Middle East, in Paris on July 8–9, 1991. A second round of talks, which took place in London on October 17–18, 1991, concluded with issuance of two documents. The guidelines for exports of major conventional weapons called on states to avoid transfers that would increase tension or contribute to instability in a region; to not introduce destabilizing military capabilities; to not contravene embargoes; to not supply arms for purposes other than legitimate defense and security needs; and to avoid sales that would seriously undermine the recipient state's economy. A communiqué on arms transfers to the Middle East included the pledge to establish arrangements for the exchange of information for the purpose of meaningful consultation. However, no requirement was made for advance notification of arms transfers to the Middle East, something that had been favored by the United States, the United Kingdom, Russia, and (less emphatically) France but had been opposed by China. The commitment covered tanks, armored combat vehicles, artillery pieces, combat aircraft, combat helicopters (the five categories mentioned in the CFE Treaty), and certain types of missiles and naval vessels that had a displacement of over 150 tons. The information submitted was not to be made public. A third round of formal P-5 talks was held at the level of experts in Washington on February 21–22, 1992.

These initiatives have to be seen not only in the context of the Gulf conflict but also against the background of the UN Study on Ways and Means to Promote Transparency in the International Transfer of Conventional Arms, which was requested by the General Assembly in 1988 and submitted in the fall of 1992. The group of experts who conducted the study, whose debate had also been influenced by the Gulf War, called for the establishment of a register on international transfers of conventional arms. On December 9, 1992, the General Assembly voted, with 150 votes in favor, to establish such a register. In addition to information of international transfers of conventional arms, it would also include information on military holdings, procurement through national production, and relevant policies.[11] A group of experts is currently elaborating the procedures for this register. A significant number of states have already indicated that they will submit the relevant information on their arms transfers for the register.

Conclusion

The Kuwait War and the breakup of the Soviet Union have profoundly changed the situation surrounding conventional arms transfers. One of the traditional expectations regarding arms transfers that was not fulfilled was that the supplier would politically support a major recipient. In addition, the United Nations mustered the unanimity and resolution necessary for effective sanctions. Arms transfers, which for so long had evaded formal international discussion and commitments,[12] have at last come to be considered an appropriate subject for international monitoring and restraint, though not (yet) for control in the proper sense. Arms transfers will continue, but in a different international environment.

Notes

1. Iraq had been able to modify some of the Scud-B short-range ballistic missiles supplied by the Soviet Union, giving the weapons a greater range but decreasing their accuracy. The modified Scud-B versions were the Al-Hussain, with a range of about 600 kilometers, and the Al-Abbas, with a range of about 900 kilometers. Under Resolution 687 of the UN Security Council, Iraq must destroy all ballistic missiles with a range over 150 kilometers.

2. Yevgeny M. Primakov, a former director of the Institute for Oriental Studies of the USSR Academy of Sciences (and now director of the Directorate for Foreign Intelligence of Russia, a successor to the KGB), was reputed to be personally close to Saddam Hussein.

3. According to the Swedish Institute of International Peace and Research (SIPRI), the United Kingdom had supplied 58 armored personnel carriers to Iraq in 1982 to 1983, and Iraq had received 45 helicopters from the United States, but the latter was a commercial deal (without U.S. government involvement).

4. In 1990, the five permanent members of the UN Security Council accounted for more than $19 billion in arms exports, out of a total of $21.7 billion worldwide—that is, about 88 percent. See Ian Anthony, "The Global Arms Trade," *Arms Control Today*, June 1991, 3–8.

5. According to U.S. government officials, Jordan may have passed on to Iraq arms components and spare parts during the war. *Financial Times*, 17 April 1991.

6. *Arms Control Today*, April 1992, 21.

7. With the Treaty on Conventional Armed Forces in Europe (CFE) entering into force on July 17, 1992, the European defense industries face increased pressure for exports to non-European countries, because the CFE Treaty limits demand within Europe. Pressures are not limited to the West European arms manufacturers, however. Having lost the competition for the advanced tactical fighter, McDonnell-Douglas and Northrop may have to focus on the export market more than before. As for Russia, arms are one of the few export products in which it is competitive.

8. Theodore Postol, "Lessons of the Gulf War Experience With Patriot," *International Security,* Winter 1991–1992, 119–171.

9. *The New York Times,* July 3, 1991, A4.

10. *Arms Control Today,* June 1991, 27.

11. Resolution A/46/36 L. Cuba and Iraq abstained; China did not participate in the vote.

12. Between 1977 and 1979, the United States and the Soviet Union had engaged in the Conventional Arms Transfers Talks, but they were broken off without conclusions being reached.

9

Oil and Power After the 1991 Gulf War

Robert J. Lieber

What are the implications of the Gulf War for the world oil market and for global energy security? On initial examination, three separate factors contribute to the conclusion that there is little cause for concern. First, the devastating defeat suffered by Iraq suggests that both past and future military threats from that country can be minimized. Second, the success with which producing and consuming countries managed to cope with the purely oil-related components of the Gulf crisis suggests that both the supply and the price of petroleum are manageable. Third, regardless of policy choices made by these countries, elasticities of both supply and demand appear to ensure that world energy markets can and will cope with potential disruptions.

However, an assessment of oil and power in the aftermath of the Gulf War provides evidence for concluding that the risks were in fact substantial and that avoidance of serious upheaval was by no means inevitable. This interpretation rests not only on an analysis of the Gulf crisis but also on the lessons of the two oil shocks of the 1970s and the experience of the following decade. In this light, the three arguments just presented are less reassuring.

In the military realm, the extraordinary victory of the U.S.-led Coalition in an air war lasting just over five weeks and a ground war of one hundred hours has given rise to a virtual consensus on the invincibility of the Coalition and the inevitability of its triumph. However, cases both old (the debacle of Australian and other British Empire forces at Gallipoli against the Ottoman Turks in 1915)[1] and more contemporary (the failure of Desert One, the U.S. effort in April 1980 to rescue the Iranian-held hostages),[2] and even the ambiguous consequences of Israel's 1982 war in Lebanon,[3] suggest that the triumph of the forces of modern or Western powers over those of less technically advanced Middle Eastern regimes cannot be taken for granted.

Moreover, timing proves to have been crucial in the 1991 Gulf War. Had Saddam Hussein's forces promptly followed up their invasion and occupation of Kuwait with a drive into Saudi Arabia, the Saudis and U.S. forces would have lacked the military means to stop them. At best, this action by Iraq might have triggered a longer, less successful (for the Coalition), and far more costly war. At worst, Saddam Hussein might have controlled the Saudi Gulf coast ports and major Saudi oil fields, leaving the United States with two unwelcome options: to mount a military campaign without the benefit of the Saudi ports and facilities, risking the kind of destruction later seen in Kuwait though on a vaster scale against the oil fields of Saudi Arabia, or to acquiesce in Iraq's control of almost half the world's proved oil reserves as well as the likelihood of Saddam's domination of the remainder of the Gulf oil producers.

The cutoff of Kuwaiti and Iraqi oil from the world's markets was accomplished at the cost of great volatility in world oil prices. Saudi Arabia increased its own oil production by more than 3 million barrels per day (mbd)—approximately the amount previously supplied by Iraq—and other countries more than made up the shortfall caused by the loss of Kuwait's production. On the demand side, the countries of the International Energy Agency (IEA), led by the United States, eventually took measures to signal their ability and willingness to reduce demand and subsequently to release oil from their strategic stockpiles. Nevertheless, the United States and the IEA countries were slow to announce their intent to draw down stocks, and these delays were unfortunate.

Although markets did work, the temporary run-up of prices proved costly in terms of inflation and in tipping a weakening U.S. economy into a serious recession.[4] Moreover, two lessons of the 1973–1974 and 1979–1980 oil shocks were that markets often overshoot and that inelasticities of both supply and demand for energy can make the adjustment process long and expensive. Indeed, even with the effects of supply and demand largely under control, initial uncertainties and market psychology caused oil prices to triple from a precrisis level of $13 per barrel in May 1990 to a peak of over $40 per barrel in early autumn before falling back to the $20 per barrel range.

In sum, the experience of the Gulf crisis—as well as the evidence of the 1970s and 1980s—leaves little reason for complacency, and the case thus deserves careful examination. In the remainder of this chapter, I first assess the problem of oil by integrating economic and political analyses. I then consider the status of oil from Iraq and the Gulf and the problems posed by the fact that two thirds of the world's proved petroleum reserves are located in the Gulf region. Next, I consider the status of Iraqi and Saudi oil during the Gulf crisis and the way in which the global oil system reacted to the crisis. Finally, I examine a number of policy implications.

Oil as a Problem in Political Economy

Understanding the role of oil in international politics and international political economy has proved elusive. Too many observers approach the subject through perspectives that are narrowly economic or, conversely, mostly political. Such interpretations, in their most pristine forms, can be considered as "ideal types."

From the vantage point of the exclusively economic perspective, it is assumed that the market mechanism will eventually provide an equilibrium between oil supply and demand.[5] Thus, if shortages of oil develop, prices will rise until the available supply matches demand. Higher prices will have the effect of causing additional supplies of oil and other forms of energy to be developed and brought to market. At the same time, higher prices will result in reduced demand as buyers seek to economize by conserving or by switching to other forms of energy.

From this perspective, policies aimed at protecting energy security or incorporating externalities are seen as largely irrelevant, and the risks of energy crises are seen as minimal.[6] However, the governmental policies implemented as a result of this perspective have had unintended consequences and have often failed. For example, during the 1970s price regulation and allocation policies for oil and natural gas did not prevent, and may even have fostered, spot shortages, gas lines, congressional stalemate, and political recrimination; ultimately, these policies were discarded. The expensive synthetic fuels program initiated by the Carter administration was also unsuccessful and later abandoned.

When used in isolation, the economic perspective is seriously deficient. For one thing, it tends either to minimize the importance of the Organization of Petroleum Exporting Countries (OPEC) in shaping the world oil system or to suggest that long-term market factors make it largely impossible for OPEC to have a lasting impact. For another, this approach tends to overlook the implications of geography—particularly the fact that 67 percent of proved world oil reserves are located in the Gulf area, politically one of the world's most unstable regions. In addition, it disregards market imperfections and barriers to market entry in terms of both cost and time; yet, regardless of market signals, many billions of dollars and many years are needed to find and develop a new oil field or to exploit particular energy sources. Finally, an exclusively economic perspective does not successfully meet the test of historical reality. That is, after the costly and disruptive cases of the 1973–1974 and 1979–

1980 oil shocks, this perspective fails to provide a convincing explanation for why such disruptions might not recur.

Conversely, analyses of oil that are essentially—or even exclusively—political also provide only a one-dimensional perspective. Such approaches tend to minimize the role of market phenomena. They have overstated the threat of oil embargoes, exaggerated the relationship between the world's oil supply and the Arab-Israeli conflict, and inflated the fundamental power of individual oil-producing countries. After both of the 1970s oil shocks, the political approach tended to assume that oil prices would continue to rise indefinitely.

Many of the prevailing economic (or political) interpretations are more complex than is conveyed by these ideal types. For example, one of the more sophisticated market-oriented interpretations, which sees economic forces pushing oil prices lower over the long term and which tends to play down the risk of future oil shocks, nonetheless incorporates policy recommendations for the United States that go well beyond merely letting the market take its course. Eliyahu Kanovsky, for example, has urged that the United States take steps to limit its vulnerability to Middle East oil supply disruptions through such actions as incentives for Third World states to pursue oil exploration and development; he also recommends the introduction of U.S. fiscal and regulatory policies to encourage domestic energy efficiency and conservation.[7] In reality, the subject of oil can be understood most effectively by integrating insights from both economics and politics. As Robert Gilpin noted, without this synthesis, political scientists tend to overlook the role of markets, and economists often neglect the importance of power and the political context of events.[8]

Oil issues in the Middle East take on a broad significance precisely because they encompass both political and economic dimensions and because they often have consequences that spread far beyond regional confines. Under certain specific circumstances, events occurring in the Gulf can reverberate halfway around the world—and can do so almost instantaneously. The most dramatic (though least common) pattern is that of an oil shock, defined as a profound disruption of the existing supply and price system. For such an event to take place, two major phenomena must be present simultaneously. One is the tight or precarious balance between supply and demand, in which the world's available oil supplies only just manage to satisfy the world's demand, and little or no additional unused production capacity exists. The second is some major event (war or revolution being the most pertinent) that triggers a disturbance in existing supply patterns. When these two circumstances intersect, the result is an oil shock.

The political economy of world oil thus involves an integrated world system. All countries that import or export petroleum are linked to it.

Developments occurring anywhere in the system that have a bearing on the demand or supply for oil, whether political or economic in nature, affect the overall balance of that system. Hence, when a serious disequilibrium occurs, the effects are felt globally. For example, even if the United States imported little or no Middle East oil, the fact that it imports any oil—and that its oil imports provide nearly 50 percent of its total petroleum supplies—means that it would be almost instantly affected by a serious disequilibrium in the system.

Iraqi and Gulf Oil

Prior to the outbreak of the Gulf crisis and war, Iraq was producing 3.4 million barrels of crude oil per day.[9] Its production in July 1990 represented a 20 percent increase over its average output for 1989 and meant that Iraq had regained its level of peak production set in 1979, the last full year prior to the Iran-Iraq War. Even at the July 1990 figure, however, Iraq's oil output accounted for just 5.7 percent of world production.[10]

By another measure, proved oil reserves, Iraq's importance to the world's oil system is significantly greater. In terms of proved oil reserves, Iraq is second only to Saudi Arabia. (See Table 9.1.) Set against a world total of just under one thousand billion barrels, the Saudis, with 260 billion barrels, hold approximately 26 percent of the current world total. Iraq has 100 billion barrels, which is equivalent to 10 percent of the world total, and is followed closely by the United Arab Emirates (98 billion barrels), Kuwait (97 billion barrels), and Iran (93 billion barrels). By contrast, the next largest group of producers, Venezuela, the former Soviet Union, and Mexico, falls in the 51–59 billion barrel range. For its part, the United States has just 26 billion barrels, or the equivalent of only 2.7 percent of the world's proved reserves.

The significance of Iraq's position, particularly during the crisis, thus becomes more evident. As of August 2, 1990, not only did Saddam Hussein's regime control both its own oil reserves and those of Kuwait—and thus some 20 percent of the world figure—but it directly menaced Saudi Arabia. Iraq thus was in position to dominate, either directly or indirectly, 56 percent of all proved oil reserves, including those of the rich but militarily inconsequential United Arab Emirates.

To grasp the implications of this situation, one must understand the importance of Gulf oil—and of OPEC more broadly—as well as the reasons why this importance seems to wax and wane at various intervals. In brief, the volatility is due to a phenomenon that one analyst has called "the OPEC multiplier."[11] For a combination of political and economic reasons, oil-importing countries have tended to rely on OPEC oil as a last resort. Where possible, they prefer to utilize domestic oil and energy

TABLE 9.1   Proved Oil Reserves

Country	Billion Barrels	Percentage of World Reserves
Saudi Arabia	260.3	26.3
Iraq	100.0	10.1
United Arab Emirates	98.1	9.9
Kuwait	96.5	9.7
Iran	92.9	9.4
Venezuela	59.1	6.0
Former USSR	57.0	5.8
Mexico	51.3	5.2
United States	26.3	2.7
China	24.0	2.4
Libya	22.8	2.3
Nigeria	17.9	1.8
Algeria	9.2	0.9
Norway	7.6	0.8
Indonesia	6.6	0.7
India	6.1	0.6
Canada	5.6	0.6
Egypt	4.5	0.5
Oman	4.3	0.4
Yemen	4.0	0.4
United Kingdom	4.0	0.4
Others	32.9	3.1
World Totals	991.0	100.0

Sources: Based on data from *Oil and Gas Journal,* December 30, 1991, for reserves recoverable with present technology and prices. Data for Saudi Arabia and Kuwait include half of the Neutral Zone. UAE includes Abu Dhabi, Dubai, Ras al-Khaimah, and Sharjah. Figure for former USSR is "explored reserves," including proved, probable, and some possible. Calculations for "others" and percentages are the author's.

resources. If they must resort to imports, they next seek supplies from non-OPEC countries. But when these other avenues are no longer available or are fully utilized, they must turn to OPEC suppliers. As a consequence, changes in the demand for OPEC oil may be disproportionate to overall changes in the world's oil demand.

When world demand falls, the reductions thus affect OPEC to a greater extent than other suppliers. In the case of the United States, when total oil demand fell by more than 3.6 mbd--or almost 20 percent--between 1978 and 1983, domestic oil production continued at near-capacity levels, and imports of non-OPEC oil actually increased. At the same time, U.S. imports of OPEC oil fell sharply, dropping from 5.7 to 1.8 mbd (a reduction of 68 percent).[12]

The OPEC multiplier works in the opposite direction as well. During the last half of the 1980s, a combination of economic growth, cheaper oil prices, and gradual decreases in U.S. oil output caused an upsurge in world oil demand. At the time, most of the non-OPEC suppliers were producing at or near capacity, and so demand for OPEC oil rose rapidly. U.S. imports of OPEC oil increased by 2.5 mbd to a level of 4.3 mbd. Global demand for OPEC oil surged from a low point of 16.6 mbd in 1985 to 24.3 mbd by spring 1990. OPEC still possessed several million barrels per day of unused capacity, but much of this capacity was concentrated within Saudi Arabia and nearby areas in the Gulf.

Status of Iraqi and Saudi Oil During the Gulf Crisis

In the weeks following the Iraqi invasion of Kuwait, the United Nations embargo against Iraq's oil exports had the effect of removing between 4.0 and 4.3 mbd of crude oil from world supplies.[13] World crude oil markets, reacting initially to the threat of war in the Gulf and then to the loss of oil from Iraq and Kuwait, saw a dramatic run-up in prices. As a result of growing tensions in the region, prices that had been as low as $13 per barrel for Saudi light crude in June 1990 had already climbed to $20 by mid-July. By August 2, the day of the invasion, oil reached the price of $24 per barrel. Not surprisingly, prices moved steeply higher in the following weeks, peaking at $40.42 on October 11.[14]

Set against the world's oil production of some 60 million barrels per day, Iraqi and Kuwaiti oil exports before the crisis amounted to approximately 7 percent of the global total. Had this 7 percent loss not been offset by production increases elsewhere, the shortfall would have been in the same range as the one that triggered the 1973–1974 oil crisis and would have been greater than the 4 percent shortfall experienced during the 1979–1980 oil crisis.[15]

Even though a supply shortage did not materialize, the economic impact of the sharply higher oil prices could have been significant. If oil had remained at an average price of $30 per barrel for all of 1991, instead of receding to $20 by late January, the industrial democracies of the Organization for Economic Cooperation and Development (OECD) would have experienced a 2 percent increase in inflation, a 0.5 percent reduction in gross national product (GNP) growth, and an adverse shift of $90 billion in the balance of trade.[16] By themselves, these effects would have been less damaging than the results of the 1970s oil shocks (the numbers for inflation and balance of trade, for example, were only one-third those of the earlier period),[17] but they could have contributed significantly to tilting the world economy into recession. The price "spike" that did occur was relatively brief, but it exacerbated economic problems in Eastern Europe and parts of the Third World and damaged certain industries (e.g., aviation, automobiles) in the more prosperous Western countries.

Actually, despite the loss of Iraqi and Kuwaiti crude oil and fears that terrorism or war could further reduce supplies of oil from the Gulf, oil producers were able to increase production sufficiently to offset the potential shortfall. Almost 80 percent of this production came from Gulf states and from other member countries of OPEC, with smaller amounts from producers elsewhere around the world.

Saudi Arabia proved to be the greatest source of increased production. Between December 1989 and December 1990, Saudi production of crude oil rose by nearly 2.9 mbd to a level of almost 8.6 mbd. (See Table 9.2). Although a great deal of additional activity took place on the world oil market—including production increases, efforts to curtail or defer demand, and, on January 17, 1991, a pledge by the twenty-one states of the International Energy Agency to make available 2 mbd from their reserves[18]—more than two thirds of the reduction in oil from the Gulf was made up by Saudi Arabia alone, with less than 20 percent coming from outside the Middle East.[19]

Other net additions to world supplies came from Iran (0.4 mbd), Venezuela (0.36), Libya (0.3), Indonesia (0.1), Algeria (0.1), and Nigeria (0.1), and smaller amounts came from a variety of producers around the world.

One important factor worked in the opposite direction, however: The continuing decline of production in the Soviet Union between December 1989 and December 1990 resulted in a reduction there of more than 1 mbd. In total, world oil production in December 1990 was 60.4 mbd. Despite the Gulf crisis, this was just 0.9 mbd below the figure of a year earlier. With a cutback in world demand of some 1 mbd in response to the sharply higher price of crude oil, as well as the subsequent decision by the United States and other IEA countries to make additional oil available from stockpiles,[20] total oil supplies remained adequate.

TABLE 9.2 Production of Crude Oil, Millions of Barrels per Day (mbd)

Producers	December 1989	December 1990	Change	
Iraq	3.000	0.425	−2.575	
Kuwait	2.090	0.075	−2.015	
Total loss:				−4.590
Estimated Global Loss (net of domestic consumption)			−4.0 to 4.3	
Additions from Gulf				
Saudi Arabia	5.696	8.570	+2.874	
Iran	2.900	3.300	+0.400	
Libya	1.201	1.500	+0.299	
Algeria	1.110	1.210	+0.100	
Qatar	0.395	0.370	−0.025	
UAE	2.406	2.400	−0.006	
Net Additions from Gulf	+3.642			
Other Major Net Additions				
Venezuela	1.977	2.340	+0.363	
Mexico	2.476	2.660	+0.184	
Indonesia	1.434	1.550	+0.116	
Nigeria	1.854	1.950	+0.096	
Total +0.759				
Other Totals				
Arab OPEC				
Gulf	16.529	15.182	−1.347	
Total OPEC	24.605	24.280	−0.325	
World	61.320	60.449	−0.871	

Source: Author's calculations from data in *Monthly Energy Review* (Washington, D.C.: U.S. Department of Energy, Energy Information Administration, March 1991), 118–19.

Thus, no real oil crisis developed. The shortfalls from Iraq and Kuwait were effectively offset. By mid-January 1991, oil prices fell below $20 per barrel (a figure returning close to preinvasion levels) and then fluctuated in a narrow range around that figure during the Gulf War and its aftermath.

In view of this result, as well as the postcrisis commitment of the Saudis to maintain high levels of oil production, the resumption of Kuwaiti oil production, and the prospect that some amounts of Iraqi oil will eventually be exported again, there might appear to be grounds for complacency: A potentially destabilizing loss of supply from two major oil producing countries was absorbed with no major crisis, and the accompanying surge in oil prices subsided within five months. A closer look, however, suggests that the world's ability to weather a potential crisis without severe disruption cannot be taken for granted.

The most important factor that helped prevent a Gulf War oil crisis was the role of Saudi Arabia. If the Saudis had been unable or unwilling to respond as they did, the history of the Gulf crisis would have been far different. An Iraqi invasion of Saudi Arabia during the earliest days of the crisis would have been beyond the ability of the Saudis themselves—or of the U.S. forces in their initial deployments—to repel. Saudi oil fields, which are concentrated in the vicinity of Ras Tanura, less than 200 miles from the Kuwaiti border, could have been seized by a determined Iraqi assault. In such circumstances, even if the Saudis had retained any kind of nominal independence, they most likely would not have been in a position to do anything except acquiesce in whatever demands Saddam placed upon them and their resources.

On August 4, 1990, just after Iraq's invasion of Kuwait, the U.S. Central Intelligence Agency (CIA) reported that Saddam's forces numbered more than 100,000 men and that the only obstacle between the Iraqis and the Saudi oil fields was a Saudi National Guard battalion of fewer than 1,000 men.[21] The U.S. deployments succeeded because they had the full cooperation of the Saudi government, access to Saudi ports, and the use of a vast infrastructure of modern airbases. (See chapters by Danspeckgruber and Yesson.) Without these requisites, a U.S. military effort aimed at driving the Iraqi invaders out of both Saudi Arabia and Kuwait would have been exceptionally difficult and costly, if the Bush administration had even attempted it. The widespread diplomatic, political, and military support that the U.S.-led Coalition enjoyed would also have been far more difficult to assemble under circumstances in which Saddam's triumph looked self-evident and the costs of reversing it unsustainable.[22]

The Iraqi destruction and torching of Kuwait's oil wells in the midst of the allied military triumph suggests that even a successful U.S. assault on the Iraqi forces in Saudi Arabia would have resulted in unprecedented destruction of oil facilities. The threatened reduction, or actual disappearance, of 8.5 million barrels of oil (Saudi Arabia's December 1990 oil production) would have triggered a disastrous crisis in world oil supplies. The consequences in shortfalls of petroleum for the world economy, staggering price increases, alliance disarray, and political blackmail are almost incalculable.

If Saddam had been in a position to exercise control over the oil resources of Kuwait and Saudi Arabia in addition to those of Iraq, 46 percent of the world's proved reserves of crude oil would have been subject to his direct dictate. With his Gulf neighbors painfully aware of his willingness and ability to use any means at his disposal, the Iraqi president would have gained access to a vast source of present and future wealth. Moreover, these resources would have permitted him to purchase the most modern forms of technology and arms, including missiles and nuclear weapons technology.

The sobering conclusion of this scenario is that oil-importing countries and Iraq's Middle Eastern and even European neighbors have been fortunate in what did *not* happen after August 2, 1990. The avoidance of disaster was by no means inevitable despite the resounding military defeat of Iraq and the destruction of much of its dangerous weaponry.

Iraq and World Oil: Past and Future Patterns

Saddam Hussein's seizure of Kuwait had multiple causes, not the least of them being the Iraqi leader's characteristic overreaching and its disastrous consequences. Nonetheless, important economic considerations are quite evident as well. During the 1980s, Iraq spent approximately $100 billion on its military. By mid-1990, the country had accumulated an international debt of approximately $90 billion,[23] on which interest payments amounted to some $8 to 10 billion per year. With world oil prices at $20 per barrel, exports of 3 mbd would generate less than $20 billion per year in revenues. Moreover, by June 1990, with both Iran's and Iraq's oil exports having increased following the end of the Iran-Iraq War, oil prices had slipped to as low as $13 per barrel. At that figure, Iraq would have earned approximately $14 billion per year, barely enough to cover debt service and imports of necessities. Because of the costs of reconstruction following the Iran-Iraq War, the demands of the Iraqi economy and popular expectations, and Saddam's continuing and grandiose military spending predilections, the Iraqi leader had to seek means of increasing his country's revenues. The income that could be afforded by the seizure of Kuwait, as well as the prospect of exerting leverage over Saudi Arabia and hence an influence over world oil prices, was tempting.

In the aftermath of the Gulf War and with the continuing United Nations sanctions on oil exports, Iraq's economy has experienced an acute need for oil revenues. This reality provides an opportunity for external actors to influence that country's conduct. Sooner or later, however, Iraq will resume oil exports. When it does, the amounts involved could grow rather quickly. Indeed, just two months after the war ended, a CIA report estimated that within three months after restrictions were lifted, which could have been as early as 1992, Iraq could have been producing 1 mbd. And, with the investment of an additional $1.5 billion to repair pumping facilities, output could have reached 2.7 mbd by the end of 1992.[24]

In light of Iraq's indebtedness, estimated costs of $30 billion to repair destruction caused by the 1991 war, and UN-mandated reparations of as much as $50 billion to pay for the destruction and looting in Kuwait,[25] Iraq will continue to have a pressing long-term need for export revenues. Thus Saddam, or his eventual successors, will be motivated to seek ways of encouraging higher world oil prices. In additon, barring major changes in existing circumstances, the motivation will remain for Iraq to continue to have its own reasons for seeking to intimidate its neighbors. Apart from efforts to shape oil production and pricing policies, such pressures could also aim at obtaining financial assistance (in less polite terms, blackmail), influencing other countries' defense and foreign policies, and causing changes in the internal regime structure of adjacent states.

As long as the United States remains unambiguously committed to regional security in the area, whether in terms of troop presence or longer-term security arrangements, this potential intimidation will not have much effect. The U.S. played a unique role in opposing the Iraqi takeover of Kuwait, in orchestrating UN condemnation and sanctions, and, finally, in leading an international coalition in a brief, devastating war against Iraq. However, if the United States proves unable to sustain a long-term commitment, or if regional states are unwilling or unable to collaborate in its maintenance, Iraq will eventually find ways to reassert strength within the region. Under such circumstances, Saddam's regime (or a successor regime with comparable interests and values) will continue to threaten both long-term regional stability and the prevailing Gulf oil regime. Even in the absence of this threat, internal and external sources of instability remain—for example, Islamic fundamentalism and the uncertain nature of Iran's role. Nonetheless, Saddam and Iraq represent the demonstrably most significant danger to their neighbors.

The oil dimension of this danger incorporates two distinct elements. One is that Iraq—having previously attacked four of its neighbors (Iran, Kuwait, Saudi Arabia, and Israel) and having had bitter quarrels with Syria and uneasy relations with other countries (such as Turkey)—could again initiate a conflict or war. If it does, the danger to oil facilities, whether international or not, would again be present. Alternatively, if Iraq succeeds in regaining regional power and influence, it may attempt to manipulate oil production for the purpose of increasing world prices. To be sure, the economic and market dimensions of the political economy of oil make it uncertain whether Iraq could succeed in such efforts. The experience of the OPEC countries in the 1980s suggests that Iraq's task would be a difficult one. Yet, if Iraq ultimately did manage to exert control over its neighbors, or succeed in intimidating them, the results could be significant.

Due to the interplay between politics and economics, if Iraq finds ways to regain a measure of economic strength and to loosen the sanctions now imposed on it, it can again translate its oil revenues into offensive military power that once more could jeopardize the security of the region. Unless a UN embargo on weapons exports can be sustained and rigorously enforced, some arms manufacturing countries will again seek markets, including the Middle East, for their exports of tanks, aircraft, missiles, chemical weapons, and nuclear weapons technology. The pressing financial predicament of the emergent East European economies, and the countries of the former Soviet Union, the problems of Latin American manufacturers such as Brazil and Argentina, and the behavior of China make this a serious long-term problem. Indeed, post-Gulf War accounts of a Czech decision to supply T-72 tanks to Syria, of China's shipment of M-9 missiles to Syria, of construction of a nuclear "research" reactor in Algeria, and of an Argentine Condor II surface-to-surface missile program financed by Iraq[26] provide evidence that any sustained effort to control the export of advanced offensive weapons to the region will face great difficulties. Even with an embargo on weapons exports, the capability of Iraq's existing defense industrial base plus the leakage of technology from outside sources (particularly from the former Soviet Union) present additional problems.

Summing Up

The principal developments in world oil since the early 1970s have come largely as surprises; many have run directly counter to conventional wisdom among policy makers, analysts, and scholars. Such developments include the tightening world oil market after 1970, the oil shocks of 1973–1974 and 1979–1980, the oil gluts (and accompanying price reductions) of 1976–1978 and especially the mid-1980s, and Iraq's invasion of Kuwait in August 1990.

The long-term pattern of oil supply and price, along with the broader stability of the Middle East, depends on a complex interplay of economic, political, and military elements. Such factors include the fate of the Ba'athist regime of Saddam Hussein, the availability of oil revenues to finance a rearming of Iraq, the durability of the U.S. commitment to regional security, the role of Saudi Arabia and the stability of its regime, the pattern of long-term oil and energy demand outside the region, the decline of Russian oil production, the inability of the United States to implement an energy policy that would reverse its increasing dependence on imported oil, and the risk of renewed warfare within the region. In other words, economic and energy variables partially determine political and military outcomes, and vice versa.

In sum, the fact that the first great crisis of the post-Cold War era did not produce a severe oil shock should not be grounds for complacency. A reconsideration of the three optimistic but widely shared notions cited at the start of this chapter suggests grounds for caution.

First, despite the crushing defeat of Iraq and the destruction of much of its military infrastructure, Saddam Hussein has survived and has conducted a bloody suppression of uprisings by Shi'ites in southern Iraq and Kurds in the north. Although Iraq has been subjected to a continuing oil and weapons embargo, the durability of these restraints is problematic over the long term. If there is no change of regime, Saddam and his Ba'athist leadership could eventually pose a renewed regional threat. Moreover, the crisis that began in August 1990 could have had a far more dangerous outcome if Saddam had sent his forces into Saudi Arabia immediately or if the U.S. administration had been less effective in gaining United Nations support, in assembling an unprecedented international coalition, and in ultimately gaining congressional approval for its actions.

Second, the ability of oil producers and consumers to weather the crisis owed a great deal to the willingness and ability of Saudi Arabia to increase production. If Saudi oil facilities had been disrupted by the crisis, or if Saudi leaders had decided not to boost production (or had been prevented from doing so), the economic and political consequences of the crisis would have been far more serious.

Third, although the market mechanism functioned successfully both in the recent crisis and in moderating the policies of OPEC countries in the 1980s and 1990s, the market does have its limits. For example, markets tend to overshoot. Thus, in the aftermath of Iraq's seizure of Kuwait, despite the factors that allowed producing and consuming countries to avoid serious disruption, panic buying caused the price of oil to spike to more than $40 per barrel. Moreover, market mechanisms cannot change geography—in this case, the concentration of two thirds of the world's proved oil reserves in the Gulf area. These supplies remain vulnerable to military or political events that have nothing to do with markets but can have an enormous impact on oil supply and price.

Indeed, even though markets have benign effects in regulating supply and demand for oil and energy, market imperfections have consequences as well. These include the role of OPEC in influencing (though by no means determining) the world's oil supply and price, and time delays before markets regain equilibrium. Although the price spikes of 1973–1974 and 1979–1980 ultimately proved reversible, the damage done to the economies of Western and developing countries during these two shocks was quite serious. By one estimate, the Group of Seven industrial countries lost $1.2 trillion in economic growth as a result of the two oil shocks.[27] The developing countries' grave problems of indebtedness, which have plagued their economies and societies during the 1980s and early 1990s, are in part a legacy of these "temporary" oil price disturbances.

The picture that has emerged of Iraq and the world oil system in the aftermath of the Kuwait War provides a measure of reassurance, but it also argues for caution. An awareness of the interrelated political and economic dimensions of the problem and a willingness to draw lessons from the 1990–1991 crisis as well as those of 1973–1974 and 1978–1979 are essential if future threats to energy security are to be avoided.

Policy Implications

Comprehension of a problem does not automatically dictate the response. The urgency of the problem will vary due to factors that may be only modestly influenced by policy choices. In the present case, these factors include future levels of oil and energy production outside the Persian Gulf, the global supply-and-demand balance for oil, and the degree of instability and conflict within the Gulf area. Nonetheless, the broad outlines of an appropriate U.S. policy can be suggested.

Iraq's invasion of Kuwait and the subsequent crisis and war suggest a continuing need for the United States to maintain some mix of forces capable of intervening effectively in the Gulf. International collaboration also appears essential if legitimacy, effectiveness, and funding are to be achieved. In the specific case of Iraq, the ability of the United States to organize and lead a coalition with the support of the UN Security Council was not only important internationally; it was also a prerequisite for obtaining congressional authorization for the use of force. The alternative to U.S. leadership in the crisis would have been international inaction.

In retrospect, Saddam Hussein's postwar survival and the resistance of his regime to compliance with UN Security Council resolutions that require identification and destruction of facilities for the production of nuclear and chemical weapons and missiles lead to the conclusion that the war was brought to a close too early. Key units of the Republican Guard that sustain the Ba'athist regime should have been destroyed. Allowing Saddam's forces to use attack helicopters against uprisings by Shi'ites in the south and Kurds in the north was also shortsighted. As long as Saddam's regime endures, the stability of the Gulf area will remain vulnerable.

The role of Saudi Arabia is paramount to other oil suppliers. If anything, the Saudis' importance to the world oil system is even greater than previously suggested. Although the most commonly reported numbers, including those officially used by the Saudis, credit the kingdom with 260 billion barrels of proved oil reserves, the actual figure is more likely to be in the range of 320–330 billion barrels.[28] This figure represents approximately one third of the global total.

After a long period of internal evolution and debate following the oil shocks of the 1970s, the Saudi political system has managed to demonstrate a much greater durability than might have been expected. Although the long-term stability of the Saudi system and its political evolution remain imponderables, the Saudi leadership has made a series of choices that commit the country to energy, economic, and security policies that align its own future with that of the United States and the other industrial democracies. It has also displayed a certain degree of pragmatism toward other regional issues and the Arab-Israeli conflict. But the Kuwait War and the unprecedented deployment of U.S. forces in the Saudi Kingdom do not mean that the Saudis have chosen to embrace a substantial and ongoing U.S. force deployment. The fact that the United States was willing to lead a worldwide coalition and to deploy a half million troops without a formal treaty most likely has led Saudi leaders to conclude that they can retain this commitment with only modest additional steps involving force deployments or signed agreements. For both Saudi Arabia and the United States, dealing with the long-term development of this security relationship will be a complex task.

More broadly, U.S. and international efforts to reduce the proliferation of missiles and of chemical, biological, and nuclear weapons in the Gulf region may contribute to stability or at least reduce the scope of destruction in the event of future wars there.

The United States must cooperate with member states of the International Energy Agency in making provisions for dealing with future crises, and must seek agreement on the earlier use of strategic stocks. Both the United States and the IEA were slow to commit themselves to announcing stock draw-downs in the 1990–1991 crisis. If they had acted earlier, they could have alleviated the kind of market panic that drove prices to over $40 per barrel. An announcement of their willingness to use the strategic reserve in August or September 1990 could have blunted the price spike significantly and thus reduced its negative economic effects.[29]

The criterion for judging U.S. domestic policies is not the unattainable goal of energy independence. Instead, it is the reduction of oil consumption and imports, and thus the lessening of U.S. vulnerability in the event that some kind of serious disruption in the world oil market arises in the future. The United States should adopt a more coherent and sustained program to encourage energy efficiency and conservation, including the use of tax policies to encourage more efficient use of gasoline.[30] It should strive for a robust, diverse energy mix, with incentives for domestic production of oil and natural gas, encouragement of clean-burning coal technologies, maintenance of a viable nuclear power option, pursuit of more ambitious policies for the research and development of new technologies (including solar energy), and an increase in the Strategic Petroleum Reserve to its originally intended target of one billion barrels.

Finally, it remains to be seen whether the need for policy in this area can correspond with the capacity for policy making, or whether this intersection represents a very "small set." The years since the first oil crisis in October 1973 do not provide a great deal of encouragement. Although elements of effective policy response do exist (e.g., the creation of the International Energy Agency, the passage of the Corporate Average Fuel Economy [CAFE] standards for automobile fuel efficiency, and the establishment of the Strategic Petroleum Reserve), these tend to be exceptions. In 1977, the Carter administration found itself in a policy stalemate over a series of energy issues, particularly natural gas, that lasted up to the oil crisis brought on by the fall of the Shah in early 1979. During the 1980s, the Reagan administration largely de-emphasized energy policy and dismantled much of what had existed.[31] The Bush administration began by seeking the development of a National Energy Strategy (NES) with the aim of reducing U.S. dependence on imported oil, but the recommendations of the Department of Energy were watered down by the White House before their release in early 1991. The remaining proposals were stalled in Congress until the issue of drilling for oil in the Alaskan National Wildlife Refuge (ANWR) was finally removed.

These experiences lead to the sobering conclusion that although the United States generally has an impressive capacity for responding to crisis, its policy process is far less effective in providing coherent policy responses in noncrisis situations. Its ineffectiveness applies especially to issues such as energy security, which are themselves complex, involve huge resource allocation choices, tend to engage the attention of tenacious advocates and institutions on opposite sides, and rarely attract strong leadership on the part of the executive branch. Thus, although the broad elements of an effective energy policy are more or less evident, their implementation may await the time of some future crisis in energy security.

Epilogue

Some three years after the end of the 1991 Gulf War and the liberation of Kuwait, the basic regional configuration remains essentially as outlined in this chapter. To be sure, changes have occurred: the defeat of George Bush in the 1992 presidential election and the onset of the Clinton administration, the return to full production of the Kuwaiti oil fields, the growing impoverishment of the Iraqi population, U.S. air attacks on Iraq for its violation of UN cease-fire agreements and for the assassination plot against former President Bush, and a somewhat greater degree of defense cooperation between a number of the Gulf sheikhdoms and the United States.

In Iraq, Saddam has demonstrated a staying power greater than most observers had anticipated in the immediate aftermath of the Gulf War. Moreover, the behavior of his regime does not seem to have been permanently modified. Saddam has refused to accept the border demarcation with Kuwait set by the United Nations and continues to threaten the sheikhdom. Until 1994, his cooperation with United Nations cease-fire terms and Security Council resolutions has been unsatisfactory. Iraq has concealed weapons of mass destruction, along with hundreds of Scud missiles and substantial missile production capability,[32] as well as biological warfare programs. The Iraqi armed forces, though reduced in number and with less advanced weaponry, have been substantially rebuilt. Terrorism remains an instrument of the regime, as evident in the Kurdish region and in the Bush assassination attempt.

Moreover, with the passage of time, additional evidence has surfaced of how serious a threat Saddam represented. The Iraqi leader and members of his immediate entourage have observed publicly that they made their worst mistake in not marching into Saudi Arabia's eastern province immediately after seizing Kuwait or at least doing so at a time when the U.S. troop presence was still in its early stages.

Even more serious is evidence that Iraq, despite being a signatory to the Non-Proliferation Treaty (NPT), had embarked on a massive nuclear weapons program. According to United Nations inspection teams sent to Iraq after the cease-fire, Saddam had engaged in a huge and secret effort, costing between $7 billion and $10 billion, that put Iraq within eighteen months of acquiring its first nuclear weapon. Moreover, the inspection teams found that despite destruction of the program, Iraq has not abandoned its nuclear ambitions. The leader of the Iraqi effort to produce the bomb told UN inspectors of new guidelines issued by the Ministry of Military Industrialization for constructing buildings better able to survive future air attacks. As the chief UN nuclear weapons inspector later observed, "If Saddam ... had waited [to invade Kuwait] until June 1992, the world would have been facing a nuclear armed Iraq."[33]

For their part, the United States and the Coalition countries have continued to enforce the cease-fire against Iraq and to monitor its behavior, but the durability of this commitment remains to be seen. Although undertaken in response to Iraqi violations of cease-fire agreements and UN Security Council resolutions, a number of the U.S. air and cruise missile strikes against Iraqi facilities have been met with an embarrassed silence or even criticism in parts of the region.

For its part, the Clinton administration, after some initial hesitation, has embraced the main features of the Bush policy. Indeed, in its initial official statement on Middle East policy, the administration elaborated a concept of "dual containment" aimed at Iran as well as Iraq.

To date, no effective alternative to U.S. leadership exists for maintaining stability in the Gulf. The European Community has been incapable of acting effectively in foreign and defense policy, despite an initial burst of optimism following the December 1991 signing of the Maastricht Treaty. Local efforts among the Gulf states to ensure their own security, for example in cooperation with Egypt, have not proved feasible. Iran, which has been unable to moderate its own behavior, remains a source of regional instability. And the United Nations Security Council has no prospect of acting effectively in the Gulf except through U.S. initiatives. In short, no practical alternatives exist to U.S. leadership that would maintain stability in the Gulf and provide the collective goods of deterrence, reassurance, and defense. The means for doing so may remain subject to debate, but the necessity continues to be compelling.

Notes

An earlier version of this chapter appeared in *International Security,* Summer 1992, Vol. 17, no. 1. Reprinted with permission.

1. A brief account of the Gallipoli expedition and debacle can be found in David Fromkin, *A Peace to End All Peace: The Fall of the Ottoman Empire and the Creation of the Modern Middle East* (New York: Avon, 1990), 150–187. For a more comprehensive treatment, see Alan Moorehead, *Gallipoli* (New York: Harper and Brothers, 1956).

2. See, for example, Gary Sick, *All Fall Down: America's Tragic Encounter with Iran* (New York: Random House, 1985), 296–302.

3. In particular, see Avner Yaniv's assessment of what he terms a "Pyrrhic Victory," as well as the unforeseen domestic and international political reverbera-

tions; Avner Yaniv, *Dilemmas of Security: Politics, Strategy and the Israeli Experience in Lebanon* (New York: Oxford University Press, 1987), 117ff., 216–84.

4. The annual *Economic Report of the President* subsequently concluded that the rapid rise in oil prices and uncertainties accompanying the crisis with Iraq were among the factors that tipped the U.S. economy, then only barely growing, into recession in the third quarter of 1990. See John M. Barry, "Administration's Annual Economic Report Presents Lower Expectations," *Washington Post,* February 6, 1992, A14.

5. For example, the initial National Energy Policy Plan of the Reagan administration held that market forces could increase petroleum investment and production and that this approach should be applied in times of crisis: "In the event of an emergency, preparedness plans call for relying primarily on market forces to allocate energy supplies." Summary of National Energy Policy Plan, U.S. Department of Energy, *Energy Insider,* Washington, D.C., August 3, 1981, 3.

6. For example, the Reagan administration initially made clear that it would not use governmental action or resources to reduce oil imports or oil consumption. And, despite the previous decade's experience with international energy instability, it held the view that "achieving a low level of oil imports at any cost is not a major criterion for the nation's energy security and economic health. Even at its current high price, imported oil is substantially less expensive than available alternatives." Quoted in *Energy Insider,* August 3, 1981, 3. Moreover, as late as 1985, the administration advocated a "moratorium" on filling the strategic reserve during the 1986 fiscal year. *New York Times,* February 5, 1986.

7. See Eliyahu Kanovsky, *OPEC Ascendant? Another Case of Crying Wolf,* Policy Papers no. 20 (Washington, D.C.: Washington Institute for Near East Policy, 1990), x, 53–56. An earlier paper by the same author argued that competition for market share and revenue needs of oil exporters, along with advances in oil exploration and production, energy efficiency, and the conclusion of the Iran-Iraq War, would hold down the price of oil for the foreseeable future. Kanovsky, *Another Oil Shock in the 1990s? A Dissenting View,* Policy Papers no. 6 (Washington, D.C.: Washington Institute for Near East Policy, 1987). See also the discussion of Kanovsky's approach by Hobart Rowen, *Washington Post,* May 12, 1991, H16.

8. Robert Gilpin, *U.S. Power and the Multinational Corporation: The Political Economy of Direct Foreign Investment* (New York: Basic Books, 1975), 4–5.

9. *Monthly Energy Review* (Washington, D.C.: U.S. Department of Energy, Energy Information Administration, March 1991), Table 10.1a, 118.

10. Percentage calculations throughout this chapter are those of the author. World crude oil production in 1990 amounted to 60.072 mbd; *Monthly Energy Review,* March 1991, Table 10.1b, 119.

11. For elaboration of the concept, see Bijan Mossavar-Rahmani, "The OPEC Multiplier," *Foreign Policy,* no. 52 (Fall 1982), 136–148.

12. In 1978, "petroleum products supplied" (i.e., total demand for petroleum) in the United States amounted to 18.847 mbd. By 1983, the figure had declined to 15.231. *Monthly Energy Review,* March 1991, 17.

13. As of December 1989 Iraq had been producing 3.0 mbd and Kuwait 2.1 mbd. By December 1990 these figures had fallen to 0.425 for Iraq and a mere 0.075 for Kuwait. Counting domestic uses of various kinds, the combined reduction of

nearly 4.6 mbd was greater than the two countries' net oil exports, estimated to total in the range of 4.0 to 4.3 mbd.

14. With the exception of the June figure, all prices are for light sweet crude oil quoted on the New York Mercantile Exchange; see *New York Times*, October 12, 1990, and March 1, 1991.

15. See Robert J. Lieber, *The Oil Decade: Conflict and Cooperation in the West* (Lanham, Md.: University Press of America, 1986), 13–43.

16. Data from "The World Economy: Third Time Lucky," *The Economist* (London), August 11, 1990, 23.

17. The increased wealth transfer from the OECD countries at $30 per barrel would have been on the order of 0.6 percent of GNP, whereas in each of the 1970s oil shocks, the figure was 2.0 percent. In addition, compared with a hypothetical OECD inflation increase of 2 percent for 1991, the actual net increase for the Group of Seven leading industrial countries (G-7) in the 1974 shock was 6.1 percent (i.e., rising from 7.9 percent in 1973 to 14.0 percent in 1974). In the second oil shock, the inflation rate of the G-7 increased to almost 6 percentage points. See "The World Economy: Third Time Lucky" (fn. 16).

18. With the aim of reducing market volatility related to the Gulf War, the IEA countries agreed to make available approximately 2 mbd from their government reserves and to take conservation measures to reduce demand by an additional 500,000 barrels per day. However, in implementing the plan at the end of January 1991, agency officials noted that its oil would be sold only if oil companies indicated a need to buy it. See Steven Greenhouse, "International Energy Agency Affirms Plan to Tap Stocks," *New York Times*, January 29, 1991. The implementation of this plan represented the first time since the IEA's creation in 1974 that its emergency draw-down system was put into effect. On March 6, shortly after the end of the war, the IEA ended emergency sales of oil. For details, see Steven Greenhouse, "International Energy Agency Ends Emergency Oil Sales," *New York Times*, March 7, 1991.

19. Figures for oil supply from the Gulf and OPEC, as well as world figures, often vary depending on the particular source quoted, differing time periods, and other factors. For reasons of consistency, information in this chapter is derived from the *Monthly Energy Review* of the Energy Information Administration, U.S. Department of Energy, except where otherwise noted.

20. OECD stockpiles would have been sufficient to provide 2 mbd for an additional 4.5 years. Data are from International Energy Agency, reported in *Economist*, August 11, 1990, 21.

21. Bob Woodward, *The Commanders* (New York: Simon and Schuster, 1991), 248. The situation remained precarious during the first two weeks of U.S. force deployments; both U.S. Chief of Staff General Colin Powell and Secretary of Defense Dick Cheney reportedly believed that Saddam's forces would have had the upper hand at that time. Woodward, 278, 282–285.

22. A counterargument is that a more powerful and threatening Iraq might have made it easier for the Coalition to muster support from other regional powers such as Iran and Syria, which might then have been expected to balance rather than bandwagon in their behavior. Moreover, Stephen Walt's work provides evidence of alliance formation in the Middle East in which state behavior is driven

by reaction to threat. See Walt, *The Origins of Alliances* (Ithaca, N.Y.: Cornell University Press, 1987). However, practical—indeed brutal—regional realities work to minimize balancing. Saddam would have achieved a fait accompli. Moreover, in view of Saddam's demonstrated willingness to use violence with extreme ruthlessness against his internal and external adversaries, as well as his ability to wield both bribery and blackmail, the ability of his neighbors to align themselves with the United States effectively would have been highly problematic. Iran in particular, having been militarily defeated after an eight-year war in which its cities were exposed to demoralizing Scud attacks, would hardly have been willing or able to play an active role in an anti-Saddam coalition, let alone a balancing role, by aligning itself with the United States (the "Great Satan").

23. Laurie Mylroie cited this figure, noting that it represented a $10 billion increase over the previous two years, i.e., from the time of the cease-fire with Iran. See Mylroie, *The Future of Iraq*, Policy Paper no. 24 (Washington, D.C.: Washington Institute for Near East Policy, 1991), 29.

24. These calculations assumed that mutual agreement on lifting the sanctions would have been achieved and that Western countries would have agreed to sell oil equipment to the Iraqis. However, Iraq rejected the UN's terms for resuming initial limited oil exports; as of April 1992, no agreement had been reached. The CIA report is described in Patrick E. Tyler, "Hussein's Ouster Is U.S. Goal, But at What Cost to the Iraqis?" *New York Times*, April 28, 1991.

25. *New York Times*, May 15, 1991, A16.

26. The Condor II project was a secret program organized by the Argentine air force, over which government officials had little control. After his election as president, Carlos Menem initially found himself in a bureaucratic battle with the air force over the program, which had become a sensitive issue in relations with the United States in the aftermath of the war with Iraq because Argentina had aided Iraq's missile development program. See Nathaniel C. Nash, "Argentine's President Battles His Own Air Force on Missile," *New York Times*, May 13, 1991, 1. Subsequently the program was halted, and in January 1993 the Argentine government delivered most of the Condor II missile components to the United States so that they could be destroyed. Nash, "Argentine Gives Missile Parts to U.S. for Disposal," *New York Times*, March 7, 1993, 9.

27. Daniel Yergin, "Crisis and Adjustment: An Overview," in Yergin and Martin Hillenbrand, eds., *Global Insecurity: A Strategy for Energy and Economic Renewal* (Boston: Houghton Mifflin, 1982), 5.

28. Author's interviews with officials in Saudi Arabia, October 8–14, 1991. The Saudi government's figure of 260 billion barrels does not include 30 billion barrels of light sweet crude oil in the more recently discovered al-Hawta field.

29. The case for early release of the Strategic Petroleum Reserve (SPR) has been made, for example, by the chairman of the Energy and Power Subcommittee of the House Committee on Energy and Commerce, Representative Philip Sharp. See Sharp, "How Bush Made the Recession Worse," *Washington Post*, December 29, 1991, C7. See also Sharp's exchange of letters with Deputy Energy Secretary Henson Moore, *Washington Post*, January 23, 1992, and February 10, 1992.

30. The OECD has noted that energy prices and energy taxes are far lower in the United States than in Western Europe and Japan; gasoline sells in the United

States for one-third its price in Italy and France. The OECD's annual report on the U.S. economy concludes that higher U.S. energy taxes would be consistent with enhanced energy security and with environmental goals. See Steven Greenhouse, "OECD Forecasts Slow U.S. Recovery from Recession," *New York Times*, November 26, 1991.

31. For an evaluation of the Reagan administration's energy policy, see Robert J. Lieber, "International Energy Policy and the Reagan Administration: Avoiding the Next Oil Shock?" in Kenneth A. Oye, Robert J. Lieber, and Donald Rothchild, eds., *Eagle Resurgent? The Reagan Era in American Foreign Policy* (Boston: Little, Brown, 1987), 167–189.

32. See, for example, testimony by the then director of Central Intelligence, Robert M. Gates, as quoted in Elaine Sciolino, "Iraqis Could Pose a Threat Soon, CIA Chief Says," *New York Times*, January 16, 1992, A9.

33. David Kay, "Bomb Shelter: A Report from Iraq," *New Republic*, March 15, 1993, 11–13.

PART THREE

Outside Powers
and the Emerging Order

10

The American Approach
to the Security of the Gulf

Amin Saikal

The security of the oil-rich Gulf has been of great concern to the United States ever since the end of World War II. Every U.S. president from Harry S. Truman to Bill Clinton has attempted to reshape the geopolitics of the region to stabilize it in line with the global interests of the United States. Despite differences in approach, all pursued a common goal: to establish and maintain U.S. dominance in the region. And all contributed incrementally toward achieving this goal, but perhaps none more than George Bush. As the United States emerged with unprecedented eminence in the Gulf[1] in the wake of the favorable regional and international situation created by the ending of the Cold War, the demise of the Soviet Union, and the Gulf War of 1991, President Bush was unusually well placed to take the greatest leap forward. He accelerated the development of what might be called a "unipolar security system" in the Gulf, which had the aim of securing a permanent security structure not just to safeguard the country's friends in the region but also to ensure the expansion of U.S. control in the Middle East as a whole in the post-Cold War and post-Soviet era. With this system he left a legacy that his Democratic successor, Bill Clinton, has evidently embraced as central to his Middle East strategy. The four key, interrelated objectives of Clinton's strategy were outlined in a policy statement as (1) to protect U.S. allies and interests—most importantly "the free-flow of ... oil at reasonable prices" from the region; (2) to enforce a "dual containment" of Iraq and Iran; (3) to promote an Arab-Israeli peace, on the basis of a linkage between this and the second objective; and (4) to stem "the spread of weapons of mass destruction and promote a vision of a more democratic and prosperous region for all the peoples of the Middle East."[2]

In this chapter, I undertake three interrelated tasks. The first is to delineate the kind of unipolar security system that U.S. policy makers have sought to put in place in the Gulf. Second, I argue that a unipolar system is unlikely to be effective in preventing conflict and bringing durable stability to the region. Third, I suggest that a better alternative to the unipolar system would be a comprehensive collective security arrangement in which all constituent states would have the option of participating without the military involvement of outside powers.

Unipolar Regional Security System

U.S. efforts to establish a favorable security system in the Gulf date back to World War II. In 1944 the United States helped construct the Dahran air base in Saudi Arabia as a means to expand its regional influence and facilitate allied operations during the war. A year later President Franklin D. Roosevelt gave secret assurance to King Ibn Saud that the United States would defend Saudi Arabia in the event of an outside attack.[3]

Roosevelt's initiative was pursued in one form or another by his successors within the frameworks of the Truman policy of containment and the Eisenhower, Nixon, and Carter doctrines, each of which came to replace its predecessor at roughly ten-year intervals between 1947 and 1980. However, although they resulted in varying measures of success, no U.S. effort until the turn of the 1980s proved as effective as the United States desired.

Against this backdrop President Ronald Reagan resolved to give teeth to the Carter Doctrine within a Reaganist framework of "strategic parity." However, the most important breakthrough for the United States came during the Bush administration with the August 1990 Iraqi invasion of Kuwait. Seizing upon this situation and the concurrent decline of the Soviet Union as a superpower, the Bush administration set out not only to reverse the Iraqi occupation of Kuwait but also to alter the regional status quo in the hope that the United States would achieve an unchallenged military position and political dominance in the region. It moved rapidly to capitalize on the success of Desert Storm by developing a security system in the Gulf that would be low-key in its political disposition and economical in its implementation. The security system would address the country's previous military shortcomings in the region but would be in tune with the post-Cold War position and objectives of the United States. Successful completion of the system was expected to provide the United States with a firm and long-term regional structure of control through which it could influence geopolitical developments and oil politics in the area and beyond with an eye to Washington's perception of what should constitute the post-Cold War international order in a single-superpower world.

To date, Washington has not revealed anything resembling a detailed blueprint for this security system. In fact, it has released only a limited amount of information, and even that in piecemeal fashion, and it has been circumspect about its dealings on the issue with regional allies. Nevertheless, enough information is available from press reports and disclosures by officials to enable us to construct a fairly clear and coherent picture of the unipolar security system.

This type of system essentially rests on the notion of one major power taking responsibility for the security of a number of small and vulnerable allies within a vital but at the same time highly unpredictable region. In return, these allies are required to provide effective political, financial, and infrastructural support for the major power, so that it can act as the external guarantor of their security with the highest degree of impunity whenever a threat arises. The system is structured into three interlocking levels: an alliance between the regional constituents, bilateral security pacts between each regional member and the major power, and an overall regionally based command center and defense network shared by the major power and the regional allies as a whole.[4]

In its operational dimensions, the system does not necessarily require the major power to station a large permanent ground force in the region, only a core of functionaries. However, the system is premised on the need of the major power to have adequate infrastructural support and sufficient military equipment stored and positioned in the allied countries to allow it to rapidly build up its forces and swoop in to preempt, to nip in the bud, or repel a threat whenever necessary. Since the system is predicated on the preponderance of the major power, the ability to determine the nature of the threat and the manner in which it should be countered lies very much with the major actor. Thus, there is enough elasticity in the system for the major power to determine largely on its own when to intervene; it cannot be forced by its regional allies into action if it does not deem action to be in its interests. In short, the system, which can be either collective (based on the notion of all against one) or partially collective (predicated on the notion of a majority against a minority),[5] is basically hegemonic, where the major power stands supreme in its relations with the regional allies.

To construct such a security system in the Gulf, the United States has been negotiating with the Gulf Cooperation Council (GCC) countries.[6] Although the overall structure of the system is still being formed and the central regional actor, Saudi Arabia, has yet to agree formally and fully to all the details of the alliance,[7] some important steps have been taken for its construction. The most substantial was the ten-year security pact signed on September 19, 1991, between the United States and Kuwait. Under the pact—the first of its kind between an Arab state and the United States—the Kuwaiti leadership gained a long-term guarantee of Kuwait's security by agreeing to full defense cooperation, which included allowing the United States to stockpile and position military hardware in Kuwait and have full access to the country's infrastructural facilities for military operations. In the wake of the signing of this pact, Washington made it clear that it expected to conclude similar treaties with the five other members of the GCC in the near future and that the agreement was part of a wider effort to "enhance security and stability" in the region.[8] U.S. talks with other GCC members were also reportedly making good progress. Although no formal military pact has as yet been signed with Saudi Arabia, for all practical purposes such a pact seems to be in place. The Saudi leadership has evidently agreed to the use of its territory and infrastructural facilities for U.S. military operations whenever needed.

To this end, the United States has positioned in Saudi Arabia an undisclosed amount of military hardware, much of which was left over from the Desert Storm campaign against Iraq. And it has given every indication that it is unlikely to reduce its naval and air power in the region to a pre-Gulf War level in the foreseeable future. Washington has continued to assist Saudi Arabia in modernizing and expanding its infrastructural facilities, especially airfields, ports, roads, and storage centers; and it has continued to sell the country as many conventional, up-to-date arms as necessary to enable it to provide backup for U.S. operations whenever required.

From Washington's perspective, a unipolar security system will have several important advantages. First, it will enable the United States to act as over-the-horizon guarantor of regional security with little troop visibility on the ground. That is, it will put the United States in a position to achieve its objectives with a low profile in peacetime, and thus it will diminish the chances of U.S. troops becoming an obvious target of those opposition forces that would like to stir up public discontent for a political-religious backlash at mass level in the region.

Second, it will place the United States in full control of the weapons systems that it deploys. Thus, it will reduce substantially the risk of their falling into the hands of unfriendly forces in the event of either an attempt by a hostile group to gain access to them or a national uprising that results in the breakdown of the command structure in one of the regional member states of the alliance. The system is designed to avoid a repetition of what happened in Iran in the wake of the shah's overthrow.

Third, it will help Washington to deter its regional allies from acquiring nuclear weapons and other arsenals of mass destruction and will help it to temper their desire for excessive conventional arms purchases from non-U.S. sources and for expansion of their armies (which in turn could enhance the risk of national military takeovers and regional arms racing).[9] By the same token, such a system could allow Washington to stage a public relations exercise in support of its pledge to establish a regime of arms control as a necessary condition for stability in the region while continuing to sell arms to the GCC members, particularly Saudi Arabia, in larger volumes than ever.[10] It is reported that during 1991–1992 the U.S. agreed to the sale of $19.2 billion worth of new arms to Saudi Arabia alone.[11]

Fourth, the system will require minimum financial contributions from the United States but maximum expenditures by the regional members to maintain the necessary infrastructural support for the alliance and U.S. operational readiness at the regional level. Consequently, the United States will sustain little financial burden, which will enable the U.S. administration to avoid aggravating its foreign deficit and causing adverse public reaction. This is, of course, an outgrowth of the burden-sharing arrangement that Washington forged with its oil-rich GCC allies in the Gulf War.

Fifth, it will give the United States legitimacy and the operational capacity to monitor, sanction, isolate, and, finally, punish those forces and movements within and on the peripheries of the region that adopt policy stands contrary to its own. Despite their triumph in the war against Iraq, the United States and its allies are concerned about (1) Saddam Hussein not only surviving the ordeal but also reconsolidating his dictatorial rule and causing anxiety for Kuwait and other GCC members; (2) a resurgent Iran, with an enhanced military capability; (3) an upsurge in the growth of anti-Western, anti-Israel Islamic radicalism, which has made its impact felt throughout the region, including in some of the United States' most prized Arab allies such as Egypt and Saudi Arabia; (4) the spread of radical political Islam and perceived Iranian activities in former Soviet Central Asian Muslim republics; and (5) the possibility of an alliance between Islamic and secular radicalism and therefore between Iran, Syria, Yemen, and Sudan as well as some of the Palestine Liberation Organization's splinter groups, particularly if the current U.S.-backed joint PLO-Israeli efforts fail to bring about a settlement of the Palestinian problem and the Arab-Israeli conflict.[12]

Sixth, it will help Washington to maintain, rather than diminish, its strategic alliance with Israel, which is opposed to any U.S. arming of Arabs that could conceivably tilt the regional power balance against

Israel, and at the same time it will not necessarily undermine Washington's interests in helping the Middle East peace process. The latter aim is embedded more clearly in Clinton's efforts than it was in Bush's. The Clinton administration hopes to promote an Arab-Israeli settlement not by pressuring Israel but rather by reassuring it of the United States' total commitment to its security and therefore minimizing any risks the Jewish state would have to take in return for an Arab-Israeli settlement. This reassurance is given not only in the form of direct U.S. assistance to Israel but also as U.S. promises to weaken and contain those regional forces that Israel claims to be threatening to its security. It is in this context that the U.S. security system in the Gulf is being sold to Israel as vital for the protection of the United States' Arab allies and interests in the region. The system is being presented as an imperative not only to control any possible threat from the GCC to Israel, but also to contain those forces that Israel fears most: the Iranian Islamic regime and its regional associates, especially the Lebanese Hezbullah, and the Palestinian radical Islamic group, Hamas. The Iranian regime, Hezbullah and Hamas have actively denounced Israel and the United States and opposed the PLO-Israeli peace agreements of September 1993. Thus that the Clinton administration has sought a U.S. security system in the Gulf that will underline a strategic link between its desire for a settlement of the Arab-Israeli conflict and its need to pursue a policy of "dual containment of Iraq and Iran," based on its understanding that one enforces the other. In this sense the U.S. approach to the security of the Gulf is designed to exacerbate a new geopolitical shift that is predicated on vilifying Iraq and Iran and their associates as the most important "enemies" of the rest in the region.

Seventh, the system will not make it obligatory for the United States to act whenever its regional allies want it to do so. Enough in-built leverage would exist for the United States to control the system and to be able to determine virtually at will when, how, and for what purpose the system should be activated.

The Drawbacks of the System

The most disturbing aspect of the system is that it will accentuate and entrench divisions within the region. For the system to function effectively, the region will need to be kept divided between those who are dependent on and vulnerable to the United States and those who are vilified as "enemies" and therefore dangerous to the interests of the United States and its allies. Thus, whatever the regional positions and threatening capacities of Iraq, Iran, and other insubordinate forces—especially those that Washington simplistically calls "Islamic fundamentalists"[13]— they have to be demonized as the "enemy." Therefore, the system cannot allow the growth of any type of collective regional cooperation and order that could render it superfluous. It is on this basis that in early 1993 President Clinton's adviser on the Middle East, Martin Indyk, declared both Iraq and Iran to be "hostile to American interests" and harboring "antagonism ... towards the U.S. and its allies in the region." He also made it clear that the United States no longer needed to build up one of these countries to balance the other, as it did prior to the Iraqi invasion of Kuwait: "As long as we are able to maintain our military presence in the region," Indyk said, "as long as we succeed in restricting the military ambitions of both Iraq and Iran and as long as we can rely on our regional allies—Egypt, Israel, Saudi Arabia and the GCC, and Turkey—to preserve a balance of power in our favor in the wider Middle Eastern region, we will have the means to counter both the Iraqi and Iranian regimes. We will not need to depend on one to counter the other."[14] He discounted any possibility of reconciliation with Iraq and the normalization of relations with Iran for as long as these states failed to comply fully with the objectives of the United States. To force such compliance, the Clinton administration proclaimed a policy of full political, economic, and military containment of those states and their supporters.

This policy raises an important question: Although this containment is central to the overall Clinton strategy, is there much substance to the claim that Iraq, Iran, and radical political Islam pose the most serious threat in the region, one that the international community should take seriously? Let us first look at the case of Iraq.

Undoubtedly, the survival of Saddam Hussein's regime and its periodic challenge to the U.S. position, mainly by defying or rejecting some of the U.S.-driven UN measures against it, have proved to be an embarrassment for Washington. But for all practical purposes the regime does not have a capacity to achieve much beyond this for the foreseeable future. It is important to be remember that much of Iraq has already been reduced more or less to the status of a UN-mandated territory without the benefits of a mandate. Saddam Hussein's control of Iraqi soil is severely restricted, and his military machine, which was once regarded as formidable, is badly incapacitated. He no longer has the necessary infrastructural capacity, the financial and economic resources, or the backing of a major power to be able to reemerge as anything more than a regional nuisance for a long time. Thus, it is not surprising that the Iraqi leader has since early 1993 grown increasingly compliant to UN demands. Of course, he may still continue his efforts to regain control over all of Iraq and keep up his saber-rattling rhetoric against his regional and international opponents to underscore his personal pride and enhance his credibility with the Iraqi people in particular and the Arab peoples in general. But, he is no longer in a position to pose a threat to Iraq's neighbors that cannot be contained and countered effectively by the GCC, Iran, or both on the basis of their own resources.

As the situation stands, Saddam Hussein is incapable of being a serious regional threat, and it is not in the interests of the United States to seek his immediate replacement with a compliant alternative. The real purpose underlying Washington's containment of Iraq is to let Saddam's regime go on indefinitely but only as a weak, demonized, and chastised force to which Washington can point to substantiate its perception of a regional enemy, which it must do for the functioning of its security system in the Gulf and for its Middle East strategy as a whole. So far, Washington has paid no more than lip service to the cost of this policy to the Iraqi people; it is simply a policy dictated by the need to ensure the success of its grand strategy.

As for Iran, the Clinton administration is essentially following a policy that has been in place ever since the success of the Islamic Revolution in 1979, except that it is the first administration to announce it formally and with a high degree of venom. It continues to rely on the residue of the bitter U.S. experiences with Iran's Islamic regime, especially the hostage crisis of 1979–1981, and on the historical, cultural, political, and sectarian differences and the general distrust that have existed between Iran and its Arab neighbors. Like its predecessors, the Clinton administration has found it quite easy to escalate both domestically and regionally its demonization of Iran's Islamic regime and to urge both U.S. allies and adversaries to join Washington in vilifying the most dangerous "enemy" of the international community.

Undoubtedly, ever since the Kuwait crisis, Iran's capacity as the Gulf's largest and potentially most powerful actor has increased. Indeed, no regional state has benefited as much from the Kuwait crisis as has Iran. When Baghdad set out to do battle over Kuwait, it found it imperative to make instant peace with its old foe, Iran, almost entirely on the latter's terms. Without firing a shot, Tehran secured the return of all of the territories occupied by Iraqi forces during the eight-year war that began in 1980. It also unexpectedly became the recipient of more than one hundred Iraqi frontline fighter planes when Saddam Hussein dispatched them to safer grounds in Iran at the start of Desert Storm.

Together with Iran's skillful adoption of a neutral position in the Gulf War, these developments enabled the government of President Hashemi Rafsanjani to press for a vigorous process of domestic reconstruction and foreign policy rationalization to end Iran's international isolation. Under his guidance Iran sought to play a constructive role in securing the release of Western hostages in Lebanon, to retrench its involvement in that country, and to make a substantial shift to a free-market economy.[15] It also endeavored to mend its relations with the GCC countries. Shortly after the Gulf War, it restored diplomatic relations with Saudi Arabia after two years of rupture; Foreign Minister Ali Valayati visited the Saudi kingdom and expressed strong interest in the formulation of any regional arrangement that placed the security of the Gulf in the hands of its constituent states.

An important message rang clear: Iran wanted better international relations and was ready to show flexibility in its global dealings, although not at the cost of certain ideological and ethical principles, including its stance on Salman Rushdie. However, the U.S. response continued to be one of treating Iran as an "outlaw" state; notably, it accelerated its efforts toward building a security system in the Gulf that could abort the Iranian efforts for greater regional and international accommodation. The Rafsanjani government, the theocratic nature of which breeds an inherent sense of insecurity, could not but feel that the United States and its allies were more than ever determined to contain the Islamic republic as a legitimate player in the region. It could even perceive that the punishment meted out to Iraq contained an important message for Iran: If you fail to recognize the dominant U.S. interests and fall in line with them, the United States now has the necessary regional and international leverage to punish you. As a result, Tehran could only strengthen its resolve to shore up its security position in an effort to avoid facing the same fate as Iraq in the event of possible recriminatory actions.

Hence, Iran set about modernizing and strengthening its military with increased arms purchases, especially from Russia and North Korea. Although Iran has repeatedly denied the U.S. allegation that it has actively sought to acquire nuclear arms, it may be aware that a capability of this kind is the ultimate deterrent in the face of such powerful and determined adversaries as the United States and Israel. Washington has pointed to Iran's actions in procuring arms as further evidence of the Iranian regime's quest for regional domination and on that basis has claimed further justification for its own hegemonic approach to the security of the Gulf.

Whatever the nature of and prospects for Iran's military buildup, its military purchases have so far been relatively modest, constituting about 2–3 percent of its GDP for 1991—a figure that falls far short, for example, of what Saudi Arabia spent on arms purchases in the same year. Further, Iran faces some real constraints on how much it can spend on the military beyond what is essential for safeguarding its national security. As admitted by its own leadership, Iran today faces a serious economic situation with a potential for widespread social unrest. Since the advent of the Islamic regime in 1979, the country has experienced a steady rise in its national consumption but a decline in its national productivity. Although its population has grown from some thirty-four million to nearly fifty-eight million, its oil income fell from a prerevolution level of over $20 billion per annum to $12 billion in 1991, and the shortfall was not substantially met by any other source, for the nonoil sector of the economy also declined noticeably. Although the official figures put the inflation rate at about 20 percent and do not clarify the rate of unemployment, according to unofficial data Iran's inflation in 1991 was running at about 50 percent and unemployment at 30 percent; its per capita income was half of what it had been just before the revolution.

The economic situation, together with the devastation that resulted from the long years of war with Iraq, has left the Iranian leadership with little choice but to devote as much of its resources as possible to national reconstruction and thus to refrain from the type of regional activities that could undermine this process. Iran is today in strong need of foreign investment and foreign borrowing. In late 1989 President Rafsanjani succeeded in securing the approval of the Majlis (the Iranian National Assembly) to borrow $27 billion as part of Iran's five-year plan. However, Iran has so far been able to attract only one third of this amount.[16]

Thus, in contrast to other oil-rich states in the region, especially Saudi Arabia, Iran does not have the necessary volume of nonhuman resources either to engage in a large-scale military buildup or to provide substantial aid to receptive states and movements for regional influence. Yet, Washington has made much of what it calls Iranian activities in fomenting anti-Western Islamic activism in the region, especially in the Sudan, Egypt, Algeria, Lebanon, and some parts of Central Asia. Although Iran has not denied its expression of solidarity with and support for a number of Islamic groups, three issues must be factored into any analysis of the Iranian role. One is that most of the Islamic movements in the region have had roots in their places of origin and have grown in response to the failure of the ruling elites of those countries to address declining social and economic conditions. Iran cannot be held responsible for the growth of these movements. Another issue is that as much pluralism exists within and between the Islamic movements as within the Muslim world, which makes it extremely difficult for any particular force to cut across ethnic, cultural, and sectarian cleavages in an attempt to gain more than a limited influence. The third issue is that Iranian support, like that of Pakistan and Saudi Arabia, for certain Islamic groups on sectarian grounds has not necessarily helped the process of government building in post-Communist Afghanistan, and there is little evidence of active Iranian involvement in support of Islamists in the former Soviet Muslim republics. Iran has avoided fueling the struggle between Islamists and their still Communist-dominated governments in these republics, especially Tajikistan. It clearly grasps that its interests are best served through cooperation with Russia (which has become its major source of arms and which has expressed opposition to the spread of Islamic radicalism from Iran) and through stability in the Central Asian-Transcaucasian region.

Yet Tehran has reason to be politically, economically, and culturally active in Central Asia-Transcaucasia. Iran, after all, shares borders and substantial ethnic and cultural ties with this region, and Central Asia-Transcaucasia has emerged as volatile, with the potential to be as problematic and destabilizing for Iran as the Gulf. The region has also become the focus for involvement by a number of Iran's regional U.S.-backed competitors, which have launched a vigorous campaign to gain access to markets and resources for both economic gain and political influence. These competitors are Turkey, whose efforts have openly focused on reviving its age-old *pan-Turkik* ambitions; Saudi Arabia, which has endeavored to buy Islamic but nonetheless anti-Iranian influence;[17] and, more significantly, Iran's archenemy, Israel, which has established diplomatic relations with five of the republics and has a booming involvement in Kazakhstan's cotton industry as well as trade ties with the country.[18] In light of this focus on the region by Iran's competitors, no government in Tehran—regardless of its ideological stance—can afford to remain disinterested in the region. This situation together with the lingering strife in Afghanistan, makes Iran seem like an island surrounded by regions of active instability on nearly all sides. The challenge that this situation and the declining internal economic conditions have posed to the Iranian Islamic regime is formidable, leaving it very little room either to remain ideologically too aggressive or to be able to achieve regional paramountcy. When all is considered, it is not surprising that Tehran has felt increasingly vulnerable and become both restless and assertive about what it regards as Iran's need for sufficient capabilities to safeguard its interests.

However, all of these factors have proven irrelevant to Washington's strategic considerations and calculations. Little evidence suggests that Washington has been interested in understanding the Iranian position and evaluating the rationale behind it and the limitations upon it. What has driven Washington is its desire to ensure U.S. dominance in the region. Its unipolar security strategy is adopted with precisely this aim, with a clear and unwavering focus on demonizing not only Iraq but also the Iranian regime and other insubordinate forces of Islamic activism and on driving more deeply the wedge between Iran and the other constituent states in the region. No matter what these states and forces do, as long as they remain outside the orbit of U.S. dominance, they are useful "enemies" for the pursuit of U.S. strategy in the Gulf in particular and in the Middle East in general. They are treated almost as a necessary substitute for the Cold War Soviet Union but for the purpose of a post-Soviet and post-Cold War regional and international order.

The Collective Security System

When examined closely, the current U.S. strategy is incapable of ensuring long-term stability in the Gulf. It is geared more toward exacerbating regional tensions and hardening dividing lines than fostering the necessary bases for cooperation and stability within the region. It contains germs of a realist or Hobbesian view of international relations that emphasizes the primacy of "self-help," "self-interest," and "competitive pursuit of power" as the best means for states to survive in an anarchical world. It thus ignores the fact that no attempt based on the Cold War mentality can improve the prospects for peace and stability in this extremely important and yet highly volatile region, whose frontiers have now expanded to include the critical area of Central Asia. It was, of course, the Hobbesian view that largely underscored the behavior of the superpowers during the Cold War struggle.[19]

An alternative that could more effectively have served the cause of stability and security would have been a comprehensive Gulf collective security system worked out within the region. This system would have included all the states of the region and no outside powers. It would have provided for a framework of security on the basis of institutionalized processes of confidence building and conflict resolution. Such a system would have been accomplished through enhanced political, cultural, economic, and military interactions and cooperation among all the constituent states. The role of a power like the United States should have been to mediate between its allies in the region and other regional states, most importantly Iran, and to support the United Nations and its agencies in serving as nonpartisan stimulants for furthering the cause of respect for national independence, human rights, and democracy within a milieu that encompasses many traditions. Only through such a system could the states have developed a sense that their security is indivisible and that the endurance of their security requires a willingness and ability on all of their parts to act as a necessary regional collective against the one who seeks to divide their security. Something along the lines of an expanded GCC, with the inclusion of Iran and Iraq, could have provided the basic structure for the development of such a security scheme.[20]

At no other time in modern history had the conditions been so ready for such a development as in the immediate wake of the defeat of Iraq and the crumbling of the Soviet Union. The United States could have played a pivotal role in this respect if it had shown foresight and achieved two preconditions as part of its Gulf War and postwar efforts. One was to go a step further in its defeat of Iraq, fostering the conditions for the process of giving rise to a more broadly based and responsible government in that country. The other was to resist the temptation, to which it had previously succumbed, to use its geopolitical gains for its own regional paramountcy and that of its allies. Further, it was in a position to reopen lines of communication with an increasingly accommodating Iran and play a positive role in support of a serious dialogue between Iran and its Arab neighbors for three purposes.

The first purpose would have been to enable the regional states to find appropriate mechanisms for a viable regional collective premised not on the idea that the security of the region simply requires military cooperation but on the belief that it needs to involve much more than a defense arrangement. The post–World War II history of the Gulf clearly demonstrates that much of the volatility in the region has had its roots deep in political and socioeconomic conditions; and, in fact, all attempts to address these conditions through force and intimidation have been counterproductive. Thus, if a regional security mechanism, whatever its origins and modus operandi, fails to have adequate political and socioeconomic dimensions, it is unlikely to provide for enduring stability in the region.[21] The second purpose would have been to provide incentives to the government of President Rafsanjani to continue its course of reform, alleviating its deep concern that the United States is intent upon destroying the Iranian Islamic regime. The third purpose would had been to facilitate Iran's participation in regional arms control negotiations and in the Middle East peace talks. The more Iran were locked into regional responsibilities the more it would have recognized its limitations and the burdens of fulfilling its responsibilities. All these objectives would have been imperative for the creation of regional collective security.

Despite their traditional differences with Iran, the United States' Arab allies could have been expected to support the U.S. moves, for three good reasons. First, the GCC countries are aware that a regionally integrated Iran would be less vulnerable to provocation than an isolated one. Second, despite their oil riches the GCC countries—Saudi Arabia and Kuwait in particular—have been experiencing a noticeable shortage of cash, which would have induced them to welcome any U.S. measures that could enhance regional stability without inflicting a heavy financial burden. Third, the U.S. defeat of Iraq had made the GCC countries so indebted to and dependent on Washington that they could not easily reject a U.S. prescription for a better understanding with Iran. However, the Bush administration evidently decided otherwise, and now its successor has resolved to build on rather than depart from the Bush legacy. The administrations have evidently given precedence to self-interest, specifically in terms of preserving and widening the U.S. status as the single superpower in the post-Soviet era, over the need for a rational calculation of what could genuinely enhance stability and security in the Gulf. Their unipolar security efforts may serve U.S. interests in the short run, but they are problematic enough to prove unviable and possibly counterproductive in the long run.

In the 1990s pressure on the Gulf region is bound to mount from a number of areas: political suppression, administrative corruption, and lack of public accountability; human rights violations; wealth and resource disparities; social divisions; the plight of national ethnic and religious minorities— most importantly the Kurds, Palestinians, and Shi'ites; migration of these minorities and political dissidents; and environmental hazards caused by the Iraqis during their occupation of Kuwait and the Gulf War. The salient point is that the present U.S. security approach provides for no dimension to help the region address the threat from these sources. If anything, the unipolar system has the potential to stifle rather than enhance reform processes for defusing the sources of the threat. Long-term security cannot be achieved in the Gulf without the necessary foundations for durable stability; and the latter cannot be attained through military power and alliances. It can only be attained through structural national reform and regional cooperation.

Notes

1. Zbigniew Brzezinski, "Selective Global Commitment," *Foreign Affairs* 70 (Fall 1991), 18.

2. See the statement delivered by Martin Indyk, President Clinton's policy adviser on the Middle East, to the Washington Institute for Near East Policy on May 19, 1993.

3. Aaron D. Miller, *Search for Security: Saudi Arabian Oil and American Foreign Policy, 1939–1949* (Chapel Hill: University of North Carolina Press, 1980), 127–128.

4. Youssef M. Ibrahim, "Gulf Nations Said to Be Committed to U.S. Alliance," *New York Times*, October 25, 1991.

5. See Mancur Olson, *The Logic of Collective Action* (Cambridge: Harvard University Press, 1971); Kenneth A. Oye, ed., *Cooperation Under Anarchy* (Princeton: Princeton University Press, 1986); Gregory Flynn and David Scheffer, "Limited Collective Security," *Foreign Policy*, 80 (Fall 1990); Charles A. Kupchan and Clifford A. Kupchan, "Concerts, Collective Security, and the Future of Europe," *International Security* 16 (Summer 1991).

6. The GCC consists of Saudi Arabia, Kuwait, Qatar, Bahrain, Oman, and the United Arab Emirates.

7. For background, see Patrick E. Tyler, "Gulf Security Talks Stall Over Plan for Saudi Army," *New York Times*, October 13, 1991.

8. Eric Schmitt, "U.S. and Kuwait Sign Pact on Troops," *New York Times*, September 20, 1991.

9. In this respect, Washington's main concern is Saudi Arabia. It is often argued that both the ruling Saud family and its U.S. backers are very conscious of the fact that a substantial increase in the size of the Saudi Arabian army could heighten the risk of domestic military takeover. However, this argument has

lately been used for different purposes by the Saudis and the United States. The Saudis have emphasized the need for a "high-tech army," with a total troop strength of about 200,000, whereas Washington has sought to moderate this emphasis by stressing that in the context of the proposed regional alliance Saudi Arabia will be protected by the United States and therefore has is no need to develop its armed forces in excess of its basic requirements. See Tyler (fn.7) and *Wall Street Journal*, November 6, 1991. For a brief background, see Richard Pfaff, "The Kingdom of Saudi Arabia," in Tareq Y. Ismael and Jacqueline S. Ismael, eds., *Politics and Government in the Middle East and North Africa* (Miami: Florida International University Press, 1991), 385–414, esp. 403–407.

10. For a succinct discussion of U.S. arms sales, see Natalie J. Goldring, *Arms Transfers to the Middle East* (Washington, D.C.: Defense Budget Project Paper, April 25, 1991); William D. Hartung, "Relighting the Middle East," *New York Times*, September 20, 1991. With regard to the sale of Patriot missiles, see *Wall Street Journal*, November 11, 1991. For more recent arms sales, see International Institute for Strategic Studies (IISS), *The Military Balance, 1992–93* (London: Brassey's, 1993).

11. IISS, *The Military Balance, 1991–92* (London: Brassey's, 1992), 117.

12. For a critical discussion of concerns about Syria, see Daniel Pipes, "Is Damascus Ready for Peace?" *Foreign Affairs* 70 (Fall 1991); Gerald F. Seib, "Saudis, Shedding Usual Caution, Play Bold Role in Peace Talks, Hope to Win Over U.S. Critics," *Wall Street Journal*, November 11, 1991.

13. For details, see Amin Saikal, "The West and Post-Khomeini Iran," *World Today* 49 (October 1993); John L. Esposito, *The Islamic Threat: Myth or Reality?* (Oxford: Oxford University Press, 1992).

14. See fn. 2.

15. See excerpts from President Rafsanjani's speech to the Group of 77 on November 19, 1991, in Tehran, in William Drozdiak, "Iran Outlines Shift to a Free Market," *Washington Post*, November 20, 1991.

16. For assessments of the Iranian economic situation. see Elaine Sciolino, "Iran Struggles to Attract Investors," *New York Times*, April 30, 1992; Caryle Murphy, "Iran: Reconciling Ideology and a Modern State," *Washington Post*, April 28, 1992; Peter Waldman, "Clergy Capitalism: Mullahs Keep Control of Iranian Economy with an Iron Hand," *Wall Street Journal*, May 5, 1992.

17. See Jonathan C. Randal, "Turkey Woos Its Ex-Communist Neighbors," *Washington Post*, February 4, 1992.

18. Hugh Carnegy, "Israel Extends Its Arm to Tie Up Central Asian Links," *Financial Times*, May 6, 1992.

19. Kupchan and Kupchan, fn. 5, 116.

20. For a discussion of a similar scheme and alternative models for post-Cold War Europe, see Adrian Hyde-Price, *European Security Beyond the Cold War: Four Scenarios for the Year 2010* (London: Royal Institute of International Affairs and Sage Publications, 1991), 3.

21. See Gordon C. Schloming, *Power and Principle in International Affairs* (New York: Harcourt Brace Jovanovich, 1991), 658–661.

11

From Kuwait to the Abyss: The Soviet Union's Last Foreign Policy

William C. Wohlforth

The Soviet Union deserves a place in the history of the Gulf War mainly by virtue of what it did not do. It did not oppose or even substantially complicate Operations Desert Shield and Desert Storm, which were led by its old superpower rival against an old regional ally. Only a few years after the war's conclusion, with the former Soviet Union mired in the routine brutalities of post-Soviet civil wars, it is difficult to recall the euphoria called forth by Moscow's cooperation with the anti-Iraq coalition. Few major participants in the Kuwait drama could imagine the Soviet Union of 1977 or even 1987 acting the way Gorbachev's crisis-ridden country did in 1990 and 1991. Soviet cooperation, more than any other factor, contributed to U.S. President George Bush's optimism about a "new world order." After all, the new order was mainly about collaboration among the major powers in defense of international stability. Collaboration among the other Gulf War partners was old news; what had changed was the attitude of the Soviet Union. Of course, the new order based on superpower collaboration was short-lived, for the life of one of the two superpowers came to an end less than a year after Desert Storm lit the night sky of Baghdad.

The Kuwait War deserves a place in the history of the decline and fall of the Soviet empire not because of any direct causal role but because of its timing. It occurred in that special period after the collapse of Moscow's outer empire but before the disintegration of its inner one. By this time, the Soviet leadership, its foreign partners, and its domestic opponents were clearly becoming aware of the extent of the country's decline and the profound depth of its internal crisis. No one could know that collapse was just around the corner, but the presentiments of further rapid decline and the possibility of eventual collapse were in the air.[1] An examination of this period thus promises to reveal clues about why the Soviet Union disintegrated when it did and in the manner it did.

This chapter has two goals: to explain Soviet behavior in the Kuwait War, and to connect that explanation to the dramatic and historically unprecedented dissolution of the Soviet state less than one year later. President Mikhail Gorbachev's strategy and tactics in the Gulf conflict provide an illustration of short-run success contributing to long-run failure. The policies that seemed to meet the immediate crisis made it impossible to meet the ultimate crisis. The story is a familiar one in political life, but it is rarely told in connection with events as epochal as the Soviet collapse.

Gorbachev's Gulf Policy and the Soviet Dissolution

The Soviet Union declined and fell more suddenly and more peacefully than any other empire or great state in history. Imperial decline has historically been a prolonged process spanning decades or even centuries during which the imperial elite is aware of the problem and tries to deal with it. Historically, imperial collapse has always been associated with large-scale violence, arising either from the imperial elite's resort to internal or external force to arrest decline or from outside powers, delivering the empire a military coup de grâce.[2] Since most political analysis is based on historical analogy, it is not surprising that all who concerned themselves with Soviet affairs failed to predict the timing and nature of the USSR's collapse almost until it began to occur before their eyes.[3]

The failure to predict or even anticipate in general terms the sudden Soviet decline and collapse resulted from two errors that could be known only in retrospect. The first was the underestimation of Soviet decline and overestimation of the country's capacity to adapt via reform. Even those observers who, before the fact, thought that Soviet decline was very advanced *and* that the system was relatively incapable of reform made the second error, namely, they overestimated the imperial elite's capacity and willingness to arrest decline by force. Few observers could imagine the Soviet *nomenklatura* rolling over and playing dead in the face of the imminent collapse of the Motherland.[4] Hence, even those who thought seriously about the collapse of the Soviet Union could not imagine its occurrence in the absence of a powerful foreign shock that would break the nomenklatura's grasp on power.[5]

The reasons why observers made these two basic errors are complicated and interdependent. Ex post facto arguments rage about poor data and poor theory, about who predicted events most accurately or most inaccurately.[6] In an examination of the connection between Soviet policy during the Kuwait War and the dissolution of the Soviet state, the focus must inevitably be narrower. The 1991 Gulf War case can help explain some of the puzzles surrounding the Soviet Union's exceptional decline and fall by focusing attention on the weakness of the reactionary forces in the Soviet Union. Why were they so ineffectual? If it was clear that the Soviet Union was headed toward disaster, why were more vigorous measures not taken to save it? The answers are numerous, as always, but one simple answer is often overlooked: It was by no means obvious that the Soviet Union was headed for disaster. And even if one was convinced that the country was on the road to ruin, it was by no means obvious that Gorbachev's policies were not the best solution to the problem.

The reasons for the difficulty in assessing the Soviet Union's power and prospects and the likely efficacy of Gorbachev's policies even quite late in the game were also numerous: poor information, high uncertainty, and a rapid pace of events, to name a few. But an additional factor, which has attracted little commentary, is the ambiguity of Gorbachev's policies. The Soviet leadership faced powerful and mutually reinforcing international and domestic incentives for ambiguity. And as the case of the Kuwait War shows, that ambiguity complicated matters for domestic reactionaries and foreign analysts alike. This illustration is fair because the argument that ambiguity frustrated the development of a reactionary opposition gets weaker the closer we get to the actual Soviet collapse. The more evidence of decline is available to contemporary political actors, the more clarity ought to be evident, and the less effective ambiguous policies ought to be in obfuscating matters. So it is particularly illuminating to examine Soviet foreign policy and the arguments of its domestic opponents during the period of the Kuwait crisis from August 1990 until February 1991.

Moscow's "Dual Policy"

Looked at in isolation, from the preceding forty-five years, the most notable feature of Moscow's Kuwait War policy was its ambiguity. In other words, once we accept as normal the possibility of close U.S.-Soviet collaboration on a vital regional conflict between partners of each superpower, what stands out about the policy was its dualism. Moscow sought to be a member of the anti-Iraq Coalition while at the same time mediating between the Coalition and Baghdad. The ambiguity led to contradictory assessments of the policy during and after the conflict. Some accounts focus on cooperation with the West; others on a "tilt toward Iraq"; and others on the policy's "dual" or "conflicted" character, resulting mainly from Gorbachev's need to appease domestic opponents.[7]

The differences between these accounts are partially due to *when* they were written and *which phase* of Soviet Gulf policy they highlight. The policy went through three phases. From Saddam Hussein's August invasion of Kuwait until mid-November 1990, Moscow supported sanctions against Baghdad but opposed the use of force to resolve the conflict. President Gorbachev, Foreign Minister Eduard Shevardnadze, and special Presidential Envoy Yevgeny Primakov all balanced their condemnations of Iraq with expressions of concern about the U.S.-led military buildup in the Gulf. Accounts written during this phase or that focused on it highlight the policy's "dual" character.[8] After the failure of Primakov's late October 1990 negotiating effort, the Soviets, in a series of crucial meetings with the U.S. administration, communicated a policy change: They would now support a Security Council resolution sanctioning the use of force, provided diplomacy were given a sufficient window of opportunity. In this phase, accounts focus on Moscow's unprecedented cooperation with the West.[9] The policy's final phase was ushered in by two developments in December 1990: the rise of conservative opposition to Gorbachev in Moscow, signaled to the world by Shevardnadze's resignation as foreign minister, and the imminence of the actual use of force by the Coalition against Iraq. This phase of Soviet Gulf policy was characterized by a renewed mediating effort by Primakov, which culminated in the Gorbachev cease-fire plan proposed in February 1991, just before the onset of Desert Storm's ground offensive. Accounts in this phase again focus on the policy's dualism.[10]

For the majority of onlookers, including not only distant analysts but also President Bush, U.S. Secretary of State James Baker, and U.S. National Security Adviser Brent Scowcroft, the ambiguity of Soviet policy derived mainly from domestic politics. According to this view, Gorbachev would have preferred a more unambiguously anti-Iraq policy but could not follow such a policy in the face of stiff domestic opposition.[11] A small minority—writing mainly during the third phase of Soviet policy as Gorbachev pushed his cease-fire plan—attributed the ambiguity to a deliberate, calculated strategy designed to recapture Soviet prestige in the Gulf region at the expense of the United States.[12] Knowledge of the war's outcome, and events leading up to and following it, particularly Gorbachev's seeming indifference to the eventual failure of his cease-fire plan and his continued eagerness to work closely with Washington, has only strengthened the majority position. Despite or, more accurately, because of the clarity conferred by hindsight, the incentives for ambiguity in Soviet Gulf policy warrant closer examination. What we find is that the ambiguity in Gorbachev's Gulf policy was overdetermined. Powerful domestic *and* international incentives for ambiguity were evident throughout the period.

Incentives and Disincentives for Ambiguity

Ambiguity is as important for politicians as it is for poets, though political scientists have (perhaps wisely) been more chary of the subject than have literary critics.[13] Any student of politics knows intuitively that it is often beneficial to politicians and statesmen to appear to be different things to different people. It is also common political sense that the actor on the stage of politics must now and then "define" him-or herself. That is, there are costs to pursuing a strategy of ambiguity too far, and woe betide the political actor who is perceived by constituents or negotiating partners to be slippery and bereft of principles. Political savvy is the deft manipulation of ambiguity—knowing when to obfuscate trade-offs and preferences and when to draw lines in the sand. These basic facts of political life are central to understanding Mikhail Gorbachev's tenure as Soviet leader and the story of the Soviet Union's collapse. They are illustrated as well by Moscow's policy toward the Gulf conflict as by other events that occurred in Soviet political life in the years after 1985.

Domestic Incentives

The domestic conservative opposition to Gorbachev's Gulf policy attracted a great deal of attention in part because public foreign policy criticism was such a novel phenomenon even in the Moscow of the glasnost era. To the observer blessed with hindsight, it is startling to learn that public criticism of Gorbachev's Gulf policy was many times more substantial than the open criticism of his policies toward the Eastern European revolutions of 1989 and the reunification of Germany—policies infinitely more momentous for Soviet prospects than any policy toward the Middle East. The foreign policy debate tends to follow a pattern of steadily increasing intensity unrelated to the apparent importance of the issues involved. Until 1990, criticism of Soviet foreign policy took traditional forms. Open opposition was limited to scholarly journals, newspaper editorials, and interviews, and even that opposition was couched within general support for the leadership's "new thinking." Opposition also took the form of delaying or sabotaging the implementation of various agreements with Western powers.

The situation changed as the Gorbachev leadership accepted German reunification in principle in January 1990 and then acceded to Western terms in June. Finally, after all the main decisions had been made and it was too late for a fundamental reversal, the foreign policy debate began to assume the contours one would expect in such dramatic circumstances. Party conservatives such as Yegor Ligachev, Chief of Staff General Mikhail Moiseev, Defense Minister Marshal Dmitry Yazov, and various lower-ranking figures publicly took up the reactionary banner. At the

February 1990 Communist Party plenum, conservatives at last jettisoned party unity and lambasted Gorbachev and Shevardnadze for a foreign policy of fecklessness and dilettantism.[14]

Several factors explain the long delay before a full-throated foreign policy debate occurred. Censorship—formal and informal, enforced and habitual—still played a role. Glasnost came later to foreign policy than to any other issue. And though the Soviet Union was democratizing, it was still far from being a democracy. Potential oppositionists outside the Communist party faced formidable obstacles to organizing substantial agitation and consciousness-raising about foreign policy issues, and critics within the party were still hamstrung by codified strictures and powerful traditions against "factionalism." Ironically, the conservative and nationalist Communists most incensed by Gorbachev's and Shevardnadze's "sellouts" took classic party rules most seriously of all. It took a lot of nudging by unambiguous events to push old party warhorses like Yegor Ligachev into open opposition to their chief.[15]

Not only did oppositionists to Soviet foreign policy during the events leading to the USSR's demise lack the means and sometimes the inclination to organize, they also lacked the time. The suddenness of the flow of events must be taken into account. The Soviet Union's reversal of fortune between the beginning of 1989, when things appeared to be going quite well for Moscow internationally, and the end of that year, when Soviet power appeared to be in unanticipated and hasty retreat, was extraordinarily rapid. Unlike earlier great-power elites, the Soviet political class did not have the benefit of a prolonged and agonizing reappraisal as the scales of power slowly tipped against it. Instead, it was presented with what could be described as nearly a historical fait accompli. The course of events did not grant politically active Soviets the time to organize the kind of mass "patriotic organizations" that had dogged, for example, the governments of Edwardian Britain and Wilhelmine Germany.[16]

The delay in the emergence of a powerful opposition to Germany's foreign policy brings us back to our central concern. The new thinking was fundamentally ambiguous. Both the strategy articulated by the Soviet leadership and its intellectual legions and the actual policy were subject to numerous equally plausible interpretations. Foreign policy doves in Moscow and the West highlighted the new Soviet commitment to cooperation and willingness to make unilateral concessions. Although not blind to that side of the policy, Soviet and Western hawks perceived a different side: a restless revisionism, a lingering animosity toward hallowed Western policies such as containment and extended deterrence, and an expansive globalism still envisioning a world-transforming role for Soviet Russia.[17] Evidence of dramatic concessions and major cooperative accords was undeniable. But so was evidence of the profoundly disruptive effects of the new policy on the key arrangements lying at the foundation of Western security policy. Even as 1989 began, Soviet proposals had propelled the North Atlantic Treaty Organzation (NATO) into an unseemly row over short-range nuclear missile modernization and the "singularization" of West Germany.

The ambiguity of the new thinking hindered the evolution of opposition by obscuring goals and trade-offs. Many hardheaded, self-described "realists" and conservatives could subscribe to or at least acquiesce in the policy because it was subject to multiple interpretations. People with different goals (competition, cooperation, domestic reform) could support the policy at the same time *and think it was working*. All could plausibly think that their preferred facet of the multifaceted policy would eventually come to the fore. Conservatives could console themselves in the evenings over vodka by noting that through all the Gorbachevian blathering about interdependence and common human values, the new thinking might finally attain long-standing Soviet objectives that had eluded Leonid Brezhnev and Andrey Gromyko, from a superpower-chaired Middle East peace conference to the dispatch of NATO.[18] The phenomenon is nowhere better illustrated than in Yegor Ligachev's memoirs, aptly titled in Russian, *The Gorbachev Enigma*. The book chronicles the earnest Ligachev's efforts over many years to puzzle out exactly where Gorbachev stood. Ligachev expressed the conviction that Gorbachev's true preference was for moderate reform but that he allowed himself to be captured by "ultra-radicals" such as Aleksandr Yakovlev.[19] The obverse of the conservatives' uncertainty was the reformers' uncertainty. Even such stalwart new thinkers as Shevardnadze, Yakovlev, and Gorbachev's foreign policy aide Anatoly Chernyaev were occasionally uncertain about whether Gorbachev was really "their man."[20]

The collapse of the Warsaw Pact and the reunification of Germany coupled with further domestic travails finally got the conservative opposition under way. However, conservative opposition to Soviet Gulf policy was hardly in evidence when that policy was formulated. On the contrary, the discourse was dominated by criticisms *from the democratic Left* (in the Soviet parlance of the times). The members of the Left denounced the policy for its refusal to support the West unambiguously. For them Saddam Hussein was a stand-in for domestic totalitarians, and U.S. soldiers and pilots were figurative democratic knights in white armor fighting despotism. The Soviet Union's commitment to Iraq symbolized the ideologically driven, militarized "imperial" policy that had bankrupted the country in the first place. Some intellectuals even argued for the use of Soviet military force against Iraq.[21] As newsworthy as the conservatives' attacks were, this "leftist" critique was extremely popular domestically. It flowed from a long-building dissatisfaction with the Soviet Union's provision of aid to various "progressive" Third World regimes—a dissatisfaction that the Afghanistan war had brought to a head.

It was only after the USSR's Security Council vote sanctioning the conditional use of force against Iraq that Soviet conservatives mobilized for their own assault against Gorbachev and (especially) Shevardnadze. They lambasted the foreign minister for "abandoning" a valued strategic ally, both a source of foreign exchange and a symbol of Soviet credibility. They exploited some incautious remarks made by Shevardnadze to accuse him of planning to introduce Soviet troops into the Gulf, an incident angrily recounted by Shevardnadze in his December 20, 1990 resignation speech. Conservatives maintained that the U.S. use of force made a mockery of the new thinking's idealistic focus on peaceful resolution of disputes. The "democratic" Americans, they noted, had no qualms about the massive use of force in defense of their national interests. And they questioned why the Soviet government sanctioned the employment of military means by the other superpower while appearing categorically to rule out its own resort to force. Furthermore, they contended that the U.S. buildup represented a major military threat near the Soviet Union's southern borders and speculated that it was likely destined to become a permanent new buttress to a NATO alliance weakened by German reunification.

Gorbachev was thus being pulled in two directions domestically, each side wanting him to decrease the ambiguity of his Gulf policy and line up more clearly with one or the other party to the conflict. This bidirectional pull was evident at all levels of the Soviet policy. Consider, for example, the imperial dimension. Whereas the Russian Federation Supreme Soviet demanded immediate withdrawal of all Soviet aid personnel from Iraq and the presidium of the Latvian Supreme Soviet requested an end to Soviet training of Iraqi military personnel at the Bolderaji naval base near Riga, the Supreme Soviets of Kirgizia, Uzbekistan, and Azerbaijan sent notes of protest against Gorbachev's pro-U.S. stance. To cite another example, as the likelihood of the Coalition's use of force against Iraq rose, numerous highly placed policy experts on the Middle East, including Yevgeny Primakov, warned that a bloody attack on Iraq could spark a violent backlash in the Islamic world— including the Soviet Islamic world.[22] And, indeed, Islamic political movements of various stripes did organize antiwar rallies in Daghestan, Kazakhstan, Kirgizia, and elsewhere in Central Asia denouncing the Soviet Union, the United States, and Israel as "aggressors." But Soviet Muslims were split just as were their coreligionists in the Middle East. Many lined up with the Gulf states, Turkey, Egypt, and Syria in supporting military opposition to Iraq's aggression against Kuwait.[23]

Closer to the actual nexus of decision making, sympathies were also divided between those who supported an unambiguous commitment to the allied Coalition and those who favored standing closer to Iraq. Analysts dubbed these tendencies "Western" and "Arabist" and suggested that they were reflected at the top by Shevardnadze and Primakov, respectively.[24] The Foreign Ministry tended to be "Western," and the fact that it was bypassed by special presidential envoy and Near Eastern affairs expert Primakov attracted commentary. Further, speeches by the two men reflected important differences between Western and Arabist lines. Though his comments were distorted by the conservatives, Shevardnadze did discuss the use of Soviet troops, and his westernizing, democratic credentials were impeccable. Divisions within the government, however, were naturally narrower than those reflected in the public debate, for inclusion within the decision-making circles tends to beget conformity. One account, for example, related that a "high-level Arabist" source complained bitterly that regional specialists even within the Foreign Ministry were kept out of the decision-making loop, but when asked what his group would have done differently, the expert could come up with only one argument—that Security Council resolution 678 should have given Soviet diplomacy more time for peace efforts.[25]

International Incentives

It would make things simple analytically if the ambiguity of Gorbachev's Gulf policy could be explained solely by reference to the domestic opposition. But the analytical waters are muddied by the fact that Moscow also faced powerful international incentives for ambiguity. The moment one accepts the Soviet Union's mediation effort as rational, all the ambiguity becomes readily explicable solely by reference to international factors. From this perspective, Gorbachev's Gulf policy follows logically from his previous policies on regional conflicts, which had been in place since 1987. In a series of conflicts from Afghanistan to Angola, the Soviet Union mediated settlements between its regional allies and their Western opponents. This policy was widely hailed in the West and in Moscow as one of the jewels in the crown of the new thinking. Indeed, Western analysts, many of whom had regarded the superpower competition in the Third World as irrational, now pointed out that the new Soviet policy on regional conflicts was not a humiliating retreat but a wiser policy reflecting learning about the world and a profound conceptual reordering, and that it met Soviet ends better than had any previous approach.[26]

An ambiguous policy is the probable result of any mediating effort by an interested great power. A neutral intermediary might convince the disputing parties of its objectivity and disinterestedness. However, no one will believe that a mediating great power, whose success depends upon its ability to sustain the disputing parties' uncertainty with regard to its true preferences, is acting disinterestedly. Each party to a dispute wants a great-power mediator who can influence the other party but is biased toward its interests.[27] A great power interested in serving as an intermediary thus has an incentive to convince both disputants that it is favorably disposed or could become more favorably disposed if the disputant made certain concessions.

Thus, when Gorbachev's Soviet Union positioned itself as a useful mediator in regional conflicts from southern Africa to Afghanistan and the Gulf, it appeared to dance around the issue of its real preferences for a settlement and the degree of its commitment to the disputing parties. In the Kuwait War case, if Gorbachev wished to have any chance of playing the intermediary, he had to induce a certain level of uncertainty in the Western camp as to the firmness of his commitment to its position. Unambiguous commitment to either camp would have vitiated Soviet influence. The same applies to the role of the United States in the Middle East peace process and dozens of other similar cases.[28]

Soviet policy in the 1991 Gulf War presents a textbook case of negotiating ambiguity. During the first phase of the conflict, for example, practically every Soviet statement coupled opposition to Iraq's seizure of Kuwait with expressions of concern about the U.S.-led military buildup, as if the latter were a separate threat to regional stability. Once Desert Storm was under way, Soviet spokesmen claimed that it was punishment well earned by Saddam but also that perhaps it was being pursued too violently and indiscriminately. Such statements were contradictory but useful as signals to both sides of the dispute, especially the Iraqis. The purpose was presumably to give Baghdad reason to think that if it was willing to negotiate about Kuwait, Moscow would become a less stalwart member of the anti-Iraq alliance. Of course, the Soviet effort to place Kremlin diplomacy rather than Western military power at the center of the conflict ultimately failed, but that failure may have been more a result of Saddam Hussein's obtuseness (or conviction that he could win militarily) than a (result of a) lack of calibrated signaling on Moscow's part. Unambiguous Soviet support for Saddam or for the allies would have reduced Iraq's incentives to negotiate.

Any ambiguous policy has costs and limits. In the case of Soviet Kuwait War policy, the key limiting factor was U.S. policy. If Gorbachev had tried to balance between Baghdad and Washington for too long, the latter could have become frustrated to the point of threatening larger Soviet goals of cooperation with the West. Tests of Moscow's real position came now and then, mainly in the form of votes on UN Security Council resolutions. The choice was clear: Oppose, support, or abstain. Much superpower diplomacy during the conflict revolved around Soviet efforts to delay these votes or to introduce ambiguity into the language of Council resolutions, both of which were done to further Soviet mediating policy. In this context, Soviet domestic criticism was useful to Soviet diplomats, for they could argue to U.S. interlocutors that the ambiguity of their policy had nothing to do with preserving Soviet influence at the expense of the United States or with "saving Saddam," but resulted exclusively from the need to "preserve Gorbachev against the Generals."[29]

Given the uncertainties of the situation—particularly surrounding Saddam's willingness to compromise and the potential costs of military action against him—Soviet coyness about setting precise goals made common sense. Although Soviet diplomats did enunciate a consistent set of objectives throughout the Gulf crisis—relations with the West; regional influence; regional peace and stability; consistency with new thinking; safety of the Soviet citizens in Iraq; return of Kuwait to the status quo ante—these objectives were also mutually contradictory. Which one was really paramount in Soviet eyes was impossible to guess. Moscow did not wish to communicate an ironclad set of negotiating priorities that might prove unattainable in practice. But, even at the time, it was clear that the Soviet Union stood a better chance of attaining the maximum number of these goals in the maximum degree if it achieved a negotiated end to the crisis that included Iraq leaving Kuwait.

The ambiguous policy had two wonderful properties from Gorbachev's perspective. First, since Gorbachev liked staying in the middle, he and his supporters could use the arguments of each side against the other. Thus, defenders of the policy could position domestic reactionaries against Washington, Washington against the domestic reactionaries, domestic liberals against reactionaries and against the Iraqis, and so on. And second, since Moscow's precise goals were carefully obscured, proponents of Soviet policy could easily claim victory after the fact. Indeed, throughout the new thinking years, Western analysts debated whether Gorbachev's Third World policy was a retreat, a continuation of the competitive strategy in a new form, or a conceptual revolution matching Soviet ends and means better than any previous approach.[30] Russian intellectuals carried out an analogous debate in Moscow, with radicals arguing that the Gorbachev team had not been able to shed Soviet imperial ways, conservatives charging the Kremlin with selling out allies, and the Gorbachevites in the middle using different aspects of the ambiguous policy to argue against both kinds of critics.[31]

In any given regional conflict, ambiguity *simultaneously* abetted Moscow's negotiating efforts, in the manner spelled out earlier, *and* helped to keep various domestic critics at bay. In many of the regional episodes leading up to the Kuwait War, from Afghanistan to southern Africa and Cambodia, Soviet leaders could and did argue that their policy preserved and even enhanced Moscow's influence in the region while facilitating conflict resolution and reducing budgetary expenditures.[32] During the 1991 Gulf War, Soviet diplomats could challenge liberals that Gorbachev's policy was an attempt to avoid war and bloodshed while reminding conservatives that the policy enhanced Soviet influence via new relations with Gulf sheikhdoms, held out the prospect of a major diplomatic coup if only Saddam would come to his senses, and would in any case help bring Moscow to the coveted but heretofore elusive position at the center of the peace process.[33]

After each major and controversial event, defenders of the new thinking policy could be grateful that the original objectives of the policy had been ambiguous and mutually contradictory. They could consequently stress whatever aspect of the policy appeared successful after the fact. In the case of the Kuwait War, as already noted, the Soviets articulated their mutually contradictory objectives throughout the conflict. They avoided dealing with the likelihood that those objectives concealed painful trade-offs implicit in the policy. Why burn bridges or close off avenues of advance or retreat until the real stakes in the trade-offs were precisely known? If, but only if, a major diplomatic coup ending the conflict without war appeared realizable, then the cost of the Bush administration's rancor could be incurred. If, but only if, Saddam offered absolutely no way out, then the cost of a total break with Baghdad could be borne. It hardly made sense to write the political checks to pay these bills until the precise amounts were known. Once the outcome was known and all the trade-offs heretofore implicit and obscure became explicit and obvious, Soviet leaders and diplomats defending Soviet policy could highlight those objectives that were met and simultaneously downplay those that were not.

The Causes and Consequences of Gorbachev's Gulf Policy

Three issues are raised by this analysis: the explanation for the ambiguity of Gorbachev's Gulf policy; the policy's immediate impact on the Kuwait conflict; and the influence of policy ambiguity on the collapse of the Soviet Union.

The Sources of Soviet Ambiguity

Puzzling out the relative importance of domestic versus international forces in explaining any country's foreign policy provides endless grist for scholarly mills. As is so often the case, the contours of the Soviet

Union's policy during the Gulf conflict seem overdetermined after the fact. Although the vast majority of observers and indeed most participants attributed the policy's ambiguity to domestic opposition, a strong case can be made in favor of the *Primat der Aussenpolitik*. After all, the basic policy was consistent with recent behavior on similar issues, it was formulated before the conservative onslaught in the fall and winter of 1990, and it was implemented consistently, despite the reactionaries' rise and Shevardnadze's resignation in December. Gorbachev's mediating effort and cease-fire proposal in January and February may not have been consistent with private Soviet diplomatic representations to the U.S. government, but they were entirely consistent with the publicly stated policy that had been in place since the beginning of the conflict. Indeed, the Soviet Union's moderate course on the Middle East proceeded steadily after Desert Storm. Moscow opened diplomatic relations with Israel and further distanced itself from radical political forces in the region in seeming disregard of the pro-PLO and anti-Israel sentiments of domestic conservatives.

The evidence of powerful domestic sources for ambiguity in Soviet policy during the conflict is also persuasive. Foreign Minister Shevardnadze's speeches and actions eloquently attest to his conviction that reactionary forces were sabotaging his policy; the same holds for his testimony after the fact. Soviet officials close to Gorbachev recalled in retrospect that though their chief had a free hand in foreign policy up to the revolutions of 1989, after that point he felt constrained by domestic critics.[34] The dramatic rise of the reactionaries' influence on domestic affairs and on Soviet political discourse as a whole in the fall and winter of 1990 lends credence to this view. Gorbachev's efforts to appease the conservative forces in this period by bringing some of their representatives into the leadership, as well as his distancing himself from celebrated reformers like Yakovlev and Interior Minister Vadim Bakatin, aroused suspicions that foreign policy must have been affected by domestic criticism. Gorbachev's move to the Right led to Vice President Gennady Yanayev, Defense Minister Dmitry Yazov, Interior Minister Boris Pugo, and KGB chief Vladimir Kryuchkov being included in the special Crisis Committee set up to monitor events in the Gulf. All these men would play roles in the August 1991 putsch attempt—just six months later. At exactly this moment in domestic politics, Primakov seemed to gain influence over Gulf policy and Gorbachev put forth his cease-fire plan calling for a cessation of hostilities and sanctions before Iraq's withdrawal from Kuwait.

Was the ill-fated Gorbachev plan the Soviet president's supreme effort to appease domestic reactionaries, or was it his supreme effort to ward off a Coalition ground invasion his advisers had told him would be bloody while salvaging the potpourri of foreign policy goals he had been articulating since August 1990?[35] Gorbachev's own preferences provide the answer, for during this period he lay at the center of an extraordinarily confused decision-making apparatus. Glasnost in foreign policy had reached new heights by December 1990; the reactionaries were making a lot of noise, but their real access to decision authority is hard to evaluate. Gorbachev's reforms had by this time sent the Soviet political system into a tailspin: The Communist Party was in decline but the new, reformed institutions of government had not yet found their feet. The USSR Supreme Soviet and its International Affairs Committee were fairly quiescent throughout the conflict, and the Supreme Soviets and foreign ministries of Russia and other republics sought to influence policy. The roles of the Presidential Council and the newly created (in November 1990) National Security Council were unclear. All the evidence suggests that the key decisions were made by Gorbachev in informal crisis groups consisting of figures from the military, intelligence, and foreign policy apparatuses.

The issue of the influence of domestic factors boils down to a simple question: Was Gorbachev's private preference for a more unambiguously anti-Iraq policy? And if so, did he tailor his publicly stated preferences to preempt or appease domestic reactionaries? The former question is simple but probably unanswerable. For, as Gorbachev put it enigmatically to an interviewer in December 1991: "Who knows Gorbachev's intentions at all?"[36] The key to Gorbachev's strategy was to obscure his preferences from the country at large and even from his closest colleagues. In the numerous interviews Gorbachev has given since resigning from the presidency of the USSR, he has spelled out his strategy and tactics in detail. The strategy is common to leaders in all circumstances, but the former Soviet president has made a persuasive case that he faced particularly powerful incentives to obfuscate. Speaking after his resignation, Gorbachev has claimed that his private preferences on most issues were more radical than he could have articulated publicly and that had he been more forthright when in power, his days as Soviet leader would have been numbered.[37] Scholars may have no recourse but to take him at his ex post word, for if he succeeded in concealing his real views from his colleagues and his people, he may well have succeeded in concealing them from the documentary record as well.

The Soviet Impact on the Gulf Crisis

The question of Moscow's influence on the Kuwait crisis boils down to a set of counterfactual queries: What would have happened had Soviet policy been more firmly in either the anti-Iraq or the pro-Iraq camp? If Gorbachev had walked in lockstep with Bush throughout the crisis, would Saddam have opted for a negotiated settlement? If the Soviet

Union had sided with Iraq, could the Coalition have reversed the occupation of Kuwait by military means? Such counterfactual questions can be spun out indefinitely. One way to limit them is to consider only those options the Soviet political system itself considered. The record of the Soviet policy debate suggests that Moscow's options were actually quite narrow.

Within Soviet decision-making circles, arguments raged over what in hindsight look like nuances. The available evidence does not suggest that anyone at the top, including Shevardnadze, opposed the policy of trying to mediate a peaceful solution to the conflict. As argued earlier, once an interested great power takes on a mediating role, it must of necessity follow a policy of regulated ambiguity. So the arguments concerned the degree to which Moscow ought to accept the U.S. approach to the conflict; the amount of room for maneuver Saddam ought to be given; the amount of time sanctions ought to be given before resorting to force. Had Shevardnadze had total control over policy, the Soviets still would have bargained with Washington on the wording of Security Council resolutions concerning the use of force. The Gorbachev cease-fire plan most likely would not have been forwarded in the form it was—if at all. Had Primakov been clearly in charge from the outset, earlier bargaining with Washington would have been tougher. The cease-fire plan obviously would have occurred just as it did. In short, it is hard to see how the total victory of either faction within governing circles would have substantially altered the history of the Gulf conflict, since both accepted the basic premises of the Soviet Union's mediating policy.

More interesting, and more speculative, is to imagine what might have happened had opinions prevailing outside Soviet governing circles come to control policy. But even here one must keep one's imagination in check, for the public debate was severely constrained as well. The controlling constraint was the unwillingness of most people to contemplate Soviet use of force in the conflict. If the Soviet Union had been willing to risk a major showdown with the West by aiding Iraq militarily or even by offering Iraq more concrete security guarantees, the effort to reverse the aggression against Kuwait might have been rendered untenable. If Moscow had been willing to deploy forces against Baghdad, Saddam might have been persuaded to withdraw from Kuwait without a fight. However, precious few voices in Moscow called for use of force or even for accepting the serious risk of the possible use of force. Some Soviet intellectuals on the pro-Washington side of the debate called for making a symbolic contribution to Desert Shield, but most were chary of military entanglement. When Shevardnadze speculated that Moscow might take forceful measures against Iraq if Saddam allowed any harm to come to Soviet citizens there, conservatives attacked him mercilessly for his recklessness. Once it was established that calls for the use of force were unpopular, no one on the conservative side advocated credible Soviet military support for Iraq or opposition to the anti-Baghdad Coalition.

The most judicious estimate of the realm of the possible is limited. Had the conservative forces prevailed, Moscow would definitely have abstained in the UN Security Council and could conceivably have vetoed resolutions calling for force or even, in the extreme case, for sanctions. That would have seriously complicated matters for U.S. policy though it would not have rendered forceful action against Iraq impossible. Had the most radical forces prevailed, Moscow would have firmly and unambiguously aligned with the U.S. policy but would not have contributed materially to the Coalition's military operations. The most one can imagine is the deployment of some naval vessels to the Gulf. Whether that limited contribution would have influenced Saddam in any significant way is a matter for experts to ponder, but it does not seem likely.

Policy Ambiguity and the Dissolution of the Soviet Union

The contours of the domestic debate on foreign policy during the Gulf conflict indicate how widespread the perception of decline had already become by late 1990. It was clear to all serious participants in the political discourse that the country was in no position to risk a military confrontation. Such aversion to military risk is not unusual among the elites of declining empires. The Byzantine, Ottoman, Manchu Chinese, and tsarist Russian imperial elites all acutely perceived the risks associated with foreign wars against more efficient rivals.[38] But all those elites, prominently including the Romanovs, were also obsessed with retaining their great power status and the integrity of their central empires. What is so striking in the Soviet case is the very late and very weak effort by a segment of the imperial elite to defend the empire's international prestige and territorial integrity.

The Gulf episode demonstrates that part of the story was the ambiguity of Gorbachev's new-thinking foreign policy, which helped prevent the formation of the kind of domestic opposition typical in declining powers. Even after the new thinking suffered what to any nationalist could only be described as devastating setbacks in 1989 and 1990, the leadership was able to continue functioning with the policy essentially intact until the country's formal demise at the close of 1991. The virtue of ambiguity is that it helps to stave off polarization, which by definition requires that clear lines be drawn in the political sand. To polarize around a policy, one must know what it is. If all major groups have a different impression of what the policy is, or if all simultenously have reason to think the policy will soon shift in the desired direction, polarization is unlikely.

In this Soviet case, Gorbachev managed repeatedly to maintain the ambiguity of his policies and keep political players uncertain about overall goals and even near-term changes. Polarization thus tended to occur after the fact. Political forces argued over the sagacity of policies after they were seen to have led to more or less irreversible outcomes. Intellectual adjustment to each new diminution of Soviet power appeared to occur well after the fact. This cognitive lag is partially an artifact of hindsight. The real meaning of major events usually becomes clear only after they occur. But in the Soviet case, that ubiquitous problem was exacerbated by the high levels of ambiguity perhaps consciously fostered by leaders playing a dangerous game of balancing among factions and staving off societal polarization. The cognitive lag was abetted by a series of other factors including the centralization of power. Because of this centralization, pressure groups and dissatisfied sectors of the elite were unusually disadvantaged in the Soviet system. The concentration of power in Gorbachev's hands also assisted him in his zigzagging strategy of fostering ambiguity about his true preferences, his Machiavellian domestic dance between radicals and conservatives, his occasional Faustian pacts with each faction, his compromising, his dissembling, his deception. All had reason to believe that Gorbachev might come their way. All had reason to wait just a bit, to see how things would develop before taking extreme measures. Was Gorbachev socialism's murderer or its last defender? People were not sure when he was in power. They argued about it after his retirement. They will doubtless still be debating it after he is dead and buried.

The case of the Kuwait War illustrates the great appeal of ambiguous policies. Leaders can have their cake and eat it too, for long periods of time. They can be everything to everybody or at least appear to offer most groups what they want—both internationally and domestically. Leaders can stave off polarization and keep enemies disorganized and at bay. The benefits are obvious in the short term, but the costs accrue over time. Ambiguity may keep opponents from organizing, but it also removes incentives for supporters to organize. If people are unsure of their leader's preferences, they are unlikely to take risks and bear costs to fight for that leader. Further, the strategy of ambiguity has a time limit. In the end, the leader loses credibility with all players: Having avoided unambiguous commitment to any one of society's factions, the leader ends up alone when in trouble. In the summer of 1987 Gorbachev told his aide Chernyaev, "I mean to go far, very far. No one knows how far I mean to go." The Soviet leader's strategy of ambiguity helped him "go very far" but left him without organized support when he faced his most serious crisis after the August putsch. In his retirement, he has bemoaned his failure to make an alliance with the democratic Left earlier in the game.[39]

The cognitive lag that characterized each step along the road to the Soviet collapse applied also to the final, fatal decisions surrounding the dissolution of the Soviet Union and creation of the Commonwealth of Independent States in December 1991. Not only was the real meaning of those decisions unclear when they were taken, but the meaning will remain unclear for years to come.

The most popular view holds that the dissolution of the Soviet Union was the inevitable fruition of fundamental forces long germinating behind the facade of Soviet power. Leninism was a spent force, and imperialism (in the classic definition of the term) had long been an anachronism in the modern international system. As Michael Dobbs of the *Washington Post* put it, "The collapse of the facade only confirmed what everybody here (in Moscow) already knew."[40] This viewpoint is accurate in that many people did anticipate the collapse of the Leninist political system and the USSR as constituted and run by the Communist Party, especially after the failure of the August putsch. But the popular interpretation is entirely misleading if it is taken to mean that "everybody already knew" before December 1991 that the old USSR would split into fifteen sovereign states. Such an interpretation suggests that "everybody" expected and accepted the borders and nationality designations drawn up by the Bolsheviks and that nobody expected or preferred a reconstituted non-Soviet Union. It implies, for example, that the Russian political elite accepted that "Russia" would henceforth be defined as the "Russian Soviet Federated Socialist Republic." Nothing could be further from the truth.

Soviet power was centered in Moscow. Neither the people nor the republics took that power. The fourteen non-Russian republics probably could not have brought down the Soviet Union individually or in combination had they tried to do so. And had they tried against the will of the Russian metropole, the Soviet dissolution would have been much less exceptional, for it would have required prolonged wars of national liberation around the periphery. Only one republic—the Russian Federation— had the strength to put a swift end to the Soviet state.

Two key developments conspired to create the bizarre situation under which "Russia" acted to overthrow the empire of which it was the center: Boris Yeltsin and the heterogeneous "Democratic Russia" movement transformed the government of the Russian Federation into a center for opposition to Communist rule, while at the same time Yeltsin steadily increased his personal control over the Russian government. Throughout 1991, therefore, increasing the Russian Federation's independence from the Soviet Union was synonymous with fighting Communist Party rule in general and Mikhail Gorbachev's leadership in particular. The Russian Republic's institutions were tailor-made for co-opting the functions of key Soviet institutions or absorbing them outright. The process by which Russia progressively took over Soviet functions and institutions was under way well before the August putsch. The failure of the putsch dramatically accelerated it.

The temporary confluence of anti-imperialism, anti-Sovietism, and anti-Gorbachevism obscured the implications of the December events. In the wake of Ukraine's vote for independence on December 1, Yeltsin suddenly switched from a position of cooperating with Gorbachev on the creation of a confederation of states to one of supporting an alliance with the other Slavic republics against the Soviet center. Yeltsin and the leaders of Ukraine and Byelarus formalized the new alliance at a meeting in the Belovezhkaya Forest outside Minsk on December 6–8 at which they adopted protocols proclaiming the demise of the USSR and the founding the Commonwealth of Independent States. Two weeks later the leaders of all the former Soviet republics except the Baltics and Georgia met in Alma-Ata, Kazakhstan, to increase the Commonwealth's membership to eleven.

These epochal decisions sparked immediate controversy. Gorbachev, of course, deplored the "Minsk maneuver" but expressed the hope that the new Commonwealth would contain as large a cooperative element as possible.[41] Extreme nationalists and conservative Communists also immediately sought to portray the maneuver as a "stab in the back."[42] Even some "democrats" criticized it as shortsighted, hasty, and ill thought-out.[43] But a surprisingly large proportion of the Russian political class not only accepted the Union's demise as inevitable but also genuinely supported Yeltsin's maneuvers as brilliant strokes that freed Russia from Soviet shackles and cleared the decks for decisive reform.[44]

The relatively muted "imperial anguish" occasioned by the formal end of the Soviet empire represented more than the temporary association of the Union with discredited Communists. The new Commonwealth of Independent States was a sufficiently ambiguous formation to be all things to all people. For many Russians, the shift from supporting a renewed Union in November to supporting the Commonwealth notion in December was slight indeed, for the Commonwealth appeared to them to be a renewed Union under another name. The entity's founding protocols speak quite clearly about independent states coming voluntarily together. They also speak just as clearly about a common defense and strategic policy, a unified economic space, basic guarantees of human and minority rights, and so on.[45] Russians easily read into such documents the expectation of Moscow's continued de facto suzerainty over much of the old Soviet Union.

Coupled with the rapid pace of events, the centralization of formal decision-making power, and the high levels of uncertainty, the ambiguous policies of Gorbachev and his successors helped smooth the way for the Soviet Union's decline and fall, making it unique in comparison with the decline of earlier empires. For that the world can be grateful. The guardians of the Soviet state's greatness and prestige were presented with a series of historical faits accomplis before they could organize effectively. In most historical cases, the imperial elite exaggerates the costs of reduced prestige and territorial expanse to individuals and social groups. In the Soviet case, the costs and risks were obscured. Should the perceived costs rise, the appeal of revisionism and restoration may grow. Since the empire was not lost by fire, its recovery in whole or in part may be thought to be a comparatively easy matter. The requirements for Western policy are clear: a tolerance for ambiguity and a willingness to help reduce the human and material costs of dissolution.

Notes

1. One did not need peculiar foresight to anticipate Soviet collapse during his period. See, e.g., G. R. Urban's spring 1989 interview with Hugh Trevor-Roper (Lord Dacre) in Urban, *End of Empire: The Demise of the Soviet Union* (Washington, D.C.: American University Press, 1993); "Z," "To the Stalin Mausoleum," *Daedalus* (Winter 1990); Zbigniew Brzezinski, "Post-Communist Nationalism," *Foreign Affairs 68* (Winter 1989–1990); and W. C. Wohlforth, "Gorbachev's Foreign Policy: From 'New Thinking' to Decline," in W. F. Danspeckgruber, ed., *Emerging Dimensions of European Security Policy* (Boulder, Colo.: Westview, 1991).

2. On the lengthiness of typical imperial declines, see Paul Kennedy, "Why Did the British Empire Last So Long?" in *Strategy and Diplomacy, 1870–1945* (London: Fontana, 1983). On the exceptionalism of the Soviet case, see Stephen Peter Rosen, "The Decline of Multinational Empires: Introduction and Overview," manuscript, Harvard University, n.d.).

3. In fairness to Sovietologists, failure to predict revolutionary events is the rule rather than the exception. For an entertaining, if sobering, compilation of predictive failures, see Timur Kuran, "Now Out of Never: The Element of Surprise in the East European Revolution of 1989," in Nancy Bermeo, ed., *Liberalization and Democratization: Change in the Soviet Union and Eastern Europe* (Baltimore: Johns Hopkins University Press, 1992).

4. Western exponents of the totalitarian model did stress the decline and unreformability of the Soviet Union more than their intellectual opponents in the modernization of developmental schools. But they focused on the regime's brittleness *not* as an argument for the likelihood of collapse but as an argument for the improbability of any liberalization. Since they believed the elite's commitment to the system was total, they could not imagine the elite embarking on reform that would destroy the system. See William E. Odom, "Soviet Politics and After: Old and New Concepts," *World Politics 45* (October 1992), 66–98.

5. The two predictions that were most accurate in hindsight are Andrei Amalrik, *Will the Soviet Union Survive Until 1984?* (New York: Harper and Row, 1970);

and particularly Randall Collins, *Weberian Social Theory* (New York: Cambridge University Press, 1986). Amalrik presciently portrayed the elite's loss of élan and the declining appeal of Soviet ideology, as well as the country's inefficiency and the disaffection of the populace. But the key to his scenario of collapse was the Soviet leadership's resort to a diversionary war with China. Eight years after *Will the Soviet Union Survive Until 1984?* was published, Amalrik published another book in which his estimate was revised, putting collapse into the more distant future, but the diversionary war theory remained central. See Amalrik, *SSR i Zapad v odnoi lodke* (London: Overseas Publications Interchange, 1978), 9–15. Collins (chaps. 7 and 8) placed the Soviet Union in an advanced state of geopolitical decline and overextension. His geopolitical theory predicted gradual dismemberment of the empire through a prolonged series of internal and external wars (although the precise level of violence was unspecified) over many decades and even centuries. See also Collins and David Waller, "What Theories Predicted the State Breakdowns and Revolutions of the Soviet Bloc?" in Louis Kriesberg and David R. Segal, eds., *Research in Social Movements, Conflicts and Change*, vol. 14 (Greenwich, Conn.: JAI Press, 1992); and Ted Hopf's letter, "Getting the End of the Cold War Wrong," *International Security* 18 (Fall 1993), 202–208, which alerted me to Collins's work.

6. Fair-minded postmortems include Robert C. Tucker, "Sovietology and Russian History," George Breslauer, "In Defense of Sovietology," and Thomas Remington, "Sovietology and System Stability," all in *Post-Soviet Affairs* 8 (July–September 1992); and Peter Rutland, "Sovietology: Notes for a Post-Mortem," *National Interest* 31 (Spring 1993), 109–123.

7. See Robert Legvold, "The Gulf Crisis and the Future of Gorbachev's Foreign Policy Revolution," in Frederic J. Fleron, Erik P. Hoffmann, and Robbin F. Laird, eds., *Soviet Foreign Policy: Classic and Contemporary Issues* (New York: Aldine de Gruyer, 1991); Olga Alexandrova, "Soviet Policy in the Gulf Conflict," *Aussenpolitik* 42, no. 3 (1991), 231–240; Graham E. Fuller, "Moscow and the Gulf War," *Foreign Affairs* 70 (Summer 1991), 55–76; Robert O. Freedman, "Moscow and the Gulf War," *Problems of Communism* 40 (July–August 1991), 1–17; and Galia Golan, "Gorbachev's Difficult Time in the Gulf," *Political Studies Quarterly* 107 (Summer 1992), 213–230.

8. See, e.g., Suzanne Crow, "Soviet Union Pursues Dual Policy on Iraq," *Report on the USSR* 2, no. 40 (October 5, 1990), 6–8.

9. See, e.g., Legvold, fn. 7.

10. The most informative account is Golan, fn. 7.

11. On the views of Bush, Baker, and Scowcroft, see Michael R. Beschloss and Strobe Talbott, *At the Highest Levels* (Boston: Little, Brown, 1993), 338–339. Beschloss and Talbott appear to share that assessment, as do Lawrence Freedman and Efraim Karsh, who wrote *The Gulf Conflict: Diplomacy and War in the New World Order* (London and Boston: Faber and Faber, 1993), which some call the most influential account of the Gulf War.

12. See, e.g., A. M. Rosenthal, *New York Times,* Feburary 22, 1992; and William Safire, *New York Times,* February 14, 1992. Freedman (fn. 7) also stressed the strategic rationality of the policy, though he cast it in a less sinister light than the two *Times* columnists.

13. The classic critical study on ambiguity is William Empson, *Seven Types of Ambiguity* (New York: Meridian Books, 1955). An exception among political scientists in this regard is James G. March, whose work deals with organization theory but is highly relevant to the study of politics. See J. G. March and Johan P. Olsen, *Ambiguity and Choice in Organizations* (Oslo-Tromsø: Universitetsforlaget, 1976); and Michael D. Cohen and J. G. March, *Leadership and Ambiguity: The American College President* (New York: McGraw-Hill, 1974).

14. On Ligachev's attack see *Pravda*, February 7, 1990, 6; on Shevardnadze's defense see *Pravda*, February 8, 1990, 3; see also Shevardnaze's April speech recorded in *Foreign Broadcast Information Service Daily Report-Soviet Union* (FBIS-SOV), 90–081, 9–10, and Gorbachev's speech accepting the USSR presidency, Moscow TV, March 15, 1990 (FBIS-SOV), 90–051, 44.

15. See Yegor Ligachev, *Inside Gorbachev's Kremlin: The Memoirs of Yegor Ligachev,* trans. Catherine A. Fitzpatrick, Michele A. Berdy, and Dobrochna Dyrcz-Freeman (New York: Pantheon, 1992).

16. For the comparison to pre-1914 patriotic organizations, consult Kennedy, *The Rise of the Anglo-German Antagonism, 1860–1914* (London: Allen and Unwin, 1980), chap. 18; and Paul Kennedy and Anthony Nicholls, eds., *Nationalist and Racialist Movements in Britain and Germany before 1914* (London: Macmillan, and St. Antony's College, Oxford, 1981).

17. As Russian Federation Foreign Minister Kozyrev later put it: "The 'new thinking' was largely an indeterminate philosophical concept, but in fact it was simply a new front" for the old policy. Interview with *Moscow News*, 1992, 23, 14.

18. As Jerry Hough noted: "The Soviet military has every reason to support Gorbachev. Although the officers were unhappy over the loss of Eastern Europe and the unification of Germany, they know that these events eliminated NATO as a threat." See Hough, "Understanding Gorbachev: The Importance of Politics," *Soviet Economy* 7, no. 2 (1991), 104.

19. Ligachev (fn. 15); and Ligachev, *Zagadka Gorbacheva* (Novosibirsk: Sibirskii tsentr SP "Interbook," 1992). Although Gorbachev's close colleagues were often unsure of his intentions, many Western analysts experienced no such uncertainty. For the view that Gorbachev was a radical reformer and even a revolutionary early on, see Stephen F. Cohen's introduction to Ligachev, *Inside Gorbachev's Kremlin* (fn. 15), and John Gooding, "Gorbachev and Democracy," *Soviet Studies*, no. 2 (1990), 195–231. For the view that Gorbachev was really a savior of the Soviet system, see Marshall Goldman, *What Went Wrong with Perestroika* (New York: Norton, 1991), written during Gorbachev's 1990 shift to the Right. The view that Gorbachev was really a Machiavellian, Ataturk-like, state-building reformer is expressed in the perestroika-era writings of Jerry Hough (e.g., fn. 18). Gorbachev's actions before and during the August coup, as well as his own testimony in retirement, have lent credence to the first view. It will surely be reflected in his memoirs.

20. Especially revealing is Chernyaev's memoir, based on his diary entries during his five-year stint as Gorbachev's close adviser; Chernyaev, *Shest' let s Gorbachevym: po dnevikvym zapisiam* (Moscow: Progress, 1993). See also Georgy Arbatov, *The System: An Insider's Life in Soviet Politics* (New York: Random House, 1993), 320–361, and Shevardnadze's testimony on this score in his interview with

Yury Shchekochikhin in *Literaturnaia gazeta*, January 22, 1992, in FBIS-SOV-92-018, 22.

21. See, e.g., Igor Belaev in *Literaturnaia gazeta*, October 10, 1990, cited by Golan (fn. 7), 215.

22. Golan, fn. 7.

23. George Stein, "Soviet Moslems Split on Gulf War," *Report on the USSR* 3, no. 8 (Feburary 1991).

24. See, e. g., Suzanne Crow, "Primakov and the Soviet Peace Initiative," Radio Liberty *Report on the USSR* 3, no. 9 (March 2, 1992), 14–17.

25. A. Vasil'ev, "Kem i kak opredelialas' positsiia Sovetskogo Soiuza v konf-likte mezhdu Irakom i Kuveitom," *Komsomol'skaia pravda*, February 16, 1991.

26. For a persuasive argument along these lines, see Richard K. Herrmann, "Soviet Behavior in Regional Conflicts: Old Questions, New Strategies, and Important Lessons," *World Politics* 44 (April 1992), 432–465.

27. See Thomas Princen, *Intermediaries in International Conflict* (Princeton: Princeton University Press, 1992), chap. 5.

28. See, e.g., ibid., esp. chap. 6.

29. Foreign Ministers Eduard Shevardnadze and Aleksandr Bessmertnykh repeatedly made this case in discussions with James Baker and George Bush. See Beschloss and Talbott (fn. 11). What is not clear is how genuine these representations were.

30. For representative examples, see Stephen Sestanovich, "Gorbachev's Foreign Policy: A Diplomacy of Decline," *Problems of Communism* (January–February 1988), 1–15; Celeste A. Wallander, "Third World Conflict in Soviet Military Thought: Does the 'New Thinking' Grow Prematurely Grey?" *World Politics* 42 (October 1989), 31–63; Mark Katz, *Gorbachev's Military Policy in the Third World* (New York: Praeger, 1989); Charles H. Fairbanks, Jr., "Gorbachev's Global Doughnut: The Empire with the Hole in the Middle," *National Interest* 19 (Spring 1990); and Herrmann, fn. 26.

31. Prior to the Gulf War, liberal critiques far outweighed conservative attacks. See, e.g., Andrei Kolosov, "Reappraisal of USSR Third World Policy," *International Affairs* (1990), 5; Georgiy Mirsky, "The USSR and the Third World," *International Affairs* (1988), 12; Andrei Kortunov, "Generosity or Wastefulness?" *Moskovskie novosti*, December 3, 1989; *Current Digest of the Soviet Press* 42, no. 2, 15.

32. See esp. Herrmann, fn. 26.

33. Richard Weitz, "The Gulf Conflict and the USSR's Changing International Position," *Report on the USSR* 2, no. 41 (October 10, 1990), 1–5.

34. Author's interviews with former Foreign Minister Aleksandr Bessmert-nykh and former aide to Gorbachev for foreign affairs Anatoly S. Chernyaev, February 1993.

35. Golan (fn. 7), 219. According to Freedman and Karsh (fn. 11), 176, Gorbachev's key military adviser, Marshal Sergei Akhromeev, projected that the war would be long and sanguinary.

36. *Nezavisimaia gazeta*, December 14, 1991, 5, in FBIS-SOV-91-248, 19.

37. Ibid. See also, e.g., his interview with *Komsomol'skaia pravda*, December 24, 1991, trans. in *Current Digest of the Soviet Press* 43: 51:7; *La Stampa*, July 15, 1992.

38. Rosen, fn. 2, 8.

39. See sources cited in fn. 37.

40. *Washington Post*, December 29, 1991, A1, A26, cited in Joseph G. Whelan, *Gorbachev's Decline and Fall: From Failed Coup to Collapse of Empire, August–December, 1991* (Washington, D.C.: Library of Congress, Congressional Research Service, 1992), 36. This book provides an excellent, concise analysis of these events.

41. See the interviews and speeches assembled in M. K. Gorshkov and V. V. Zhuravlev, *Gorbachev-Yel'tsin: 1500 dnei politicheskogo protivostoianiia* (Moscow: Terra, 1992), 429–434.

42. See citations in Whelan, fn. 40, sec. C; and the articles reprinted in Gorshkov and Zhuravlev, fn. 41, 437–443.

43. The best example here is Aleksandr Tsipko. See his interview with *Komsmol'skaia Pravda*, January 14, 1992, trans. in *Current Digest of the Post-Soviet Press* 44, no. 6, 12–14.

44. See Vera Tolz and Elizabeth Teague, "Russian Intellectuals Adjust to the Loss of Empire," *RFE/RL Research Report* 1, no. 8 (February 21, 1992).

45. See Whelan, fn. 40, appendix D, for the texts of the protocols.

12

Moscow: The 1991 Gulf Crisis and Its Aftermath

Irina Zviagelskaia

The 1991 Gulf crisis occurred during a period marked by drastic changes in international relations especially within the Soviet Union. In the time since the crisis, it has become obvious that the allied victory and the unprecedented Soviet-U.S. cooperation within the UN and abroad, important as they were, left many Middle East issues unresolved. New problems lay ahead— not only for the Middle East, but also for the Soviet Union, which ceased to exist as such in December 1991. The Kuwait crisis turned out to be an additional cause for political struggle in Soviet society—the struggle that resulted in the disintegration of the country. A few signs of the approaching collapse could be discerned earlier, but they were overshadowed by the dramatic events in the Gulf.

The Gulf crisis differed from previous military clashes in the Middle East in that it was the first regional conflict following the end of the Cold War. That period of confrontation between the USSR and the United States had seriously affected not only the bilateral relations of the two superpowers but regional developments as well; the Soviet-American rivalry, however, was not in itself a source of the regional conflicts. The internal causes, such as territorial, national, and religious contradictions among the parties involved, and the ambitions of certain regimes and political leaders, had always existed.

Still one can assume that the Cold War confrontation between the two superpowers had a profoundly negative effect on international relations, adding fuel to local disputes and, in fact, imposing upon them a global pattern of political behavior. During the Cold War, the Soviet Union perceived U.S. policy as the main threat to its interests. The same perceptions (or misperceptions) dominated American political thinking. The USSR eagerly supported any regime or movement in the Third World that proclaimed its intentions of building socialism and countering imperialism, irrespective of its true nature and potentials; the United States was no less busy searching for Communist plots in societies that were not ready for even rudimentary capitalism.

In the framework of a zero-sum game, both powers considered regional conflicts as instruments of enhancing influence; the participants of the conflicts were accordingly divided into "their clients" and "our clients." Such classification involved a great deal of arrogance and make-believe. "Clients" were not puppets but were regimes with interests of their own—which did not necessarily correspond with the interests of the patrons. Moreover, in any conflict with their neighbors, "clients" tried, for their own reasons, to draw in friendly outside powers and demanded more and more sophisticated arms, political commitments, and even direct military support.

Patron-client relations were complicated enough, but they were complicated further by the Soviet-American rivalry, which made it still easier for proxies to capitalize on the mutual paranoia of the two powers. It is therefore doubtful that during the Cold War the United States and the Soviet Union had a great deal of control over events because of any influence they exerted over their regional allies. Obviously, both superpowers exerted some leverage and coercion; but, on the one hand, the allies preserved room for maneuver and, on the other, both superpowers, absorbed by their rivalry, were not always willing to constrain their friends. Mutual suspicions made the situation worse. In the Middle East, for example, both powers had long understood that the continuation of the Arab-Israeli conflict with its regular crisis stages had become detrimental to their interests, but this realistic conclusion did not prevent them from rejecting or treating with suspicion any peace proposal advanced by either a global rival or a regional ally.

In the context of the Kuwait crisis, ideological approaches could have easily dictated the behavior of the USSR and the United States, thus creating the threat of a third world war. Fortunately (if this word can be used in the circumstances), the crisis occurred when a new détente was gaining momentum and when the end of the East-West confrontation paved the way to cooperation between the former global rivals. However, the approaches of the two countries were not necessarily the same, and frictions and misunderstandings were produced by the crisis. Behind these differences lay Soviet and U.S. misinterpretations of each other's motives and the remnants of traditional mistrust and competition, as well as reflections of the Soviet Union's internal political struggle.

Nevertheless, both nations perceived the nature of the threat in the Middle East and were ready to counter the aggression. Their attitude toward the Kuwait crisis contributed positively to the activities of the United Nations, which not only condemned the aggressor but applied sanctions toward it, including the mandate to use force.

The posture of the Soviet leadership toward the Gulf crisis did not meet with the approval of some political movements within the country, and the anti-Gorbachev forces used the crisis as a pretext for a campaign against the government's policy. It was not the situation in the region itself that caused debate in the USSR: Even those people who appeared to be advocates of Saddam Hussein did not really care for him, and most of them had no knowledge of Middle East problems and controversies. At stake, though it was not yet clear to all observers, was the future of the reforms in the Soviet Union. Those in opposition to democratic change found in the Gulf crisis an opportunity to flex their muscles.

The heated debate in the Soviet Union over the Gulf War was a result of the democratization of Soviet society. Never before had a foreign policy issue commanded such public attention and stirred such passions. Even the ill-fated Soviet invasion of Afghanistan had been met with total public silence. Under President Mikhail Gorbachev, political institutions were no longer a mere facade for executive power; through their election, the members of those institutions had won an opportunity to make their voices heard. The reforms did not and could not produce a system of clear-cut power functions by the time of the Kuwait crisis, but they put an end to the closed style of Soviet policy making.

The stormy public response to Soviet policy during the Kuwait crisis was also caused by dramatically increased political interest in Soviet society. Under the existing domestic circumstances at the time, almost any issue could turn into a lever of political strife. This was especially true of Soviet policy towards Iraq where two main political approaches clashed.

The first approach manifested itself through greater coordination with the West and through the de-ideologization of foreign policy. At the domestic level, its proponents supported a market economy and the transformation of Soviet political structures. Outside the domestic realm, this general trend had an impact on foreign policy, including Middle East policy. On one hand, that policy became more pragmatic. On the other, the manner in which the Soviet leadership tended to abandon its former allies in Eastern Europe and in the Third World caused great concern in certain Arab countries. It was not so much the changed Soviet attitude toward Saddam (who was not greatly respected throughout the Arab world) but rather the new principles of the Soviet Union's international behavior that made some Arabs feel abandoned and even deceived. At the time of the crisis, a new Soviet Middle East policy was in the making, but the burden of the old approach could still be felt. The understandable desire of Gorbachev's team to eliminate the latter as soon as possible, and the new priority given to Soviet-American relations, resulted in Moscow's policy in the Gulf being, at least in the initial stage, heavily influenced by the "Western trend."

The opposing bloc, which might be described as conservative-nationalist, was made up of those who insisted that the Soviet Union should take a stand of its own (different from that of the United States) because the interests of the two powers were antagonistic. Included were those who depicted the anti-Iraq policy as the result of "Zionist plotting;" those who adhered to old Communist dogma; and those who were simply inclined to criticize the government for any political course.

At the initial stage of the crisis, the Soviet government itself invited strong criticism. For example, the statements of Foreign Minister Eduard Shevardnadze, in which he acknowledged that participation of a Soviet military contingent in the multinational force was a possibility, evoked a negative reaction in the country, which was chiefly motivated by the "Afghan syndrome." The tragic Afghan war was and is still haunting public conscience. Many families still mourned their dead, many men still remained in Afghan captivity, and those who had come back still experienced difficulties in adjusting to civilian life. And the Gulf issue was complicated by the possibility of hostages. Before Yevgeny Primakov's mission to Iraq in October 1990, the public shared the concern that the lives of the Soviet specialists and other workers in Iraq might be in danger as a result of the Soviet Union's opposition to Iraq's aggression.

At the fourth session of the Supreme Soviet of the USSR on October 15, 1990, Shevardnadze tried to calm public passions, but the damage had already been done.[1] The critics' activities reached a high point in the parliament of the Russian Federation. There, the conservative parliamentary grouping "Russia" made use of the situation by introducing a draft of an appeal to the president of the USSR and the Supreme Soviet of the USSR that expressed concern "over the military and political developments in the Gulf area" and pleaded "to prevent the Soviet Union's involvement in a military conflict." The appeal was passed by the Congress of Peoples' Deputies of the Russian Federation on December 11, 1990. By frightening the deputies with the threat of a dispatch of Soviet troops to the Gulf area (which was not a real threat at the time), the conservatives used to their advantage the unpopularity of Soviet military activities abroad. Moreover, they capitalized on the position of those democratic deputies who refused to vote for the appeal. The latter, opposed to any involvement of Soviet troops, thought the appeal would damage the prestige of the president and impair Soviet-American understanding. Right or wrong in their evaluations, the 161 deputies who voted against the appeal were depicted by the conservatives as antipatriots and proponents of a dangerous cause of "new thinking."

An article in the weekly *Literaturnaya Rossia* provides a good example of this kind of criticism. After visiting Baghdad, a *Literaturnaya Rossia* correspondent wrote, "The new thinking has led us today to the situation where we, utterly impoverished, but still powerful militarily, will pay with the blood of our sons and with the remainder of our money for the interests of the richest imperialist countries and of the emirate that thrived at the expense of its natural resources."[2]

The debate over the Gulf policy revealed both the structure of the opposition and the populist methods to which the opposition adhered. Anti-Communist Russian nationalists sided with the most ardent Communists. They managed to attract to their camp some politically inert but very popular groups. The Soldiers' Mothers Committee, for example, held a meeting on December 24, 1990, near the Arbatskaya metro station, where the members popularized the slogan, "We shall not let our sons go to the Persian Gulf."

In the Russian Federation those in opposition to the government continued to use the same tactics after the Gulf crisis. Nationalists and neo-Bolsheviks organized mass demonstrations in the center of Moscow on January 9, 1992, this time appealing primarily to socially insecure strata of the society.

The debate over the Gulf issue could not be separated from domestic developments because it reflected an acute political struggle. That struggle could be seen, for example, during the first days of work of the Congress of Peoples' Deputies of the USSR, which opened on December 17, 1990. The efforts of the conservatives to set up "a strong center" and their obvious longing for "an iron hand" found expression in the so-called 53's Appeal, which propounded the need to introduce a state of emergency and presidential rule in "major conflict zones." The document was signed by some intellectuals of "Russian-patriotic" orientation, heads of the military-industrial complex, high-ranking military officials, and the minister of culture. The appeal, which again demonstrated the existence of a more or less organized opposition, was followed at the Congress session of December 20 by Eduard Shevardnadze's resignation in protest of "advancing dictatorship."[3]

At the time, some observers thought that sharp criticism of his Gulf policy might have been a reason for the minister's resignation. However, later developments showed that the Gulf issue had nothing to do with Shevardnadze's decision. On January 13, 1991, blood was spilled in Vilnius, and in August 1991, a coup d'état, which had been anticipated for some time, took place. The interconnection of foreign and domestic policies became clear when the "putchists" turned toward the Middle East. They could not afford to antagonize the West (because of the need for its economic support) by making a direct hostile step. But a volte-face in Middle East policy, which at the time still symbolized Soviet-American cooperation, would be less dangerous and could be interpreted by old ideological friends as an important signal. A delegation was hastily dispatched to Iraq. The coup junta did not last long and did not have time to return to the pre-perestroika political track. Still, its signals were understood.

Some former Soviet allies in the Gulf region longed for the days when, because of the Soviet-U.S. confrontation, they were important to the USSR's military-industrial complex and could exploit that situation for their own ends. The support for the putchists expressed by Saddam Hussein, Muammar Qaddafi, and some radical Palestinian leaders who felt better under the patronage of the Soviet Communist regime, was based on the hope that the Soviet Union might again become an adversary of the West.

Joint or parallel actions of the Soviet Union and the United States in the context of the Gulf crisis did not mean that their interests were identical or that the superpowers had equal opportunities to secure their interests. Since both powers acted autonomously and had different tactical goals, misunderstandings and bad feelings arose concerning some of their actions. One example is Yevgeny Primakov's mission, especially his visit to Iraq in February 1991.

The Gulf policy advocated by Shevardnadze and the Primakov mission reflected two Soviet approaches to the conflict. As the political analyst Andrei Kortunov put it:

> The first approach ... favored steady support of the United States and the West as a whole, up to the readiness to sacrifice long-term allied relations with Baghdad for the sake of protecting norms of international law and going ahead with Soviet-American cooperation. The second approach ... favored the possibility of the Soviet Union's greater dissociation from the West and proceeded on the assumption that Moscow should play an independent role in the conflict if an opportunity arose to act as a mediator between Washington and Baghdad.[4]

The two political lines also bore the characteristics of rivalry between Primakov and Shevardnadze and between different state structures. No wonder that in the wake of the crisis rumors were circulating that Primakov might be nominated for the post of foreign minister.

Primakov's efforts to find a last-minute compromise were met with suspicion in the United States. The USSR was looked upon as trying to steal victory from the allies, to save the Iraqi regime, and to capitalize on anti-American feelings in the Arab world. Frictions between the two powers developed, and some experts raised the question of political trust.

Victor Kremenyuk, for example, a deputy director of the Institute of the USA and Canada Studies, wrote in *Moskovskie Novosti*:

> The Soviet peace initiative bewilders. If it is seen as part of the common effort to settle the crisis, why then did the Soviet people and coalition partners know nothing about it? Gorbachev's peace plan was made public ... after it had been handed to the Iraqi side at separate talks. What were the proposals put forward for and on whose behalf? On behalf of the entire coalition or on behalf of the Soviet Union staying away from armed action? And did that plan take into account the positions of the other parties to the anti-Iraq coalition?[5]

The fact that such questions were even raised, however, demonstrates that a new attitude to Soviet-American relations was gaining currency, at least in the academic community—that is, a readiness to take the other party's concerns into consideration. Unfortunately, during the Gulf crisis such an attitude could not always be applied to the politicians. It might have helped to minimize tensions, although it would hardly have excluded them completely. The main causes of possible misunderstandings lay in the asymmetry of the local interests of the two powers, which were to become even more vivid with the collapse of the Soviet Union and the creation of the Commonwealth of Independent States (CIS).

Before perestroika, Soviet national interests in the Middle East had never been properly defined. On the one hand, the geographical proximity of the region to the USSR made it important to the latter for security reasons. On the other hand, the Soviet leaders, obsessed with the East-West confrontation, tended to explain all unfavorable developments in the area as "imperialist conspiracy." In practice, the Soviets transformed security concerns into a search for spheres of influence: The Soviet presence often became an end in itself.

To a great extent, such ideological considerations were behind the Soviets' ill-fated decision to invade Afghanistan. Those who were responsible for the decision ignored all warnings, seemingly unable to grasp the idea that their recipe for a socialist future did not fit Afghan society. The picture had been drawn in black and white: A progressive regime was fighting against outcast groups of counter-revolutionaries aided by imperialist forces and by the United States in particular. Undoubtedly, the situation in Afghanistan and U.S. activity in the area were of concern to the Soviet Union. But the methods chosen by the Soviets had nothing to do with the goal of making the Soviet Union more secure. The Soviet actions contributed to further destabilization in the region and were ultimately devastating for Soviet society.

The Iraqi aggression occurred at the time when Soviet Middle East policy was still in a state of flux. It was clear (but probably not to everyone) that the old policy priorities had to be revised. As for new approaches, there were more questions than answers. Some officials had made an effort to apply principles of the new political thinking mechanically. Ideas such as the necessity to "repudiate the image of the enemy" or "to give priority to values common to all humanity" found favorable response at the global level but were not applicable to countries of a region fraught with acute conflict. In addition, these principles were too universal to meet the specifics of oriental societies, their political culture, and their historical heritage.

At the same time, Soviet interests in the area became clearer than ever before. When stripped of ideological trappings, they were concentrated on the goal of securing stability in the Middle East for the following reasons:

1. *The USSR's geostrategic considerations.* Military hostilities near the Soviet frontiers (as close as 250 kilometers) might be dangerous for the country. Even a medium-range missile could hit its territory. In view of the scale of the arms race in the Middle East and the possession of weapons of mass annihilation by certain states in the region, developments in the Middle East were of concern to the Soviet Union. The USSR could also be heavily affected by the ecological consequences of war. Iraq's aggression aroused all these concerns.

2. *Nationality and religious considerations.* Soviet interests had to take into account the feelings of 55 million Soviet Muslims (some 20 percent of the population of the USSR) who were part of the Arab-Muslim culture. This factor had been ignored by Soviet policy makers for a long time. They had preferred to believe that the Muslim republics had undergone such profound changes since the establishment of Soviet rule that they had nothing in common with the outside Muslim world or even with neighboring countries. However, this assumption proved to be wrong.

Though the Soviet Muslims were no less split on the issue than the Arab world itself and Soviet society as a whole, they became more vociferous during the Kuwait crisis. In October 1990, a representative of the Muslim Board for the Caucasus wrote: "As for Kuwait, we'll liberate it. I say 'we' because 5,700 Muslims in the Caucasus are already prepared to go and join the ranks of Kuwaiti resistance voluntarily. Allah will help us to free Kuwait!" Other Muslim voices differed. The spokesman for the Muslim Board for Transcaucasia (which unites mostly Shi'ites) noted: "Unless the Palestinian question is settled, no other problem will be resolved in the Persian Gulf region. And since Iraq is in the forefront of actions concerning the solution of the Palestinian question, its position should be backed up."[6]

It would be incorrect to portray the Soviet Muslims as pro-Iraqi, but their posture had to be taken into consideration. Moscow could not afford to take steps that might be interpreted as a direct confrontation with the Arab world. Thus, the feelings of the Soviet Muslims contributed to the decision not to send Soviet troops into the Gulf and to the efforts of Soviet diplomats to prevent military action and remove Saddam from Kuwait by political means.

3. *Global considerations*. The cessation of the East-West confrontation and the new level of Soviet-American understanding that followed made the world more secure and opened the door for mutually advantageous international cooperation in various areas. Then as today, the task of economic modernization of the former republics has been closely linked to Western assistance. Thus it would not have been in Soviet interests to allow developments in the Middle East to become an obstacle to improved East-West relations and to the process of arms reduction.

These three principal interests were inherited by the Commonwealth. However, the issues are becoming more complicated as each member-state develops its own perceptions of its interests and the means to secure them.

The quest of the former Soviet republics for sovereignty and independence was greatly advanced by the aborted coup d'état of August 1991. First, by demonstrating that the central government could become a threat to the members of the Union, it gave new incentive to the notion of secession. Second, it produced an example to be followed—that of the successful struggle of the Russian authorities against the Union's political structures. The victory of the Russian leaders has turned out to be a mixed blessing, however. On the one hand, it undermined the regime, although the government still had enough power to impede reforms. On the other hand, it sped up the disintegration of the state, including the Russian Federation itself at a time when autonomous republics and regions were demanding sovereignty.

For the authorities in the former republics, foreign policy is acquiring special importance as a means of legitimizing newly elected presidents and of securing the recognition of sovereign republics. However, the former Soviet republics are still newcomers in international relations. Whatever their interests are, and however much they may differ from the interests of the former Soviet Union, the republics possess comparatively limited means to support any desired international status. For them, the choice is one of partners and the intensity of international ties. With the exception of Russia (which claims to be the legitimate successor to the USSR), no republic is ready to develop a regional, let alone global, policy of its own. Instead, the republics are focusing on establishing and developing bilateral relations, mostly with countries that are geographically, historically, ethnically, and culturally close to them. Because of the great number of Muslims living in the territory of the former USSR, Middle East policy is becoming especially relevant.

Although the republics are making foreign policy choices for themselves, they are also the object of foreign policy choices being made by external forces and states interested in cooperating with the periphery of the former USSR for their own ends. Among these states are Turkey, Iran, and Saudi Arabia.

The republics' attitudes toward Middle East developments will no doubt be affected by their historical, ethnic, and religious ties with neighboring countries and with Arab and non-Arab Muslim states. Depending on the amount of assistance and support they receive from their partners, they will have to take into consideration the approach of certain Muslim states to the basic problems of the region.

The behavior of the former Soviet Muslim republics in the international arena will be also dictated by purely pragmatic considerations. All of them, despite obvious differences in their level of development, are now facing grave economic problems that will have to be solved to ensure social stability. To the leaders of some of these republics, Muslim prescriptions for boosting the economy may seem inviting. But the importance of the technology and the know-how of the West and of the most developed oriental countries, such as South Korea, Taiwan, and others that do not belong to the Muslim world, cannot be denied.

Many of the former Soviet republics with newly acquired independence and sovereignty will have to adapt to a modest and humble existence in the international community. They will have to accept that, at the present time, the standards of some underdeveloped countries are the maximum they can count on. To overcome economic and political barriers, they will have to combine traditionalism and modernization. The Muslim republics are turning toward the Muslim world, but at the moment they can hardly afford to alienate the West. During the transitional period, pragmatic considerations will be as important as their Muslim ties—a fact that may counter some of the more extreme manifestations of the latter.

The role of Islam in the former Soviet republics should be analyzed at different levels. At the domestic level, it is, no doubt, growing. Still, one should not project growing Islamist currents into foreign policy. The Islamic factor cannot be treated as the only factor that will determine the Muslim republics' political behavior—even in the most sensitive area, namely the Middle East. In this context, it is no surprise that Kyrgyzstan,

Uzbekistan, Kazakhstan, and Azerbaijan are eagerly developing economic ties with Israel despite their ties to the Muslim world.

Certain forces in the republics may become an obstacle to conflict reduction in the Middle East because of their connections to Muslim extremists. But the republics as a whole will not work against stability in the region. The easing of tensions in the Middle East will contribute to the republics' realization of their pragmatic goals and will save them from a difficult and uncomfortable choice in the future. At the same time, their urgent need for hard currency and for overcoming economic backwardness as quickly as possible might, in the absence of central control, have negative consequences. For example, press reports have indicated that Iraq and Libya have an eye on nuclear materials and experts in some of the Muslim republics.

The main burden of the USSR's foreign policy heritage, including its Middle East policy, will be shouldered by Russia, whose potential is more limited than that of its predecessor. Economic difficulties, strained relations with certain autonomies, and unresolved problems with the independent states limit Russia's capabilities to deal with the whole spectrum of foreign policy issues, including the Middle East.

The post-Kuwait War situation accentuated the urgency of creating a security system in the Middle East, for it instigated a new round of arms races in the area. Several factors contributed to the heightened arms race. First, the war accentuated the insecurity of the Middle East actors. The Arab countries were unable to defend themselves and could have never stopped the aggression without international help, the bulk of which consisted of U.S. forces. Even Israel was vulnerable and, for political reasons, had to rely upon the American forces in defending itself. Further, the Arab feeling of insecurity has been heightened by a new balance of forces in the region that is unfavorable to the Arab countries. Three non-Arab nations—Iran, Turkey, and Israel—have moved ahead since the war, thus making the Arabs even more concerned about the future. Second, despite political and ideological differences, the Arabs have always considered the Iraqi military potential as an integral part of their collective military might. With this potential gone, they have felt a strong incentive for acquiring more sophisticated weapons to compensate for the loss. Third, arms transfers to the Middle East have increased markedly. In addition to the traditional arms suppliers, a lot of newcomers have appeared, including Third World countries. They are entering new markets and making good use of the growing demand for weapons.

These trends have aggravated the situation in the region and can easily undermine a search for security there. One must even question whether the region is ready for a security system. The European experience cannot be applied to the Middle East, where borders have not been defined, economic interdependence is missing, and rivalry and hostilities seem to dominate. The concept of a Six-Plus-Two alignment as a basis for future regional cooperation has turned out to be premature. Further, the Kuwait crisis created a situation in which the containment of Saddam Hussein proved to be more important for the members of the Coalition than ideological differences and regional ambitions: Iraq's aggression against Kuwait was equally dangerous for all participants of the Coalition. Baghdad's claims on the territory of its rich neighbor and Saddam's quest for regional hegemony were meant to intimidate other Arab states. Iraq's territorial expansion and its proclaimed intention to distribute the oil wealth equally among the Arab states were perceived as a most acute threat by the Gulf oil producers—and that perception only intensified when the Iraqi slogans elicited a favorable response on the Arab street and in the ruling circles of some not-so-well-to-do Arab countries.

For Egypt and Syria, the prospect of Iraq playing a decisive role in Arab affairs was especially unpalatable. Their vigorous opposition to Saddam's moves was dictated not only by ideological contradictions with the Iraqi regime but first and foremost by realpolitik.

After the war, centrifugal tendencies in the Arab world again began to dominate.[7] The Gulf states have shown a preference for bilateral relations with the United States over the uncertainty of a regional defense alliance, particularly as it is not clear what Iraq's future role will be, how a reliable regional security system can be established without Iran and Yemen, and whether there will be any progress at the Arab-Israeli peace talks. All in all, it seems that the main burden of security in the Gulf area will have to be shouldered by the United States.

The Soviet performance in Madrid was far from impressive, but the Russian government cannot ignore Moscow's commitment to the peace process. Russia's participation in the talks was perceived as important by the parties to the conflict and helped confirm its status as the legitimate successor to the USSR. Because, for economic reasons, Russia will remain an arms supplier,[8] Moscow will have additional leverage on the arms recipients, but at the same time, its role as an arms supplier may contribute to regional instability, especially if peace talks come to a halt.

All in all, the problems of Middle East security have not lessened. They demand attention and responsibility, on the part of both local actors and outside powers, including Russia and other states of the Commonwealth that remain historically, geographically, ethnically, and culturally linked to the region.

Notes

1. *Izvestia,* October 16, 1990.

2. *Literaturnaya Rossia,* December 7, 1990.

3. *Izvestia,* December 21, 1990.

4. *Moskovskie Novosti,* January 13, 1991.

5. *Moskovskie Novosti,* March 3, 1991.

6. *Ogonyok,* January 1991, 5.

7. See "A Survey of the Middle East," *The Economist,* September 28–October 4, 1991.

8. *Izvestia,* January 18, 1992.

13

Germany and the Kuwait War

Helmut Hubel

The Iraqi raid on Kuwait on August 2, 1990 initiated the first international crisis since the end of the East-West conflict and led to the forced liberation of the Kuwaiti emirate by a worldwide Coalition headed by the United States. The circumstances and development of this conflict illuminated the extent of the change that had occurred in global political conditions since the end of the Cold War. This change exposed Germany, in the process of unification at the time of the 1991 Gulf conflict, to special burdens: The country suddenly realized that its traditional understanding of its role on the world stage, which had been evolving for forty years, was no longer valid. The United States and other partners expected unlimited solidarity, whereas the Federal Republic sought to adhere to its traditional, self-imposed military restraints. Influenced by the crisis, however, Germany began to change its thinking and made its first moves toward a new foreign policy stance. After the end of the fighting in the Gulf, the Federal Republic for the first time provided military units for an area of crisis outside NATO (North Atlantic Treaty Organization) territory. Moreover, Germany intensified its efforts to assume a European security identity.

The Cold War had not formally ended at the time the Iraqi dictator Saddam Hussein sent troops into his rich but militarily weak neighbor Kuwait. The Cold War was officially terminated during the Conference on Security and Cooperation in Europe (CSCE) in Paris in November 1990, which a U.S. observer later appropriately called the *"Ersatz"* ("substitute") Peace Conference.[1] Nevertheless, by the summer of 1990 important decisions to overcome the division of Europe and to legalize the unification of Germany had already been made by the international community. The Iraqi aggression raised the question of whether this new and cooperative relationship between the former superpowers of the West and the East would remain solid in the Gulf region, an area of important world economic and political interests.

Earlier, the United States and the Soviet Union had cooperated with significant success on solutions to regional conflicts in Afghanistan, Angola, and Cambodia.[2] But the Kuwait crisis was especially sensitive from the Soviet point of view, since Iraq was one of the USSR's closest Third World political, military, and economic partners. Moreover, the action was taking place in proximity to Soviet territory, a factor of importance to the Soviet military. The instantaneous joint U.S.-Soviet denouncement of Iraq's aggression against Kuwait was impressive and indicated that in the face of this provocation, these former antagonists would now work together. Indeed, this cooperation proved to be the decisive precondition for the UN Security Council to rule shortly thereafter for stringent international sanctions: Resolution 678 of November 29, 1990, empowered members of the world community to enforce the UN sanctions, even by military force, if necessary. For the first time since the formation of the United Nations, the United States, the Soviet Union, and the other permanent members of the Security Council were cooperating and utilizing all UN resources to maintain international order.

Tensions escalated when Iraq refused to desist despite universal denouncement of its aggression and despite the economic sanctions. Saddam Hussein's calculations that the U.S.-led Coalition of nearly thirty countries would not counterattack and that even a military conflict with the alliance was preferable to acquiescing to the United Nations and its Security Council led him to ignore the sanctions—which resulted in the Coalition initiating military operations for the liberation of Kuwait. The United States and its allies took the opportunity during these operations to conduct air strikes against the most dangerous of Iraq's weapons installations, especially the ABC weapons (atomic, bacteriological, and chemical) and production facilities. Following the 1980s, the proliferation of weapons of mass destruction became a matter of great concern.[3] In the case of Iraq—a Third World country with apparent nuclear and chemical capabilities—the United States and its allies attempted, for the first time, to force disarmament by specific and limited air strikes. This same goal (of disarmament) was later incorporated into the cease-fire agreement of April 3, 1991, which empowered the UN to verify, control, and destroy those Iraqi weapons.

The 1991 Gulf War contrasted sharply with developments in Europe and in other parts of the Third World, where the end of the East-West conflict and the settlement of regional antagonisms were achieved by diplomacy. In Cambodia, for instance, where Japan had considerable interest, there was now realistic hope for a political solution. Even the liberation of

East and Central Europe in 1989/1990 and the unification of Germany occurred peacefully and facilitated far-reaching disarmament. The war for the liberation of Kuwait, however, struck a different note, confronting the world with the unpleasant fact of a new and unexpected war of vast technical and strategic dimensions. This painful experience was to be repeated and intensified in the war among the former Yugoslav republics, which began in 1991.

The Role of the United States

Soviet President Mikhail Gorbachev cooperated with U.S. President George Bush, assuring him that he would not oppose any action the United States took in response to Iraq's aggression. During the Cold War, an American president who mobilized sizable U.S. troops against an ally of the Soviet Union would have risked a global confrontation and the possibility of a third world war. With this danger apparently past, the United States had considerable political and military freedom to act.

Although they were determined to repel Iraq's aggression, President Bush and Secretary of State James Baker first gathered support for their plans from U.S. allies and the UN Security Council. Thus, military action against Iraq was instituted only after the Security Council gave its approval on November 29, 1990, and after the deadline of January 15, 1991, given by UN resolution had expired. Furthermore, by cooperating with the leaders of Saudi Arabia, Egypt, and Syria, the Bush administration succeeded in isolating Iraq from its Near East and Middle East friends. Finally, Washington endeavored to avoid regional escalation of the Arab-Israeli dispute as well as infringement upon the alliance by ensuring that Israel would not enter the war and convincing Tel Aviv not to retaliate even in the face of Iraqi Scud missile attacks.

The end of the Cold War also permitted the United States to transfer U.S. troops from Europe to the Gulf in quantities that would not have been feasible before 1990. On November 8, 1990, when President Bush announced the doubling of U.S. forces in Saudi Arabia, which meant the allies would gain an "offensive option," he had already ordered the transfer of U.S. elite armored units, among them the VIIth Corps, from Germany. The Coalition command could thus rely on important components of U.S. forces that had been stationed in Western Europe, that is, in Germany, as well as on NATO's transport and maintenance infrastructure. Within a few weeks, the Coalition was able to station a fighting force of one half million soldiers in Saudi Arabia with the attendant sophisticated arsenal.

At the beginning of the crisis, NATO members had agreed that this deployment would not activate mutual treaty obligations. However, all member states—including Germany—supported, without reservation, the military deployment by the United States, Great Britain, and the other NATO members directly involved. These countries contributed appropriate transport facilities, military equipment, and munitions. Even Europe's neutral countries, such as Austria and Sweden, as well as East European Warsaw Pact countries, such as Hungary, facilitated allied operations by opening their air spaces.

In the first phase of the crisis the U.S. government attempted to protect Saudi Arabia and its vast oil reserves from Iraqi advances, but with the doubling of the troops in November 1990 the United States opened the way for pushing back and disarming the aggressor. Determined to avoid a repetition of the U.S. experience in Vietnam at all costs, President Bush made every effort to assure a decisive victory and a speedy conclusion to the military operation. He gave his military leadership a free hand and allowed mobilization of all the necessary troops and defense equipment. In addition, the president and his military advisers understood that U.S. public support for the operation could be maintained only if military losses were kept to a minimum. Indeed, whether losses could be kept low was questioned in the face of the Iraqi threat to use chemical weapons—but that threat certainly reinforced the allied intent to eliminate Iraq's facilities for the production and development of nonconventional weapons of mass destruction. Saddam Hussein, meanwhile, reinforced his troops and prepared for a bloody ground battle, hoping to inflict as many allied casualties as possible.

The U.S. war strategy deliberately addressed these potential problems. Intensive electronic surveillance and countermeasures to weaken Iraq's air defenses and more than five weeks of concentrated air strikes against command centers, weapons factories, and other military targets prepared the way for a final, hundred-hour ground operation to repel Iraqi troops. Despite the surprisingly fast victory, President Bush kept to the prestated goal of liberating Kuwait and did not permit the allied occupation of Baghdad. To avoid further involvement of U.S. forces, Bush declined to interfere directly in the Shi'ite and Kurdish uprisings (even given the likelihood of victory) against Saddam's regime.

Implementation of the U.S. strategy required great logistical effort and considerable expense; total costs have been estimated at U.S.$ 75 billion.[4] Even a healthier U.S. economy than that at the time of the crisis would have been severely burdened by this enormous financial outlay. As it was, the U.S. economy and balance of trade showed a large deficit at the time. Thus, the Bush administration could hope for congressional approval only by proving that its allies and partners would assume a considerable share of the financial burden.

Besides receiving financial support from Saudi Arabia and Kuwait as early as August 1990, the U.S. government asked for substantial support from its economically strong allies, Germany and Japan. In January 1991, after the beginning of the air strikes, Washington endeavored to get additional, sizable financial pledges from its partners.

European Reactions During the Kuwait Crisis

At the beginning of the Kuwait crisis, the governments and peoples of Europe were mesmerized by the dramatic developments that had ended the East-West conflict on their own continent. The governments of both Eastern and Western Europe were almost unanimous in denouncing Iraq's aggressions and approving the decisions of the UN Security Council. In addition, they expressed concern for the fate of foreigners detained by Saddam in Iraq and Kuwait as pawns for his power politics. Fearing impairment of their political and economic relations with the Arab world, most European governments preferred a peaceful solution to the crisis and felt that such a solution was, indeed, possible. France, for instance, attempted to offer Saddam a face-saving retreat hours before the UN ultimatum ran out. For a long time, the prevailing expectation was that this conflict—like many others—might be resolved peacefully. The shock was therefore great, particularly in Germany, when the Coalition began extensive air strikes against Iraq and all efforts at mediation failed. The Coalition's offensive was to be the most powerful strategic operation carried out since 1945.

After Iraq invaded Kuwait, members of the West European Union (WEU), at the behest of France, attempted to streamline their response. As part of this effort, the WEU coordinated the mobilization of naval units in the Gulf from some of the member states. Because Germany had sent a flotilla of minesweepers to the Mediterranean in August, the German Navy did not participate in the Gulf marine detail coordinated by the WEU. But once the crisis unfolded, the WEU efforts, as well as other multilateral efforts (such as the European Political Cooperation [EPC] of the European Community [EC]), lost relevance in the larger strategy picture of the European NATO members.

Although France, Italy, and other West European countries had pursued a peaceful diplomatic solution to the crisis for some time, the British government was emphatic that only a complete and unconditional Iraqi retreat from Kuwait was acceptable. Prime Minister Margaret Thatcher, who received significant military assistance from the United States in the 1982 Falklands war against Argentina, advocated a strong military response during a meeting with President Bush at Aspen, Colorado, on August 3, 1990.[5] The British government maintained this position of solidarity with the United States even after Thatcher's resignation on November 22, 1990. Besides principal considerations, Britain's leadership felt a historical responsibility for Kuwait. In addition, the British welcomed the opportunity to reaffirm their traditionally special relationship with the United States—especially since President Bush had offered to Germany a "partnership in leadership" only the year before.[6]

But the Kuwait crisis created tough problems for France, for whom both Kuwait and Iraq were important economic partners.[7] In the wake of the oil crisis in 1973, France and Iraq had forged an especially close relationship: In exchange for preferential terms in the delivery of oil, France granted Iraq far-reaching industrial technological support, especially in the development of nuclear energy but in the realm of arms transfers as well; also, France was Iraq's strongest ally during the eight-year Iraq-Iran War. The French government found it both significant and problematic that the Iraqi president had now begun a second war with weapons delivered from France, among other countries. For these reasons, President François Mitterrand had to consider major domestic policy issues in addition to the critical foreign policy aspect of Iraq's aggression. As a result of France's sixteen-year collaboration with Baghdad, a powerful "Iraqi lobby" influenced French foreign policy in Paris. It represented the interests of all the major parties to the collaborative efforts and, in particular, the exporting industry, which was eager not to sever the long-standing connections with this attractive partner.[8] Iraq's enormous debt of several billion French francs to its French suppliers was another concern. Since Iraq had been in arrears on its debts for some time, France had stopped all deliveries of weapons as of May 1990.

Among members of the French government, Defense Minister Jean-Pierre Chevènement was especially inclined toward Iraq and was hence a leading member of the Iraqi lobby. In the first phase of the crisis he worked hard for a peaceful solution, and even after the allied air strikes had begun, he ordered French planes to confine their attacks to Iraqi positions in Kuwait. President Mitterrand eventually rescinded this limitation, and Chevènement resigned his post in January 1991. Subsequently, French elite troops played an important role in the Coalition pincer movement in February 1991, in which Coalition forces surrounded Iraqi troops and advanced deep into Iraqi territory.

The French president was most concerned that France live up to its "role and stature" as a major power.[9] Thus, as early as August 21, 1990, after consulting with pertinent governments, he ordered French troops to Saudi Arabia and to the United Arab Emirates. France increased the level of its military engagement in the Gulf considerably when the Iraqis occupied the French embassy in Kuwait.

Mitterrand cultivated close cooperation with the United States, as he had done during the Middle East crises of the 1980s. In fact, shortly after the Iraqi raid on Kuwait, France reportedly provided the United States with detailed information about its earlier weapons deliveries to Kuwait.[10] More than Middle East political considerations were at stake: French observers pointed out that Mitterrand considered it essential to keep the United States in Europe "to balance the Soviet Union militarily and Germany politically."[11]

The German Role

When Iraq invaded Kuwait on August 2, 1990, Europe was no longer divided, and the basic political decisions about German unification and its continued NATO membership had been made by the major powers and the Germans. Nonetheless, unification and the formal ending of the Four Power rights (Great Britain, France, the United States, and the USSR) did not come until October 3, 1990, and during those intervening months, the government of the newly unified Germany was anxious to see that nothing kept these agreements from becoming reality. Its main concern was to not agitate the Soviet Union, whose parliament still had to ratify both the agreements and the order to withdraw Soviet troops from the former German Democratic Republic. In the fall of 1990 the influence of conservative political forces in the Soviet Union became more noticeable, and finally, on December 20, 1990, resulted in the spectacular resignation of Foreign Minister Eduard Shevardnadze increasing Germany's concern. The German government was anxious to avoid giving Moscow's reactionaries any reason to torpedo the agreements. Germany's concern waned only after February 1991, when it became clear that the Soviet leadership had acceded to allied military action against Iraq. On March 4, 1991, the Soviet parliament finally ratified the Two-Plus-Four Treaty for Germany. This was the treaty among the four victorious powers of World War II, namely the United States, Great Britain, France, and the Soviet Union as well as the (FDR) Federal Republic of Germany (Western) and the (GDR) German Democratic Republic (Eastern).

For the German population and its leadership, the process of German unification was of overriding importance. The first all-German elections took place on December 2, 1990, and the election campaign was imprinted with the issue of unification. To many Germans, having just witnessed the peaceful solution of the forty-year East-West conflict in Europe, the development of the Gulf crisis and subsequently the war for the liberation of Kuwait came as a shock. Opinion polls in January 1991 showed that a clear majority of Germans were opposed to any direct involvement by German soldiers, even though about three quarters of the population shared the view that the Coalition's actions against the Iraqi dictator were justified, an opinion also proportionately held by other European countries. This attitude, however, was contrary to the views held by France and Great Britain.[12]

Public opinion in Germany was reflected less by this "silent majority" than by the protest of the minority that opposed any military force whatsoever and even failed to denounce the Iraqi missile attacks against Israel. The reactions of this minority confirmed the observation of Hans-Peter Schwarz, a political scientist from Bonn University, who some years before had criticized German *Machtvergessenheit* (obliviousness of power).[13] This minority feared that Iraqi Scud missiles could carry warheads filled with poison gas, a fear intensified by the belief that some German companies had provided Saddam with chemical weapons. Fortunately, the Iraqi missiles that hit targets in Israel and Saudi Arabia carried only conventional warheads.

The German government and parliament were ambivalent in their reactions to the allied operation. Although Chancellor Helmut Kohl emphasized on January 14 and again on January 17, 1991, that the allied military operation was fully justified and that the responsibility for this war rested solely with the Iraqi leader, the speakers of the German parties and German President Richard von Weizsäcker voiced "concern" over the offensive and the desire for a rapid end to the armed conflict.[14]

German political leaders, in a somewhat misleading way, highly publicized the protests by the minority opposing military force. These protests and the fact that German troops did not participate in the war while Coalition soldiers risked their lives for the liberation of Kuwait aroused strong reactions among Germany's allies during January and February 1991. Additionally, the possibility of an Iraqi attack against Turkey, a NATO member, caused an odd debate on the prerequisites of the *Bündnisfall* (the activation of NATO's mutual defense obligations) and thereby about German assistance for Turkey. When Germany dispatched air defense missiles to southeastern Turkey to protect eighteen German Alpha Jet ground support planes that had been sent there at the beginning of January 1991, organizational difficulties within the German and NATO contingencies emerged as well.

At times, all of these developments left the public impression that Germany had assumed a rather neutral position in the Gulf War. In fact, however, since the beginning of the crisis, the Federal Republic assisted its alliance partners with elaborate organizational and significant financial contributions. Germany, being the site of the U.S. military headquarters in Europe and, as such, the main point of strategic support for U.S. troops in Europe, was involved in the allied strategy throughout the war and particularly when U.S. troops were dispatched to Saudi Arabia. The

Bundeswehr (federal armed forces) and other German institutions supported the U.S. military without reservation in all issues such as logistics, supplies, transportation, etc., especially when, at the behest of President Bush, the number of U.S. soldiers in the Gulf was more than doubled. In addition, Germany provided extensive logistical support when the United States transferred the entire VIIth Corps from its quarters in Germany to Saudi Arabia on very short notice. Germany also provided substantial support to other allies, such as Great Britain, although this activity was largely unknown by the general public.

In accordance with NATO agreements, the *Bundesmarine* (Federal German Navy), as already mentioned, dispatched five minesweepers to the Eastern Mediterranean in the fall of 1990. At the beginning of March 1991 these minesweepers were ordered to the Gulf to assist with the detection and removal of mines. The German government declared this operation to be a "humanitarian mission," with the intention of circumscribing the *Grundgesetz* (Basic Law), which at that time prohibited the assignment of German troops outside "NATO territory." Under this humanitarian label, this naval operation gained the support of even the parliamentary opposition, that is, the Social Democrats (SPD) and the "Greens," and followed the proposition of the WEU to deploy naval units in a joint operation. Thus the *Bundeswehr* took an operational, though limited, role within the WEU.

In April 1991 additional units of the *Bundeswehr* took part in the international relief effort (Operation Provide Comfort) to assist Kurdish refugees who fled the Iraqi army to southeastern Turkey and Iran. In this case, the center of German operations was in Iran, and German participation was instituted during an unsecured cease-fire—once again outside NATO's area as circumscribed in the North Atlantic Treaty, Article 6. In view of the possibility of severe casualties among the Kurdish refugees, the German parliamentary opposition approved this humanitarian action as well. German units, however, did not participate in the military operations on behalf of the refugees that took place on Iraqi territory. Since June 1991, civilian and military experts from Germany supported by transport planes and helicopters have taken part in UN inspections in Iraq aimed at eliminating the threat of Iraqi weapons of mass destruction in accordance with Resolution 687.

This extensive engagement in the UN inspections was undertaken in response to the repeated national and international reproaches that German experts and businesses had assisted in Iraqi weapons programs. Although it later became known that Israeli authorities had not found any Western components in the debris of Iraqi Scud-B missiles fired against Israeli cities,[15] these accusations eventually led to significant legal proceedings against alleged exporters in German courts.

German financial contributions supporting U.S. efforts in the Gulf War totaled 18 billion D-Marks. Financial and other aid was granted to the United States amounting to more than 10 billion D-Marks, which included a direct payment of U.S.$5.5 billion toward U.S. military measures. Bonn also provided financial and other assistance to participating NATO members including France, Great Britain, and Israel. Finally, Germany made payments for the support of the Near Eastern partner countries—Egypt, Jordan, and Syria, as well as Turkey—that had been particularly hurt by the UN economic sanctions imposed on Iraq.

All in all, except for the fact that it did not provide actively participating troops to the Coalition forces, Germany should not be accused of a "lack of solidarity." Yet, the German government did little to provide proper information to its public and the citizens of its partner countries regarding the actual degree of its contributions to the allied war effort.[16] In misjudging public reaction for too long, Bonn's politicians left public opinion making in the hands of a (loud) minority opposed to any German involvement and thereby contributed to a contradiction between the actual German deeds and support and the (misguided) perception at home and abroad.

Conclusion

Although preoccupied with its own unification, Germany fully abided by the UN resolutions and supported the international alliance against Saddam Hussein logistically and financially. Yet the widespread impression among international observers was that Germany had opted out during the crisis. Japan, which also did not contribute armed forces to the Coalition, faced similar reproaches. In its military abstinence, the federal government of Germany (like that in Japan) acted according to the long-standing convictions of a majority of its population and the parliament. Memories of World War II were still much alive. Saddam's aggression reminded Germans of the catastrophe Adolf Hitler had brought upon the world and themselves. On February 13, 1991, when the inhabitants of Dresden saw on their televisions the high-precision air raids against targets in Baghdad, the scene awakened painful memories of the firestorm the three air raids against their own city had created just forty-six years earlier.

The Gulf conflict demonstrated that Germany's major allies no longer agreed with the German (and Japanese) reservations against extensive international military involvement, particularly in a case of so blatant a violation of international law. This experience also intensified the domestic debate about unified Germany's future international role. Two aspects of the debate are the future German military contribution to international peacekeeping under the auspices of the United Nations and the future German role outside the areas defined by the NATO treaty and within WEU.

Thus, the Gulf War was a catalyst in Germany for questioning the nation's self-image as a "civilian power."[17] The failure of diplomacy and the use of military force in the Gulf shattered the fundamental belief that only peaceful solutions should be undertaken in international problems—a belief widely embraced by the German democracy since World War II. Political forces in Germany were now arguing more strongly for a "return to normalcy" (*zurück zum Normalzustand*). Several experts of Germany's most powerful parliamentary group, the conservative Christlich Demokratische Union/Christlich Soziale Union (CDU/CSU), have since advocated unrestricted German military participation in all kinds of multilateral peacekeeping and peace enforcement missions, whether within the UN, NATO, or the WEU, and the liberal coalition partner FDP has proposed German participation not only in UN peacekeeping ("blue helmets") but in all forms of UN missions. Yet the Social Democratic opposition party, SPD (not to mention the Green party), from whom votes were necessary to obtain a two-thirds majority for changing or clarifying the *Grundgesetz* (the constitution) did not seem willing to tolerate more than UN "blue helmet" missions.[18]

German participation since 1991 in UN peacekeeping missions in Cambodia, Somalia, and the Adriatic Sea has demonstrated that the Kuwait crisis initiated a profound change in German attitudes. The redefinition of Germany's international role has clearly been confined to multilateral action—a fact that can be used in the internal debate against those who have resisted any "participation in power politics." At issue has been Germany's complete solidarity with its allies and partners—no more and no less.

Notes

This chapter was translated from German by Marianne Donath and edited by Wolfgang Danspeckgruber.

1. Zbigniew Brzezinski, "The Consequences of the End of the Cold War for International Security," in *New Dimensions in International Security,* pt. 1 (London: IISS, Adelphi Paper no. 265, 1992), 33.

2. Helmut Hubel, "Die amerikanisch-sowjetischen Beziehungen und regionale Konflikte," in *Internationale Politik 1987–1988* (Munich, 1990), 47–61.

3. Vgl. ders., "Neue Waffen in der Dritten Welt und Ihre Folgen" (New Weapons in the Third World and Their Consequences) *Europa Archiv,* 15 (1990), 453–460.

4. See the analysis in Karl Kaiser and Klaus Becher, "Deutschland und der Irak-Konflikt. Internationale Sicherheitsverantwortung Deutschlands und Euro-

pas nach der deutschen Vereinigung" (Germany and the Iraq Conflict: Germany's and Europe's International Security Responsibility After the German Unification). Forschungsinstitut der DGAP, Working papers for International Politics, No. 68, p. 53 ff., Bonn, 1992.

5. See Margaret Thatcher, "No Time to Go Wobbly," *The Downing Street Years* (London, 1993), 816.

6. See speech of President George Bush at Mainz, May 1989, *Europa Archiv* 12 (1989) 357.

7. See Helmut Hubel, "Western Europe and Iraq: The Cases of France and West Germany," in Amatzia Baram and Barry Rubin, eds., *Iraq's Road to War* (New York: Gustav Heinemann Center for Middle East Studies, University of Haifa, 1993), 273–285.

8. The French weapons sales to Iraq between 1977 and 1985 were estimated to have reached the amount of 56 billion French francs. Compare Kenneth Timmerman, "Un nouvel Iraq?" in *Politique Internationale* (Winter 1985–1986), 173.

9. See Mitterand's talk after the cease-fire, reproduced in *Le Monde*, March 5, 1991.

10. See *International Herald Tribune*, August 14, 1990.

11. Dominique Moïsi, "The Gulf Crisis: A Roundtable Discussion," *France Magazine* (Spring 1991), 10.

12. For results of opinion polls during January–February 1991, see Helmut Hubel, *"Der Zweite Golfkrieg in der Internationalen Politik"* (The Second Gulf War in International Politics) with selected documents, Forschungsinstitut der DGAP (Bonn: Working Papers for International Politics, 62, 1991), Kaiser/Becher, 27.

13. Hans-Peter Schwarz, *Die Gezähmten Deutschen: Von der Machtbesessenheit zur Machtvergessenheit* (The Subdued Germans: From the Obsession with Power to the Oblivion of Power) (Stuttgart, 1985).

14. See Hubel, fn. 7, 20.

15. See statement of Jürgen Möllemann, minister of economics, in *Die Welt*, March 21, 1991.

16. For a critical assessment, see Michael J. Inacker, *Unter Ausschluss der Oeffentlichkeit? Die Deutschen in der Golfallianz* (Excluded from Publicity? The Germans in the Gulf Alliance), Bonn/Berlin, 1991.

17. For more on this concept, see Hanns W. Maull, "Germany and Japan: The New Civilian Powers," in *Foreign Affairs*, vol. 69, No. 5, Winter 1990–1991, 91–106.

18. Standing for peace keeping—or peace making operations under the auspices of the United Nations. For a good summary of the different positions, see Ronald Asmus, *Germany After the Gulf War*, Rand, N-3391-AF (Santa Monica, CA, 1992), 20.

14

Trial of an Ideal: Japan's Debate Over the Kuwait Crisis

Masaru Tamamoto with Amy Cullum

The Iraqi invasion of Kuwait and the subsequent U.S. demand that Japan contribute to the Coalition's military effort precipitated a major foreign policy debate in Japan. At issue were the two pillars of postwar Japanese foreign policy—Japan's alliance with the United States and its constitutional renunciation of overseas military activities. The Gulf crisis showed that these two pillars, which for so long had reinforced each other, could be at odds with one another.

The Gulf crisis pushed Japan, which has been a politically hesitant power, closer to the center of the world stage. The question for Japan's leaders is no longer whether their country should be involved in the troubles of the politically and geographically distant Middle East (the answer to which had been a resounding "no" since 1945); it is now, how should Japan become involved? This dramatic change in the way Japan's leaders see the role of their country in world affairs came about as a response to a military crisis that forced the country to confront another difficult question: Does active participation in world politics include the exercise of military power?

The constitutional debate that began in Japan shortly after Iraq's invasion of Kuwait focused on the feasibility and wisdom of dispatching the Japanese Self-Defense Force (SDF) to the Persian Gulf to bolster the U.S.-led multinational force. Sending the SDF would have constituted Japan's first military foray overseas since World War II. The debate concerned one of the core values of postwar Japan's foreign policy and a fundamental source of its postwar national identity—its strictly nonmilitary involvement with the rest of the world. The Kuwait crisis precipitated the first real trial of Japan's pacific ideal as set forth in its constitution.

The Peace Constitution

Demilitarization came to the Japanese as a gift of its occupiers following World War II. The Japanese constitution that the American occupiers drafted and imposed upon the defeated Japanese in 1946 heralds peace as a cornerstone of postwar Japanese politics and society. Its preamble states the following:

> We, the Japanese people, desire peace for all time and are deeply conscious of the high ideals controlling human relationship, and we have determined to preserve our security and existence, trusting in the justice and faith of the peace-loving peoples of the world.

These lofty words are backed up by Article 9 of the Japanese Constitution, the War Renunciation Clause:

> Aspiring sincerely to an international peace based on justice and order, the Japanese people forever renounce war as a sovereign right of the nation and the threat or use of force as means of settling international disputes.
>
> In order to accomplish the aim of the preceding paragraph, land, sea, and air forces as well as other war potential will never be maintained. The right of belligerency of the state will not be recognized.

According to a strict reading of these words, the Japanese concept is a Gandhian, nonviolent peace.

Although the Japanese constitution has not been amended since its promulgation, its original intent was compromised early on. With the outbreak of the Korean War in 1950, General Douglas MacArthur, the supreme commander of the allied powers in occupied Japan, ordered the Japanese prime minister to establish a National Policy Reserve Force of 75,000 men and to equip it with tanks, artillery, and other instruments of war. The authority of the supreme commander was paramount, and his directive was law. MacArthur, who earlier had issued the directive abolishing the Japanese military and was highly regarded in Japan as the father of the peace constitution, made his case for the constitutionality of the National Policy Reserve Force in his New Year's address to the Japanese people in 1951: He told them that the constitution does not proscribe the sovereign right of all nations to self-defense.

Henceforth, the status of Japan's pacific ideal was reduced to a game of words. Tanks for the National Policy Reserve Force, for example, were referred to as "special vehicles." Soon after Japan regained its independence in 1952, the National Policy Reserve Force was renamed the Self-Defense Force. Even though Japan's military budget is the third largest in the world today, the Ground Self-Defense Force is still not referred to as the army, for the word "army" indicates a war potential and thus would violate Article 9 of the constitution.

For decades after the inception of the SDF, the Japanese continued to debate its constitutionality without reaching any consensus or definitive answer. By keeping the SDF's status vague, Japanese officials avoided being locked into a rigid position. This vagueness allowed for policy flexibility—permitting Tokyo, for example, to strengthen its defense capability steadily in response to U.S. demands. In 1989 a consensus finally emerged in Japan on the status of the SDF. After years of debate, it was agreed that as long as the purpose of the SDF is limited to the defense of Japanese territory, its existence is within the legal framework.

The consensus on the SDF was made possible by an important shift on the part of the Socialist party, Japan's main opposition party. In an effort to make itself more acceptable to the Japanese public, the Socialist party retracted its long-standing platform advocating the abolition of the SDF. That platform had been the hallmark of the party, which for decades had portrayed itself as the self-appointed guardian of the original intent of the peace constitution. Its position that the country should maintain unarmed neutrality had attracted much support in the 1950s and 1960s, but by the late 1980s, the public no longer found this idea credible. Continuing the postwar tradition of fuzzy, even contradictory attitudes toward the SDF, the Socialists in 1989 adopted a new stance—that the SDF is "legal yet unconstitutional." With the Socialist party's acquiescence over the legality of the SDF, a debate that had pitted the ruling Liberal Democratic party (LDP) against the opposition Socialist Party for over four decades came to an end. (This cleared the way for the formation of an LDP-Socialist coalition government in 1994.)

The consensus did not last long, however. Barely a year after the Socialist party recognized the legality of the Self-Defense Force, the LDP government succumbed to U.S. pressure and adopted a plan to send troops to the Persian Gulf, thus rupturing the year-old understanding that the purpose of the SDF was limited to territorial defense. The government's decision was a major turning point for postwar Japan and immediately sparked another constitutional debate.

By agreeing in October 1990 to send Japanese troops abroad, the government of Prime Minister Toshiki Kaifu opened itself up to charges that it had betrayed the national ideal of peace. Led by the Socialists, the opposition parties were not about to let pass what they and the vast majority of Japanese saw as a clear violation of the constitution. Having no legal basis for its plan to send troops abroad, the government attempted to secure one by introducing the "United Nations Peace Cooperation" bill into parliament. A bitter fight ensued over the bill, the fundamental orientation of Japanese foreign policy, and the pacific identity of Japan as set forth in the constitution.

The Iraqi Invasion of Kuwait

Nearly three months after the Iraqi invasion of Kuwait, the Kaifu government presented its plan to parliament to send an unspecified number of SDF troops to the Gulf to provide logistical support to the U.S.-led multinational force. Kaifu's delay was deliberate, as will be discussed in the following paragraphs. The events that finally persuaded Kaifu to adopt the plan reveal much about how Japan sees itself in the world, and about the weight the United States continues to carry in the formulation of Japanese foreign policy.

Toshiki Kaifu is a Japanese pacifist. He had intended to use August 1990 as a time to project his vision of a peaceful Japan. August is a somber month in Japan. August 6 and 9 are the anniversaries of the atomic bombings of Hiroshima and Nagasaki, and August 15 is the anniversary of Japan's surrender in World War II. For the Japanese, these anniversaries serve as reminders of the horrors of war and provide a powerful affirmation of the nation's desire for peace.

To underscore his commitment to a peaceful Japan, the prime minister not only attended the memorial ceremonies at Hiroshima and Nagasaki but also traveled to the southern island of Okinawa, where 110,000 Japanese soldiers and more than 160,000 civilians perished in one of the fiercest battles of World War II. Antiwar sentiments continue to run deep in Okinawa, the only Japanese home island invaded during the war. To this day, Okinawans blame Emperor Hirohito for the loathsome war. During his reign, which ended with his death in early 1989, Hirohito did not dare visit the island because of the depth of feelings against him. Kaifu's visits to Hiroshima, Nagasaki, and Okinawa were meant to be meaningful symbolic gestures, for no prime minister before him had made such a pilgrimage to all three places in a single August. But the Iraqi invasion of Kuwait on August 2 overshadowed these events.

In the wake of the invasion and the rapid U.S. military buildup in the Middle East, the Japanese public wondered how Kaifu would deal with the U.S. call for Japan, an alliance partner, to share the defense burden. Kaifu did not respond in any major way to the new Gulf crisis for nearly a month after the invasion. Fearing he might be drawn into making commitments for which he was unprepared, the prime minister cancelled a previously scheduled visit to the Middle East. Kaifu behaved as if he were hoping the crisis would be settled before he, as the head of a great power, would be forced to make any difficult choices. But that was not to be.

The United States continued to strengthen its expeditionary force, and the militaries of France, Britain, and other U.S. allies joined in. American pressures on Japan "to join the team" grew stronger with each passing day. President George Bush and his top aides called Kaifu regularly asking the prime minister to send Japanese minesweepers and oil-supply ships to the Gulf. The U.S. secretary of state emphasized to Kaifu the need for a timely and visible Japanese contribution, and the president's national security adviser stressed the importance of the Japanese flag being displayed on ships and planes sent to the Middle East. U.S. officials told Japan to prove to the world that it was fully committed to the path Washington had taken. The message was clear: Sending money was not enough.

On August 30, with no end to the crisis in sight, Kaifu announced that Japan would provide $1 billion for the multinational force. When Kaifu reported his plan to Bush, he must have sensed that the president was not satisfied, for within two weeks, Kaifu arranged for an additional $1 billion for the multinational force and $2 billion for refugee and economic aid to Turkey, Jordan, and Egypt. Although $4 billion is not a sum to be taken lightly, U.S. pressure on Japan for a visible contribution—the display of the Japanese flag in the Gulf—intensified.

At the root of the impasse between Washington and Tokyo were the contradictory ways in which the United States and Japan view the world and each other. The United States, the hegemonic power and keeper of Pax Americana, perceives the world in economic, political, and military terms. Japan, as a subordinate power and a major beneficiary of Pax Americana, sees the world primarily in economic terms. Since 1945, the United States has provided Japan with military protection and political leadership, which has allowed Tokyo the luxury of defining its role in world affairs largely in terms of trade. For that reason, Japan has gotten in the habit of dealing with the world as if it were simply a marketplace. But today, with the relative economic decline of the United States, the end of the Cold War, and the American desire to see itself as a leader among equals, the United States is no longer willing to allow Japan to live in such a selectively and narrowly defined world.

The United States, in the name of burden-sharing, urged Japan to play a larger political and military role in the world. Japan's political leaders responded to the U.S. change in attitude by the "internationalization of Japan" (a national slogan in vogue since the early 1980s) with the goal of supporting Pax Americana while maintaining Japan's subordinate place in it. To accomplish this objective, Japan greatly expanded its military and foreign aid budgets, its financial support for U.S. forces stationed in

Japan, and its contribution to pillar organizations of Pax Americana such as the World Bank and the International Monetary Fund. In keeping with an economic definition of its role in international affairs, Japan saw fit to fulfill its greater political responsibilities in the world through monetary means. But how could an internationalizing Japan meet U.S. demands for it to shoulder military burdens more directly?

When President Bush requested in mid-August that Japan dispatch minesweepers and oil-supply ships to the Gulf, Kaifu explained that the obstacles to such an action were threefold: The constitution, parliament, and public opinion. The explaination was meant as a refusal of the request, but Bush did not see it as such. He was mystified by Kaifu's response, unable to figure out whether the answer was yes or no. Kaifu, certain that he had made his position clear to Bush, did not bother to instruct the Foreign Ministry to prepare a response to the president's request.

Kaifu's behavior reflected an attitude toward the United States that is ingrained in many Japanese leaders. Seeing their country as subordinate to the United States, many Japanese, including political leaders, act like sons who expect parental understanding when dealing with the United States. This naive approach to state-to-state relations is the primary cause of the U.S. frustration with and incomprehension of Japan's international behavior.

When officials at the Japanese Foreign Ministry, who are more experienced in dealing with Washington than are Japanese politicians, heard of President Bush's request for a military contribution, they realized the gravity of the situation and immediately sought to formulate a response to the president's request even though the prime minister had not asked for one. Based on its more realistic and less naive understanding of international relations, the ministry put together a plan to contribute monetarily to the multinational force. That plan became the basis for Kaifu's August 30 offer of $1 billion.

Ministry officials did not seriously consider sending military support; from the beginning the issue was money. Given the depth of pacifist sentiment in Japanese society, the idea of sending the military was beyond the realm of the possible even for the "realists" at the Foreign Ministry. Although relatively more sophisticated in their dealings with the United States and the world in general, Foreign Ministry officials never seriously considered the military option. Like Prime Minister Kaifu, they still saw Japan's role in the world primarily in economic terms, and their actions bore the distinct mark of Japan's psychological dependence on a "paternal" United States.

The Japanese Foreign Ministry asked the U.S. government how much it planned to spend for Operation Desert Shield, but the answer, of course, was that the United States did not know. The ministry, in search of a "respectable" contribution and a "proper" percentage of the total bill, was temporarily at a loss. When U.S. Treasury Secretary Nicholas Brady arrived in Tokyo in early September and put forth the figure of an additional $3 billion in Japanese contributions, Foreign Ministry officials were relieved. They felt comfortable with, and felt they could accommodate, this kind of U.S. request.

The Japanese public was generally indifferent to the crisis in its early weeks. To the average Japanese, the crisis was "a fire across the river"—a problem that was of no direct concern and therefore better left alone. This indifference reveals some important aspects of Japanese attitudes toward the use of force in international relations and toward Japan's assuming a larger role in world affairs. Although more than 60 percent of Japan's oil imports come from the Persian Gulf, the Japanese showed no great concern about a potential oil crisis. They seemed confident of their economy's ability to adjust to an oil price hike, as it had done quite successfully in 1973 and 1979. For Japanese industrialists, what mattered most was international competitiveness. As long as an oil price hike affected all industrial economies equally, they saw no compelling reason to worry about the price of oil or to urge that Japanese troops be sent to the Middle East to secure the flow of cheap oil.

This response was quite a departure for a people who until recently seemed obsessed with the vulnerability of their resource-poor country. When the U.S. government had demanded Japanese participation in its military effort, it had mistakenly assumed that the Japanese would readily agree to this demand because they wanted and needed U.S. help to protect their oil supply. One might argue that the Japanese could afford to be indifferent precisely because Washington had dispatched the U.S. military so swiftly to the Middle East to defend Saudi Arabia. But, in fact, their indifference sprang from something more fundamental. It reflected a growing understanding that their country did not need U.S. protection except in the case of a direct military attack. Until the Gulf crisis, it had been assumed that Japan depended on the United States to "protect" Japanese interests in Southeast Asia, the Middle East, and elsewhere. But with the end of the Cold War, it has become apparent that the Japanese feel less strongly that such "extended protection" is necessary.

Even though most members of the Japanese public disapproved of Iraq's invasion of Kuwait, they could not, given their pacifist inclinations, fully support the military response chosen by the United States. They remain haunted by memories of the last time Japan ventured abroad. Accustomed to living in a world dominated by U.S. leadership, they were unprepared and unwilling to engage in constructive thinking about international politics.

The Gulf crisis revealed another fundamental feature of the Japanese state today and of Japanese attitudes toward international relations. The postwar Japanese state has shown a greater willingness than the United States to negotiate when its citizens are taken hostage. Whereas the United States has been willing to sacrifice its citizens in pursuit of abstract principles such as the national interest or international law and order, the Japanese state, as it was constituted by the United States forty-five years ago, does not have a mandate to sacrifice the lives of its citizens for abstract principles. In general, the Japanese place a higher value on individual life than on reasons of state. International relations theorist Nicholas Onuf has attributed this difference to the fact that the final responsibility for Japan's physical security from external threat—which is the primary justification of a state's existence—resides with the United States, not Japan itself.

This difference of views over the role of the state was apparent in the way Japanese shipping companies and airlines responded to Kaifu's request to provide transportation for the multinational effort in the Gulf. Executives at Japan Air Lines knew they could not turn down the prime minister's request, but they were worried about the safety of their employees held hostage in Kuwait. They therefore considered painting over the company's name on planes to be flown to the Gulf and having their planes fly together with planes from other Japanese airlines so that their company would not be singled out for retaliation by Iraq. They also insisted that their planes carry only nonmilitary cargo, such as medicine, for the multinational force.

What MacArthur Giveth, Bush Taketh Away?

At the end of September, Prime Minister Kaifu traveled to New York and addressed the UN General Assembly, where he reiterated Japan's condemnation of Iraq and Tokyo's support for UN efforts to resolve the crisis. His speech also called for the arms manufacturing nations of the world to reach an agreement among themselves to cease the export of arms; further, he implied that those who sold arms to Iraq bear some of the responsibility for Saddam Hussein's invasion of Kuwait.

As the head of a nation with a strict ban on arms exports, Kaifu was in a unique position among great-power leaders to make such an appeal. His proposal was a real effort by a Japanese prime minister to seek a transformation of the norms of world politics so as to further the peace ideal embedded in the Japanese constitution. This approach to foreign policy was the type of approach the Japanese constitution had stipulated. Unlike his predecessors, who had used the constitution as an excuse for distancing their country from world politics and as a justification for

Japan's insular foreign policy, Kaifu appeared to be setting out on a more active, internationalist path. But his proposal fell on deaf ears at home and abroad and was overshadowed by the agreements he made in a meeting with President Bush shortly thereafter.

To the surprise of those around him, Kaifu, who had not even allowed the words "Self-Defense Force" to be mentioned in earlier discussions about the Kuwait crisis with Japanese cabinet and Foreign Ministry officials, announced after meeting with Bush that he would send the SDF to the Middle East. Little is known about the conversation between the president and the prime minister. But some Japanese commentaries have portrayed Bush as the puppet master and Kaifu as the puppet, reinforcing the impression in Japan that the prime minister was beholden to the U.S. president for having put him in power.

Kaifu, who had not been a strong figure in the LDP prior to assuming the prime ministership in August 1989, had become the head of government at the behest of the party's elders. Tainted by the 1989 Recruit bribery scandal, in which LDP politicians were found to have accepted illegal gifts from the Recruit company, the LDP needed a "Mr. Clean" to occupy the prime minister's seat. The party therefore sought someone who was not important enough to have been implicated in the scandal. Kaifu was supposed to be a temporary selection, one who would weather the storm but who was not expected to last long in office. To the surprise of the party elders, however, Kaifu became popular, which in turn greatly enhanced his stature in the LDP. According to opinion polls, on the eve of the Kuwait crisis, Kaifu enjoyed a level of public support.

This popularity was in large part a result of the recognition that the president of the United States had bestowed upon the Japanese prime minister. Frequent telephone calls from the White House, which the prime minister's office did not hesitate to publicize, had been especially effective in boosting his ratings in the polls. With the eruption of the Gulf crisis, however, the calls from the White House requesting a military contribution became cumbersome for the pacifist Kaifu. At his September meeting with Kaifu, Bush called in his debts. Without doubt, Kaifu was indebted to Bush for much of his domestic popularity, but it is hard to imagine that any prime minister would have been able to resist the heavy pressure President Bush put on Kaifu to show the Japanese flag in the Gulf.

Although Kaifu's change of mind introduced a whole new set of problems for Japan's leaders, it offered them a way out of a problem that had been nagging at them since the beginning of the crisis. They did not want to be confronted with the question they feared they would be asked if U.S. soldiers died in the war against Iraq: How many yen is a U.S. soldier's life worth? It was a question to which the Japanese leaders had no answer. In this regard, the plan to send Japanese troops offered a solution. If Japanese troops were to march beside U.S. troops in even a limited way, Japan's leaders would be spared from having to answer this question if a shooting war broke out.

To dispatch the SDF beyond Japan's borders, however, the Kaifu government needed to get the "United Nations Peace Cooperation" bill through parliament. This bill challenged the interpretation of the constitution that limited the scope of SDF operations to territorial defense. Instead of attempting to amend Article 9 of the constitution, Kaifu took the position that the act of sending the SDF abroad in a noncombatant role (such as transporting medical support, etc.) to a potential war zone would not violate the constitution. His position was tenuous, and the debate that ensued in parliament exposed its political folly.

Much of that discussion verged on the comical. Kaifu stated that the troops would not be sent to "dangerous" areas, and because they would not be directly engaged in fighting, their dispatch would not violate the constitution. The opposition questioned whether the troops would be armed. At first, Kaifu said no; then he reversed himself and said yes, they would carry small arms. The opposition wanted to know whether small arms meant pistols or assault rifles and whether the troops would be allowed to shoot back if fired upon.

The debate did seem to acquire some substance when Kaifu, hinting at a reinterpretation of the constitution, stated that the SDF is permitted to engage in collective security under UN auspices. But the opposition quickly pointed out that the multinational force in the Gulf was not a UN force, and the director of the legal bureau in the prime minister's own office testified that the constitution did not allow the SDF to engage in collective security. Subsequently, the debate degenerated once again, reverting to the question of whether the SDF would constitute a military force if it were dispatched to the Middle East to provide logistical support to U.S. soldiers.

Kaifu's mistake was in trying to find a technical solution to the problem of sending troops abroad while maintaining that such an act did not infringe on the constitution. In effect, he simultaneously tried to preserve and to break the constitution. His futile attempt to have it both ways contributed to the uninspiring and disappointing way in which the debate was conducted.

The Socialists also deserve some of the blame for the insipid nature of the debate. They were presented with opportunity to provide theoretical arguments in defense of Japan's pacific national identity as set forth in the constitution—and they proved incapable of doing so. In a telling episode broadcast on television, two leading Socialist members of parliament were asked where in the constitution it says that the SDF cannot be sent abroad. Instead of answering "nowhere"—because, according to the constitution, the SDF does not exist—they responded with embarrassed, blank stares. The Socialist Party chose to fight the bill on technical grounds instead of appealing to the lofty principles of the constitution. Its tactic was to prolong the hearings so that no vote could be taken before November 10, the deadline for the end of the session of parliament that was convened to debate the bill. For this reason, members of the opposition led by the Socialists bombarded the government with questions about pistols and assault rifles, reducing the trial of the national ideal of peace to a question of technicalities.

During the debate, Kaifu had to contend with more than just the objections of the opposition. The LDP, which for years had been advocating a revision of the "occupation" constitution, split over Kaifu's proposal. The older members—those who had experienced the Pacific War firsthand and belonged to the generation that had built a peaceful Japan after the war—tended to be openly skeptical of the idea of sending troops. They remembered the meaningless deaths of their comrades and were not about to order today's youths into battle.

The fifty-seven-year-old Kaifu, a generation younger than those who had been traumatized by the experience of World War II, instinctively rejected the military option at first. However, he soon reversed himself, concluding that the primary foreign policy task of the postwar Japanese prime minister was to maintain good relations with the United States. Kaifu acted according to what he thought were the responsibilities of his office. In contrast, Ichiro Ozawa, the party's secretary general, a chief rival of Kaifu's for the prime ministership, and a member of the same generation, saw the situation differently. From the beginning, he argued that Japan must cease pretending to be a "special state"; it must recognize that the use of military force is an integral part of the foreign policy of a great power. He argued that if Japan acted otherwise, the United States would not be satisfied. His point of view was not a new one. It had gained ground in recent years as memories of the Pacific War faded and the United States stepped up its pressure on Japan to act like a great power.

In addition, both Kaifu and Ozawa feared Japan's isolation in the world, which in the country's postwar political language meant isolation from the United States. That fear is as potent for this postwar generation as the loathing of war was for the generation that had been traumatized by the Pacific War.

With public opinion and even a large part of the LDP opposing the dispatch of troops, Kaifu's plan did not have much of a chance. Two days before the November deadline, the government withdrew its bill.

The lull in the debate did not last long, however. As the costs of the Gulf War soared, and U.S. disenchantment with the Japanese government's perceived unwillingness to send tangible aid to the Gulf grew, more demands were made on the Japanese pocketbook. A U.S. request for $9 billion in Japanese aid for the Kuwait War, with no strings attached, met with a new wave of opposition in Tokyo. The possibility of dissent by the opposition which controlled the upper house of parliament forced Kaifu into a compromise position that allotted the funds to purchases of nonlethal equipment. A new tax was introduced to fund this contribution.

This attitude took a surprising turn following the end of the Gulf War. The Japanese people, so vehemently opposed to their country's role in the fighting, were tepid in their response to the dispatch of four Japanese minesweepers to the Gulf in April 1991. The fighting in the Gulf was over, and so too, it seemed, was the fighting in parliament.

After the Gulf War

In September 1991 the prime minister introduced the "Peace-Keeping Battalion" bill to parliament. The bill, which authorized the participation of up to 2,000 Self-Defense Force members in UN peacekeeping operations during cease-fire activities, was expected to pass. Indeed, in December 1991 the bill passed in the lower house, backed by the new prime minister, Kiichi Miyazawa. Yet, by December 1, the bill was dead.

The abandonment of the bill by the opposition-controlled upper house served once more to underline the fundamental conflict between "passive and active pacifism." The "passive" proponents of a strictly defined pacifist posture maintained that Japan's ability to wage war must never be restored. "Active" pacifists argued that given aggressive actors like Saddam Hussein, such a policy is unrealistic and even detrimental to world peace. In their point of view, Japan, as a power in the new world order, must commit itself to a larger role in enforcing peace. "Passive" pacifism was, in their eyes, irresponsible isolationism.

In February 1992, by which time the controversy had reached new levels of intensity, the Ozawa Committee, formed by the Japanese government, published a report that attempted to redefine Japan's global role in the post-Cold War world and to outline the debate between passive and active pacifism. Commenting on the legislative and moral standoff that had been occurring in Japan since the beginning of the Gulf War, the committee pointed to the fundamental differences between the preamble of the Japanese Constitution and Article 9.[1] The preamble's emphasis on the need for international cooperation in the preservation of global peace and prosperity seemed to conflict with Article 9's pacifist doctrine. The debate now focused on both interpretation and prevalence. Should the preamble take prevalence over Article 9?

In March 1992, when the United Nations Transitional Authority in Cambodia (UNTAC) requested that Japan provide one third of the esti-mated $2.8 billion necessary for its peace mission in Cambodia, these questions had yet to be answered in legislative fashion.

Prime Minister Miyazawa and the Japanese legislature reached a stormy compromise in June 1992. During two weeks of ongoing debate, and amid threats of a walk-out by the Socialist Party, the Diet passed a watered-down bill to allow the participation of up to 2,000 members of Japan's Self-Defense Force in UN peacekeeping missions. Miyazawa's success in bridging the gap of opinion be-tween his party and the opposi-tion parties was achieved at the expense of giving the legislature final authorization for the Cambodia and future UN missions and restricting the scope of the jobs to be performed by the troops. The legislation paved the way for a Japanese role, albeit a limited one, in UN peacekeeping.

Japan's decision to send peacekeeping forces to Cambodia as a part of the UN peacekeeping mission is not a solution that promises to be perma-nent. The troops that left Japan by mid-October 1992 had, in accordance with Japanese legislation, a very limited role. They provided construction and engineering assistance for building infrastructure and medical and transportation assistance. They were lightly armed, authorized to fire only in self-defense, and not allowed into dangerous areas.

The peacekeeping debate will inevitably intensify if Japan pursues a greater role in the new world order, quite possibly as a member of the UN Security Council. Such a move, which has been alluded to by the UN as well as Japanese officials,[2] would require a reopening of the deployment discussion. At a time when the United Nations is taking steps to improve its military capability in the areas of peacekeeping and peacemaking, Japan's compliance with Article 43 of the UN Charter, which requires the provision of troops to the UN by member states, will be expected. Quite likely, the current compromise is only the calm before the storm.

Notes

An earlier version of this chapter was Published in *World Policy Journal*, Winter 1990–1991.

1. The Preamble includes statements such as the following: "We desire to occupy an honored place in an international society striving for the preservation of peace, and the banishment of tyranny and slavery, oppression and intolerance for all time on earth. ... We believe that no nation is responsible to itself alone, but that the laws of political morality are universal; and that obedience to such laws is incumbent upon all nations who would sustain their own sovereignty and justify their sovereign relationship with other nations."

2. See Boutros Boutros-Ghali, *An Agenda for Peace* (New York: United Nations, 1992). John Lee, *Peacekeeping and Peacemaking: A Summary* (Washington, D.C.: International Economic Studies Institute, 1992).

Suggested Readings

Asai, Motofumi, "Pacifism in the New International Order," *Japan Quarterly* 38 (April–June 1991).

Chuma, Kiyofuku, "An End to the Cold War," *Japan Quarterly* 34 (July–September 1990).

Eto, Jun, "The Japanese Constitution and the Post-Gulf War World," *Japan Echo* 18 (Autumn 1991), 62.

Martin, Jurek, "Japanese Foreign Policy in the 1990s," *Asian Affairs* 21 (October 1990), 268–276.

Miyazaki, Katsuji, "Time to Reevaluate the Security Treaty," *Japan Quarterly* 37 (October–December 1990).

Nakanishi, Terumasa, "The U.N. and Japan's Place in It," *Japan Echo* 19 (Special Issue 1992), 66.

Nakao, Eiichi, "Japan's Role in the 1990s," *Vital Speeches of the Day* 57 (July 1, 1991), 549–552.

Okita, Saburo, "Japan's Quiet Strength," *Foreign Policy* 75 (Summer 1989), 128–145.

15

The Impact of the Kuwait Conflict on the United Nations and the Security Council: Developments and Perspectives

Helmut Freudenschuss

This chapter focuses on the impact the Kuwait conflict has had, and may have in the future on the United Nations. It does not attempt to give an account of the conflict itself or of the United Nations's involvement in it.

The Kuwait conflict was rife with misperceptions. The most significant one regarding the UN was that the Security Council (SC) was in the driver's seat. In reality, the Security Council was being driven by the United States, quite skillfully and successfully, both in substance and in terms of public relations. Another misperception was that the UN would, once the crisis was over, play—or at least be allowed to play—a large role in tackling, if not settling, the problems of the region.

Some other misperceptions do not fall within the purview of this chapter, such as those of Saddam Hussein himself, for example, that the "Arab masses" would revolt, that the Coalition would not hold, that Israel would inevitably be drawn into the conflict, that moderate Arab regimes would fall, and that the conflict would degenerate into a large, and disastrous shooting match. Finally, there remains what may be the greatest misperception of all—the often-proclaimed "new world order"—on which the jury is still out.

Changes in the Involvement of the Security Council

In comparison to its conduct in other conflicts, from the onset of the Kuwait crisis the Security Council acted more speedily, decisively, and comprehensively. The reasons were many, including improved cooperation between its five permanent members (P-5), especially between the United States and the Soviet Union, the non-confrontational attitude of China, the split among the 70 odd nonaligned members (NAM), and the willingness and ability of the United States to assume a leadership position.

Why did the United States make use of the Security Council to an extent not seen since the Korean War? For one thing, UN approval helped the Bush administration to secure and maintain domestic support.[1] But also, the Security Council's engagement gave the U.S.-suggested actions an international cover, thereby making the proposed plan easier to sell as well as easier to swallow. Security Council involvement made not only the imposition of fairly comprehensive sanctions more palatable but aided approval of the authorization for the use of force and the terms of the cease-fire. It also helped the Arab members of the Coalition to save face, so to speak, in their own populations and those of fellow governments, and it made the sanctions more effective than if they had been imposed unilaterally.

The split among the nonaligned members of the Security Council also helped to secure for the United States the nine votes necessary for the passage of a decision. With China usually abstaining, the United States could count on the support of the United Kingdom, the USSR, France, Canada, Finland (replaced by Belgium and Austria in January 1991), and Romania. In addition, it had the support of Zaire, Côte d'Ivoire, and Ethiopia (which had its own score to settle with Iraq). Thus, including its own vote, the United States could command at least ten votes. The remaining countries—Cuba, Yemen, Colombia, and Malaysia—which became known as the "Gang of Four," tried valiantly to get the Security Council to consider and adopt alternative approaches but were ultimately unsuccesful. The split among the NAM, which had been felt before on other issues, had thus come to light in the present situation. When, as in the case of Resolution 678, an "impressive" result of the Council vote was extremely important to the United States, and when Washington consequently exerted its influence, whether with carrots or sticks, Colombia and Malaysia often voted with the United States as well. After January 1, 1991, with Colombia, Ethiopia, and Malaysia replaced on the council by Ecuador, Zimbabwe, and India (and the outcome of the Kuwait conflict no longer in doubt), the voting patterns remained essentially the same although the climate had changed in the Security Council. The sometimes frantic efforts and debates within the council to change its course had ceased, the heated rhetoric had largely subsided, and a sense of anticlimax had set in.

China's attitude—"abstentionism" in most cases, passive cooperation in some—was widely considered to be a result of its desire to make up for the Tiananmen Square events of June 1989. It was generally perceived within the UN that Washington was rewarding China for its vote when, on the day after China abstained on Resolution 678, the Chinese foreign minister was invited to visit Washington. The position of the USSR—Yevgeny Primakov's last-minute efforts in Baghdad notwithstanding—was widely interpreted as a result of its assessment of the advantages of better ties with the West, with the Soviet diplomats (and the economists) allegedly getting the upper hand over the military.

Among the permanent members of the Security Council, cooperation reached an unprecedented peak during the crisis and remains high in its aftermath. The roots of this close relationship can be traced to 1986–1987, when the P-5 began to work together during the conflict between Iran and Iraq. The cooperation continued with regard to events in Namibia and Cambodia. By the time of the Kuwait crisis, the P-5 had virtually formed a "politburo"; after having established a general agreement among themselves, they "informed" the other members of the outcome of their deliberations with the expectation—usually correct—that they would quickly ratify (or rubberstamp) that outcome by giving it the council's official approval.

As mentioned, the end of hostilities in the Gulf did not bring an end to this cooperation; instead, it continued with the passage of a series of resolutions. In fact, the P-5 now "pre-clear" the reports or plans of the UN Secretary General that are required by Resolution 687, as well as subsequent texts, before they are submitted to the Security Council as a whole.

Thus, in a short time, the P-5 have gone from paralyzing the council to running it. Subjectively, this new state of affairs can be frustrating for the nonpermanent members.[2] But, objectively speaking, for the Security Council to be effective, the P-5 must cooperate closely. And one must also bear in mind that, according to the UN Charter, all fifteen members of the Security Council, not just the P-5, act on behalf of the UN members. As long as the decisions of the council are accepted by the international community, its legitimacy will remain intact. A problem would arise, however, and the legitimacy of the Security Council and the prestige of the UN as a whole would be put into question if such a universal or at least broad international acceptance was no longer in evidence or if, for instance, a double standard was applied. Thus, within the council considerations of short-term expediency must be measured against their longer-term implications.[3]

The Limited Role of the UN Secretary General

The Secretary General's role at the height of the Kuwait crisis, notwithstanding his trip to Baghdad on the eve of the January 15 deadline, was quite limited. Not having been given a specific mandate of clear negotiations or bridge building in the first Security Council resolution, he absented himself on an extended trip to Latin America. Despite the later efforts of the "Gang of Four" to give him a mandate (Resolution 598 on the Iran-Iraq conflict comes to mind as a comparison), the closest he came to receiving a mandate was in Resolution 674, passed in late October, in which the Security Council "reposed its trust in the Secretary General to make available his good offices and, as he considers appropriate, to pursue them and to undertake diplomatic efforts in order to reach a peaceful solution." Still, this carefully drafted formulation clearly did not give the Secretary General a mandate. It was included in the resolution which served other purposes (see Appendix for further details) only to accommodate, to an extent, some of the nonaligned council members.

Consequently, the actions of the Secretary General were restricted to efforts to secure the release of foreigners held by Iraq, to oblique warnings of the consequences of war in general, and to statements about the public perception of the UN and the importance of its retaining the trust of all the peoples of the world. The significance of the Secretary General's trip to Baghdad and his meeting with Saddam Hussein on January 12, 1991 remains unclear. Even though he did not have a mandate from the council, he did have the support of some of its important members. Yet, some of this support may have been extended in spite of the expectation that he would come back empty-handed. In his report to the Security Council upon his return from Baghdad and in his statement to the press on January 15, the Secretary General outlined the elements of the "package" he had offered the Iraqi leader, including efforts to comprehensively address the Arab-Israeli conflict and the Palestinian question. Although some controversy arose afterward about the veracity of the Iraqi version of the minutes of this meeting, it seems safe to say that both sides offered too little too late.

The Secretary General's involvement in the conflict increased considerably, however, following the cessation of hostilities. Many of the conditions set by the Security Council in Resolution 687 involved executive tasks, including the deployment of assistance from the UN Iraq-Kuwait Observation Mission (UNIKOM) with the demarcation of boundaries, the development of a plan for creating special commissions to supervise the destruction of certain Iraqi weapons and missiles, and the administration of a fund to pay compensation for claims against Iraq. The policy making was done either by the Secretary General and the Security Council or was assigned to special commissions.

The other area in which the Secretary General could have become increasingly involved and in which his help would, indeed, have been welcomed, was the humanitarian field, first through the Ahtisaari missions to Iraq and Kuwait and then, following the passage of Security Council Resolution 688, through the Suy mission and the appointment of Sadruddin Aga Khan as the coordinator for all relief efforts. Various specialized organizations and agencies in the UN system made efforts to get involved, but the UN's disorganized and slow response led to criticism.

Such a limited and largely reactive role for the Secretary General is probably appropriate in times when the Security Council is functioning effectively. Those who see the council as dominated by one member, however, may well deplore the absence of the Secretary General as part of a system of checks and balances. The performance of the UN system in response to the humanitarian challenges arising from the Kuwait conflict has already prompted calls for the next Secretary General to have considerable managerial qualities.

Sanctions

Although the sanctions imposed on Iraq failed to result in a reversal of the aggressor's position, they did possess some interesting features including the following:

- The comprehensiveness of the sanctions (e.g. Security Council Resolution 661, later complemented and refined in Security Council Resolutions 665, 666, and 670)
- The creation of a comparatively strict and efficient implementation mechanism in the form of a Sanctions Committee within the Security Council (created by Resolution 661; its mandate was later enlarged by Resolutions 666, 669, 670, and 687)
- The establishment of guidelines for states "to facilitate the full international implementation" of the arms embargo rather than reliance on the initiative of each state to regulate the application of sanctions on a purely national level.

However, sanctions can be effective only with the broadest international cooperation and support. Such support, in turn, may well be influenced by the impact of the implementation of sanctions on national economies. The insufficient attention to the difficulties created by the observance of sanctions during and following the Kuwait conflict could well dampen the enthusiasm of states to support and implement these sanctions in the future.[4]

Security Council Resolution 678 (1990)[5]

The relevance of Resolution 678 lies in its rather general character and in the way it was used rather than in its authorization of the use of force; other resolutions have served the latter purpose.

There is no need to describe here how this authorization came about. What matters is the extensive way in which the authorized force was carried out, and what kind of impact this will have on the future of collective security. Some have argued that in the absence of controls on accountability within the Security Council the use of force was excessive and that no further blanket authorizations of this kind should be given. Others have pointed to the special nature of the Kuwait crisis and have voiced their assumption that future authorizations would carry more fine print on how to apply and command that force. Still others have expressed concern that, in the light of the success of the "678 procedure," it might be tempting to seek authorization from the Security Council to use force in other cases rather than to apply more time-consuming measures such as those enumerated in Chapter VI of the UN Charter to resolve a conflict.

On a more general plane, some observers seemed to remember only vaguely what they had read in their undergraduate textbooks about the UN and collective security and went on to pronounce the UN's involvement in the Kuwait crisis as exactly what the "Founding Fathers" had originally intended. I do not share this view. For one thing, authorization by the Security Council to take certain measures does not suspend the right to continue to act without (or outside) council authorization in the exercise of the inherent right of self-defense under Article 51 of the charter.[6]

Further, collective security, as originally intended, meant applying not only Articles 40 and 41 but also Articles 42, 43, and so on, of the Charter, which implied a UN command, agreements between the UN and states on the provision of troops, a role for the Military Staff Committee, and so forth. None of these conditions has yet come to pass, and given the exigencies of modern warfare, none probably will. I (having attended a number of Security Council meetings) find it difficult to imagine war being waged, and forces if not actually commanded at least to an extent being controlled, by representatives of fifteen diverse countries.[7]

In effect, a viable alternative to the infeasible concept of collective security in its classic sense has emerged. A new instrument has been created that, like earlier UN peacekeeping operations, cannot be found in the UN Charter but responds to a need and gives both the Security Council and the states the flexibility they desire.[8] This "new" collective security force—authorized but not controlled by the Security Council—could have the additional advantage of being a step closer toward substituting multilaterally authorized enforcement for unilateral action under the guise of self-proclaimed self-defense. For this to happen, however, a broader application of this new practice would have to take place, so that a climate of trust among major powers could be established in the Security Council's ability and preparedness to exercise its powers in a fair and equitable way and perform its tasks for world peace and global security.

Terms for the Cease-Fire and the Cessation of Hostilities (Security Council Resolutions 686 and 687)

In many instances, victors have dictated the terms of a settlement to the vanquished. What distinguishes the Kuwait situation is that the terms of settlement first drafted by the United States, then reworked in consultation with the United Kingdom, then with France, and finally with the other two permanent members of the UN Security Council were "ratified" by the Security Council in Resolutions 686 and 687. Although the settlement terms came into being without any real input from the ten nonpermanent members, these terms now wear the cloak of international approval. They are also without precedent in the following respects:

- They provide for the (indirect) settling of an international boundary (that between Iraq and Kuwait) and the guarantee of its inviolability.
- They create a peacekeeping organization (PKO) in a Chapter VII resolution.
- They provide for the liquidation of weapons of mass destruction and of material usable for nuclear weapons under the supervision of a Special Commission and the International Atomic Energy Agency (IAEA), with provisions for future ongoing monitoring and verification of Iraqi compliance.
- They establish a compensation regime for war damages.

Time will tell to what extent these provisions and mechanisms are working. If they are working well, a strong precedent would be set for the consequences of future aggression. The message would be clear: Crime does not pay.

The UN Iraq-Kuwait Observation Mission (UNIKOM)

Peacekeeping operations (PKO) are among the original inventions and success stories of the UN. Their development thus deserves particular attention. UNIKOM is, compared to a "classical" PKO, an innovation in several respects:

- Its mandate is based on two Security Council resolutions (687 and 689), both of which are mandatory Chapter VII decisions.
- Consequently, the traditional requirement of consent of the host countries for the deployment of the PKO was deemed unnecessary. More important, however, the PKO does not have to be withdrawn if one host country so wishes.
- Indeed, the termination of UNIKOM requires a decision by the Security Council: Its mandate is, contrary to usual practice, indefinite and not subject to the normal extensions.
- There has been no lack of volunteers in this instance. Typically, troop-contributing states are reluctant to participate in a PKO without the explicit consent of the host countries (if not of all parties to the conflict) because of their concern for the safety of their personnel.
- The objections of a host country (Iraq) to individual troop-contributing states were not taken into account. The P-5 not only told the Secretariat what UNIKOM's role should be but also how to set up the mission. For example, they rejected the Secretariat's idea of a defined region of thinned-out military personnel and armaments adjacent to the Demilitarized Zone (DZ), because a considerably higher number of UN personnel would have been required. The result was a curious mixture of military observers and support and protection personnel.
- Units of the P-5 are themselves participating in UNIKOM. Some of the P-5 countries even insisted on disproportional representation. Although this development is not unique, it is unusual. "Classical" peacekeeping theory holds that only countries without national agendas in a given conflict can be impartial peacekeepers. A strong argument has been waged, however, in favor of the participation of the P-5, since its participation lends a stronger political backbone to the PKO vis-à-vis the parties.

So far, UNIKOM seems to be working well—despite or because of its peculiarities. Both parties to the conflict are cooperating with it.

Humanitarian Issues

Shortly after the liberation of Kuwait, the members of the Security Council were contacted informally by the Palestine Liberation Organization (PLO), which expressed a deep concern about reports alleging Iraq's mistreatment of Palestinians in Kuwait. However, the majority of the council members considered this to be an internal matter for Kuwait to handle. Some of them sought and received, on a bilateral basis, assurances from the government of Kuwait that all was well.

After a massive flow of Kurdish and Shi'ite refugees toward and across the borders of Turkey and Iran, caused by the repression of insurgencies by the Iraqi government, the Security Council, on the initiative of France, adopted the quite unprecedented Resolution 688 by a vote of 10:3 (with Yemen, Cuba, and Zimbabwe voting against it), with 2 abstentions (China and India). Although the text of this resolution confirms a threat to international peace and security, it also demands that Iraq immediately end this repression, allow unhindered access to international humanitarian organizations, and make available all necessary facilities for their operations and it appeals to all countries to contribute to the humanitarian relief efforts.

It was this formulation that the United States, the United Kingdom, and France invoked when they started to send troops into northern Iraq to create "safe havens" for the Kurds, with the idea of turning them over to the UN as soon as possible. The United Nations' own relief efforts were slow in getting off the ground, but the UN members did realize that the organization needed to provide some sort of protection to reassure the Kurds of their safety. Iraq did not agree to the UN's sending in a force, however, and the Security Council did not make another mandatory decision in this regard (as it had in the case of UNIKOM because of the concerns of council members about intervention in internal matters). Eventually, the Secretary General dispatched a small contingent of UN "guards" to perform some policing, a measure to which Iraq acquiesced. The matter was never discussed in the Security Council.[9]

One might ask whether Resolution 688 was indeed the Security Council's first step toward the emergence of a right of humanitarian intervention, as some would like us to believe,[10] or whether it will remain a one-time exception to the usual resistance of those who continue to regard state sovereignty and territorial integrity as the highest values.

The point has been made that the Security Council would not have authorized the Coalition to save the Kurds (or to march to Baghdad). Legally this issue is open to interpretation. Resolution 678, which authorized the use of all necessary means, includes the phrase "to restore peace and security in the area." The political interpretation given to this clause at the time was a narrow one. With the benefit of hindsight, the military operation could well have turned out differently at this stage.

Conclusion

Only time will tell whether we have witnessed something unique in the history of the UN or whether the UN's operations for the liberation of Kuwait can be viewed as the beginning of a truly new role in world politics. The answer will depend in part on the lessons learned from the Kuwait conflict experience. Some of these lessons could be:

- An understanding of the importance of what has been called "conflict termination ability." The UN has so far had experience only with deploying PKOs, not with dealing with humanitarian problems on a large scale or with laying down the terms for what amounted to, in the present case, an unconditional surrender and its follow-up.
- The importance of the UN and the Security Council developing a preventive capacity, either in finding ways of stationing UN deterrent forces before a conflict breaks out or, after a constant and close watch over a situation, in preauthorizing sanctions or the use of force, should aggression occur.[11]
- The need for further study of the parameters of future Security Council authorization of the use of force.[12]
- The need for studying what elements a situation must have if it is to be defined not as an internal matter but rather as having an international character with implications for international peace and security, and thereby qualifying for UN involvement.[13]

Postscript

During the three years since this Security Council operation took place, some things have changed but others have not. Cooperation among the permanent members of the UN Security Council is still working but less smoothly and closely than during and immediately after the Kuwait conflict. The United States is still in a position to dominate the Council but is less inclined to do so. Criticism of the Security Council is more muted, but demands for a change in its composition have increased. The role of the Secretary General has shifted under the present incumbent, Dr. Butros Butros-Ghali, from secretary to general. Most important, the precedents created by both Resolution 678 and Resolution 688 have neither led to the establishment of a real system of collective security nor to the emergence of a right of humanitarian intervention. The zenith reached by the Security Council in 1993 with its authorization to use force for humanitarian purposes in Somalia may indeed also become its nadir. It serves as a sharp reminder that the Security Council is not the powerful conscience of a mythical "international community" but remains at best a mechanism for the coordination of national interests.

Notes

1. Oscar Schachter viewed the UN resolution authorizing force of decisive importance in Bush's obtaining congressional approval. "UN Law in the Gulf Conflict," *American Journal of International Law,* Vol. 85 (1991), 452–460. For critical views from the "Right," see, e.g., Sofaer, "Asking the UN Is Asking for Trouble," *Wall Street Journal,* November 5, 1990; and Krauthammer, "The Unipolar Moment," *Foreign Affairs,* Vol. 70, No. 1 (1990/1991), 25. For views from the "Left," see, e.g., Ball, "The Gulf Crisis," *New York Review of Books,* December 6, 1990; and Lewis, "A Promise Betrayed," *World Policy Journal,* Summer 1991, 539. For views on legal grounds, see Weston, "SC Resolution 678 and Persian Gulf Decision Making: Precarious Legitimacy," *American Journal of International Law,* Vol. 85 (1991), 516.

2. See, e.g., the statements made by UN representatives from Colombia, Cuba, and especially Malaysia in the debate in the General Assembly on the report of the SC, doc.A/45/PV.63,32.

3. The UN Secretary General, in his address at the University of Bordeaux on 24 April 1991, doc. SG/SM/4560, warned that "when the permanent members agree on the course of action to be followed by the Council, they wield enormous powers, which can overshadow the role of the other members of the Council ... and affect the public perception of the UN as an impartial intermediary for peace. ... A disequilibrium in this respect may, I fear, prove dangerous in the future." See also Maksoud, "The Arab World's Quandary," *World Policy Journal,* Summer 1991, 551: Weston, fn. 1, 517, and Stanley Hoffmann, "The Price of War," *New York Review of Books,* January 17, 1991, 6.

4. See the article by the UN Legal Counsel Fleischhauer, "Wirtschaftliche Zwangsmassnahmen in Recht und Praxis der Weltorganisation," *Vereinte Nationen* Vol. 2 (1991), 41.

5. Security Council Resolution 678 and others are described in more detail in the Appendix.

6. For a detailed discussion of this point, see Franck and Patel, "UN Police Action in Lieu of War: The Old Order Changeth," *American Journal of International Law,* Vol. 85 (1991), 63, Rostow, "Until What? Enforcement Action or Collective Self-Defense?" *American Journal of International Law,* Vol. 85 (1991), 506; and Schachter, fn. 1.

7. Ball, fn. 1, p. 8, expressed the opposite view, however.

8. Weston, fn. 1, 522, agreed (despite his misgivings about the present case) that a new precedent has been set that may, if wisely fine-tuned, prove salutary over the long run. Both the UN Secretary General in his Bordeaux address quoted in fn. 3, p. 5, and Schachter, fn. 1, p. 472, stressed the need for more adequate reports to the Security Council to enable its members to make an informed judgment on the necessity, proportionality, and ends sought by the means employed.

9. Schachter, fn. 1, 469.

10. Parsons, "The UN Charter and International Intervention in Iraq," *MEI*, 19, April 1991, 20. Even the UN Secretary General, fn. 3, p. 6, saw "what is probably an irresistible shift in public attitudes towards the belief that the defense of the oppressed in the name of morality should prevail over frontiers and legal documents."

11. Particularly instructive in this regard is Urquhart, "Learning from the Gulf," *New York Review of Books*, March 7, 1991, 34. See also Russett and Sutterlin, "The UN in a New World Order," *Foreign Affairs*, Vol. 70, No. 2 (Spring 1991), 69, and Johansen, "Lessons for Collective Security," *World Policy Journal*, Summer 1991, 561.

12. See fn. 7. The Austrian representative to the Security Council, Hohenfellner, in quoting a speech by U.S. Representative Pickering, made this suggestion after the adoption of Resolution 687, doc. S/PV.2981, 121, of April 3, 1991.

13. Such a proposal has been made by this author as the Austrian representative in the Special Political Committee of the 45th General Assembly, doc. A/SPC/45/SR.19 of November 21, 1990.

16

Epilogue:
Reflections on the Kuwait Crisis
as Part of an International Triple Crisis

Wolfgang F. Danspeckgruber

The Kuwait crisis signaled an end to the Cold War and indeed to the entire bipolar post-World War II order with dramatic live ammunition fireworks created by high-technology weapons, inaugurating a supposedly better, less antagonistic, and more peaceful "new" world order. In retrospect, the crisis was arguably intertwined with, or at least influenced by, two other major instances of turmoil: the breakup of the Soviet Union and the disintegration of Yugoslavia. One could say that all three crises converged into an international triple crisis that has lingered since 1989 and escalated in 1991. In that year, some months after the liberation of Kuwait, the other two parts of that triple crisis increased in intensity due to the cataclysmic effect of the 1991 Kuwait War, with the attempted coup in the Soviet Union in August and the radicalization and armed confrontation in the unexpected violent disintegration of Yugoslavia in July. All of these events happened within an unipolar international system with the United States as the one superpower, and they all occurred during the ongoing unification of Germany, Japan's process of identifying its new role as a world power, and the search for functioning new global structures and organizations.

By 1992—actually the year the European Community created the Single European Market—signs had begun to appear that Russia and its (conservative) leaders would not relinquish the lost empire but would instead recreate Russia's "near abroad." One can argue that Iraq's aggression against Kuwait and the subsequent war, as well as the trauma of the Kurds, shook the entire region from Baghdad to the Bosporus and became an incendiary for the ensuing developments in Belgrade and Moscow. This triple crisis, however, also caused closer European Union (EU) cooperation in foreign and security policy (CFSP), influencing the Maastricht negotiations in 1991 as well as influencing a surge in the international activities of an increasingly imperious Germany and the reorientation ("internationalization") of Europe's neutrals. Furthermore, both the Kuwait War and the Balkan War have shed doubt on the capability of international organizations such as the UN to make and keep peace.

In contrast to the original perception of the liberation of Kuwait under UN auspices as the commencement of a new world order, the Kuwait crisis appears today to be the last major and perhaps culminating demonstration of Cold War thinking and military operations.[1] Nevertheless, it also introduced an unstable and unpredictable transition phase, suggesting mechanisms and problems to come in the aftermath of the Cold War in bilateral and multilateral relations, and international crisis management. The Western military and humanitarian assistance (following the liberation of Kuwait) on behalf of the Kurds in northern Iraq (Operation Provide Comfort) demonstrated new forms of intervention but also shaped international expectations vis-à-vis the involvement of major outside powers.[2] Most ominously, though, these events depict emerging issues in the European system at the end of the twentieth century, such as armed confrontation, geopolitical expansion, intensified integration, centrifugal and centripetal dynamics, the rise of regional hegemons and spheres of influence, xenophobic nationalism, the making of alliances, and an emerging system of anti-U.S. cooperation and networks. Such opportunistic realpolitik has become translated by a ruthlessly operating leadership testing the dynamics and limits of foreign involvement and has resulted in a variety of diplomatic and strategic moves including new interactions between such regions as the Balkans and the Gulf. In the post-Cold War international system, and due to interdependence and global media networks, crises may henceforth become interconnected even if presumed to be independent. At the same time, the value of economic sanctions and their influence on the target states' performance and cooperation have appeared much more complex and less effective against certain target states.

Many aspects of the Kuwait War, including the eminent power of the media, their all-consuming global real-time information and concomitant emotionalization, introduced, if not triggered, through graphically transmitted *sentiment de guerre* during Desert Storm a new level of brutalization and radicalization in the otherwise surprisingly smooth and orderly transition that had been occurring since 1989 in Central Eastern Europe and the Balkans. The media display of twenty-first century warfare to an astonished worldwide community of observers may have contributed to the acceleration of conflict and inhumanity in the breakup of Yugoslavia as well as to the climax in the Soviet Union.[3]

The developments that surrounded the Kuwait-Soviet-Yugoslav triple crisis demonstrate how one crisis can induce the radicalization of leadership and political-strategic destabilization in other regions, especially where instabilities are already brewing. Such personal, strategic, and socio-political interrelations, combined with historical patterns, may offer important clues for future crisis management or prevention.

This Epilogue analyzes and summarizes some of the relevant aspects and mechanisms of the Kuwait crisis in an effort to clarify its impact on and legacy for the international system and Europe. The chapter is divided into four sections: a section elaborating on regional implications of the crisis; a discussion of the crisis as part of an international triple crisis; a discussion of the international framework at the time of the crisis; and finally, a conceptual section, in which conclusions for policy, Europe, and the emerging international system are offered.

National and Regional Dimensions

Kuwait and the Gulf States

In large part the Kuwait crisis and what followed is the story of how an indebted dictator attempted to extort cash from wealthy neighbors. In the aftermath of the liberation of Kuwait, something akin to austerity measures could be seen in the Gulf Cooperation Council (GCC) member states. Gone are the days when oil kingdoms like Saudi Arabia paid in cash for billion-dollar arms or other major foreign purchases. The combined effects of financing a significant war effort, low oil prices, and reduced global demand for oil made deferred payments, credits, and loan guarantees a new reality for Saudi and several other Arab leaders. Today, as a result of these conditions, the financial and military ties between the United States and Saudi Arabia are central to the stability of the region (as demonstrated by Erik Yesson's and Amin Saikal's chapters in this volume).

The significant interdependence that now exists between the Gulf states and the West, especially the United States, includes the needs of the conservative sheikdoms as a bulwark against the spread of threatening and revolutionary fundamentalism (see Amin Saikal's chapter in this volume). What would be Washington's or Brussel's position and NATO's attitude if al-Sa'ud (or another friendly government) were to fall to Islamic fundamentalists? Would it be acceptable to permit the local oil reserves to come under the control of groups that would align themselves with radical governments and antagonize Israel and the rest of the Arab friends? These questions, which evoke memories of the fall of the Iranian shah Rezah Pahlevi, are likely to occupy U.S. and European decision makers for years to come. But this interdependence also includes the reliance of the United States and the Organization for Economic Cooperation and Development (OECD) on the free flow of oil, a situation that has converted the region into a zone of interest or a sphere of influence for the United States. Likewise, the U.S. declaration by inaction in the Yugoslav breakup may be an indication of the United States' granting the Russians a sphere of influence in the Balkans.[4]

At the prompting of the democratic Carter administration, and as part of the Carter Doctrine of 1979–1980, the Saudis invested heavily in an array of Western military technology and infrastructure following the Soviet invasion of Afghanistan.[5] The Saudi military alliance with, if not dependence on, the United States is exemplified by King Khalid Military City (KKMC), a vast complex 200 miles north of Riyadh, designed to accommodate U.S. forces in wartime.[6] Constructed to support U.S. military preparations against a Soviet invasion of the Gulf, this infrastructure proved invaluable to U.S. forces in preparing for the liberation of Kuwait. It was large enough to house more than 500,000 Coalition soldiers. In the most complicated and extensive logistical operation since the Korean War (1950–1951), the U.S. Army shipped approximately two million tons of matériel, ammunition, and spare parts to Saudi Arabia.[7] Further, CentCom had drawn up detailed logistical plans for transporting an expeditionary force to Saudi Arabia. The extensive military infrastructure in that country, including special ports, housing, commando posts, and facilities for more than 2,500 military planes, provided for a uniquely favorable circumstance of preparation, operation, and strategy for Coalition forces.[8] Decision makers would be wise to keep in mind this unparalleled relationship between the United States, NATO, and the Royal House of al-Sa'ud when considering potential new military involvements of the United States or NATO in future conflict scenarios other than the Gulf.

Following Kuwait's liberation, public sympathy in the United States and the West for several Arab oil states appears to have changed, except with regard to their involvement in the Arab-Israeli peace endeavor. Publicized scandals, or at least damaging reports, surrounding leading Arab families, especially regarding finances and corruption, did not bode well in the West for courting sympathy and support after the (perceived) sacrifice of U.S. and NATO soldiers for the liberation of Kuwait and the reduction of Iraqi military capabilities. The continuing absence of democracy in the region, the illegal financial activities of Gulf banks, the reported extravagant lifestyles of members of royal families, and insights into the Kuwaiti government's public relations campaign designed to influence U.S. and Western public opinion did little to improve general Western views.[9] Nevertheless, soon after Kuwait's liberation, Western companies, especially from the United States, France, and Great Britain, began to reap large profits by rebuilding Kuwait, its power supplies and infrastructure, and the arms arsenals of its neighbors. Clearly, money is involved in all calculations and can certainly soothe adverse perspectives quickly.

A renewed crisis occurred in October 1994 that was brought about by Iraq's military buildup—with significant outside help, as will be described later—of some 70,000 troops, tanks, and 20,000 stateless Arabs north of Kuwait's border on the eve of the UN General Assembly's debate about continuing economic sanctions.[10] This buildup allowed the Clinton administration to demonstrate a clear strategic policy. Saddam's militarization of southern Iraq (occurring, incidentally, at the most unfortunate moment for Iraqi interests) represented a breach of UN resolutions and caused a forceful U.S. and British reaction, including reinforcing the desire of certain Arab states to eliminate Saddam's leadership once and for all. But it also brought to the limelight an increasing divergence between U.S. and British positions, on the one hand, and Franco-Russian attitudes and interests regarding sanctions against Baghdad, on the other. Some of the behaviors and positions of these powers in this regard are comparable to their attitudes concerning the Balkans and Yugoslavia.

Iraq

Although Iraq lost the war in 1991 on the battlefield, Saddam continues to reign in Baghdad, which constitutes something of a political victory for the Iraqi leader. Having voiced his acceptance to the Security Council resolutions for the inspection and destruction of Iraq's chemical, bacteriological, and nuclear weapons facilities, he has continuously tested the resolve of U.S. and UN leadership in enforcing the relevant resolutions and no-fly zones. Saddam's longevity remains particularly unsettling to those who wished for his downfall during the war, especially citizens of Kuwait, Saudi Arabia, and the Gulf states. The Ba'athist regime has proven its capability of continuously menacing internal groups such as the Shi'ites and the Kurds. In addition, the Iraqi leadership has apparently been successful in remaining insulated from popular sentiment, although significant evidence exists of opposition, and the Iraqi people suffer painfully and increasingly under the UN economic embargo, which has resulted in major rationing and a deteriorating economy. The UN Food and Agricultural Organization has argued that "massive deprivation, chronic hunger, endemic malnutrition [exists] for the vast majority of the population."[11]

Iraq does play an important role in the strategic framework in the Middle East, especially as a counterweight against Iran—supposedly perceiving itself as the major regional power, supporting fundamentalism and interested in strengthening its own influence despite its major economic crisis. Yet, as was reported, "there is also a sense of increasing despair in Iraq over the apparent indifference of the West to the sufferings of the population. The sentiment is encapsulated in the widespread Iraqi and Arab view, that the West has an interest in maintaining Saddam Hussein in power."[12] This view may help Saddam—at least indirectly—who has not given up efforts to stay in control and rebuild Iraq's (military) capabilities and power.[13] This development also confirms the argument that economic sanctions contribute to the strengthening of the leadership in place, i.e. that rallying effect.

Turkey

Power relations in the larger region of the Middle East, that is, the countries further from the Gulf have changed dramatically since 1991. On the one hand, a peace arrangement has taken form and shape between Israel, the Palestinians, and other Arab states. On the other hand, Saudi Arabia, Iraq, Iran, and Turkey are still contesting the role of regional power.

Under President Turgut Ozal, Ankara took clear sides with the Christian West, NATO, and the European Community (EC) during the Kuwait conflict and—after some initial apprehension—permitted the Coalition to station various forces, including German units, at the air base of Incerlik and to "attack Iraq from Turkish territory." Turkey also accepted hundreds of thousands of refugees from Iraq. In the end, it emerged as a major player in the region, and its power was enhanced by the subsequent collapse of the Soviet Union.[14]

Ankara demonstrated its clear stance with NATO and the UN during the Kuwait conflict and might be asked to do so again in the Balkans, even in the face of Greek opposition. Iran and Turkey share a common border, and both aspire to greater influence in the former Soviet republics in Central Asia—Turkmenistan, Tadjikistan, and Uzbekistan.[15] Turkey is a key power behind the emerging Black Sea Cooperation Zone, "whose economic function may well mask political ambitions."[16] Turkish elites envision themselves as leaders of a new regional order in (Turkish) central Asia, and Turkish businessmen flock throughout the region to demonstrate the power of trade in these areas. But three significant regional challenges appear: a revitalized Iran, a reemerging Russia with strategic interests around the Bosporus talking about "near abroad" and trying to solidify influence in the former Caucasian and Central Asian USSR republics; and Turkey's geostrategic position and Ankara's capability to hold in check popular emotions about Bosnia.[17] The geopolitical connection between the Gulf and the Balkans—like a revolving door—rests on the critical geostrategic location of Turkey, with two prominent issues defining the situation: the Greek-Turkish relationship, and the strength of the Kurds and Islam. The fate of the Kurds has always been dramatic, but they suffered yet again after the Gulf War. Iraq's treatment of the Kurds has influenced not only the relationship between Baghdad, Ankara, and Tehran but also the position of NATO and the European Union (EU). In many ways the absence of central authority in Iraq in general, but particularly in northern Iraq, appears disadvantageous for Turkey, as it creates instability due to tensions, leads to further flights of people from the south, and results in intensified operations of the PKK. Greater independence for the Kurds south and north of the Turkish-Iraqi border would obviously infringe upon Ankara's interests.[18]

Regarding religious and historical links with the Balkans, Turkey's relations encompass two of the three existing alliance structures: Turkey maintains close cooperation with Albania, Bulgaria, Macedonia, and, as much as possible, with Kosovo, which extends west and east of Greece. This "system" is opposed by a cooperative structure between Serbia, Greece, Romania, and Russia.[19] The variably powerful domestic pressure in Turkey to undertake action in support of the many relatives of the several hundred thousand Bosnians may be encouraged by religious arguments and cries for help from Bosnia-Hercegovina and will certainly aggravate Turkey's relations with Athens.

The Kuwait Crisis as Part of an International Triple Crisis

The following evaluation has the advantage of an ex post facto analysis. Today one can argue that the Iraqi occupation of Kuwait, the ensuing, highly publicized military buildup, and the air and land war for the liberation of Kuwait contributed cataclysmically to significant change in the international atmosphere at that time. Further analysis suggests an interdependence between the Kuwait crisis and those in Yugoslavia and the Soviet Union. That interdependence, in addition to being influenced by the developments in Kuwait, resulted also from the fact that both Iraq and Yugoslavia had been cooperating actively as leading members in the nonaligned movement and that Moscow had sympathies for Baghdad and increasingly for Belgrade (particularly via Slav and orthodox links and via the military, but also because the Milosevic government is considered the last remaining Communist leadership).[20] By 1990, in the aura of German unification and the threatening dissolution of the Soviet empire, President Mikhail Gorbachev himself began to search for means to stabilize the domestic situation within the USSR—especially in the independently minded Baltic Soviet republics. Any opportunity for a relatively unnoticed chance to clean house and stabilize his domestic power was therefore more than welcome. The international reaction to Tiananmen

Square, so harmful to the image of the Chinese government, and the great Soviet need for Western economic support limited the options available.

But, one cannot say that any of the individual parts of this triple crisis would not have developed independently. (Similarly, that could not be said about the 1956 Hungarian-Suez dual crisis either.) However, many indicators suggest that mutual reinforcement, acceleration, and intensification were evidenced in the triangle of Baghdad-Belgrade-Moscow following the August 1990 invasion of Kuwait by Iraq.

The Soviet Union—The Beginning of Its End

The outcome of the Kuwait War struck a major blow to President Mikhail Gorbachev's fate. With the Soviet Union having already "lost" its Eastern European empire, including the German Democratic Republic (GDR), and given in to the unification of Germany and its NATO membership (which de facto started the ringing of Gorbachev's domestic death knell), the Kuwait War represented, as one analyst put it, "just the kind of regional conflict that Gorbachev had hoped to avoid. It could damage U.S.-Soviet relations and escalate in unpredictable directions."[21] Contrary to the USSR's stance during the earlier crisis and the 1973 Yom Kippur War, Gorbachev was willing to accept the UN sanction of the use of an international coalition (in effect, a U.S. force), but only after the unilateral mediation efforts of Yevgeny Primakov failed.[22] This policy, fashioned according to Western strategy, became part of the final act of the former USSR and Gorbachev's tenure as president. The Kuwait crisis illustrated the faltering of his leadership and the overextension of his performance at home as well as the dilemma he faced in trying to satisfy both domestic needs and foreign expectations.[23] (See the discussion in the chapters by Irina Zviagelskaia and William Wohlforth.)

Unfortunately, Soviet behavior toward Iraq displayed —especially to the USSR's traditional Third World allies—a message of unreliable Soviet support and the new readiness of the Soviet Union to give in to U.S. domination of the UN Security Council. In addition, the conflict demonstrated the astounding technological inferiority of Soviet weapons systems. The Soviet military leadership was therefore hit particularly hard by the outcome of the 1991 Gulf War. (See the chapters in this volume by William Wohlforth and by Lawrence Freedman and Ephraim Karsh). The Soviet military had hoped to envision a U.S. Army stalemated by Soviet equipment and strategy and eagerly sought to redress Soviet prestige following the losses of Eastern Europe and especially the German Democratic Republic (GDR) in 1989–1990. When the opposite took place and disaster struck the Iraqi defense forces, the Soviet military had to rethink a great deal of its assumptions about the quality differences of weapons systems and the nature of warfare in the late twentieth century—and once again it blamed Gorbachev, its supreme commander.[24]

After Eduard Shevardnadze's surprise resignation (see Irina Zviagels-kaia's chapter), two significant changes could be seen in Soviet behavior: A sudden stalemate occurred in the Conventional Disarmament in Europe (CDE) arms negotiations, and Soviet airborne units and "black berets" (troops of the Interior Ministry) were sent into operation in Vilnius and Riga on January 12, 13, and 15, 1991 following the intensification of independence movements. Subsequently, there was considerable draft evasion in the Baltic states.[25] This operation caused some twenty civilian deaths but did in no way reduce the independence drive of the Soviet Baltic republics. Apparently imitating Nikita Khrushchev's strategy in 1956 towards Hungary, Gorbachev was attempting to exploit the international attention on the Kuwait crisis, the United States, and the UN, hoping that the eyes of the world would remain focused on the Gulf and not on his actions. He permitted the sending of Interior Ministry special forces to round up and silence demonstrators, stop draft dodging, and prevent the breaking away of the Baltic republics. When these operations met with resistance and turned into violent clashes, Western (Swedish) television camera teams were on hand to broadcast the demonstration of brutal Soviet force à la Stalin. Similar to the events of Tiananmen Square two years earlier, the pictures touched a sensitive nerve particularly among the European public and leadership, which reacted immediately by placing conditions on the ongoing negotiations over financial and economic support between Brussels and Moscow. For instance, the British government under the then new Prime Minister John Major threatened at once to veto EC financial support to the Soviet Union of Ecu 1 billion.

Gorbachev became caught up between Europe's disappointment in "Gorbymania," domestic damage control, and the need for substantial EC economic help. By not trying to challenge the opposition to the latter, he became paralyzed to act decisively and put an end to the erosion of the Soviet empire.[26] That development took place in the shadow of the international public's attention toward Kuwait, particularly around January 15, 1991, in similar fashion as in the fall of 1956 when Soviet Secretary General Nikita Khrushchev smashed political reform in Hungary while the world's attention was focused on British and French operations to internationalize the Suez Canal. The double Baltic-Gulf crisis of 1991 hence represents in some ways a repetition of the double Hungarian-Suez crisis of 1956, although with two critical differences: The Soviet Baltic operation was unsuccessful largely because of the presence of sophisticated real-time communication technologies and the mounting international support for Baltic independence, and Khrushchev succeeded in 1956 in the absence of such technology and with Budapest perceived as being within the accepted Soviet hegemonic parameter.[27]

Yugoslavia—Its Last Days

Since the 1960s, Yugoslavia and Iraq—both non-aligned countries—have closely cooperated in economic and industrial relations, oil exploration, and the training, education, and equipment of their armed forces,[28] which has included officer training (up to general staff level).[29] Also, they have shared common experience, as both armies have deployed weapons of Warsaw Pact (WTO) and NATO origin (i.e., Soviet, French, and British systems—see Christopher Klaus's Appendix for further detail). Their military connections were intensified during the eight years of the Iran-Iraq War, aided in part by triangular defense industry deals.[30] Yugoslavia has always made a point of balancing its Soviet and WTO military equipment with NATO matériel for political and economic reasons, while Iraq has been equally interested in obtaining French, British, and German matériel. Yugoslavia has also supplied Iraq with Yugoslav equipment[31] and has taken part in several cooperative military industrial projects and maintenance contracts with Iraqi defense industries.[32] Furthermore, Iraqi-Yugoslav cooperation in politics and education and multiple economic-industrial bilateral links (especially Yugoslav oil imports from Iraq and exports of finished and semi-finished industrial products to Iraq) have existed.[33] As evidence of the ties between the two countries, a significant Iraqi community resides in Belgrade. At times, several thousand Yugoslav military advisers have supported the training and education of Iraqi armed forces, and many Iraqi Flag officers have completed Yugoslav general staff training. And finally, a significant part of the Iraqi military infrastructure was planned and constructed with Yugoslav assistance and by Yugoslavian companies, all financed under a barter trade agreement that provided for the exchange of products and services for oil.

The liberation of Kuwait and the end of the Gulf War in February 1991 coincided with the beginning of the violent disintegration of the Socialist Federation of Yugoslavia. Arguably, the intensification of the tensions between Ljubljana and Zagreb, on the one hand, and between Belgrade, on the other, involved a radicalization of resistance to independence (certainly in Belgrade) and a Serbian leadership emboldened by the international attention devoted to the Gulf War.[34] A new alliance was forged between President Milosevic and the JNA, closely following the example of the Baghdad regime. The exchanges on sanctions—nonpayment of federal duties, freezing of funds, stopping of exports, and so forth—between Slovenia, Federal Yugoslavia, and Croatia, and a presumed intensification of Laibach's and Agram's intentions to leave the federation, developed after January 1991.[35] Croatia and Slovenia may have perceived a strengthening of their position through the unification of Germany and through rather encouraging signals from Bonn and Vienna that ensured, among other things, future economic and political support for a new state.[36] At that time, however, no one counted on the actual deployment and live fire use of federal troops, the JNA, in the escalation.[37]

Several factors may have contributed to the course of events in Yugoslavia: U.S. and French interests in maintaining a unified Yugoslavia, the unlikelihood of another U.S. military effort so soon after the Gulf War, Washington's understanding of the Yugoslavian crisis (Yugoslavia being part of Europe's backyard) and, finally, at least the indirect support from Soviet conservative and military circles for the last remaining Socialist leadership, particularly after the USSR's profound disappointments resulting from losing Central Eastern Europe and Germany and from the showing in Iraq.

The Belgrade government certainly felt the implicit encouragement from France and the United States to maintain a unified Yugoslavia and deny secession. Indeed, during his visit to Belgrade on June 21, 1990, U.S. Secretary of State James Baker indicated the U.S. interest in preserving stability in Central Europe, particularly after the German unification, through a united Yugoslavia. He also suggested that all differences between Ljubljana and Zagreb would be regarded by the United States as internal affairs of Yugoslavia and an independent Slovenia and Croatia would not be recognized by the United States.[38] One may thus compare Secretary Baker's role in Yugoslavia with Ambassader April Glaspie's role in Iraq.[39] After the United States' enormous military and financial efforts for the liberation of Kuwait, Baker's suggestions likely found further confirmation around Milosevic and in the JNA command: It seemed highly unlikely that the United States would commandeer another major military effort, especially in what Washington considered to be Europe proper.

And a further green light lit up for the Belgrade government: the passivity of President Bush, who first commanded his forces to fight Saddam and the Republican Guards, but was now letting the Iraqis brutally clamp down on the resurrection of the Kurds and Shi'ites within the range of the U.S. military still on Iraqi soil. The U.S. passivity may have encouraged the Belgrade government to go ahead with its active denial of Slovenian and Croatian independence efforts.[40] Moreover, neither the United States nor any European state or institution had undertaken major steps of reprisal after the killing of thirty-one people by Yugoslav federal security forces in the uprisings of Pristina and Kosovo the year before.

It has been said that the Milosevic regime found many sympathizers in the Soviet Parliament and among Russian conservatives and the military. As the West showed increasing outrage toward Serbian power projection and the brutality in Croatia and Bosnia-Herzegovina, it seems that the Soviet experience in Iraq, and its catastrophic outcome, increased the degree of Russian sympathy for Milosevic and the Serbian cause. Also, Slobodan Milosevic and Saddam Hussein were among the first congratulants for the supposedly successful putschists after the coup attempt on August 20, 1991. At that time the Serbian military had been cooperating intensely with its Soviet counterparts, and, in fact, several months before, Yugoslav Defense Minister Kadijevic had made a secret trip to Moscow to negotiate a U.S. $2 billion arms deal. Two days before the attempted coup in August 1991, the Romanian defense minister arrived in Belgrade to talk about the transport of these weapons across Romanian territory. The degree to which the deal was consummated has not been revealed.[41]

The International Framework

The United States

When President George Bush sought to galvanize U.S. and world public opinion in support of a military operation against Iraq—incidentally much like President Clinton in October 1994—he spoke in terms of the need for securing access to oil supplies, the right of Kuwait as a state to remain free and independent, and the need to create a new world order after the fall of the Berlin Wall and the demise of communism. Whether intended or not, the Gulf War left many people hopeful that U.S. policy in the new world order would involve "global policing"—that is, halting aggression and intervening on behalf of oppressed minorities to re-create law and order and uphold human rights.[42] Strategic humanitarian efforts after the war, such as Operation Provide Comfort, reinforced this hope. Even Washington's search for financial contributions from OECD allies (see chapters by Helmut Hubel and Masaru Tamamoto in this volume) was accepted by the major economic powers.

However, since the aftermath of the Kuwait War the Clinton administration has been very selective with interventions. So far it has avoided a similarly forceful and concerted effort to assist Bosnia and has not taken decisive action to bring stability to the Balkans. Some in the Muslim world have drawn direct comparisons between Kuwait and Bosnia and have concluded disappointedly that Western leaders find it easier to mobilize the public against Muslims in Iraq than Christians in Serbia and Croatia. However, inasmuch as the victims of aggression in both cases were part of the Islamic civilization, the argument goes that Muslims living on top of a sea of oil are more likely to receive military assistance than those who are not. Whether the United States, as the dominant power in today's unipolar system, will have the will and stamina to intervene in future complex situations like Bosnia or whether it defines its sphere of interest according to U.S. strategic cost-benefit analysis remains to be seen.

The significant U.S. effort for Kuwait, in addition to bringing about a quick and decisive victory, was designed to put an end to the *Vietnam syndrome* and to boost the United States out of its economic malaise. When the political calculations failed, and George Bush had to leave the White House, a rejoicing Saddam immediately tested President Clinton's resolve.[43] Subsequent to an apparent assassination attempt against George Bush during his visit to Kuwait in April 1993, Clinton responded with a cruise missile attack against Iraqi intelligence service headquarters (ISHQ) in Baghdad.[44] Presumably Saddam was surprised that the apparent assassination attempt as well as Iraq's second major challenge through military deployment (in October 1994) resulted in President Clinton, the U.S. military, and the UN responding rapidly, decisively, and with unexpected determination. The response created a more visible and permanent U.S. presence in the Gulf but also shaped the overall U.S. strategy vis-à-vis Iraq today and Iran for the future, especially in light of a perceived Islamic challenge.

Overall, however, the Kuwait crisis demonstrated a profound and recurring dilemma for the United States in the new global order: In whatever direction it turns and operates, it will attract criticism. On the one hand, despite winning the war, the United States was accused of not necessarily winning the peace. Although not much would have been undertaken to liberate Kuwait in 1991, and certainly not as quickly and decisively, without the clear leadership of Washington, this criticism was still raised—a phenomenon to be repeated in the case of the Balkan crisis and Somalia. Kuwait was liberated and Iraq was not invaded, as agreed upon by the UN, but the United States was criticized for the excessive use of superior force and the failure to eliminate the culpable Saddam Hussein once and for all (see chapter by Gustav Däniker in this volume).[45]

On the other hand, several voices have claimed that the West and Washington instigated the Kurds in the north and the Shi'ites in the south to try to assert themselves and rise against Baghdad.[46] Arnold Hottinger, a senior Swiss analyst, even argued that units of the Iraqi elite forces would have been ready to side with the revolutionaries if they were assured the support of the United States. But, according to Hottinger, once it became obvious that they would not receive U.S. support, the Iraqi forces withdrew their offer and joined fully with Saddam against the uprising.[47] The Kurds and Shi'ites both wanted rightful representatives, if not a new government, and acting on the misguided assumption of

Western help began to revolt—as they understood that such an action would be seen as a suggestion for outside support. In the end, nobody came to help, and Saddam punished them severely while the world looked on.[48] Atkins argues that the increasing Iranian support for the Iraqi Shi'ites galvanized the Iraqi armed forces around Saddam and helped his own domestic survival. In the U.S., reportedly, the civilians pleaded for U.S. military support but the officers around Colin Powell objected to such an operation. In retrospect, one can say that the dramatic fate of the Kurds in the north and the Shi'ites in the south, as a consequence of international (U.S.) hesitation following the liberation of Kuwait, neutralized many of the hopeful impressions for a 'just new order' that had been created by the end of February 1991. Some have even viewed the denial of U.S. assistance as the major cause of contemporary anti-U.S. feeling in Iraq and other Arab states.[49] However, many of today's upbeat references to Kuwait disregard these dramatic developments that occurred right after the Coalition victory, caused tremendous suffering for the Iraqi population, and blurred the shining peace.

In debating why U.S. military operations were terminated in February 1991, little consideration has been given to the fact that many people, especially the Arab allies and the government of France had not the least interest in violating Iraq's territorial sovereignty, nor in completely eliminating the Hussein government and risking chaos, civil war, and Iraq's disintegration. The outcome of such actions was perceived to be too unpredictable, and the only powers that were assumed to benefit therefrom were Iran and Syria. The Arab Coalition members did not want to aggravate the situation further, as Saddam had already broken one taboo by invading an Arab country. For them to intrude into Iraq would have violated yet another taboo and strained the alliance to a maximum. And, at the same time, the action would have offered Saddam significant possibilities for breaking up the Coalition and activating the PLO-Israel dimension.[50] France, for its part, had, over the years, become one of Iraq's most important creditors and had, as a result, increasingly appeared as a "political debitor" (see chapter by Helmut Hubel in this volume). The French economy was therefore in no position to write off the significant Iraqi debt (apparently exceeding U.S.$20 billion). Thus Paris had to overcome significant internal political divergence over whether to support the U.S. initiative. Today, because of the Iraqi debt, France has great interest in diminishing the UN sanctions against Iraq and envigorating trade. However, Saudi Arabia and the other OPEC countries relish the fact that Iraq is still under economic embargo and prohibited to export oil. They are producing more oil than required, so world prices are very low. If Iraq were to suddenly export again, oil prices would collapse and with them the vital revenues of the Gulf economies—an important consideration for these states which have paid dearly for the war against Iraq (see Robert Lieber's chapter in this volume).

Germany

The Gulf War challenged both the leaders and the public of the newly unified German state (see Helmet Hubel's chapter).[51] Nevertheless Germany contributed massive logistical support to the Coalition and sent some troops, anti-aircraft weapons, a few minesweepers, and eighteen Alpha Jet close air support fighters. Further, Bonn provided extensive financial support to the war efforts, namely U.S.$6 billion in direct payments to the United States, another U.S.$6 billion in payments to the United Kingdom, France, and NATO, and assistance for Patriot SAMs for Israel.[52] Germany also offered its military bases to the United States and even supported Turkey, Egypt, Jordan, Syria, and Saudi Arabia economically.

Nevertheless, the absence of a true German combat force in the Gulf has left some people wondering how Europe's emerging leading nation can live up to its great power status if it does not offer military assistance to its allies outside Europe.[53] As Helmut Hubel explained in Chapter 13, the war also led to a reexamination of the nation's constitutional restrictions on the use of force outside NATO theaters of operation. Major tensions had developed concerning Articles 24, 26, and 87a of the *Grundgesetz.* (Some observers have argued that these legal dimensions served as an ideal excuse for not pressing through domestically sensitive military participation abroad and out of the NATO area.) Chancellor Helmut Kohl, according to one source, felt "a need to repay the United States for its support over [unification]" but bowed to domestic pressure that military action was impossible.[54] However, following the Kuwait War, as Germany became more assertive in the foreign policy realm, it immediately faced major dilemmas.[55]

The German Kuwait experience brought to the fore, and the Bosnian catastrophe dramatically emphasized, the extent of that new German power dilemma. On the one hand, Germany is being asked and expected by its allies to be more actively involved in international peace making; on the other hand, it is creating worries among friends and foes once it does so. To imagine German peacekeepers in Sarajevo and Thessaloniki seems simply preposterous.[56]

The European Community and the West European Union

The rising tensions in the Gulf and the armed confrontation offered the first major involvement for the reactivated West European Union (WEU) outside the European area and subsequently became the first common European defense operation. In addition, the Kuwait liberation, the conflict in Yugoslavia, and the attempted coup in the Soviet Union all happened just before the European Community's Intergovernmental Conference (IGC) held in Maastricht in December 1991. The formation at that Conference of a Common Foreign and Security Policy (CFSP) as the second pillar of a (future) European Union was thus surely influenced by these international developments, which demanded stronger intra-European cooperation.[57]

During the Kuwait crisis the WEU, with its ten members, reacted relatively quickly, dispatching naval units (minesweepers), air, and even active military detachments to the Gulf region. But the effort soon brought to light problems in terms of cooperation and command structure between NATO and the WEU, and these difficulties were repeated and exacerbated in the Adriatic operation during the Balkan conflict and the blockade against Serbia. Also the WEU members' responses during the Gulf War exhibited a "variety of nuances and emphasis" and significant domestic political considerations.[58] The European Community has argued since the war that NATO should remain the principal North Atlantic instrument of European security.[59] Nevertheless, the WEU, which includes all of the EU member states except Denmark and Ireland and is soon to admit Greece, will most likely become the increasingly relevant organization for Europe's defense as such, and as the defense arm of the CFSP within the EU. The question will be the terms on which the United States will "lend" military hardware to European defense missions.

NATO

For NATO, the Kuwait crisis became a demonstration of outstanding coordination; combined transport, command, and control, and the appropriate adoption and application of advanced strategies like Follow On Forces Attack (FOFA), including the pre-positioning of matériel at Diego Garcia and elsewhere. Some have stated that this supply and maintenance operation was the most modern and extensive to date. NATO even managed to enlist the aid of Turkey, Italy, France, and Spain. In addition, the conflict offered a major display of the most recent NATO armaments, which gave the alliance its first opportunity to employ all its capabilities including strategy, troops, and equipment, in a tremendous show of force. Domestic considerations played a significant role for the participation of the European allies in the NATO effort, although all of the European allies, at least clandestinely, cooperated to a degree unforeseen by even the greatest supporters of NATO. France, after some hesitation, broke with its Gaullist past and offered much cooperation behind the scenes in areas of intelligence and information on Iraqi military and armament; plus it allowed U.S. combat aircraft to be based on French bases. At the same time, however, France vigorously promoted the role and future of the WEU, and there was a consistent concern that Paris might try to perform independent diplomacy.

Spain was perhaps one of the most secretive NATO supporters of the United States but was nevertheless highly active in this role. Its clandestine operation seemed appropriate because of "strong antipathies in Spain against the United States in general," certain "pro-Iraq sentiments in neighboring Arab countries," and the Spanish support for a Mediterranean Conference on Security and Cooperation (CSCM).[60] Therefore the government of Spain under Prime Minister Felipe Gonzalez decided to conduct its support for the United States Air Force out of the limelight of the media. Only via an indiscretion did it become known "that Spanish (and German) air force planes transported large quantities of ammunition to the Morón Air Base, where it was reloaded into American B-52 bombers, which flew their sorties over Iraq and Kuwait directly from Spanish territory. Indeed, more than one third of all U.S. transports to the Gulf were carried out over Spanish territory." Apparently, the first round of the Middle East Peace Talks took place in Madrid "in an attempt to restore Spain's tarnished image in the Arab world and acknowledge its contribution to NATO."[61] All other NATO members, such as Belgium, Denmark, Holland, Italy, Greece, Turkey, and Portugal, participated after some hesitation and to varying degrees and, as in the case of Athens and Ankara, with significant consideration of bilateral implications.

The Neutrals

The Kuwait War caused a major shift in policy for the permanent neutral states in Europe. Unlike during the U.S. raids on Libya in 1986, Austria permitted the United States and NATO air forces to use its airspace, as they transported troops and material to Saudi Arabia, thereby reducing the parameters of its neutrality. Austria also allowed the U.S. Army to use its railroad network to transport mechanized forces from German to Italian ports via the Brenner Pass. For the first time since 1936, even Switzerland participated in international economic sanctions (against Iraq), although it did not open its airspace. Its participation was a major change in the position of an avowed neutral country; Switzerland's position demanded and introduced previously unthinkable global solidarity and showed the limits of classical permanent neutrality in the post-Cold War international system.

The three European neutrals—Finland, Sweden, and Austria—also participated for the first time actively and fully in UN economic sanctions (against Iraq).[62] In doing so, they acted in a manner appropriate to the emerging role and perception of permanent neutrality. Their active participation in global cooperation and universal solidarity was considered to be beyond the traditional rules for neutral abstention in case of conflict.[63] Comparable to other European governments, the Austrian government tried to avoid domestic tensions by making simple solutions, such as giving quick permission for north/south transfers by NATO out of the public limelight. Its digression from the classical interpretation of neutrality was repeated and intensified in the disintegration process of Yugoslavia, when Austria, particularly in the person of Foreign Minister Alois Mock, took a significant position in support of the two northern republics of Slovenia and Croatia.

The United Nations

In the world's view, the Kuwait crisis substantially altered the role and perception of the United Nations, its Security Council, and its processes of peace making and peacekeeping. In leading the UN mission against Iraq, the United States, for the first time, insisted on active and extensive financial contributions from wealthy OECD states such as Germany and Japan. Washington's insistence demonstrated the economic limits of U.S. global power, even in a supposedly unipolar structure, but it also demonstrated the financial challenges of major UN military operations.[64] Because the conflict was prosecuted under the United Nations' flag, the Kuwait War revived the notion of collective security and the legitimacy of marshaling international forces to overturn outright aggression. The war unified the international community and resuscitated the UN Security Council (which had for many years been driven by superpower vetoes) as an organ of collective security.[65]

For the first time since the Korean War, the United Nations intervened to reverse an outright act of aggression. Its action could have indicated that in other cases of aggression the United Nations would be willing to act with large scale force; but the case of Bosnia has shown that this hope could not be sustained. Its action during the Gulf War created a false precedent. But the decisive UN response to the Kuwait crisis does demonstrate the need for agreement or, even better, leadership within the Security Council and among its permanent members (see Helmut Freudenschuss's chapter in this volume).

The International System

The main reason for the interconnectedness of the Kuwait-Soviet-Yugoslav triple crisis seems to be that Iraq's attempted annexation of Kuwait and the ensuing international military operation invited a crackdown by Moscow in the Baltic republics and a radicalization in the internal tensions and dispute between Ljubljana, Zagreb, and Belgrade. Gorbachev's failure to succeed in Tallinn and Riga was Moscow's last attempt to stop the disintegration process between the center and certain Soviet republics—and to save Gorbachev's presidency. The situation became aggravated by the international acceptance of the Bush initiative concerning Kuwait, the failure of Gorbachev's peace initiatives in that region, and the apparently dismal performance of Soviet military equipment and (WTO)-trained personnel in Iraq. With regard to Yugoslavia, its President Milosevic became encouraged by Saddam's political survival and the supposed absence of any potential U.S. military involvement in Europe following the Kuwait War. Finally, the accelerated Soviet disintegration and the formation of a strategic vacuum from Belgrade eastward encouraged the disintegration of Yugoslavia. Although any of these crises could have occurred independently, in the prevailing international situation there is much to be argued in support of a direct connection among them.

Today, several regional power centers have emerged: Bonn, Belgrade, Baghdad, and, as always, Moscow. Following the developments in South Eastern Europe, it may be argued that the Balkans and the former Yugoslavian territory have always been and will always be divided into Russian Orthodox, Germanic Christian, and Turkish Muslim spheres of influence and that they are rather outside the U.S. sphere, which, however, clearly includes the Middle East. This situation reintroduces such geopolitical concepts as spheres of influence, alignments, balancing of threats, bandwagoning for profit, and, hence, balance of power into the European and international system—despite the great hopes that were put into the development of an all-integrated Europe.[66] The post-Soviet and post-Yugoslav crises also raise questions about the efficiency of the peacekeeping effort and humanitarian protection by the UN and the effects of sanctions.

In the international system during and after the Kuwait War, several additional factors played a role, including the media, environment, costs, linkage—or the interrelation between multiple and simultaneous crises—and refugees. Consider, for instance, the much-debated problem of Iraqi-caused environmental disasters, such as fire and oil spillage, as part of Iraq's warfare strategy.[67] On the one hand, this strategy raised a dramatic (and fascinating) specter particularly for the media; on the other, the use of environmental means in warfare is as old as the conduct of warfare itself. Throughout the ages, warring parties have employed fog, smog, water, and even avalanches to support their military efforts. During the Kuwait War, we saw the first major use of oil to create massive fires and to cause one of the worst oil slicks ever, which covered more than one fifth of the Gulf.[68] The thick smog from the fires caused surprisingly few problems for the Coalition, thanks to the modern electro-optic equipment the Coalition forces used, but the burden it placed on the respiratory systems

FIGURE 16.1 Systemic Graph

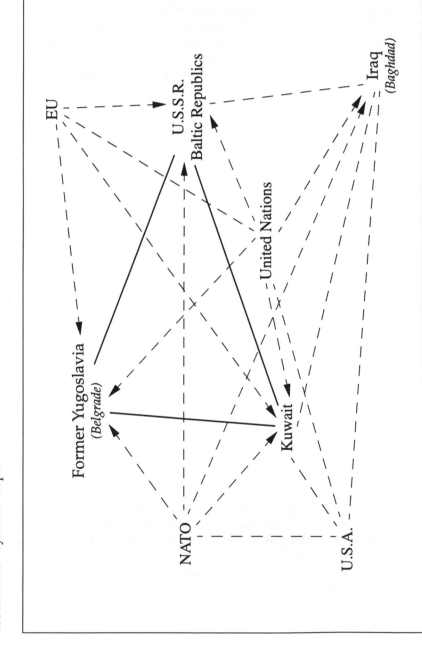

of individual soldiers and the civilian population was significant. More-over, the oil slick killed thousands of species in the Gulf, even though it disintegrated relatively rapidly. Although the financial burden caused by this Iraq strategy was staggering, the ultimate results were not nearly as dramatic as originally assumed.[69]

The Interaction Between Internal Politics, Internal Concerns, and Foreign Policy Considerations

The triple crisis also demonstrates the effects of the influence on inter-nal policy making of major external events; the distribution of informa-tion, sentiment, and mood, and therefore public attitude; and certainly the readiness and daring of the leadership. The international media, via the power of real-time information, typically create a certain amount of information that remains intellectually undigested but that promotes emotional reactions sometimes far removed from the real picture. To a significant degree, these reactions enhance media operation and agitation in democracies, introduce tensions within allies, and render appropriate and effective foreign policy making difficult. In addition, the media con-glomorates have an economic interest in creating great national excite-ment which would result in higher profits.

Linkage Among, or Interrelations Between, Multiple and Simultaneous Crises

The Kuwait-Soviet-Yugoslav triple crisis illustrates the linkage and interrelationship between potential crises in our time. Mutual interaction, nurturing, and enhancement renders crisis management and the timing of intervention difficult and demands new ways of severing or eliminat-ing these interrelationships. The links are created by the real-time trans-mission of news and related reactions, support needed by the embattled, consequential alliance formation, the *sentiment de guerre*, and the concom-itant overall radicalization of the international environment. Interrela-tionships can thus emerge due to necessity, similar fate and sympathy, geographical neighborhood, simple interests, or opportunism of the lead-ership. Even pariah states may use modern technology in the same way as does the free world—only to oppose it.

Sanctions

The imposition of a UN military ultimatum on Iraq to withdraw from Kuwait or face a military response resulted largely from the belief that sanctions would fail to coerce Saddam into relinquishing his claim on Iraq's "nineteenth province." Despite a strong movement in favor of letting the sanctions work, the course of the war and the subsequent maintenance of the sanctions have left the impression that an embargo would not have forced an Iraqi withdrawal. Sanctions did succeed in prying open Saddam's military installations after the war, but only after Coalition aircraft had torn the country asunder by thoroughly pounding its economic and industrial infrastructure. Thus, the military operation paved the way for the subsequent maintenance of sanctions. Unfortunately, few of the lessons about the shortcomings of sanctions in Iraq were applied to the Serbian situation. Some authors have even contended that Belgrade's leadership has learned from Baghdad how the latter overcame the disrupting consequences of economic embargoes. The situations in Iraq and Rump Yugoslavia have proved that economic sanctions alone may not work to the degree expected.[70]

UN sanctions against these two states and their respective economic capabilities also demonstrate that the learning curves of the target states are much steeper than are those of the states that apply them. Centrally controlled and/or autocratic states and less developed countries (LDCs) may offer greater possibilities for evasive maneuvers to their government and allow the individual consumer to survive better under international sanctions than higher developed states, but industry and trade-oriented companies will be seriously hit in both cases. Nevertheless, sanctions against authoritarian states contribute to the longevity of a target government because of an internal rallying effect which, in turn, offers such a government the opportunity for radical domestic policies. Among target states, reactions to sanctions include domestic evasive operations, improvisation, hidden and/or deliberate breaking of sanction rules, and international cooperation and alliance formation, all of which are difficult to control, especially in rough terrain as in the Balkans and the Black Sea area. Showing the learning curve of the targeted countries, the Iraqi Defense Minister Ali Hasan al-Majid stressed in 1992 that "Iraq has always seen Yugoslavia as a friend and as the only country which understands the scope of sanctions imposed by the world organization."[71] As will be explained later, his words imply that the longer sanctions continue, the greater the tendency for the formation of a Pariah network and the greater the intensification of cooperation between the targeted states.

Military Strategic Lessons

The immediate lessons of the Kuwait War for Iraq were summed up nicely by a member of the Indian General Staff: Don't contemplate war with a superpower before having developed your own nuclear weapons. Iran and North Korea seem to have learned this from the Kuwait War, and so did the United States and NATO, both of which are actively seeking to prevent the spread of nuclear weapons to other international pariahs. Part of the U.S. objective certainly was to diminish, if not eradicate, the Iraqi nuclear and mass destruction capability as well as its conventional army for a long time to come.[72]

The battle for the liberation of Kuwait illustrated several firsts in military strategic dimensions: complete involvement and interaction of all four strategic dimensions—sea, land, air, and space—which was built around the air-land battle doctrine; the most successful execution of a combination of high-mobility, sophisticated technology, large-scale maneuver warfare, and enormous firepower; the defensive frenzy regarding the danger of the use of weapons of mass destruction, including chemical and related threats of (nuclear) escalation; the employment of last-generation weapons such as stealth fighters and J-stars; and the full strategic use of space and satellite communications, intelligence, and command and control (see chapters by Lawrence Freedman and Ephraim Karsh and by Erik Yesson in this volume). The war also demonstrated the limits of real-time information, the nearly overwhelming capabilities of most sophisticated defense equipment and sensor and laser technology, the devastating reality of "friendly fire" and the amassing of the greatest firepower and tank formation in history.[73] It furthermore uncovered once again a rivalry between branches of the U.S. armed forces and certain shortcomings in inter-allied cooperation that ultimately resulted in casualties caused by friendly fire.

The battlefield results of the Kuwait War are, however, unlikely to be duplicated elsewhere. Among the many lessons learned from the war is that the U.S. military apparently aims to conduct war in an all-out fashion— sometimes even beyond the necessary application of force and in possible disregard of political consequences and future solutions. Because of the desert terrain and Iraq's neutralized air power, it could deploy full-scale armored units. Further, the combination of the preparations taken by Saudi Arabia, as discussed earlier, Iraq's lack of allies (besides the USSR), and U.S. technology and strategy, among other factors, indicate that the Kuwait operation will not be reproduced anytime soon; that fixed and fortified military installations appear to be of limited value against laser-guided ammunition, and that sophisticated electronic equipment and weapons systems not only intensify the force of war but also complicate warfare. The great advance in battlefield information systems and the vast amount of data and images available can cause confusion and misinformation about performance and battlefield reality for military leaders and the public alike.

In retrospect, the Kuwait crisis also demonstrated the profound difference between a large-scale armored military operation in tank-friendly terrain and a low-level conflict operation in mountainous and difficult topography, such as that waged to help the Kurds.[74] The fact that the United States and its Coalition partners were capable of carrying out an operation as large scale as that in the Gulf within a limited period of time demonstrates the significant logistical and operational legacy of the Carter Doctrine. It bears repeating that advanced technology is no panacea, and its involvement dissipates outside of the flat desert terrain and adverse weather conditions. Advanced technology did not solve the riddle of mobile Scuds or the search for Saddam in his bunkers. Unfortunately, it also did not help to convince the international leadership beforehand that an Iraqi invasion of Kuwait was imminent; thus Saddam managed to achieve a complete strategic surprise. Furthermore, friendly fire goes along with advanced technology: One in four fatalities of Coalition forces resulted from non-Iraqi ammunitions. Failure in the electronic guidance, poor gunnery, and so forth, contributed to casualties among Coalition forces. The principal lesson: Sophisticated weapons systems are less forgiving than older, simpler ones and demand greater training and discipline. The most recent incident of friendly fire, as of this writing, occurred in April 1994 when U.S. Air Force planes shot down two helicopters carrying UN personnel over northern Iraq.

The Coalition's strategic air campaign failed to destroy Saddam's nuclear, biological, and chemical weapons facilities. Unarmed UN inspectors, however, did manage to find and eliminate the vast majority of the Iraqi weapons complex in the years following the April 1991 cease-fire.[75] The penultimate question of service in any military operation, namely the number of casualties inflicted, proved surprisingly limited for the Coalition and addresses an important question for the United States and its Western allies: Do these states have forces ready and equipped to kill but not to die? The prewar discussions of preparations for fatalities (body bags) and the actual numbers of U.S.-inflicted casualties ran between 5,000 and 25,000. Sophisticated evaluation systems were expected to offer detailed information in the heat of war; surprisingly, however, variations appeared, contributing to confusion and chaos, especially where Iraqi civilians and armed forces were concerned. These discrepancies demonstrated that the wealth of data provided by the latest technology may confuse highly trained analysts, may offer excitement to the media, and can easily be exploited by staged propaganda, which in turn can intensify emotions and again lead to military escalation.[76]

Personal Leadership

Desert Storm demonstrated that as a precondition to engaging troops in combat, U.S. leaders may have to demonize the opponents and project them as "Hitlers" before obtaining public support. Saddam's behavior easily lent itself to such characterizations.[77] The related outpouring of U.S. nationalism and even outright jingoism during the Gulf War proved that even on the eve of the year 2000, the public can be mobilized by rhetoric, the painting of a foreign leader as cruel and despotic, and the praising of a battle as a crusade for good against evil. The Bush administration not only wanted Saddam out of Kuwait but also intended to smash and punish him with the enormous power of the latest military technology. The crisis of 1990–1991 certainly included an element of personal rivalry between Bush and Saddam as well. In the year before a presidential election, Bush must have felt the need to prove his foreign policy capabilities. Therefore, it is plausible that several missions were undertaken to eliminate the Iraqi head of state despite the U.S. legal code demanding otherwise.[78] Saddam's resilience is testimony to the survivability of targeted despotic leaders and should be kept in mind as a lesson for the future.[79]

For President Bush, high personal stakes were involved as well, not only because he, having been a Navy fighter pilot, must have felt betrayed and personally challenged by Saddam but also because he felt a messianic mission to create some form of working just world order to prevent the recurrence of such situations—and to keep intact the new thaw with the Soviet Union under Gorbachev while nevertheless pursuing U.S. interests in an increasingly unipolar world. Moreover, Bush could exploit Saddam's challenge as a national rallying feature, perhaps galvanizing the country and guiding it out of (domestic economic and other) problems. It was George Bush who mobilized the world against Saddam Hussein.

Saddam Hussein, in turn, was clearly playing on Arab nationalism to demonstrate how the technologically powerful, capitalist world was mistreating the poor Muslim man in the street, how anti-Arab sentiments were threatening the Muslims and the Arab cause, how Saddam was daring to take on the Zionist powers of the United States and Israel, and, finally, how a small country could challenge the global superpowers.[80] He invoked Islamic symbols and communities, including the declaration of jihad although the latter was not approved by the clergy—as he addressed and attempted to mobilize the Arab masses. He deployed brutality in dealing with his staff, eliminating virtually anyone with a dissenting opinion[81] and thereby diminishing any chance that he would be exposed to neutral, objective, and reliable information about the world outside Iraq. This aspect of Saddam's rule has to be kept in mind for it clearly affects all messages and signals from the West. In addition, he played an extremely sarcastic game when he employed Western mass media and their power to touch upon Western sensitivity by showing him tweaking the cheeks of children, presenting fighter pilots, and calling weapons production facilities "baby milk factories."

In retrospect, Saddam's survival and long-range influence and the effect of his survival on the violent split up of Yugoslavia are astounding. One can argue that the military manner in which the Western Coalition operated in and around Kuwait, as well as Saddam's continued political survival even after military defeat, encouraged leaders of the caliber of a Slobodan Milosevic, a Franjo Tudjman, or a Radovan Karadjic and their like to take daring military steps toward the fulfillment of their blunt strategic objectives.[82]

These radical nationalists of the former Yugoslavia appear to have confidently followed Saddam's model: first, employing force to create a fait accompli (something that would have been unthinkable during the bloc rigidity of the bipolar, antagonistic environment, in which there was much less flexibility for individual leadership)—and only then suing for peace and recognition. All of them carried out their actions knowing they would have a good probability of being readmitted to the international community, because the West and its media tends to minimize (and simplify) annoying problems and to forget quickly.[83] This pattern of action and pragmatism encourages revanchiste forces to intensify collaboration with them and provide material, conceptual, and perhaps ideological support. Any third force willing (or needing) to tap their resources and use their experiences is welcome; hence, a network between outcast (or radical) leaders can develop. Once any of its members has access to special materials such as radioactive substances, all may benefit against the rest—a turn of events which would put the rest of the world at the brink of major (nuclear) disaster.

In Russia, the ascendance of nationalism, symbolized by the rise of Vladimir Zhirinovsky to international prominence, has encouraged new links in an alliance of rogue states. If an aggressive and nationalistic leader like Zhirinovsky were to succeed Boris Yeltsin as president, how long would it be before Russia violated the embargo against Iraq and lobbied to end the UN weapons inspections? When Iraq is permitted to sell oil again, Saddam will be able to provide Russia with much-needed hard currency in exchange for sophisticated weapons sold at bargain prices. Such a new alliance could also expand through linkages to Belgrade and other states in the Black Sea region.

Russia has continuously tried to shield Serbia diplomatically from further UN and NATO military action. With someone in power like Zhirinovsky, Russia's pan-Slav ties to Serbia would almost certainly be expanded and Russia would likely supply Serbia with more weapons. In future conflicts, one can anticipate the development of an international network of all such leaders who have similar interests, especially if their own survivals were at stake. They may employ terrorists, share military intelligence, or complement the various needs of one another (e.g., trading products and knowledge for natural resources). They would be unified by their hatred of everything American or Christian and in their common experience and perception of being international outcasts. Their bonding would create animosity toward them from the outside world, and their respective ideologies and drive for political and geographical expansion would contribute to that animosity.

New Alliances, Networks, and Spheres of Influence

With the disintegration of the cohesive bipolar structure of the Cold War magnified by the Kuwait War, the ensuing Balkan crisis, and the disintegration of the USSR, a new international network seems to have emerged. The centralizing factors were Washington's unipolar leadership, which provided both cause and orientation for the new network, and the limitations to U.S. global policing which began to offer greater flexibility to opposing leaders. International sanctions, for instance, especially against Iraq and the former Yugoslavia, have put the respective leaders under tremendous pressure and made otherwise unacceptable measures seem appealing. Survival, pragmatism, and opportunism became the leitmotif. The situation has encouraged cooperation among members of the network according to economic, military, and strategic needs, sometimes even when such cooperation has been in conflict with traditional, ideological, and religious considerations. Cause and objective of cooperation are simply pragmatic.[84] It follows that the longer conditions prevail that encourage such cooperation, the deeper the cooperation will become. This is an important point in the evaluation of the effects of international sanctions.

In 1990 President Bush formed a global coalition that combined European countries, Arab states, and Israel, states of the former Soviet empire, and Asian allies, and he did so under the auspices of the United Nations.[85] Saddam Hussein tried to break this coalition. The coalition's critical part was Israel, but Jordan and the USSR were also important. For these countries, the modus operandi was determined by the other partners' willingness to cooperate. It was impossible to determine how far the Arab members would go in siding with Western Christians against Iraq, which was still considered a "brother country" to the Arab nations.

Saddam's future political survival, like the ability of Slobodan Milosevic to maneuver between sanctions and remain in power, encourages anti-U.S. resistance and the formation of a pragmatic and antagonistic *anti-establishment* network. In such an alliance among international pariah, or rogue, states (such as North Korea, Iran, Libya, and Serbia), mutual antagonisms are overshadowed by an even greater hatred toward the common enemy, the United States and its (Christian) allies. This situation may be further encouraged by a change in regime, and the diminishment of democratic forces and the enhancement of the military's impact in Russia. The Iraqi information minister Hamadi Youssef Hammadi called such a possible development part of "a new world disorder," and the Serbs apparently perceive it as the logical response to being bran-dished as outcasts.[86] Today's renewed and intensified relationship between Belgrade engaged in "ethnic cleansing" against Bosnian Muslims ("Turks" as they are referred to by Serbs) and Baghdad runs counter to logical expectation although both may be considered outcasts. Despite historically good relations between Belgrade and Saddam, a longtime secular socialist, who has been trying to Islamicize Iraq and to win new allies by enhancing his pro-Islamic image, the Belgrade-Baghdad axis exists while Serbia encourages ethnic cleansing in Bosnia-Herzegovina against Muslims and has clearly become the archenemy of Islamic countries as well as many in the West. Consequently, public dem-onstration of too great a friendship appears politically risky for Baghdad and Belgrade at a time when both are struggling to improve their image in the West so that UN sanctions will be eliminated.

Iraq is awash with oil, claiming it can now produce 6 million barrels a day, but it has a serious lack of military spare parts, machinery, and main-tenance expertise. Yugoslavia, in turn, is critically in need of oil but has a surplus of military hardware, ammunition, and spare parts—exactly what the Iraqis need. In addition, Yugoslavia had, in the past, always ser-viced a large part of the Iraqi air force and sold major systems to the Iraqis. But certainly the Serb-Yugoslav armed forces are also in need of sophisticated missile guidance and other technologies that the Iraqis have and may learn from the Iraqis strategies for how to survive major threat-ening bomb attacks. Thus, the two countries can exchange experiences and can support each other in systematically exploiting geographical and strategic cracks in the UN embargo that prohibits trade to or from either country.[87] Recent reports confirm that the Serbian military is now devel-oping a medium-range ballistic missile with Iraq that is based on the Russian Scud-B. According to Slovenian Ambassador Anton Bebler, Bel-grade is interested in intensifying scientific cooperation with a primary emphasis on "components for missiles of a new generation."[88]

On a practical level, major geographical obstacles at numerous border crossings over tightly supervised areas work against such cooperation. But the importance of a functioning exchange is so high, the issues are so vital, and the financial needs of the various governments are so great that even Iran turns a blind eye to border trade with official enemies and in violation of UN sanctions. It seems that anything can cross these borders in exchange for money. The triangular trade relations between Iraq, Iran, and Turkey have officially been denied but it has been argued that there has been strong increase in trade across Iraq's eastern frontier with Iran, "particularly at the southern border crossing of Shalamcheh. Iraq uses neighboring Iran as a transit point for Yugoslavia-bound oil, and Turkey as the route for inbound military spare parts."[89] Iran's hatred toward the

United States and mistrust toward the UN has overpowered Tehran's antagonism toward Ankara. Turkish officials, in turn, have conceded privately that the border is difficult to police. "There's . . . only money" [that rules,] an Iraqi trader explained, "you can get anything across, . . . for a price."[90] Thus, Iraq has managed to rebuild and reequip its army with Serbian support and maintenance, and Serbia has obtained sophisticated defense technology and is building missiles. The line interaction between Iraq, Iran, Turkey, and Serbia via Greece and Macedonia or Bulgaria and Romania, and vice versa, is expected to operate especially effectively with the anticipated support of the military in Russia and the Black Sea area (including the Caucasus), with the Russians' motivation being sympathy for Iraq and Serbia and potentially antagonistic strategy against Turkey's interests.[91]

The eventual development of this situation should influence the application of international sanctions and the selection and brandishing of certain states, as it may cause potentially negative and dangerous consequences. Being cornered or declared an outcast creates not only domestic, sociopolitical, and psychological effects, but also foreign policy effects. Similarly, being sanctioned may force a leadership to all kinds of unpredictable and aggressive responses if the leadership is not willing to give in or lose face, including the formation of alliances of need that are quite unexpected but are directed by feasibility and effective benefits for survival. It also aggravates tensions in the international situation which causes escalation and renders crisis management more difficult. Consideration of such networks is hence important before enacting sanctions and corresponding operations. And, once they are enacted, international leaders ought to be prepared for anticipated responses *and* the continuation of (diplomatic) contacts.

Finally, following the end of the Cold War, the Kuwait and Yugoslavian crises also have reactivated and intensified perceptions of and operations along accepted spheres of interest and resulting influence. The international demands on the newly unified Germany to participate in the Kuwait operation and to play an active role in the European security structure have certainly stimulated German foreign policy activities; however, these, in turn, may have caused the specter of an emerging German Central European (*Mitteleuropa*) sphere of influence that includes Slovenia, Hungary, and Croatia. That development has subsequently stimulated reciprocal Russian strategic interest in the adjacent areas including Serbia and the concept of the Russian "near abroad," as well as British and French counterreactions. The longer the crisis in the Balkans and the Black Sea area lasts, the deeper the division will be. All of these developments will affect cohesion and intra-European cooperation in the EU, WEU, NATO, and OSCE. Similarly, the Kuwait crisis and the continued U.S. policy toward Iraq and Saudi Arabia have encouraged the perception of a sustained U.S. interest in that region (Israel and oil being major reasons).

Mass Media and International Conflict

The mass media coverage of the Gulf War revolutionized the manner in which democratic countries conduct warfare. The transmission of real-time information via CNN to a global audience has tended to simplify the complexities and nuances of international conflict. News shaped in sound bites and video clips is generally easy to digest and quick to understand and is certainly extremely powerful when packaged in dramatic fashion.[92]

Saddam Hussein's invasion of Kuwait readily fit the uncomplicated nature of televised drama, featuring the good vs. the bad; while U.S. authorities tried to apply all the lessons learned from the Vietnam War in dealing with the press. The reporting of the conflict also demonstrated once again the dichotomy between commercial and power interests from each part of the media, with the different parts increasing switch-on or air times to enhance revenues. The drama and hype presented to outdo competitors seemed justified. Certainly, any limitations imposed could have been considered in conflict with the "freedom of information." Also, the parties involved had a clear interest in politically exploiting the available coverage.

The shooting war in the Gulf was the first major armed conflict transmitted in real time (on CNN) around the world. The televised coverage of the war was a harbinger of things to come in Russia, Somalia and the Balkans.[93] This coverage was much easier to present than the very complicated situation in and around Sarajevo.

On the other hand, coverage of events in the former Soviet Union, the live pictures provided by Western (Scandinavian) camera teams from the Baltic republics informed EC leaders within hours about Gorbachev's intention to prevent the secession of the Baltic states. Clips showing soldiers firing on civilians in the streets irrevocably damaged Gorbachev's last attempt to halt the disintegration of the Soviet Union.

Further, the landing of U.S. amphibious forces in Somalia took place in front of TV cameras and arc lights, much to the consternation of the units involved. Television also changed the course of the war in Bosnia. After a mortar shell killed more than sixty people in a Sarajevo marketplace, the mutilated bodies were almost immediately displayed on worldwide television. The resulting public outrage in the United States goaded President Clinton to order NATO's immediate response.

Television creates short attention spans and simplistic "we-they," "black-white," and "good-bad" dichotomies that tend to cover over all shades of gray. Complicated issues simply cannot be explained in depth in thirty-second sound bites. Complex issues are thus more easily denied by the public than simple ones. How does one escape the powerful force of pictures showing violated women and children? One can either lash out in rage, disregard the pictures or deny the violations occurred. The more complex things get, the better one feels by either abstaining altogether or searching for the culpable party in order to simplify one's understanding.

Unfortunately, the use of public sentiment to stimulate public opinion and to influence governments has been a longstanding strategy in the conduct of politics and international crises. But the employment of (expensive and highly specialized) public relations companies for this purpose has occurred less frequently. It demands the availability of substantial financial resources and a mentality that allows one to use the suffering of one's own people as a marketing tool. This scenario leads to a sad conclusion: The richer and wealthier a supposed victim is, the greater the chance to mobilize appropriate international public opinion and a relevant response. Conversely, poor, or unimportant, countries without resources are not likely to obtain much attention or assistance.

Notes

The author is grateful to Richard Falk, Robert Gilpin, Joanne Gowa, Elizabeth Prodromou, Edgar Rachlin, Charles Tripp, and William Wohlforth for comments on this chapter and to Marianne Donath, Eric Yesson, and Dusan Djuric for their editorial and research assistance. The paper was written under the auspices of the Center of International Studies at Woodrow Wilson School, Princeton University, and the author is indebted to the Pew Charitable Trust, and the Austrian National Bank (*Jubiläumsfond*) for financial support.

1. Included here were the military strategies used. For instance, the planning and strategies employed by Central Command (CentCom) were based on those originally developed under the Carter Doctrine against the expansion of the Soviet armies toward the Arab oil states.

2. David H. Finnie, *Shifting Lines in the Sand: Kuwait's Elusive Frontier With Iraq,* London: I. B. Tauris & Co., 1992; Chapour Haghighat, *Histoire de la crise du Golfe: Des origines aux consequences,* Brussels: Editions Complexe, 1992, 479; Harvey Morris and John Bullock, *Saddam's War: The Origins of the Kuwait Conflict and the International Response,* Faber and Faber, 1991, 192; Walid Khalidi, *The Gulf Crisis: Origins and Consequences,* Washington, DC: Institute for Palestine Studies, 1991; Richard N. Schofield, *Kuwait and Iraq: Historical Claims and Territorial Disputes: A Report Compiled for the Middle East Programme of the Royal Institute of International Affairs,* London: Morris & Bullock, 1991. Norman Friedman, *Desert Victory: The War for Kuwait,* Annapolis, MD: Naval Institute Press, 1991, 435; Gerd Linde, *Krieg um Kuwait: Der Weg zur "Mutter aller Schlachten,"* Köln: Bundesinstitut für Ostwis-

senschaftliche und Internationale Studien, 1991, 46; *The Iraqi Aggression on Kuwait: The Truth—and the Tragedy*, Encyclopaedia of the Islamic World, The Encyclopaedia, 1412–1992, 149; M. Weller, ed., *Iraq and Kuwait—the Hostilities and Their Aftermath*, Cambridge: Grotius Publications, 1993; Marshall Windmiller, *Prelude to War With Iraq, 1990–1991: A Chronology of Crisis Mismanagement,* San Francisco: Dept. of International Relations, San Francisco State University, 1991, 134.

Also see Willy Brandt, "Eine Friedensordnung für den Nahen Osten," *Europa Archiv,* 46(5), March 19, 1991, 137–142; Hans-Joachim Heintze, "Die vorherige Nichtbefolgung des Völkerrechtes als förderndes Moment für die irakische Aggression gegen Kuwait am 2. August 1990," *Archiv des Völkerrechts,* 19(4), 1991; Eckart Klein, "Völkerrechtliche Aspekte des Golfkonflikts 1990/91," in *Archiv des Völkerrechts,* 29(4), 1991, 421–435. For outstanding overall treatments, see Richard Atkinson, "Crusade," 1993, and Lawrence Freedman and Efraim Karsh, *The Gulf Conflict, 1990–1991,* Princeton: Princeton University Press, 1993.

3. It may even have helped trigger and accelerate the inhuman developments among Croatians, Slovenians, and Serbs just a few weeks after the silence of arms in Kuwait; whereas the abominable performance of Soviet weapons may have been the last that conservative military forces were ready to accept under a Gorbachev presidency—the (political) bill was presented in August and December of 1991.

4. A general of the Russian armed forces explained to this author in November 1993 that "the Balkans have always been, are certainly now, and will always remain a zone of vital strategic interest to Russia."

5. See Scott Armstrong, "Eye of the Storm," *Mother Jones,* November 1991, 30.

6. It is really known as Emerald City. Rick Atkinson, *Crusade—The Untold Story of the Persian Gulf War,* Boston: Houghton Mifflin Company, 1993, 426.

7. The U.S. armed forces transferred approximately 12,000 tanks and armored tracked vehicles, 103,000 wheeled vehicles, and 26,000 containers to Saudi Arabia. Lothar Rühl, "Der Krieg am Golf—Militärischer Verlauf und politisch-strategische Probleme" (The Gulf War—Military Developments and Political-Strategic Problems), *Europa Archiv,* Folge 8/1991, 237–242. For this operation the U.S. military used 40 seaports, its entire strategic transportation fleet, and more than 1,000 sea freighters. Also, CentCom employed major forces from NATO Europe via European air-and seaports, depots, and reserves, including 750 freight trains of the German railroads and 1,300 transport trucks.

8. Rühl, fn. 7, 239.

9. The Washington public relations firms of Ruder Finn and Hill & Knowlton, Inc. were the premier public relations companies behind the Kuwaiti efforts, launching media and political salvos and costing the Kuwaitis hundreds of thousands of dollars. They may be "best remembered for producing the phony witness who testified before a U.S. congressional committee about the alleged slaughter of Kuwaiti infants after the Iraqi invasion of Kuwait." (The "witness" was apparently the daughter of the ambassador of Kuwait to the United States.) Peter Brock, "Dateline Yugoslavia: The Partisan Press," *Foreign Policy,* p. 160.

10. However, recently new information has surfaced, putting in doubt the accuracy of U.S. satellite pictures. The argument is that old satellite images have

actually been used in order to mobilize U.S. public opinion, although there was no real threat developing.

11. George Joffé, "Iraq—The Sanctions Continue," *Jane's Intelligence Review,* July 1994, 315. Joffé argued that the Iraqi dinar (ID) had collapsed: from US$1 = ID0.3 in 1990 to US$1 = ID256 in February 1994 and to US$1 = ID510 in May 1994. Also see Amatzia Baram, "Ba'athist Iraq and Hashemite Jordan: From Hostility to Alignment," *Middle East Journal,* 45(1) Winter 1991, 51–70; M. Weller and E. Lauterpacht, eds., *Iraq and Kuwait: The Hostilities and Their Aftermath,* Cambridge, UK: Grotius, 1993; Robin Wright, "Unexplored Realities of the Persian Gulf Crisis," *Middle East Journal,* 45(1) Winter 1991, 23–29.

12. Joffé, fn. 10, 316.

13. It has even been reported that there are suspicions of the smuggling of enriched plutonium out of Russian military nuclear facilities into Iraq.

14. Eric Rouleau, "The Challenges to Turkey," *Foreign Affairs,* November–December 1993, 113–115.

15. Morton I. Abramowitz, "Dateline Ankara: Turkey after Ozal," *Foreign Policy,* Fall 1993, 165.

16. Abramowitz, fn. 14. The free trade zone to be created comprises Russia, Ukraine, Georgia, Moldavia, Romania, Bulgaria, Greece, Turkey, Armenia, and Azerbaijan and should lead to reduced trade barriers, free circulation of capital, common infrastructure, and environmental and telecomunications interaction. See also Anna Raycheva, *The Black Sea Cooperation Zone,* Princeton University, Woodrow Wilson School, Senior thesis, 1994.

17. The Western portion of the Islamic world has undergone profound changes since the Gulf War. Algeria, Morocco, and Egypt are now home to significant domestic Islamic forces, and the secular governments of Algeria and Egypt are besieged by fundamentalist Islamic revolutionary movements. The Algerian government is attempting to fend off fundamentalists who had won a popular election only to find that the government would not relinquish power. Islamic groups in Egypt also waged a campaign of violence against the government. Both groups have targeted foreigners and foreign economic interests in an effort to bring down governments that they accuse of having collaborated with enemies of Islam. Obviously, the Islamic challenge has become one of the most critical problems in the Mediterranean and may soon be evidenced as far north as Bosnia-Herzegovina if the (Christian) world continues to disregard the suffering of the Muslim population. It may even become a critical problem for Spain and France and hence contribute to a rift of interests between south and west, north and east, within the EU. Iraq and Turkey are certainly the linchpins in the southeastern corner.

18. Arnold Hottinger, "Die arabische Welt nach dem Golf Krieg," *Europa Archiv,* 439.

19. Ali L. Karaosmanoglu, "Die neue regionale Rolle der Türkei" (The new regional role of Turkey), *Europa Archiv,* Folge 15, 1993, 427.

20. Wolfgang Danspeckgruber, "The Balkan Web," *The Washington Post,* May 10, 1993, C4.

21. Richard K. Herrmann, "Soviet Behavior in Regional Conflicts," *World Politics,* 44 (April 1992), 449.

22. Richard Herrmann argued that U.S. officials considered the prospect of a negotiated haggle over a form of sequential linkage that would tie Iraqi withdrawal to a broader international focus on the Palestinian question "a nightmare scenario." *The New York Times,* December 19, 1990, p. 6, quoted in fn. 20, 452.

23. Tatiana V. Nosenko, "Soviet Policy in the Persian Gulf," *Mediterranean Quarterly,* 2(1), Winter 1991, 71–77.

24. On several occasions, reports surfaced, obviously launched by Russian officers, indicating that contrary to official U.S. and Coalition reports, major battles were fought in southern Iraq between U.S. and Iraqi armored units that ended with dozens of U.S. M1A Abrahams MBTs destroyed and proved the quality of the forces and equipment (T-72s) of the Iraqi Republican Guards.

25. "Zur Lage im Baltikum," *Österreichische Militärische Zeitschrift,* Heft 2/ 1991, 171–174; Eberhard Schulz, "Die Doppelkrise im Baltikum und am Golf," *Europa Archiv,* Folge 3/1991, 71–80.

26. William Odom, *The New Russian Threat.*

27. With the creation of the Russian Federated Republic and a host of newly independent states, today the Russian military and the conservatives look at their so-called "near abroad" as a zone of vital strategic importance. The Serbs, Ukrainians, and Crimean, Baltic and Central Asian Russians are all considered to be within the Russian sphere of influence. This has increasingly affected the situation around Iraq as well and Boris Yeltsin has been pushed by hardline nationalists to reassert such Russian influence on Iraq.

28. Andrzej Rybak, "Infernal Duo," *Die Woche,* 29 April 1993, 24, in *FBIS-EEU-93-083,* May 8, 1993, 59. Rybak reported that before the Gulf War some twenty-three Yugoslav companies and more than 2,600 Yugoslav experts worked in Iraq, and Baghdad supposedly was the biggest purchaser of Yugoslav defense material.

29. Iraqi officers were trained during the Iran-Iraq War at a naval center in the Adriatic port of Split. At that time, suspicions arose that Iraqis were being trained by Yugoslavs in the use of chemical weapons. See "IRNA Cites Belgrade Weekly on Arms in the Gulf War," IRNA, Tehran, January 23, 1987, in *FBIS-EEU-II,* January 27, 1987, I1.

30. "Guns manufactured by Bofors and a fire control system from Svenska Philips have been exported further, contrary to Swedish weapons export rule, from Yugoslavia to Iraq. They were to be installed on a Yugoslav frigate. The Yugoslav armed forces then sold the frigate to Iraq." In "Sweden/Iraq: Swedish Report of Re-export of Swedish Weapons to Iraq," Stockholm Home Service, March 4, 1985, and *BBC Summary of World Broadcasts,* Part 2, Eastern Europe Weekly Economic Report, March 21, 1985.

31. "Document: Yugoslavia's Iraq Connection," *Middle East Defense News,* Vol. 4, No. 24, September 30, 1991. Strong evidence exists about Yugoslavia's support of Iraq's military not only in maintaining airplanes and tanks but also in developing, producing, and deploying chemical weapons and supplying an especially designed multiple rocket launching system (MLRS, M 87, Orkan). This document demonstrated purchases of propellant powder for use in manufacturing 130mm artillery charges from Unis Associated Metal Industry of Sarajevo by the Al Qaqaa State Organization for technical industries (Org. Unit 12003, Iskanderiyah). The

principal chemical weapons facility in Yugoslavia is the Miloje Zapic plant, near Krusevac, Serbia.

Yugoslavia was apparently also "responsible for supplying Iraq with the technology to produce Sarin chemical weapons in 1986 and was instrumental in the construction of a chemical factory for the same weapons" 1983 to 1885 (the al Muthena State Establishment near Samarra.) The Yugoslav firms Bratstvo and Zrak also built a factory to produce 122mm howitzers near Fallujah, code named Kol 7 Saad 5. The Iraqis refer to this plant as the Saddam State Establishment. The Iraqis called the Yugoslav MLSR the Ababil 50 or the Ababil 100 both of which had twelve 262mm rockets with ranges between 50 and 100 kilometers and were designed to carry chemical warheads or cluster submunitions.

32. Orkan (see fn. 31) was apparently realized with financial and technological support from Iraq. The Iraqi Air Force also has had longstanding naval and air service and maintenance contracts with the Yugoslav National Army (YNA)—for instance, for the MiG 21 and MiG 23. Andrzej Rybak, fn. 27. There were several reports of training flights of "military aircraft with Iraqi symbols" over Zagreb. Plus, there have been several reports that they were "taking off from the Zmaj Air and Technical Repair Institute." "Croatia Accuses Presidency of Breaking Sanctions," Radio Belgrade TANJUG, in *FBIS-EEU*-90-188, September 27, 1990, 50.

33. On August 11, 1990, Yugoslav Foreign Minister Jovanovic stated that the "world should know that Yugoslavia has its stake in numerous Iraqi building sites, amounting to business of U.S.$ 1 billion. Yugoslavia has 10,000 workers there, while 50,000 people work in Yugoslavia for the Iraqi market." "Boycott Adversely Affecting Economy," Radio Belgrade TANJUG, in *FBIS-EEU*-90-188, September 27, 1990, 51.

34. Gustav Gustenau, "Zur Lage in Jugoslawien," *Österreichische Militärische Zeitschrift*, Heft 4/1991, 351–354.

35. John Zametica, "The Yugoslav Conflict," *Adelphi Paper*, 270, IISS, London, Summer 1992.

36. It has been widely argued that the Slovenes and the Croats have found the supportive German official position, especially that of then Foreign Minister Hans Dietrich Genscher, the Austrian support—particularly from Foreign Minister Alois Mock—and the verbal support of the Holy See rather encouraging.

37. Interview with Austrian, Hungarian, and Slovenian officials by this author, Summer 1994.

38. Speech by Secretary of State James Baker, *Öesterreichische Militärische Zeitschrift*, Heft 5/1991, 391.

39. John Waterbury, ed., Toward New Orders in the Middle East, Center of International Studies, Monograph Series, No. 2, Princeton, 1991.

40. Soon after Secretary Baker's visit, indications accumulated that the JNA would employ operation Bedem 91 to appease Slovenia. The degree to which the Belgrade government was informed about the military planning and preparations remains unclear. Cited in "Zur Lage in Jugoslawien," *Österreichische Militärische Zeitschrift*, Heft 5/1991, 91.

41. The deal included tanks, missile launchers, and helicopter gunships and was negotiated with Soviet Defense Minister Dimitri Yazov. Misha Glenny, *The Fall of Yugoslavia—The Third Balkan War*, New York, Penguin Books, 1993, 61.

42. Charles Krauthammer, "The Unipolar Moment," *Foreign Affairs: America and the World*, Vol. 70, No. 1 (1990–1991); Christopher Layne, "The Unipolar Illusion—Why New Great Powers Will Rise," *International Security*, 17 (4), Spring, 1993.

43. On several occasions Iraqi anti-aircraft batteries (AAA) locked target acquisition radar on U.S. aircraft patrolling the no-fly zones.

44. Twenty U.S. sea-launched cruise missiles destroyed the ISHQ in Baghdad on June 26, 1993. The United States performed a similar attack against a plutonium facility south of Baghdad six months earlier.

45. It was also clear that the Coalition's declared objective to destroy Saddam's military and nuclear apparatus was not achieved in Desert Storm although his armed forces were rendered relatively less threatening to the neighboring states (but, alas, not to the Iraqi people).

46. In a speech by President Bush on April 13, 1991, his comment, "It deems the Iraqi people to decide itself about its future," was interpreted by the Kurds and the Shi'ites as an indirect call for revolution. Le Monde, 16, April 1991, quoted in fn. 11, Arnold Hottinger, "Die arabische Welt nach dem Golf Krieg" (The Arabic World After the Gulf War), *Europa Archiv*, Folge 15–16, 1991, 440, 441.

47. Report of the Committee on Foreign Relations of the United States Senate, May 2, quoted in *Le Monde*, AFP, May 4, 1991; that Iraqi officers contacted Iraqi opposition to receive proof of suggested U.S. support and offering conditional support. There were signs that the United States wanted either a new Ba'ath government or a weakened Saddam Hussein, who could be directed by orders, to remain in power. Hottinger, fn. 46, 440.

48. Gustav Gustenau, "Zur Lage in Jugoslawien," *Österreichische Militärische Zeitschrift*, Heft 4/1991, 350. See also "After a Sure-Footed March to Victory, Baffling Missteps," *International Herald Tribune*, March 26, 1991.

49. I am grateful to Mark Fineman for this observation.

50. I am grateful to Abdlatif Al-Hamad for this observation.

51. See Karl Kaiser and Klaus Becher, *Deutschland und der Irak Konflikt. Internationale Sicherheitsverantwortung Deutschlands nach der deutschen Vereinigung*, Bonn, 1992, 114–126.

52. Uwe Nerlich, "Deutsche Sicherheitspolitik und Konflikte ausserhalb des NATO-Gebietes" (German Security Policy and Conflicts Outside NATO Area), *Europa Archiv*, 10/1991, 307.

53. According to the Basic Law, called the *Grundgesetz*, "The Federation may enter a system of mutual collective security; in doing so it will consent to such limitations upon its sovereignty as will bring about and secure a peaceful and lasting order in Europe and among the nations of the world," and "The Federation shall build up Armed Forces for defence purposes ... apart from defence, the armed forces may only be used to the extent explicitly permitted by the Basic Law." Quoted in Trevor Salmon, "Testing Times for European Cooperation: The Gulf and Yugoslavia, 1990–1992," *International Affairs*, 68(2), 1992, 237, and fn. 11. Also Helmut Hubel, "Das Vereinte Deutschland aus Internationaler Sicht—Eine Zwischenbilanz" (The unified Germany in international opinion), *Arbeitspapiere zur Internationalen Politik*, 73, 1992, 79, 80.

54. Trevor Salmon, p. 239.

55. German Foreign Minister Hans Dietrich Genscher suggested strongly that Germany—and the EU—recognize the sovereignty of Slovenia and Croatia, bringing to public attention the cases of German unification and the Baltic republics as well as certain historical prejudices against the Serbs. Because Germany's position influenced Bosnia to seek independence as well, tensions in the Balkans were exacerbated. Many have blamed the Germans for recognizing a state that had a Nazi puppet regime (Croatia) and another (Slovenia) that maintains close ties to German-speaking Austria.

56. Just the sight of German troops patrolling Sarajevo, even in UN blue helmets, would bring panic to those with historical memory of Nazi Germany's occupation of Yugoslavia and would raise similar emotions in Russia and countries allied with the Serbs.

57. Trevor Salmon, 241, 242.

58. Salmon, fn. 52, 239.

59. See Andrew Bennett, Joseph Lepgold, and Danny Unger, "Burden-Sharing in the Persian Gulf War," *International Organization*, 48(1), Winter 1994, 39–75; Martin Landgraf, "Die Europäische Gemeinschaft und die Kuwait Krise," Ferhad Ibrahim and Mir A. Ferdowski, eds., *Die Kuwait Krise und das regionale Umfeld. Hintergründe, Interessen, Ziele*, Berlin, 1992, 42–47; Helmut Hubel, *Der zweite Golfkrieg*, Bonn, 1991.

60. Friedemann Buettner and Martin Landgraf, "The European Community's Middle Eastern Policy—The New Order of Europe and the Gulf Crisis," in Tareq Y. Ismael and Jacqueline S. Ismael, eds., *The Gulf War and the New World Order*, University Press of Florida, 1994, 96.

61. Ismael and Ismael, 96, and fn. 64.

62. Sigmar Stadlmeier and Heinz Vetschera, "Dauernde Neutralität und kollektive Sicherheit im Lichte des Golfkrieges 1990/91,"*Österreichische Militärische Zeitschrift*, Heft 4/1991, 314–320; *Neue Zürcher Zeitung*, August 9, 1990.

63. Wolfgang Danspeckgruber, "Neutrality in the Emerging Europe," in Wolfgang Danspeckgruber, *Emerging Dimensions of European Security,* Westview Press, Boulder, Colorado 1991.

64. Hans Arnold, "The Gulf Crisis and the United Nations," *Aussenpolitik: German Foreign Affairs Review,* 41(1), 1991, 68–77. Charles Saint-Prot, *Saddam Hussein: Un Gaullisme Arabe?* Paris: A. Michel, 1987. *The United Nations and the Iran-Iraq War: A Ford Foundation Conference Report,* New York: Ford Foundation, 1987. Eric Chauvistre, "The Implications of IAEA Inspections Under Security Council Resolution 687," New York: United Nations, 1992.

Serge Sur, "Security Council Resolution 687 of 3 April 1991 in the Gulf Affair: Problems of Restoring and Safeguarding Peace," New York: United Nations, 1992. Ian Johnstone, *Aftermath of the Gulf War: An Assessment of UN Action*, Boulder, Colorado: Lynne Rienner Publishers, 1994. Cameron R. Hume, *The United Nations, Iran and Iraq: How Peacemaking Changed*, Bloomington: Indiana University Press, 1994. Claude Le Borgne, *Un discret Massacre: l'Orient, la Guerre et Apres,* Paris: Editions F. Bourin, 1992.

65. Robert Springborg, "The United Nations in the Gulf War," in Tareq Y. Ismael and Jacqueline S. Ismael, eds., *The Gulf War and the New World Order,* University Press of Florida, 1994, 96.

66. Randall Schweller, "Bandwagoning for Profit—Bringing the Revisionist State Back in," *International Security,* 19 (1), Summer 1994, 72–107; John Lewis Gaddis, "International Relations Theory and the End of the Cold War," *International Security,* 17 (3), 5–58; Paul Schroeder, "Historical Reality vs. Neo-Realist Theory," *International Security,* 19 (1), Summer 1994, 108–148.

67. Saul Bloom, ed., et al., *Hidden Casualties: The Environmental, Health and Political Consequences of the Persian Gulf War,* Berkeley: North Atlantic Books, 1994. Djamchid Momtaz, *Les règles relatives à la protection de l'environment au cours des conflits armés et à l'epreuve du conflit entre l'Irak et le Koweit,* Annuaire français de droit international, vol. 37, 1991, 203–219; Richard S. Williams, Jr., Joanne Heckman, and Jon Schneeberger, *Environmental Consequences of the Persian Gulf War, 1990–1991: Remote Sensing Datasets of Kuwait and Environs,* Washington, D.C.: National Geographic Society, 1991, 48.

68. R. A. Bladon, S. Miller, and M. W. Freeman, A Study of Tank Farm Fires in Kuwait, London: Home Office Fire and Emergency Planning Department, 1992.

69. Paul Aarts, "Democracy, Oil and the Gulf War," *Third World Quarterly,* 13(3) 1992, 525–538; Edward N. Krapels, "The Commanding Heights: International Oil in a Changed World," *International Affairs,* London, 1993; Gareth Kingdon, *The Impact of the Gulf Crisis on the Global Oil Industry,* London: Gulf Centre for Strategic Studies, 1991, 57; Petra Seifert and Arne Seifert, *Kuweit: Erdöl, Banken, Beduinen,* Berlin: Deutscher Verlag der Wissenschaften, 1991; Mary Ann Tetreault, "Independence, Sovereignty, and Vested Glory: Oil and Politics in the Second Gulf War," *Orient,* 34(1), March 1993, 87–103.

70. Laurie Rosensweig, *United Nations Sanctions Debated: Problems and Potential—A Proposal to Create More Effective Sanctions,* Princeton University, Senior thesis, 1993. Why did the United Nations sanctions fail? The four most significant factors were the following: First, the premature military response to the Iraq aggression by the international community destroyed any hope for the success of peaceful enforcement measures through sanctions. Second, the reliance on the domestic implementation of sanctions to enforce United Nations demands undermined the sanctions from their original imposition on August 6, 1990. Third, the poorly designed sanctions effort hindered the international community's ability to influence Iraq's behavior. Finally, the international community's unrealistic expectations about the potential for success of the sanctions and the amount of time necessary to induce an Iraqi withdrawal from Kuwait were damaging to the impact of the sanctions on Iraq.

71. He added that the "Yugoslav assets on Iraq's sites were protected and that they would continue to be so until international conditions became favorable for work to continue." Quoted in "Iraqi Defence Minister Expresses Support for Yugoslavia," Yugoslav News Agency, June 4, 1992, in *BBC Summary of World Broadcasts,* Part 2, Eastern Europe, June 8, 1992.

72. David A. Shlapak and Paul K. Davis, *Possible Postwar Force Requirements for the Persian Gulf: How Little Is Enough?* Santa Monica, CA: Rand Corporation, 1991, 29.

73. The war for the liberation of Kuwait saw the single biggest amassing of main battle tanks (MBTs) with all sides combined having approximately ten thou-

sand MBTs. In contrast, there were approximately 8,000 MBTs for the battle of Kursk in July of 1943 between Hitler's Germany and the Soviet Union, which was, until the Gulf War, the greatest tank battle in history. See Atkinson, fn. 2, 252.

74. Bruce W. Watson, et al., *Military Lessons of the Gulf War,* Novato, CA: Presidio Press, 1991.

75. The Coalition also could not destroy the Republican Guards. Some 50 percent of the Republican Guards' armored units escaped and more than 130 Iraqi aircraft were flown to Iran, which would not release them anymore.

76. See the debate between John G. Heidenreich, "The Gulf War: How Many Iraqis Died?" *Foreign Policy,* 90, Spring 1993, and William Arkin and Timothy R. Coté, letter to *Foreign Policy,* 91, Summer 1993. Heidenreich argued that in 1991, according to the Defense Intelligence Agency (DIA), there were apparently 100,000 people killed in action, and approximately 300,000 wounded in action in the Gulf. In 1992, the House Armed Services Committee released a report estimating 9,000 Iraqis killed in the air campaign and 17,000 wounded. According to that report the combined estimate of 120,000 Iraqi dead and wounded was calculated, but the report did not differentiate between those two categories. In "Triumph without Victory" *U.S. News and World Report* argued that there were about 8,000 Iraqi dead and perhaps 24,000 wounded. Heidenreich himself calculated military casualties as some 700 to 3,000 or perhaps 4,000 Iraqi dead and between 2,000 and 7,000 wounded. He argued that Iraqi civilian casualties were perhaps fewer than 1,000 dead.

77. Ahmad Al-Hamad, "The Effects of the Iraqi Aggression Against Kuwait," 2nd Liechtenstein Colloquium, Vaduz, May 1991.

78. In contrast to public statements, the Coalition undertook efforts to eliminate Saddam Hussein and thus decapitate the Iraqi leadership. One such effort involved numerous detailed air attacks with specially designed "barrel bombs." These 4,700-pound "penetrator" bombs (GBU-28), developed out of surplus artillery barrels, were dropped in precision air strikes to detonate deep in the ground at Saddam's supposed hideouts—fortified bunkers. The allied companies that constructed the bunkers provided Coalition command with detailed plans. Another such effort was the well-known air attack on a convoy of U.S.-made recreation vehicles after one widely televised Saddam interview in a trailer. See Atkinson, fn. 2, 274, 274, 473.

79. Andy McNab, *Bravo Two Zero,* London: Bantam Press, 1993.

80. See Ephraim Karsh and Mari Rautsi, *Saddam Hussein: A Political Biography.* New York: The Free Press, 1991.Several instances have been reported in which Saddam rewarded disobedience or perceived dissenting opinion or even just wrong perceptions with the utmost punishment and cruelty, such as executions on the spot, sometimes carried out by himself personally with his own pistol.

81. As Ahmad Al-Hamad indicated: "However, Saddam, who basically never travels, was blatantly ignorant of how the world had changed. His confidence in assessing the world situation was supported by the following facts:

- The West had supported him in his fight to destroy Iran as a radical threat to the region.

- His special relationship with the former Soviet Union for arms and political and technical expertise was so strong that on August 2, 1990, 14,000 Soviet military personnel were stationed in Iraq.
- His isolation and total disregard for any advice from those around him distorted his view of the changing scene of international politics.

Saddam Hussein believed that by gaining control of the Gulf and, more importantly, control of the world's largest oil supplies, he would have enough political leverage to influence the international community." Paper prepared by Ahmad Al-Hamad, "The Effects of the Iraqi Aggression Against Kuwait," 2nd Liechtenstein Colloquium.

82. Former Yugoslavians have cited nasty nicknames that describe the relationship between Yugoslavia and Iraq, such as "MiloSoddam."

83. For an excellent characterization of the personality of Slobodan Milosevic, see Aleksa Djilas, "Serbia's Milosevic: A Profile," *Foreign Affairs*, Summer 1993, 81–96.

84. Wolfgang Danspeckgruber, "The Balkan Web," c 4.

85. Robert A. Kann, "Alliances Versus Ententes," *World Policy*, 28, July 1976, 611–621; Stephen M. Walt, "Alliance Formation and the Balance of World Power," *International Security*, 9(4), Spring 1985, 3–43.

86. Mark Fineman, "When Two Outcasts Join Forces: A Yugoslav General Went to Iraq," *Los Angeles Times*, June 15, 1993, A1.

87. Fineman, fn. 86. In addition, the Iraqi experience demonstrated ways to rebuild a destroyed army, industry, and economy within a relatively short time after a most devastating air war.

88. Andrzej Rybak, "Infernal Duo," *Die Woche*, April 29, 1993, 24, in *FBIS-EEU-93-083*, May 8, 1993, 59. The Yugoslav armed forces have worked on a missile program since the 1960s. Plamen had a range of 15 kilometers, Oganj, a range of 27 kilometers, and the Orkan (1987), some 50 kilometers.

89. Despite the hatred between Iraq, Iran and Turkey, as well as the UN embargo, border traffic continues. Turkish officials have explained that it is difficult to police the legal trade in food, medicines, and other goods. There is "routine commerce from Turkey to Iraq, with some prohibited items passing through at the border town of Zakhu in the autonomous Iraqi region of Kurdistan." Fineman, fn. 86.

There has been traditional Yugoslav-Iraq oil trade via Turkey, beginning in 1986. The shipments—some 350,000 tons of Kirkuk Crude p.a.—were delivered overland via Turkish trucking services as a compensation deal. In the relation between Yugoslavia and Iraq the shipments serve as payments for construction projects by Generalexport in Iraq. Between Iraq and Turkey they serve to settle outstanding accounts. Most of the crude was to be refined near Skopje in Macedonia. Nada Stanic, "Yugoslavs Get Iraqi Crude Overland via Turkey in 3-Sided Countertrade," *International*, Belgrade, October 27, 1986, 1.

90. "On borders, whether Iraq's or the Serbs', there's simply no politics—only money," the Iraqi trader said, explaining how such trade has taken place despite the UN embargoes. "You can get anything across—anything, I tell you, for a price." Fineman, fn. 87.

91. The instability and potential danger of change, if not confrontation, in the Aegean Region have been aggravated by the tremendous recent arms flow into Greece and Turkey. Under the Cascade Program, which offers arms supplies free of charge to smaller NATO states from states that have to reduce their armament due to the CDE agreements, the two countries have received enormous quantities of military hardware. According to the report, Greece and Turkey received, in 1992–1993, from Germany and the United States, 2,822 tanks, 1,084 armored combat vehicles, 303 large caliber artillery systems, 28 attack helicopters, and 14 warships. Turkey received some 1,017 main battle tanks (almost as many as the entire holdings of the British Army); Greece obtained 725 MBTs. Although much of the equipment is secondhand, it presents a huge improvement over existing Greek and Turkish stock. Most of the tanks are U.S. M-60s or the German *Leopard I*, with much more sophisticated electronic equipment than the M-48, which has been the mainstay of both armies until recently.

These statistics were compiled by the British American Security Information Council and the Berlin Information Centre for Transatlantic Security. Bruce Clark, "NATO Arms Pour into Greece and Turkey," *The Financial Times*, July 7, 1994, 2.

92. John E. Rielly, "Public Opinion: The Pulse of the '90s," *Foreign Policy*, 90, 79–91; Beatrice Fleury-Vilatte, *Les medias et la guerre du Golfe*, Nancy, France: Presses universitaires de Nancy, 1992, 155.

93. W. Lance Bennett and David L. Paletz, *Taken by Storm—The Media, Public Opinion, and U.S. Foreign Policy in the Gulf War*, Chicago: The University of Chicago Press, 1994.

Appendix A:
Resolutions of the United Nations Security Council Regarding the Situation Between Iraq and Kuwait, August 1990–April 1995

On August 2, 1990 Iraqi forces invaded and occupied sovereign Kuwait. Starting with its condemnation of the invasion in Resolution 660, the United Nations Security Council adopted a total of 30 resolutions directly relating to the situation between the two countries. Fifteen resolutions were adopted prior to or during the crisis, with a further 15 adopted in direct relation to the implementation of the cease-fire accords (Resolution 687). In addition to the Security Council resolutions, a number of United Nations investigative bodies and organizations were established to oversee and insure the implementation of Resolution 687.

Resolution 660
August 2, 1990
Condemned Iraq's invasion of Kuwait and demanded an unconditional withdrawal of Iraqi forces. Called for a negotiated settlement to be worked out between the two countries.

Resolution 661
August 6, 1990
Imposed mandatory arms and economic sanctions on Iraq. Cited Iraq's refusal to comply with Resolution 660 and its "usurpation of the legitimate authority of the Government of Kuwait" as the basis of the sanctions. Allowed limited foodstuffs and medical supplies to be delivered to Iraq for humanitarian reasons.

Resolution 662
August 9, 1990
Declared to end Iraq's occupation of Kuwait illegal and called upon all states to refrain from recognizing Iraq's claim. Passed in an effort to end Iraq's occupation of Kuwait and restore the legitimate authority of the Kuwaiti government.

Resolution 664

August 18, 1990

Held Iraq fully responsible for the health and safety of foreign nationals in Iraq and Kuwait, demanded that Iraq allow their immediate departure and that no action be taken to jeopardize their safety or health. Demanded that Iraq rescind its orders for the closure of diplomatic and consular missions in Kuwait. Demanded that Iraq reinstate the immunity and other privileges of foreign diplomatic and consular missions.

Resolution 665

August 25, 1990

Established a naval blockade of Iraq. Called on UN member states with naval forces in the region to halt all inward and outward maritime shipping to ensure the strict implementation of the sanctions imposed by Resolution 661.

Resolution 666

September 13, 1990

Expressed humanitarian concern over foodstuff shortages within Iraq. Directed member states that any food provided to Iraq should be done so through the UN in cooperation with the International Committee of the Red Cross.

Resolution 667

September 16, 1990

Strongly condemned Iraq's violations of diplomatic missions and personnel in Kuwait, including third party nationals. Demanded the release of all foreign nationals and that Iraq protect the well-being of diplomatic personnel and premises within Iraq and Kuwait. Warned Iraq to take no action that would hinder diplomatic and consular missions and further demanded Iraq allow such missions access to their nationals being held in Iraq and Kuwait.

Resolution 669

September 24, 1990

Regarded requests for assistance concerning the sanctions imposed in Resolution 661. Entrusted the Committee established under that resolution with the examination of such requests for assistance.

Resolution 670

September 25, 1990

Expanded blockade by limiting air traffic into and out of Iraq. Regarding compliance with the economic sanctions imposed in Resolution 661, specifically restricted air traffic to and from Iraq and occupied Kuwait to UN-sanctioned relief flights. Called on states to detain Iraqi vessels in their ports and deny overflights of any aircraft bound for Iraq. Reminded states of their obligations under Resolution 661 to freeze Iraqi assets and protect those of the legitimate Kuwaiti government.

Resolution 674
October 29, 1990

Condemned Iraq's holding of third-state and Kuwaiti nationals as hostages. Also expressed grave concern over Iraq's treatment of the Kuwaiti populace, including forced departures, relocations, destruction of demographic records, and seizure of property. Held Iraq liable for loss, damage, or injury that results from the illegal occupation of Kuwait. Called on states to collect relevant information regarding any such losses or damage. Stressed that a peaceful solution to this crisis was still being sought.

Resolution 677
November 28, 1990

Expressed grave concern over Iraq's ongoing attempts to alter the demographic composition of the population of Kuwait and to destroy the civil records maintained by Kuwait.

Resolution 678
November 29, 1990

Set January 15, 1991 as the deadline for Iraq to fully implement all resolutions relating to the occupation of Kuwait. Authorized member states to use "all means necessary" to force compliance if Iraq failed to comply with all such resolutions by that date.

Resolution 686
March 2, 1991

Set conditions Iraq must meet for a formal cease-fire. Noting the suspension of offensive operations by coalition forces, demanded that Iraq fully implement all twelve resolutions regarding the crisis. Specified measures to be undertaken by Iraq to allow for a formal cessation of hostilities, including rescinding claims on Kuwait; accepting liability for loss, injury, or damage incurred to Kuwait and third states, releasing of all Kuwaiti and foreign nationals, return of all Kuwaiti property, cessation of provocative or hostile actions, releasing of all prisoners of war; designating of military commanders to meet with counterparts to discuss a cease-fire; and providing the UN information regarding mines, booby traps, chemical and biological weapons in Kuwait.

Resolution 687
April 3, 1991

Established the terms of a formal cease-fire and end to the conflict. Major points of the cease-fire included Iraqi recognition of Kuwait and its full disclosure of its weapons programs. Called for the destruction of Iraq's nuclear-biological-chemical programs (NBC) and prohibited Iraq from pursuing any such programs in the future. Established a UN Special Commission to carry out on site inspections. Demanded that Iraq cooperate with any such on site inspections and provide the UN investigative teams with full information regarding "weapons of mass destruction." Demanded that Iraq pay for damages to Kuwaiti property.

Resolution 689

April 9, 1991

Set out specifics regarding the United Nations Iraq-Kuwait Observer Mission (UNIKOM). Specified that the mission's activities were to be reviewed by the Security Council every 6 months.

Resolution 692

May 20, 1991

Formally established a Compensation Fund and a commission to organize and oversee Iraqi reparations to Kuwait and third states that incurred loss, damage, or injury as a result of Iraq's actions.

Resolution 699

June 17, 1991

Formally granted the Special Commission established in Resolution 687 and the International Atomic Energy Agency (IAEA), the authority to investigate and pursue the destruction or removal of weapons systems outlined in Resolution 687. Called on member states to provide maximum assistance, but held the government of Iraq financially liable for the full costs of carrying out the authorized tasks.

Resolution 700

June 17, 1991

Established guidelines for a continuing arms embargo on Iraq and called on all states and international organizations to act in accordance with such guidelines.

Resolution 705

August 15, 1991

Specified that compensation to be paid by Iraq not exceed 30 percent of the annual value of the exports of petroleum from Iraq.

Resolution 706

August 15, 1991

Expressed concern over the nutritional and health situation in Iraq. Permitted the sale of limited quantities of Iraqi oil, with the payments for that oil to be deposited directly into an escrow account. Such funds would be used for financing the humanitarian effort in Iraq as well as for purchasing foodstuffs and medicines essential for civilian needs. These essentials would then be distributed to the civilian population within Iraq. A portion of the money would also go toward funding the continuing Special Commission and IAEA investigations of Iraqi weapons programs. Expressed concern over missing Kuwaiti property and nationals that were seized during the occupation and demanded their release.

Resolution 707

August 15, 1991

Expressed grave concern over the Iraqi government's flagrant violations with regard to Resolution 687. Condemned the Iraqi government for its non-compliance with the IAEA and Special Commission inspections. Demanded the full cooperation of the Iraqi government with regard to such inspections. Demanded that the Iraqi government provide full disclosure of all information regarding its "weapons of mass destruction" and allow Special Commission and IAEA teams unrestricted access to any and all facilities, sites, areas, records, or means of transportation they wish to inspect.

Resolution 712
September 19, 1991
Expressed further concern over the humanitarian situation in Iraq and established guidelines regarding the purchasing of foodstuffs and medicines for Iraq. Requested the release of the first one-third portion of the funds deposited in the escrow account for the purchase of such essentials.

Resolution 715
October 11, 1991
Authorized the continuation of IAEA inspections throughout Iraq and called for the development of a system to monitor any future sales to Iraq of items relevant to the inspections. Demanded that Iraq unconditionally meet all of its obligations under Resolution 687.

Resolution 773
August 26, 1992
Listed decisions regarding the demarcation boundary between Iraq and Kuwait.

Resolution 778
October 2, 1992
Authorized the seizure of Iraqi funds outside of Iraq obtained from the sale of petroleum products paid for after August 6, 1990. Specified that such funds would be deposited in the UN-administered escrow account and used to fund humanitarian relief efforts in Iraq or IAEA investigative teams. Instructed states holding petroleum products belonging to the Iraqi government or Iraqi corporations to arrange for the sale of such products and to deposit the funds in the escrow account.

Resolution 806
February 5, 1993
Specified the international boundary between Iraq and Kuwait. Expressed concern over Iraqi violations of Security Council resolutions and border incidents. Requested the strengthening of UNIKOM forces to enable direct action against violations of the DMZ or demarcation line.

Resolution 833
May 27, 1993
Specified the demarcation boundary between Iraq and Kuwait.

Resolution 899
March 4, 1994
Concerned Iraqi private citizens who remained in Kuwaiti territory following the demarcation of the international boundary.

Resolution 949
October 15, 1994
Reviewed the situation in Iraq.

Resolution 986
April 14, 1995
Analyzed the situation between Iraq and Kuwait.

UN Bodies Established During
the Iraq and Kuwait Conflict

The United Nations Iraq-Kuwait Observer Mission (UNIKOM)
Established to monitor the demilitarized zone between Iraq and Kuwait, including the Khawr'Abd Allah waterway. Its mission was to observe and deter any violations or hostile actions by one state toward the other. Its mandate was later strengthened to enable UNIKOM to take direct action to prevent violations of the DMZ or demarcation line.

The United Nations Special Commission
Established in Resolution 687 to oversee the destruction or removal of Iraq's "weapons of mass destruction." These included all Iraq's chemical and biological weapons along with all associated facilities and capabilities. Iraq's ballistic missiles with a range of over 150 kilometers were also targeted for destruction. The Special Commission was also to work closely with IAEA inspection teams in dismantling Iraq's nuclear weapons program.

The Iraq-Kuwait Boundary Demarcation Commission
Established to demarcate the international boundary between Iraq and Kuwait. To determine the demarcation boundary the commission was to follow terms set out in the "Agreed Minutes between the State of Kuwait and the Republic of Iraq regarding the Restoration of Friendly Relations, Recognition, and Related Matters," signed in October of 1963.

The United Nations Compensation Commission
Established to administer the compensation payments made by Iraq. The commission, composed of experts in the fields of finance, law, accountancy, insurance, and environmental damage assessment, would control the fund through which Iraq was to pay compensation for any direct damage, loss, or injury caused by its invasion of Kuwait. As of January 1994, well over two million claims for compensation had been filed.

Security Council's Sanction Committee

Established in Resolution 661 to monitor the arms embargo on Iraq. The committee was to report to the security council every ninety days.

Appendix B: Chronology

August 2, 1990 – Iraq invaded Kuwait. The United Nations Security Council passed Resolution 660 condemning the invasion and calling for the withdrawal of all Iraqi forces from Kuwait. The United States froze all Kuwaiti and Iraqi assets and imposed a trade embargo on Iraq.

August 4, 1990 – Saudi Arabia mobilized its forces, and French and British warships began to move toward the Gulf. The European Community announced sanctions against Iraq, including the interdiction of all oil and arms transactions with that country.

August 6, 1990 – The United Nations Security Council passed Resolution 661 imposing comprehensive mandatory economic sanctions on Iraq. China and Yemen abstained from the vote. This resolution prohibited all trade and financial transactions, and all diplomatic and cultural relations and services with Iraq.

August 7, 1990 – Turkey closed its pipelines to the shipment of Iraqi oil to the Mediterranean Sea and authorized the transfer of U.S. combat aircraft to Turkish air bases.

August 8, 1990 – Iraq formally annexed Kuwait.

August 9, 1990 – The United Nations Security Council passed Resolution 662, which declared the Iraqi annexation of Kuwait to be null and void. The first U.S. troops, the 82nd Airborne Division, arrived in Saudi Arabia.

August 10, 1990 – The Arab League voted to send troops to Saudi Arabia.

August 12, 1990 – Saddam Hussein linked the Kuwaiti conflict with the Israeli occupation of Arab lands. President Bush ordered U.S. naval vessels to stop all Iraqi oil exports in addition to all ships carrying cargo embargoed by UN Security Council Resolution 661.

August 15, 1990 – Iraq withdrew from territory it occupied during the war with Iran, freeing troops for action in Kuwait.

August 16, 1990 – Iraq detained foreign nationals in Iraq and Kuwait with the intent of using them as shields at key military installations.

August 18, 1990 – The United Nations Security Council passed Resolution 664 demanding the immediate release of all foreign nationals in Iraq and Kuwait. U.S. naval vessels fired the first shots of the conflict across the bows of Iraqi tankers trying to run the UN blockade.

August 25, 1990 – The United Nations Security Council passed Resolution 665 authorizing the use of any "necessary measures" to halt and inspect all shipping in order to ensure strict implementation of the embargo against Iraq.

August 28, 1990 – Iraq declared Kuwait to be its nineteenth province.

September 9, 1990 – President Bush and President Gorbachev met in Helsinki. The two presidents condemned the Iraqi invasion of Kuwait and demanded Iraq's withdrawal.

September 10, 1990 – Iran and Iraq announced the resumption of normal diplomatic relations.

September 25, 1990 – The United Nations Security Council passed Resolution 670 declaring that aircraft and air transportation were included in the sanctions against Iraq.

October 29, 1990 – The United Nations Security Council passed Resolution 674, further condemning Iraqi mistreatment of Kuwaitis and foreign nationals in Iraqi-occupied areas. The vote was 13–0; Cuba and Yemen abstained.

November 4, 1990 – Syrian troops arrived in Saudi Arabia.

November 8, 1990 – President Bush ordered the deployment of 200,000 additional U.S. troops to the Gulf, giving the Coalition greater offensive capabilities.

November 15, 1990 – Egypt, Saudi Arabia, and Syria rejected calls for an Arab summit, seeking first to defeat Saddam Hussein.

November 23, 1990 – President Bush met with Syrian President Hafez al-Assad to discuss the situation in the Gulf, rewarding Syria's support for the Coalition against Iraq.

November 28, 1990 – The United Nations Security Council passed Resolution 677 condemning Iraqi attempts to alter Kuwaiti demographic records.

November 29, 1990 – The United Nations Security Council passed Resolution 678 authorizing the use of force against Iraq if the crisis was not resolved by January 15, 1991. This vote represented the first time in modern history that an international peace-keeping organization voted to use force to halt aggression. The vote was 12–2, with China abstaining and Cuba and Yemen opposing the decision.

November 30, 1990 – President Bush proposed diplomatic talks with Iraq. Saddam Hussein accepted but insisted that Palestinian problems be linked to the conflict in Kuwait.

December 7, 1990 – Iraq released all foreign hostages being held in that country.

December 11, 1990 – Soviet Foreign Minister Eduard Shevardnadze announced that the Soviet would make no troop commitment to the Coalition forces.

December 13, 1990 – The U.S. embassy staff left the embassy in Kuwait.

December 21, 1990 – Saddam Hussein announced that Iraqi forces would not withdraw from Kuwait by the appointed January 15 deadline.

December 23, 1990 – Saddam Hussein declared that Israel would be the first target if fighting began. He hoped to split the Coalition by urging its Arab members to subordinate their opposition to Iraq to their older quarrel with Israel.

December 28, 1990 – The USS *Roosevelt* and the USS *America*, both aircraft carriers, sailed for the Gulf.

December 29, 1990 – Poland joined the Coalition, sending two ships and various medical personnel to the Gulf.

December 30, 1990 – Saddam Hussein called for an Islamic meeting to discuss a Holy War should the Coalition attack Iraq.

January 8, 1991 – President Bush formally asked the U.S. Congress to authorize the use of force against Iraq.

January 9, 1991 – U.S. Secretary of State James Baker and Iraqi Foreign Minister Tariq Aziz met in Geneva. The meeting ended in a deadlock.

January 12, 1991 – The U.S. Congress authorized the use of force to carry out United Nations resolutions.

January 15, 1991 – The United Nations-appointed deadline passed without a Coalition attack. Iraq closed its border with Turkey.

January 16, 1991 – The French National Assembly approved the use of force against Iraq, and placed French forces under U.S. control. Greece authorized the United States to use its military bases and ports.

January 17, 1991 – Desert Storm began at 0230 Baghdad time. U.S. and allied aircraft launched an attack on missile launching sites, airfields, telecommunication centers, and other strategic sites in Iraq. Turkey opened its air bases for Coalition use in attacks against Iraq. Jordan and the PLO condemned the Coalition attack.

January 18, 1991 – Iraq fired eight conventionally armed SCUD missiles at Israel, striking Haifa and Tel Aviv. A U.S. Patriot ground-to-air missile intercepted a SCUD missile aimed at Dhahran.

January 19, 1991 – The Coalition attack had reportedly destroyed all of Iraq's nuclear, chemical, and biological weapons facilities.

January 20, 1991 – Iraqi SCUD missiles struck Israel and Saudi Arabia again and the United States sent Patriot missile units to Israel. Iraqi television aired interviews with U.S. and British prisoners.

January 21, 1991 – Iraq announced it would use Coalition prisoners as human shields. The United States and the International Red Cross denounced this behavior as a violation of the Geneva Convention.

January 22, 1991 – Saddam Hussein ordered the destruction of Kuwaiti oil wells. Another SCUD missile exploded in Tel Aviv, killing many Israelis. These attacks against Israel failed to garner Egyptian and Syrian support, strengthening the Coalition forces.

January 24, 1991 – The President of Yemen declared that the United States was seeking the destruction of Iraq. Morocco, Algeria, and Tunisia approached the United Nations Security Council in hopes of arranging a cease-fire agreement but did not succeed.

January 25, 1991 – Iraq began to pour millions of barrels of oil into the Gulf, endangering the ecology of the waters, threatening Saudi desalinization plants, and hindering the operation of warships.

January 26, 1991 – Two dozen Iraqi aircraft were flown for safekeeping to Iran. Soviet Foreign Minister Alexander Bessmertnykh warned the United States not to destroy Iraq in its bombing raids.

January 27, 1991 – Fifteen more Iraqi aircraft were flown for safekeeping to Iran. Saddam Hussein threatened to use unconventional weapons, such as poisonous gas, against Israeli civilians.

January 29, 1991 – More than 90 Iraqi aircraft had arrived in Iran seeking refuge from Coalition attacks.

January 30, 1991 – Iraqi troops crossed the border into Khafji, Saudi Arabia, provoking the first ground action of the war.

January 31, 1991 – United States and Saudi forces retook Khafji, capturing 500 prisoners.

February 1, 1991 – France granted permission for the overflight of U.S. bombers taking off from English airfields. The U.S. Department of State accused Jordan of violating the United Nations sanctions by purchasing Iraqi oil.

February 3, 1991 – The total Coalition missions flown had reached 44,000.

February 4, 1991 – Iraq began to move its military equipment into civilian areas, recognizing that the Coalition forces sought to avoid attacking areas in which significant civilian casualties could occur.

February 5, 1991 – Reports stated that 80 percent of Iraq's oil refineries have been destroyed. The Iraqi government ceased the sale of all fuels to civilians.

February 6, 1991 – Iraq broke off diplomatic relations with Egypt, France, Italy, Saudi Arabia, the United Kingdom, and the United States. King Hussein of Jordan inched closer to support of Iraq in a speech criticizing Western policies in the Middle East.

February 14, 1991 – The United Nations Security Council began closed sessions to discuss the war in the Gulf.

February 15, 1991 – Iraq offered to withdraw from Kuwait, but attached so many conditions to the withdrawal that the Coalition rejected the offer immediately.

February 16, 1991 – Reports indicated that U.S. ground forces were prepared to launch a ground assault if necessary.

February 17, 1991: The International Red Cross reported that Iraq denied it the right to visit Coalition prisoners inside Iraq. India refused to allow U.S. military aircraft to refuel at Indian bases. Iraqi Foreign Minister Aziz arrived in Moscow to discuss an end to the conflict.

February 19, 1991 – The United Nations Security Council authorized the International Red Cross to send water purification equipment to Iraq to alleviate civilian suffering. China declared that it is skeptical of U.S. intentions in the Gulf region.

February 20, 1991 – President Bush issued an ultimatum to Iraq saying that it must withdraw from Kuwait within 4 days, release all prisoners, and disclose the location of all Iraqi mines. U.S. ground forces captured nearly 500 prisoners.

February 22, 1991 – Soviet President Gorbachev announced a peace plan agreed to by Iraq whereby Iraq would begin a withdrawal within one day to be completed within 3 weeks, and all United Nations Security Council resolutions would be cancelled. President Bush offered Iraq 24 hours to begin its unconditional withdrawal but specified that the withdrawal be completed in one week. The United Nations Security Council did not endorse either plan.

February 24, 1991 – Iraq rejected the U.S. ultimatum, President Bush ordered the start of the ground war, and U.S. and allied forces invaded Kuwait.

February 25, 1991 – A SCUD missile landed in a barrack in Dhahran, killing 28 Americans. The Iraqi army was encircled and began a full retreat towards the Euphrates River.

February 27, 1991 – At 2300 hours Iraq informed the United Nations that it accepted Security Council resolutions.

February 28, 1991 – President Bush ordered a cease-fire. Desert Storm ended at 0800 hours Gulf time.

March 2, 1991 – The United Nations Security Council passed Resolution 686 demanding that Iraq cease all hostile actions, return all hostages and prisoners, rescind its annexation of Kuwait, return all seized Kuwaiti property, disclose the location of all mine fields, and accept liability for war damages. A retreating Iraqi unit of Republican Guards attacked U.S. troops.

March 4, 1991 – Iraq began the release of allied prisoners.

March 6, 1991 – President Bush announced the end of the war in a message to Congress.

March 7, 1991 – Shi'ite and Kurdish rebellions began to spread, facing resistance from the Republican Guards.

March 8, 1991 – The first U.S. troops arrived home.

March 13, 1991 – President Bush warned Iraq against using helicopters to combat the regime's opponents, specifically the Kurds in northern Iraq.

March 14, 1991 – The emir of Kuwait returned to Kuwait City.

March 16, 1991 – Saddam Hussein announced that the revolt in southern Iraq had been suppressed.

March 20, 1991 – A U.S. F-15 shot down an Iraqi fighter for violating the cease-fire.

March 22, 1991 – The United Nations Security Council lifted restrictions on food and critical humanitarian supplies to Iraq.

April 3, 1991 – The United Nations Security Council passed Resolution 687 establishing a cease-fire for ending the war. It demanded that (1) Iraq and Kuwait respect the international boundary; (2) Iraq accept the destruction of all of its chemical and biological weapons and all ballistic missiles; (3) Iraq reveal the location of these weapons; (4) Iraq agree not to acquire nuclear weapons or any related material and to place all of its nuclear weapons under the control of the International Atomic Energy Agency; (5) Iraq agree to on-site inspection and destruction of all such weapons; and (6) the sanctions against Iraq continue.

April 4, 1991 – The Kurdish rebellion in northern Iraq collapsed.

April 5, 1991 – The United Nations Security Council passed Resolution 688 condemning Iraq's repression of its civilian population and demanding that Iraq permit international humanitarian organizations to have immediate access to all parts of Iraq.

April 7, 1991 – U.S. aircraft began delivering humanitarian aid to Kurdish refugees.

April 9, 1991 – The United Nations Security Council passed Resolution 689, thus deploying the United Nations Iraq-Kuwait Observer Mission (UNIKOM) to the Gulf region. UNIKOM's task was to ensure that no military personnel and equipment existed within the demilitarized zone. The World Health Organization launched a 3-month emergency plan to help Kuwait meet its emergency health needs.

April 10, 1991 – The UN secretary-general appointed Major General Gunther Greindl of Austria as UNIKOM's chief military observer.

April 11, 1991 – Paul Noterdaeme of Belgium, president of the Security Council, formally acknowledged Iraq's acceptance of the terms of Resolution 687, making the formal cease-fire effective.

April 22, 1991 – The secretary-general of the United Nations named Rolf Ekeus of Sweden as executive chairman of the Special Commission on Iraqi disarmament.

May 1991 – The Special Commission on Iraqi disarmament dispatched expert teams to oversee the transfer and destruction of Iraqi weapons. Iraq submitted to the IAEA director-general a declaration specifying the amounts, types, and locations of all weapons, as required under Resolution 687. The United Nations Security Council created the United Nations Compensation Fund in Resolution 692, to cover claims against Iraq resulting from the August 2, 1990 invasion and occupation of Kuwait. In response to an Iraqi protest, the secretary-general suggested that this compensation not exceed one-third of the annual value of Iraq's petroleum exports. The Iraq-Kuwait Boundary Demarcation Commission was established pursuant to Resolution 687.

June 1991 – The United Nations Security Council passed Resolution 699, declaring that Iraq should bear the full cost of the destruction of the weapons within Iraq. On June 9, Iraq rejected this liability for the cost of destroying its chemical weapons. In Resolution 700, the United Nations Security Council approved a new set of guidelines to implement the international arms embargo against Iraq as outlined in Resolution 687. Accordingly, the Sanction Committee was to monitor the embargo and report to the Security Council every 3 months. On June 28, the Security Council discussed reports that Iraqi military authorities had denied an inspection team immediate access to a military facility.

July 1991 – The nuclear inspection teams discovered evidence in Iraq of the research and development of techniques for electromagnetic isotope separation and programs for uranium enrichment. The IAEA Board of Governors condemned Iraq for noncompliance with the safeguards agreement. Chemical inspectors reported that Iraq's chemical weapons program was four times greater than acknowledged by Iraq. The Iraq-Kuwait Boundary Demarcation Commission authorized an independent survey and mapping of the entire border. A special fact-finding mission reported on the situation of displaced groups in southern Iraq, describing a significant military presence and activity against the people of the area. On July 18, Iraqi military forces and Kurds clashed in Suleimaniya and Arbil; casualties were estimated at 500. The Food and Agriculture Organization of the United Nations issued a special alert to donors to help ease the food emergency in Iraq.

August 1991 – Kuwait reported that Iraq was still detaining over 2,000 prisoners. Iraq began to return Kuwaiti gold, coins, and banknotes. On August 15, the United Nations Security Council partially lifted a ban on the sale of Iraqi oil. In Resolution 705, the Security Council stated that Iraq's compensation payments should not exceed 30 percent of the annual value of Iraq's petroleum exports. Resolution 706 set the terms for the limited sale of Iraqi oil and oil products to meet essential civilian needs. The Security Council, in response to several incidents in which Iraq blocked inspection teams access to facilities and documents, demanded that Iraq comply with the disarmament measures. The Special Commission declared that it would have to undertake its own high-altitude aerial surveys to locate further Iraqi sites for inspection. UNIKOM reported increases in the activity on the Iraq-Kuwait border, with shots being fired on August 14 in the DMZ. On August 27, the United Nations Security Council considered a plan to monitor and verify Iraq's weapons of mass destruction. Kuwait claimed that Iraqi forces attacked the island of Bubiyan on August 28.

September 1991 – Iraq began to return valuable items stolen from Kuwait's national library. The United Nations Security Council passed Resolution 712 on September 19, setting the terms for the implementation of Resolution 706. The first major detention drama occurred on September 24: Iraqi authorities demanded that all inspections cease and detained the inspectors. Four days later, the inspection team was released. On September 23, the United Nations Security Council met to discuss Iraq's refusal to let United Nations inspection teams overfly Iraqi weapons sites with their own helicopters.

October 1991 – The United Nations Security Council decided that the sanctions against Iraq should continue. The UNIKOM mandate was extended until April 9, 1992. The Iraq-Kuwait Boundary Demarcation Commission approved a final plan for surveying and mapping the border area.

November 1991 – The Memorandum of Understanding was extended until June 30, 1992. The first shipment of enriched uranium was flown out of Iraq in compliance with Resolution 687.

December 1991 – The United Nations General Assembly appealed to all member states, nongovernmental organizations, and intergovernmental organizations to assist in the study and mitigation of the environmental consequences of the Gulf War. Special Commission Chairman Ekeus reported that Iraq formally acknowledged its nuclear weapons program on the December 4. The IAEA announced that Iraq had established a large and highly successful procurement network for its uranium enrichment and weaponization efforts. The Security Council decided that the sanctions against Iraq should continue.

January 1992 – United Nations representatives and Iraqi authorities held talks on the possible resumption of Iraqi petroleum exports. Demonstrators confronted the chemical inspections team in Baghdad on January 27.

February 1992 – U.S. Permanent Representative Thomas Pickering, president of the Security Council, declared that Iraq's failure to acknowledge its obligations under Resolutions 707 and 715 constituted a breach of Resolution 687. The Security Council decided that the sanctions against Iraq should continue.

March 1992 – The IAEA announced its decision to destroy all Iraqi facilities and equipment dedicated to the production of nuclear weapons. The Iraq-Kuwait Boundary Demarcation Commission reports the completion of its work in the border area. The Security Council announced that it was prepared to authorize the sale of Iraqi petroleum and petroleum products.

April 1992 – The Security Council warned Iraq of serious consequences if it failed to allow the Special Commission to conduct aerial surveillance flights over Iraqi territory. The council also agrees to extend the UNIKOM mandate until October 9, 1992.

May 1992 – The Security Council decided the sanctions against Iraq should continue.

June 1992 – The Special Commission initiated systematic aerial inspections of Iraqi sites using helicopters. The commission further reported that Iraq still failed to comply with its obligations. The Security Council stressed to Iraq the inviolability of the international boundary set by the Iraq-Kuwait Boundary Demarcation Commission.

July 1992 – On July 5, Iraq denied the United Nations inspection team access to the Ministry of Agriculture and Irrigation building in Baghdad, claiming that the search would violate its sovereignty. Twenty-two days later, on July 26, the team was allowed to enter the building and proceed with its inspection. A United Nations guard was killed on July 16 in the Governorate of Dohuk, in Kurdish territory. The Security Council decided the sanctions against Iraq should continue.

August 1992 – The Security Council adopted Resolution 773 guaranteeing the inviolability of the international boundary between Iraq and Kuwait. On August 11, Special Rapporteur of the Commission on Human Rights Max van der Stoel reported on the human rights situation in Iraq, warning that the food blockade against the Kurds in the north and the Shi'ites in the south could result in a major famine. The United States, the United Kingdom, and France demanded that Iraq cease all aircraft flights over the southern part of Iraq, in an effort to prevent the armed repression of the Shi'ite Muslim population in that region.

September 1992 – The Special Commission began the destruction of nerve agents in a newly commissioned hydrolysis plant. Under-Secretary-General for Humanitarian Affairs Jan Eliasson stated that security problems existed for the personnel carrying out the humanitarian program in Iraq. The Security Council decides the sanctions against Iraq should continue.

October 1992 – The Security Council assumed control of Iraq's assets frozen outside of Iraq in order to compensate the victims of the Iraqi invasion and occupation of Kuwait. The Security Council passed Resolution 778 comdemning Iraq's failure to comply with its obligations under the United Nations resolutions. The Memorandum of Understanding was extended until the end of March 1993.

April 1994 – Two U.S. Army UH-60 Blackhawk helicopters were shot down by USAF F-15s over northern Iraq. The F-15 pilots mistook the Blackhawks for Iraqi Mi-24 Hind gunships flying in violation of the "no fly zone" and engaged them with air-to-air missiles. Twenty-six people died in the incident, including 15 U.S. military advisers. A chain of human errors was found to be the cause behind the incident.

October 1994 – Some 40,000 U.S. troops and close to 600 U.S. aircraft were rushed to the Gulf in response to an Iraqi buildup on the Kuwaiti border. Hoping to force an end to the crippling sanctions imposed in 1990, Saddam moved an estimated 80,000 troops along with supporting armor and artillery into an area just north of the DMZ. Mass demonstrations involving Bedouins who had been expelled from Kuwait were also staged in Iraq. The rapid U.S. response to the buildup resulted in a speedy Iraqi withdrawal. By resorting to the use of force, Saddam seemed to have quashed any chance there had been of an early lifting of UN sanctions.

August 8, 1995 – Two high-ranking Iraqi officers, Lieutenant General Hussein Kamel and his brother, Saddam Kamel, fled Iraq and were granted asylum in Jordan. General Kamel reportedly headed Iraq's secret weapons programs since the mid-1980s. His brother, Col. Saddam Kamel, was the former head of Iraq's special forces. Both men were married to daughters of Saddam Hussein and brought their wives with them into Jordan. Both were seen as valuable intelligence assets to the West.

List of Abbreviations

AA	Anti-Aircraft (Artillery or Missile)
AAA	Anti-Aircraft Artillery
AAM	Air-to-Air Missile
AAV	Assault Amphibian Vehicle
AAW	Anti-Air Warfare
ABM	Anti-Ballistic Missile
ACAV	Armored Cavalry Assault Vehicle
ACC	Arab Cooperation Council
ACR	Armored Cavalry Regiment
ACV	Armored Combat Vehicle or Air Cushion Vehicle
AD	Air Defense
ADE	Armored Division Equivalent
ADP	Automated Data Processing
AEW	Airborne Early Warning
AFB	Air Force Base (US)
AFR	Air Force Reserve
AFSOC	Air Force Special Operations Command
AFV	Armored Fighting Vehicle
AG	Air/Ground
AI	Airborne Interception or Air Interdiction
AIFS	Advanced Indirect Fire System
AJIL	American Journal of International Law
ALARM	Air Launched Anti-Radiation Missile
ALB	AirLand Battle
ALCM	Air Launched Cruise Missile
AMRAAM	Advanced Medium Range Air-to-Air Missile
ANG	Air National Guard (US)
ANWR	Alaska National Wildlife Refuge
APC	Armored Personnel Carrier
APDS	Armor-Piercing Discarding Sabot
APDS-T	Armor-Piercing Discarding Sabot-Tracer
APERS	Anti-Personnel
APFSDS	Armor-Piercing Fin-Stabilized Discarding Sabot
AR	Airborne Refueling
ARM	Anti-Radiation Missile
ARNG	Army National Guard
ASM	Air-to-Surface Missile

ASMD	Anti-Ship Missile Defense
ASMP	(French) Medium Range Air-Surface Missile
ATACMS	Army Tactical Missile System
ATAF	Allied Tactical Air Force (NATO)
ATAS	Air-to-Air Stinger
ATBM	Anti-Ballistic Missile
ATC	Air Traffic Controller
ATF	Advanced Tactical Fighter
ATGM	Anti-Tank Guided Missile
ATM	Anti-Tank Missile
AWACS	Airborne Warning and Control System
BAAF	Bahrain Amiri Air Force
BAI	Battlefield Air Interdiction
BBC	British Broadcasting Corporation
BDA	Bomb Damage Assessment
BFV	Bradley Fighting Vehicle
BM	Ballistic Missile
BW	Biological Warfare
CAB	Combat Aviation Brigade
CAF	Canadian Air Force
CAFE	Corporate Average Fuel Economy
CAP	Combat Air Patrol
CAS	Close Air Support
Casevac	Casualty Evacuation
CB	Counter Battery
CBU	Cluster Bomb Unit
CCV	Control Configured Vehicle
CEM	Combined Effects Munition
CENTCOM	Central Command (US)
CFE	Conventional Forces in Europe Treaty
CFSP	Common Foreign and Security Policy
CI	Counter Intelligence
CIA	Central Intelligence Agency
CIC	Combat Information Center (Navy)
CINC	Commander-in-Chief
CINCCENT	Commander-in-Chief, Central Command
CINCEUR	Commander-in-Chief, European Command
CINCSOC	Commander-in-Chief, Special Operations Command
CIS	Commonwealth of Independent States (Former Soviet Union)
CM	Cruise Missile
CNN	Cable News Network
COE	Corps of Engineers
COMSAT	Communications Satellite
CoS	Chief of Staff
CP	Command Post

CPB	Charged Particle Beam
CT	Counter Terrorism
CTC	Combat Training Center
CW	Chemical Weapons
C2	Command and Control
C3	Command, Control, and Communications
C3I	Command, Control, Communications, and Intelligence
D-Mark	Deutsche Mark
DOD	Department of Defense
DP	Displaced Persons
DZ	Demilitarized Zone
EC	European Community
ECM	Electronic Counter Measures
ECCM	Electronic Counter-counter Measures
ELINT	Electronics Intelligence
EPC	European Political Cooperation
EPW	Enemy Prisoner of War
ERA	Explosive Reactive Armor
ERAM	Extended Range Anti-Armor Munition
ET	Emerging Technologies
EU	European Union
EUCOM	European Central Command
EW	Electronic Warfare
FA	Field Artillery
FAC	Forward Air Controller
FAE	Fuel Air Explosive (Closely related to napalm)
FBI	Federal Bureau of Investigation
FBIS	Foreign Broadcast Information Service
FBIS-NESA	Foreign Broadcast Information Service-Near East and South Asia
FBIS-SOV	Foreign Broadcast Information Service-Soviet Union
FLIR	Forward Looking Infra-Red
FMS	Foreign Military Sales
FO	Forward Observer
FOB	Forward Operating Base
FOFA	Follow-On-Forces-Attack
FROG	Free Rocket Over Ground (Outdated Soviet Surface-to-Surface Missile)
FSX	Stealth Fighter Experiment
FY	Fiscal Year
GBU	Guided Bomb Unit
GCC	Gulf Cooperation Council
GCI	Ground Control Interceptor
GHQ	General Headquarters

GNP	Gross National Product
GP	General Purpose (conventional iron bombs or "slicks")
GPNS	Global Positioning Navigation System
GPS	Global Positioning System
HARM	High-Speed Anti-Radiation Missile
HAS	Hardened Aircraft Shelter
HET	Heavy Equipment Transporter
HF	High Frequency
HMMWV	High Mobility Multi-Purpose Wheeled Vehicle, "Hummer"
IADS	Integrated Air Defense System (Iraq)
IAEA	International Atomic Energy Agency
IAF	Israeli Air Force or Italian Air Force
ICBM	Intercontinental Ballistic Missile
ICM	Improved Conventional Munition
(S)ICV	(Soviet) Infantry Combat Vehicle
IDF	Israeli Defense Forces
IEA	International Energy Agency
IFF	Identification Friend or Foe
IFV	Infantry Fighting Vehicle
IIR	Imaging Infra-red
IIS	Iraqi Intelligence Service
IISS	International Institute for Strategic Studies, London
IMF	International Monetary Fund
IMI	Israeli Military Industries
INS	Inertial Navigation System
IR	Infra-red
IRCM	Infra-red Countermeasures
JCS	Joint Chiefs of Staff
JFC	Joint Forces Command
JFC-E	Joint Forces Command - East
JFC-N	Joint Forces Command - North
JFLC	Joint Forces Land Component
JSTARS	Joint Surveillance and Target Attack Radar System
JTACMS	Joint Tactical Missile System
JTF(ME)	Joint Task Force (Middle East)
KAF	Kuwaiti Air Force
KE	Kinetic Energy
KIA	Killed in Action
KKMC	King Khalid Military City
kT	Kilotons (Yield or size of nuclear device)
KTO	Kuwait Theater of Operations
LABS	Low Altitude Bombing System

LAI	Light Armored Infantry
LAMPS	Light Airborne Multipurpose System (Helicopter employed on US naval vessels)
LANTIRN	Low Altitude Navigation and Targeting Infra-red for Night
LAV	Light Armored Vehicle
LAW	Light Anti-Tank Weapon
LCAC	Landing Craft, Air Cushion
LCM	Liechtenstein Colloquium, Vaduz
LDC	Less Developed Country
LDP	Liberal Democratic Party (Japan)
LF	Low Frequency
LGB	Laser Guided Bomb
LGW	Laser Guided Weapon
LL(L)TV	Low Light (Level) TV
L of C	Line of Communication
LOS	Line of Sight
LRSOM	Long Range Standoff Missile
LST	Laser Spot Tracker
LZ	Landing Zone
MAC	Military Airlift Command
MARCENT	Marine Forces, Central Command
MARDIV	Marine Division
mbd.	Millions of Barrels per day (Measurement of oil production)
MBT	Main Battle Tank
MCM	Mine Counter Measures
MEB	Marine Expeditionary Brigade
MEDEVAC	Medical Evacuation
MEF	Marine Expeditionary Force
MEU	Marine Expeditionary Unit
MEL	Mobile Erector Launcher
MET	Medium Equipment Transporter
MEU	Marine Expeditionary Unit
MG	Machine Gun
MIA	Missing in Action
MICV	Mechanized Infantry Combat Vehicle
MIMI	Ministry of Industry and Military Industrialization
MLRS	Multiple Launch Rocket System
MoD	Ministry of Defense
MOU	Memorandum of Understanding
MP	Military Police
MPF	Maritime Prepositioning Force
MPT	Multi-Purpose Tracer
MRCA	Multi-Role Combat Aircraft
MRE	Meal, Ready-to-Eat (Rations)
MRL	Multiple Rocket Launcher
MSC	Military Sealift Command

MULE	Modular Universal Laser Equipment
NAC	Northern Area Command
NAM	Non-Aligned Members
NAS	Naval Air Station
NATO	North Atlantic Treaty Organization
NAVCENT	Naval Component, Central Command
NAVEUR	Naval Forces, Europe
NAVSTAR	Navigation System with Timing and Ranging
NBC	Nuclear, Biological, and Chemical
NCP	Non-U.S. Coalition Partner
NES	National Energy Strategy
NGFS	Naval Gunfire Support
NIC	National Intelligence Council
NOD	Non-Offensive Defense
NSA	National Security Agency
NSC	National Security Council
NTC	National Training Center (Fort Irwin, CA)
OCA	Offensive Counter Air
OECD	Organization for Economic Cooperation and Development
OMG	Operational Maneuver Group
OP	Observation Post
OPCOM	Operational Command
OPEC	Organization of Petroleum Exporting Countries
OPV	Observation Party Vehicle
PACOM	Pacific Command
PBS	Public Broadcasting Service
PFLP	Popular Front for the Liberation of Palestine
PFLP-GC	Popular Front for the Liberation of Palestine - General Command
PGM	Precision Guided Munition
PISGA	Palestinian Interim Self-Governing Authority
PKO	Peace Keeping Operations
PLO	Palestine Liberation Organization
PM	Prime Minister
POL	Petrol, Oil, and Lubricants
POMCUS	Prepositioned Overseas Material Configured to Unit Sets
POW	Prisoner of War
PSYOPS	Psychological Operations
P5	Five permanent members of the United Nations Security Council
QEAF	Quatari Emiri Air Force
R & D	Research and Development
RAAMS	Remote Anti-Armor Mine System

RAF	Royal Air Force
RAP	Rocket-Assisted Projectile
RCC	Revolutionary Command Council
RDF	Rapid Deployment Force or Radio Direction Finding
RDM	Remotely Deployed Mine
Res.	Resolution (United Nations)
RG	Republican Guards (Iraq's best trained, equipped and loyal troops)
RO/RO	Roll-on/Roll-off (Large transport ships designed to carry heavy equipment such as tanks and other AFVs)
ROE	Rules of Engagement
RPG	Rocket Propelled Grenade
RPV	Remotely Piloted Vehicle
RRF	Ready Reserve Fleet
RSAF	Royal Saudi Air Force
RSLF	Royal Saudi Land Force
RSNF	Royal Saudi Naval Force
RV	Rendez-Vous
SAAF	Saudi Arabian Armed Forces
SAC	Strategic Air Command (U.S.)
SAM	Surface-to-Air Missile
SANG	Saudi Arabian National Guard
SAS	Special Air Service (British special forces; similar to US Delta Force or Green Berets)
SATCOM	Satellite Communications
SAW	Squad Automatic Weapon
SBM	Security-Building Measures
SBS	Special Boat Service (Special forces branch of the Royal Marines similar to US Navy SEALS)
SBU	Small Boat Unit
SC	Security Council
SDF	Self-Defense Force (Japanese)
SDI	Strategic Defense Initiative (STAR WARS)
SEAD	Suppression of Enemy Air Defences
SEAL	Sea, Air and Land (Naval special forces troops trained for unconventional and paramilitary operations)
SF	Special Forces
SFG	Special Forces Group
SG	Secretary General (United Nations)
SITREP	Situation Report
SLCM	Sea Launched Cruise Missile
SNF	Short-Range Nuclear Forces
SOCCENT	Special Operations Command, CENTCOM
SOF	Special Operations Forces
SOJ	Stand-Off Jammer
SOP	Standard Operating Procedures

SRAM-T	Short-Range (Air-to-Surface) Attack Missile - Tactical
SRBM	Short Range Ballistic Missile
STO(VL)	Short Take-Off (and Vertical Landing)
SWB	Summary of World Broadcasts
TAC	Tactical Air Command (U.S.)
TACAIR	Tactical Air
TACINTEL	Tactical Intelligence
TACON	Tactical Control
TADS	Target Acquisition and Designation Sight
TAF	Tactical Air Force
TALD	Tactical Air Launched Decoy
TASM	Tomahawk Anti-Ship Missile
TBM	Tactical Ballistic Missile
TEL	Transporter, Erector, Launcher
TF	Task Force
TFS	Tactical Fighter Squadron (USAF)
TFW	Tactical Fighter Wing
TIS	Thermal Imaging System
TNF	Tactical Nuclear Forces
TGSM	Terminally Guided Sub-Munition
TGW	Terminally Guided Weapon
TLAM	Tomahawk Land-Attack Missile
TNW	Tactical Nuclear Weapon
TOW	Tube-launched, Optically Tracked, Wire-guided (US anti-tank missile)
TWV	Tactical Wheeled Vehicle
UAE	United Arab Emirates
UAEAF	United Arab Emirates Air Force
UAV	Unmanned Aerial Vehicle
UK	United Kingdom
UN	United Nations
UNIKOM	United Nations Iraq-Kuwait Observation Mission
U.N.S.C.	United Nations Security Council
UN-SCR	United Nations-Security Council Resolution
UNSCOM	United Nations Special Commision
UN-SG	United Nations-Secretary General
UNTAC	United Nations Transitional Authority in Cambodia
U.S.	United States (of America)
U.S.A.F.	United States Air Force
USAFE	United States Air Force, Europe
USAR	United States Army Reserve
USAREUR	United States Army, Europe
USEUCOM	United States European Command
U.S.M.C.	United States Marine Corps

U.S.S.R.	Union of the Socialist Soviet Republics
VLS	Vertical Launch System
V/STOL	Vertical/Short Take Off and Landing
WAAM	Wide Area Anti-Armor Munition
WEI	Weighted Effectiveness Index
WEU	Western European Union
WIA	Wounded in Action
WW I	World War I
WW II	World War II

About the Book and Editors

The war for the liberation of Kuwait following the Iraqi invasion in 1990 rekindled the international community's geopolitical interest in the Gulf and helped define a new regional order. This book analyzes the political, strategic, and economic dimensions of the second Gulf War, with particular focus on military aspects. An international roster of experts treats issues of strategy, weapons technology, arms transfers, and the impact on the Arab state system. Of special interest is the exploration of the implications of the war for Japan, Germany, Russia, and Europe.

Wolfgang F. Danspeckgruber, lecturer at Princeton University, chairs the Liechtenstein Colloquium on European and International Affairs in Vaduz, Liechtenstein.

Charles R.H. Tripp is chair of the Center of Near and Middle Eastern Studies, School of Oriental and African Studies, University of London.

About the Contributors

General Walter E. Boomer
Assistant Commandant, United States Marine Corps
General Boomer led the attack of the USMC into Kuwait, 1991.

Dr. Christian Catrina
Deputy to the Representative of the Chief of the General Staff for Politico-Military Affairs, Federal Military Department, Bern, Switzerland

Mrs. Amy Cullum
Research Associate at John Snow Research and Training, Washington, D.C.

Dr. Gustav Däniker
Major General, Swiss Army (ret);
President, Dr. Farner Public Relations, Zurich, Switzerland

Dr. Wolfgang F. Danspeckgruber
Lecturer in Politics and International Affairs and Executive Director, Liechtenstein; Research Program on Self-Determination, Woodrow Wilson School, Princeton University; Chair, Liechtenstein Colloquium on European and International Affairs, Vaduz

Dr. Lawrence Freedman
Professor, Chair, Department of War Studies, King's College, London

Dr. Helmut Freudenschuss
Counsellor, Alternate Representative of Austria to the UN Security Council 1991–1992; now, Federal Ministry of Foreign Affairs, Vienna

Dr. Abdlatif Y. Al-Hamad
Director General, Arab Fund for Social and Economic Development, Kuwait; formerly, Minister of Finance, Kuwait

Dr. habil. Helmut Hubel
Dozent, Senior Fellow, Forschungsinstitut der Deutschen Gesellschaft für Auswärtige Politik, Bonn

Dr. Ephraim Karsh
Reader, Department of War Studies, King's College, London

Christopher H. Klaus
Department of Politics, Princeton University

Dr. habil. Gudrun Krämer
Dozent, University of Bonn; Research Associate, Stiftung Wissenschaft und Politik, Ebenhausen

Dr. Robert J. Lieber
Chair, Department of Government, Georgetown University, Washington, D.C.

Dr. Laurie Mylroie
The Washington Institute Center of International Affairs; formerly, Harvard University

Dr. Amin Saikal
Chair, Department of Government,
Australian National University, Canberra, Australia

Dr. Masaru Tamamoto
Senior Fellow of the World Policy Institute at The New School for Social Research, New York

Dr. Charles R.H. Tripp
Senior Lecturer in the Politics of the Middle East,
Chair of the Center of Near and Middle Eastern Studies, School for Oriental and African Studies, University of London

Dr. William C. Wohlforth
Assistant Professor, Department of Politics, Princeton University

Dr. Erik Yesson
Lecturer, Department of Politics, Brown University

Dr. Irina Zviagelskaia
Associate Director, Institute of Oriental Studies, Academy of Sciences, Moscow